BEHIND THE HEADLINES

A History of Investigative
Journalism in Canada

Cecil Rosner

OXFORD
UNIVERSITY PRESS

OXFORD

UNIVERSITY PRESS

70 Wynford Drive, Don Mills, Ontario M3C 1J9
www.oup.com/ca

Oxford University Press is a department of the University of Oxford.
It furthers the University's objective of excellence in research, scholarship,
and education by publishing worldwide in

Oxford New York

Auckland   Cape Town   Dar es Salaam   Hong Kong   Karachi
Kuala Lumpur   Madrid   Melbourne   Mexico City   Nairobi
New Delhi   Shanghai   Taipei   Toronto

With offices in
Argentina Austria Brazil Chile Czech Republic France Greece
Guatemala Hungary Italy Japan Poland Portugal Singapore
South Korea Switzerland Thailand Turkey Ukraine Vietnam

Oxford is a trade mark of Oxford University Press
in the UK and in certain other countries

Published in Canada
by Oxford University Press

Library and Archives Canada Cataloguing in Publication

Rosner, Cecil, 1952–
Behind the headlines : a history of investigative journalism / Cecil Rosner.
Includes bibliographic references.

ISBN 978-0-19-542733-2

1. Investigative reporting—Canada—History—Textbooks.
I. Title.

PN4914.I58R68 2008   070.4'30971   C2007-905968-6

Cover Image: Nick Schlax/iStockPhoto

1 2 3 4 – 11 10 09 08
This book is printed on permanent (acid-free) paper ∞.
Printed in Canada

Contents

Preface

I have a favourite example I relate to students whenever I try to explain the difference between investigative journalism and conventional daily reporting. It involves an analysis of how the media covered a rooming-house fire in Winnipeg a number of years ago. One of the city's daily newspapers told the story of how a local radio announcer happened on the fire while walking to work. He pounded on doors, sounded the alarm, and helped everyone to escape unharmed. He was the hero of the day. The city's other daily had a very different story. A cab driver was in the area, spotted the fire, and roused the residents to safety. He was the real hero. The first account made no mention of a cab driver, and the second story was silent when it came to wandering radio announcers.

What, I ask my students, do they make of these two accounts? Which one is true? The answer, of course, is not possible to glean from the media stories alone. Perhaps the radio announcer was lying, and wasn't there at all. Maybe the cab driver was embellishing his story. It's possible they were both present, at separate times, and can lay equal claim to being heroes. Or maybe an alarm system sounded well before either arrived on the scene, making their intervention pointless. No amount of reading and re-reading the stories can throw any further light on the matter.

While it's a relatively trivial example, what makes it useful is how typical and representative it is of most daily journalism today. Journalists gather information, speak to people, and report their stories, often without bothering to ascertain the real truth of a situation. It's good enough to report what the police chief, or a politician, or a public relations spokesperson says. To ensure balance, and seemingly to demonstrate objectivity, the modern journalist makes sure that comments are sought from opposing sources. If the Conservatives are quoted on a matter, it is incumbent on the reporter to quote Liberals, the NDP, and perhaps the Bloc Québécois. If a company executive pronounces on a labour dispute, a union official provides the opposing opinion.

Unfortunately, most daily reporting doesn't stop to ask: what if the company and the union were both lying? What if the Liberals and Conservatives and NDP were all incorrect in their statement of facts? What if the cab driver and radio announcer were making it all up? What if Joseph McCarthy didn't really have a list of 53 communists in the State Department? What if George Bush and Tony Blair were simply wrong in their claim that Saddam Hussein possessed weapons of mass destruction? Were the reports of all these claims still balanced and objective, despite being false? Or did the journalists fail in what is arguably their most important mission: finding the truth?

The vast majority of modern journalism is reactive, subject to manipulation, and inevitably filled with inaccuracies. Reporters will argue that they have tight deadlines, and the best they can do is to provide balance by seeking out two or more opinions on all stories. While it's true that deadlines are a major constraint, what is less clear is why we should accept this form of balance as a substitute for digging out facts. In historian Mitchell Stephens' view, modern journalists 'attempt to chain opinions to their opposites, hoping, it seems, that these beasts will annihilate each other, leaving what passes in journalistic thinking for the truth. This technique conveniently frees journalists from responsibility for looking beyond competing arguments to find the truth.'[1] Investigative journalism has a simple objective. It aims to find the truth. And it often begins when all the daily reporters have typed their quotes, securely chained opinions to their opposites, and left the scene in search of their next scoop.

While the desire to seek the truth is a prerequisite for investigative journalism, it is scarcely the whole story. What truths are important to discover? Clearly, those that have a major impact on society. Those that serve the interests of the vast majority of people. Those that will help people understand how their world really works, allowing them to take informed actions. Usually, the facts such reporters seek to uncover are not easily obtained. There may be powerful interests intent on hiding them. Or they may involve analyzing data in a way no one has thought to do before. In either case, defenders of the status quo often feel threatened by the work of investigative journalists, and they have never been shy about striking back.

Canada has a long and largely undocumented history of investigative journalism, dating back almost to the very beginning of newspapers in this country. That it is undocumented and essentially unanalyzed should not be completely surprising. Barbie Zelizer, a former journalist and now an academic, says scholars have historically had trouble taking journalism seriously. The academy, she notes, pays more attention to journalism only when it turns into a non-journalistic phenomenon, such as history or literature. 'Why is journalism not easily appreciated at the moment of its creation, with all of its problems, contradictions, limitations, and anomalies?'[2] A passionate believer that journalism matters, Zelizer crafts a framework for rethinking journalism and revisiting the explanatory frames scholars have used to review journalistic practice. She identifies five distinct definitional sets by which journalism can be described and explained. These include studying journalism as a profession, as an institution, as a text, as people, and as a set of practices.[3] Though there is significant overlap among the different frames, I have largely concentrated on examining investigative journalism as a specific set of practices. Such an approach allows for a comparison between investigative journalism and more conventional forms of news reporting. Critical to this approach is an inquiry into the practitioners of the genre, and their struggles to employ and refine their practices in the face of social and institutional obstacles.

This book, then, is an attempt to begin the process of defining investigative journalism in Canada, describing its evolution, and explaining the development of the particular set of practices that make up the genre, in the context of changing social and historical forces.

James Aucoin, in his study of American investigative journalism, put forward the idea that the genre could be understood as a social practice. 'If one is to adequately describe a social practice and how it is developing (or not developing), the historian must consider the biographies of practitioners, especially those who have influenced how journalism is done; the ideals held by practitioners about the craft; and the cultural and social setting of the practice.'[4] I have endeavoured to heed that advice in these pages, but my intention isn't to turn the entire narrative into an examination of the social practice concept Aucoin borrowed from Alasdair MacIntyre in his book *After Virtue*. Though such an examination is beyond the scope of this book, there are useful concepts in MacIntyre's analysis that illuminate the tensions between practitioners and the institutions that employ them. Modern mass media organizations are devoted to generating profits and shareholder value, an undertaking that doesn't comfortably embrace heroic muckrakers tilting at the status quo. While MacIntyre doesn't discuss investigative journalism or journalism at all in this context, he identifies a contradiction generally, and points to the necessity of practitioners professing and exercising specific virtues to overcome the obstacles posed by the institutions.[5]

> Institutions are characteristically and necessarily concerned with what I have called external goods. They are involved in acquiring money and other material goods; they are structured in terms of power and status, and they distribute money, power, and status as rewards . . . the ideals and the creativity of the practice are always vulnerable to the acquisitiveness of the institution, in which the cooperative care for common goods of the practice is always vulnerable to the competitiveness of the institution. In this context the essential function of the virtues is clear. Without them, without justice, courage, and truthfulness, practices could not resist the corrupting power of institutions.[6]

Justice and courage were key attributes for many of Canada's early nineteenth-century journalists, who were among the leading advocates for reform and responsible government. They raised their voices against the institutions of colonial state rule, the cliques and family compacts, often paying a heavy price. Many journalists were vilified, attacked, charged, even jailed for their activities. The radical editors displayed tenacity and unbending resolve in their oppositional writings.

But for all their bold opposition, many of the early journalistic firebrands exhibited only one side of the modern investigative journalistic impulse. They held the powerful to account, and they editorialized incessantly about the need for reform. Their desire to dig a little deeper in their journalism arguably qualifies some of them to be called muckrakers, a term coined by US President Teddy Roosevelt to describe a turn-of-the-century group of American newspaper and magazine writers who exposed everything from municipal corruption to workplace hazards. But not all of them paid attention to illustrating how institutions and structures really worked. Many were content with denunciations and polemic.

What elevates aggressive reporting that challenges the status quo to the plane of investigative journalism? There is no precise formula, but there are common characteristics of investigative journalists that help to illustrate the point. They display a keen sense of outrage, exposing injustice wherever it exists. They question why things have worked the way they traditionally do, and are skeptical of conventional explanations. They feel a need to hold powerful, vested interests to account. They have a devotion to seeking the truth, even when it means endangering their careers and personal well-being. They are often obsessed with information, data, documents, and proof. They are not content merely with opinions, or chronicling the work of others—they want to do their own work. They adopt scientific methods for truth seeking, always remaining open-minded and free of distorting allegiances. In many cases, like true scientists, they are willing to revise or renounce their original beliefs when the weight of evidence points them in another direction. Without scientific methodology, muckraking is easy to dismiss and devoid of any lasting impact. Investigative journalists are the most skilled of the muckrakers.

The word investigative derives from the Latin *vestigium*—footprint. It's an apt term for a profession that mimics detective work in the way it searches for clues to illuminate reality.[7] In the course of telling the stories of investigative journalists in Canada, I have paid special attention to their methodology, which has steadily improved and become more refined. The best investigative journalists use a rigorous method for collecting, sifting, and assessing their material. The very earliest investigators sought out official documents that were hard to access. Later, human sources became important, and interviews became crucial tools for journalism. In the twentieth century, reporters began using specialized tools in their quest for the truth. Access to information techniques, hidden cameras and recording devices, undercover work, and other techniques—many of them ethically debatable—became commonplace. Today, the best investigative journalists study the nuances of how questions ought to be asked, how information should be gathered and sorted, and how the principles of corroboration should be applied in their craft.

From a theoretical perspective, investigative journalism is rooted in a long tradition of Enlightenment ideals that gave rise to concepts of press freedom and liberty. Herbert Altschull joins other historians in tracing this tradition back to John Milton, who wrote an impassioned defence of free expression in 1644.[8] Milton's *Areopagitica* was an appeal to Parliament in favour of unlicensed printing. He had come under attack for writing articles supporting the concept of divorce, and Milton responded by constructing a theoretical argument to oppose English censorship provisions. If printing were to be regulated, he argued, so must all recreation and pastimes, from music to dance.[9] Truth and lies should be free to compete in the marketplace of ideas, Milton argued. Truth, he suggested optimistically, would prevail—'she needs no policies, nor stratagems, nor licensings to make her victorious.' A self-righting principle would ensure the supremacy of truth, according to this theory, rendering authoritarian prohibitions and censorship unnecessary.[10] In an era of burgeoning pamphleteering and opposition to authority, Milton's argument was an early justification for freedom of the press.

Enlightenment thinkers in Britain and France, and later in America, developed theories of liberty and democracy that inevitably had broad implications for journalism. John Locke may be best known for inspiring republican ideals in his writings, particularly his *Two Treatises of Government* published in 1690, but his theories also lent support to the concept of an unshackled press.[11] By their very nature, argued Locke, men were free, equal, and independent. It followed that any attempts to remove those basic liberties were inherently unjust. 'Whenever the legislators endeavour to take away and destroy the property of the people, or to reduce them to slavery under arbitrary power, they put themselves into a state of war with the people, who are thereupon absolved from any further obedience . . .'[12] Locke didn't care whether the legislative transgressions came as a result of 'ambition, fear, folly, or corruption'.[13] It all constituted a breach of trust, and a forfeiture of power. People had every right to resume their original liberty through revolution. It was this legalizing of force and violence, Altschull argues, that undergirds the media's notion of its role as a watchdog over lawmakers.[14]

Similar ideas infuse the writings of the French and American philosophers who inspired respective revolutions in their countries. Thomas Jefferson's celebrated preference for newspapers without government over a government without newspapers was the kind of sentiment that eventually found expression in the enshrinement of press freedom in the First Amendment of the Constitution of the United States. Newspapers began to be regarded as a fourth estate, a crucial adjunct to the political process, charged with keeping an eye on matters of state. The pursuit of truth by newspapers and journalism generally seemed to be a principle that could be embraced across many political and ethical spectrums. But as the newspaper industry matured and expanded by the late nineteenth century, and devoted itself more and more to enhancing profitability, journalism's mission became less clear. How could the newspaper be a watchdog and a check on the status quo if it was part of the status quo itself? It was this 'unresolved social contradiction between public expectation and private purpose (the publisher's pursuit of profit)', in historian Minko Sotiron's phrase, which led to a re-evaluation of journalistic responsibility.[15] The most celebrated attempt to graft a new theoretical framework onto traditional media values came with the idea of a 'social responsibility theory' of the press in the 1950s, first popularized in a widely read book called *Four Theories of the Press*, from the University of Illinois.[16] The analysis looked at authoritarian, libertarian, and Soviet concepts of what the press should be, but its analysis of a social responsibility theory was the most influential. This idea drew significant inspiration from the Hutchins Commission on Freedom of the Press, a post-war attempt to restore credibility to an American newspaper industry that had lost significant public support over a number of decades.[17] The theory's major premise was that the press, which enjoys a privileged position in society, was obliged to be responsible to that society by carrying out some essential tasks. Key among them were providing information and debate on current affairs, enlightening the public to make it capable of self-government, and serving as a watchdog over government.[18] The theory spread widely through journalism schools and among reporters and editors themselves, giving rise to intense discussions about who ought to hold the media to account for their social responsibilities. Academics at the University of Illinois, where the original idea had been hatched, revisited the theory four decades later and outlined some serious shortcomings. They showed how the original book's dismissal of the Soviet media model was rooted in Cold War politics, and not in an objective critique of Marxist thought.[19] Even the social responsibility theory had drawbacks. 'Certainly the theory expects some kind of stewardship of media resources on behalf of the public; certainly it expects the media to be educators. But at the same time it avoids detailing structural changes (including government regulation) that would allow performance of these functions.'[20] Still, the idea of a socially responsible press remains powerful for those who believe journalism should aspire to a higher purpose. Hugo de Burgh argues that 'its most extreme manifestation' is a journalism that challenges authority and opposes attempts by authority to define the issues. 'At its most bold and most impertinent, this journalism is investigative because it applies forensic skills to what we have been told.'[21]

How widespread is the influence of a bold, impertinent media applying forensic methodology to challenge powerful interests? Instead of a cantankerous, obstinate press constantly prodding authority, Edward Herman and Noam Chomsky see media that mobilize support for the forces that dominate the state. They postulate a 'propaganda model' of the press that ensures the selection of topics, and the framing of issues, keeps discourse within the bounds of acceptable limits.[22] The model suggests the media's purpose is 'to inculcate and defend the economic, social, and political agenda of privileged groups that dominate the domestic society and the state'.[23] Communications theorist Harold Innis wrote extensively as well on the media's monopolization of knowledge, which allows powerful interests to define reality and control belief systems.[24] Marxists, meanwhile, view journalism as having a class character that serves to meet the economic and political goals of the ruling class. For them, concepts of freedom and liberty applied to the media in a capitalist environment are abstractions that ignore existing reality and serve to perpetuate inequalities.[25]

Real-life examples of the propaganda model can be found in abundance, though Herman and Chomsky are quick to point out that the media are not a unified monolith on all issues. Rivalries and disputes among powerful interests can lead to challenging journalism, but one always has to wonder whose interests are being served by the reporting. They even take issue with the idea that the Watergate affair is an exemplar of modern-day investigative journalism in the public interest.[26] They point out that successive US administrations had established a pattern of targeting left-wing, radical, and popular movements with illegal break-ins and disruptive activity. Yet these illegalities received scant press coverage, to be superseded by a story detailing an attack on the Democratic Party headquarters. Their propaganda model of the media suggests that 'as long as illegalities and violations of democratic substance are confined to marginal groups or distant victims of US military attack, or result in a diffused cost imposed on the general population, media opposition is muted or absent altogether. This is why Nixon could go so far, lulled into a false sense of security precisely because the watchdog only barked when he began to threaten the privileged.'[27]

While it is important to consider all the different philosophical foundations and theories touching on journalism generally, it is also crucial to remember the unique nature of the media business. The industry generates profits, ideas, propaganda, enlightenment, and occasional nasty blows to government leaders and vested interests.

The interplay between media institutions and the journalists they employ is complex and worthy of close study, and while it is crucial to conceptualize underlying realities, it has proved notoriously difficult to predict specific journalistic outcomes. Even Edward Herman, in a revisiting of his propaganda model a decade after its introduction, adds this afterthought: 'In retrospect, perhaps we should have made it clearer that the propaganda model was about media behavior and performance, with uncertain and variable effects. Maybe we should have spelled out in more detail the contesting forces both within and outside the media and the conditions under which these are likely to be influential.'[28]

This book offers an examination of those various contesting forces in the Canadian context of investigative journalism, a field that has been virtually unplowed to this point. I propose to concentrate mainly on identifying the key players, and describing their work in the context of their place in time. Where possible, I attempt to offer explanations for the specific ebbs and flows of investigative journalism in Canadian history. I hope more works in the future will provide additional research and further analysis of this important genre of journalism.

Chapter 1 starts not at the beginning of the story, but purposely towards the end. I have sketched some of the more contemporary examples of Canadian investigative journalism, from the Shawinigate affair to the sponsorship scandal. The emphasis is on political scandal and stories that strike at government credibility. My intention is twofold: first, to show the relationship between practitioners, their institutions, and the government; second, to highlight the state of investigative journalism's modern methodologies, which constitute a highly developed set of practices. It is possible to analyze these stories from a variety of theoretical perspectives. I have tried to facilitate that examination by exposing the motivations of journalists, along with the institutional settings in which they operated.

Modern Canadian investigative journalism, for the most part, is a phenomenon that begins in the second half of the twentieth century. But there are important historical antecedents, and I have endeavoured to survey them in Chapters 2 and 3. The influence of Enlightenment ideals is evident in some of the radical editors of the eighteenth and nineteenth centuries. Politics and journalism were thoroughly intertwined during this period, and journalistic courage was often met by political repression. I have used this historical survey, in part, to show how methodologies progressed through the years. Some were driven by technological advances, others by individual journalists who were eager to discover the best obtainable version of the truth. In this context, William Lyon Mackenzie's work stands out both for its trenchant political dimension and its devotion to a more rigorous methodology. While the era was filled with muckrakers of varying skill levels, I have concluded that Mackenzie can be seen as Canada's first true investigative journalist.

Chapter 4 continues the brief historical survey from the turn of the century to the 1950s. Commercialization of the press, and the influence of the two world wars, had a significant impact on the media. Few journalists and fewer institutions were invoking the rhetoric of watchdogs and tribunes of the people. There were sporadic exceptions, especially among independent and alternative journalists, a theme I examine and return to at different points in the narrative. Still, a number of isolated individuals working in the mainstream press demonstrated that the path was not completely blocked. An interesting feature of the late 1950s and early 1960s was the Canadian debate over capital punishment, a discussion that was nurtured and fuelled by some impressive examples of investigative reporting. Meticulous exposés of wrongful convictions in this period showed how journalists could turn from daily reporting to intensive investigation. Isabel LeBourdais, for instance, spent six years interviewing people and poring over documents to expose the deficiencies in Steven Truscott's murder conviction. However, while some talented journalists were coming to the fore, the genre was still being framed mostly in the context of bigger and better scoops, and not as rigorous reporting that held powerful interests to account.

The advent of broadcasting added a new dimension to Canadian journalism, as did the entry into the marketplace of a public broadcaster. Many critics have argued that public broadcasting has contributed to the enlargement of a public sphere of discourse, an essential aid to citizens that private media don't provide.[29] Chapter 5 looks at the role of public broadcasting journalists in the 1950s and 1960s, and how they influenced investigative journalism. Pioneering efforts of Douglas Leiterman, Patrick Watson, Ross McLean, and Beryl Fox created a new language for public affairs reporting, along with important new methods. They weren't mired in the old work habits of the commercial press, and they had no hesitation devoting extensive resources to research individual stories of importance. Using the unique attributes of television, they developed intensive accountability interviews as a new technique for calling the powerful to account. In documentary work, they pioneered techniques of cinéma-vérité, surreptitious recording, and hidden-camera work in an effort to get closer to the truth. These were used to document a variety of important topics, from racial intolerance in the southern US to the horrors of war in Vietnam. Their ultimate clash with the institution that employed them, the CBC, provides useful insights into the relationship between journalists and their institutions.

Harold Innis believed change emanated from the margins. People on the periphery of established order developed their own media of expression, as they were denied access to the mainstream.[30] These new media allowed them to challenge the established order. In Chapter 6, I examine how the alternative media in the 1950s and 1960s developed new forms of communication and contributed to the evolution of investigative journalism both in the US and Canada. By the mid 1950s, a variety of social and political factors both inspired and amplified the messages from the margins. Some of the foundations of the established order throughout the world were beginning to wobble. An anti-colonial struggle raged through Asia, Africa, and Latin America. Cuba was waging a successful revolution. Chinese communism posed an ideological challenge both to the West and to the Soviet Union. Domestically, support for the US administration began to weaken, a process that only accelerated with the widening of the war in Indochina. Ideas were being challenged in many spheres, and alternative thoughts were peeking into the mainstream. I.F. Stone's independent journalism exercised a profound impact on public policy, challenging the US version of events in the Korean War, and providing an alternative viewpoint to the subservient mainstream press. Other voices that sought to hold powerful interests to account with verifiable facts began to be heard. The *Village Voice* was founded in 1955, *Liberation* in 1956, and suddenly the journalism of exposure was growing. In the mainstream, Edward R. Murrow of CBS denounced Joseph McCarthy's witch hunts. His seminal *See It Now* exposé of McCarthy in 1954 encouraged a new generation of journalists who were eager to challenge the dominant ideas of the status quo. Ralph Nader's automobile safety warnings started to emerge at the end of the 1950s. Rachel Carson challenged the widespread use of chemicals and raised concerns about their effect on the environment.[31] With the growing youth and student movement in the 1960s, a new era of aggressive journalistic inquiry emerged. Seymour Hersh's exposé of the My Lai massacre, and the success of Bob Woodward and Carl Bernstein in helping to topple a president, provided enduring inspiration to journalists. Against this international backdrop, this chapter shows how Canadian alternative journalists contributed to the genre of investigative journalism, and how many of them brought their enhanced sensibilities and more rigorous methodology to mainstream pursuits.

Though Herman and Chomsky dispute its overall significance, there is little doubt that the Watergate affair had measurable impact on investigative journalism. Chapter 7 describes how the success of Woodward and Bernstein, and the subsequent idolization of their characters in a Hollywood movie, brought investigative journalism widespread attention and prestige. It also succeeded in turning investigative journalism into a saleable commodity. Just as major American magazines had vied with each other to print muckraking articles at the turn of the century for commercial advantage, newspapers and the networks rushed to assemble investigative teams in an effort to capture readers and viewers. During this period, the CBC experimented with consumer and ombudsman journalism, eventually bringing journalists once more into conflict with their institutional managers. The same was true of Henry Aubin, the Quebec journalist who visited six countries and interviewed more than 400 people to produce a detailed and controversial account of foreign property ownership in Montreal.[32] Even though mainstream media institutions desired investigative work as a commodity, they were careful not to let journalists go too far in attacking a status quo they themselves wished to preserve. This ongoing tension eventually led to a movement on the part of individual journalists to concretize the set of practices that constituted investigative journalism, free from the constraints imposed by their employers.

Chapters 8 through 10 principally examine advances in methodology that characterized the rapid development of investigative journalism in the 1970s. Though the groundwork had already been laid by the early public broadcasting pioneers, the team that produced the *Connections* series on organized crime took investigative research to a new plateau. Their multi-year project, with its exhaustive research model and array of innovative reporting techniques, was unique in both its topic and ambition. Chapter 8 describes the method used in these and other projects of this era. The continued success of investigative journalism led the CBC to make the genre an important component of a new television series in 1975. Chapter 9 describes how this came about, and provides context for the rivalry among competing networks in the field of investigative journalism. Methodology is once again the focus in Chapter 10, which describes the career and working methods of John Sawatsky. By tackling difficult subjects most other reporters couldn't crack, Sawatsky developed a specific method of work that became important in influencing a new generation of investigative reporters. In many ways, he was responsible for setting the genre on a more solid, social scientific footing.

The disaffection between individual investigative journalists and their mainstream institutions played a role in the establishment of a Canadian organization to further the ends of the genre. Chapter 11 describes the process and traces the early history of the Centre for Investigative Journalism, which was founded in 1979.[33] Some of the most skilled and motivated investigative journalists in Canada realized that mainstream media owners weren't and never could be consistent supporters of challenging journalism. Large-scale media organizations wanted scoops and exclusive exposés that could draw an audience, but they had no interest in unleashing a tide of oppositional assaults on an established order that included their major shareholders. If the genre were to mature and grow, individual journalists realized they needed to band together and do it themselves.

Up to this point, the narrative follows a largely chronological structure, progressing from the nineteenth-century historical antecedents to the beginning of the 1980s. Beginning with Chapter 12, I break out several important issues and practices relating to investigative journalism, while still maintaining a rough chronological framework. The first issue deals with one of the most important and controversial methods of investigative journalism. A brief history of undercover and hidden-camera journalism is offered, together with an examination of its ethical justification. There were some important Canadian examples of this method in the immediate post-Watergate context.

Though investigative journalism mushroomed in the 1970s, and initial steps had been taken to professionalize its practice, the genre was still far from mature. Organizations continued to dabble in investigative work even if they had no clear idea about best practices and basic professional standards. This led, in the early 1980s, to a series of spectacular lawsuits that had the inevitable effect of chilling the practice, even in those institutions where journalists paid careful attention to sound methodology. Chapter 13 describes these lawsuits and shows how they emboldened a variety of vested interests into using the threat of court action as a club against inquiring journalists.

Chapter 14 discusses the range of techniques used to attack investigative journalists, from the overt to the subtle. Around the world, journalists who try to hold powerful interests to account are often assaulted and murdered. That has been an infrequent occurrence in Canada. But other kinds of pressure have been applied. Most troublesome for journalists is when government itself launches the attack, and this chapter looks at two case studies, three decades apart, which bear many similarities.

One of the key additions to the investigative journalist's toolkit in the 1980s was Canada's Access to Information Act. Though its effectiveness has often been questioned, it helped drive the career of one of Canada's most unique investigators, Ken Rubin. Chapter 15 looks at Rubin's work in helping create, and then in systematically mining, the legislation that nominally allows citizens the kind of access and scrutiny a watchdog press would require to discharge its democratic obligations.

Chapter 16 is meant to be an echo of Chapter 1, bringing the narrative full circle. Investigative journalism not only concerns contemporary affairs, it strives to find the hidden keys to unlock meaning in historical events. Harvey Cashore's investigation of the Airbus affair began while Brian Mulroney was still prime minister. It continued long after he had left office. Cashore's methodology is worth studying, as is his tenacity. Even though he was tilting against a former prime minister, he faced pressures very similar in nature to those encountered by his colleagues who were dealing with sitting government leaders.

The final two chapters bring the narrative to the present day, and suggest directions for the future. Chapter 17 examines a modern tool available to the Canadian investigative journalist, computer-assisted reporting, and tries to understand its significance. The last chapter offers a brief attempt to predict where the genre will go from here. Throughout the book, I have highlighted the interplay between practitioners and institutions, on the one hand, and the social and political context on the other. The commodification of modern investigative journalism, which accelerated in the post-Watergate era, has continued and assumed new forms. By the mid-1990s the major American newsmagazine programs were flourishing, offering nightly versions of exposés. But it was clear that entertainment values were driving most of the topics, not the desire to examine intensively issues and institutions of importance in society. Tens of thousands of dollars were spent exposing a single corrupt garage mechanic, while other investigations focused on such relatively inconsequential matters as the amount of dirt found on hotel bedspreads. The ephemeral nature of the pseudo-investigations became apparent when game shows and reality television began forcing the newsmagazines to abandon almost all of their public affairs content in favour of celebrity journalism and shock television. In the United States, routine television collaborations with police forces to entrap sexual predators are now presented as investigative journalism, though in truth they are nothing more than marketing devices to attract audiences. The trend to trivialization of the airwaves, coupled with a downgrading of discourse in the public sphere, appears to be affecting broadcasters around the Western world in varying degrees. In Canada, as in other countries, it is difficult to secure funding for a project that doesn't have the promise of commercial and audience success, no matter what the internal worth of the idea. The same trend is also evident in print media, as institutions struggle to maintain readership in an increasingly competitive marketplace.

Young people currently contemplating careers in journalism are seeing a far-different mainstream landscape than the one that existed in the 1970s. But from the margins there might emerge a new generation of investigative journalists, just as there did in the 1960s. The Internet offers an access and reach to ordinary people that is without precedent in communications history. It will be important to monitor how developments online affect the practice of investigative journalism.

At its best, investigative journalism in Canada has exposed odious and corrupt practices, some of them embedded in the very nature of society, and demonstrated the true inner workings of important institutions, both public and private. It has held powerful interests to account, fearlessly demanding answers and accountability. Along the way, those same interests have retaliated, using economic, political, and legal pressures to blunt the attack. And the counter-thrusts have sometimes inflicted more damage than the original exposés. Through the years, investigative journalism has ebbed and flowed, rising in prestige one year only to be beaten back the next. How it develops in the twenty-first century—indeed, whether it continues to survive in its current form—remains an open question.

Acknowledgements

The idea for this book began with a proposal to the Michener Awards Foundation, which generously awarded me a Michener-Deacon Fellowship. I would like to thank Clark Davey, Edward Zebrowski, and other foundation officials for their advice and support. I would also like to acknowledge the assistance of the Canada Council for the Arts. This project could not have been completed without the ongoing support of John Bertrand, regional director of CBC Manitoba, and many other colleagues at the CBC.

Along the way, I received help, advice, or encouragement from a variety of people. I have noted many of them in the text, but some deserve special mention, including Sig Gerber, Ross Rutherford, Christian Cote, David Studer, Maxine Ruvinsky, Kelly Crichton, David Nayman, Henry Aubin, Nick Fillmore, David McKie, Dan Henry, Michael Hughes, Edith Cody-Rice, Vera-Lynn Kubinec, Glen MacKenzie, Bryan Cantley, Clifford Newman, Katherine Skene, Peter Chambers, and Marta Tomins. There are many other colleagues, students, and fellow journalists I have encountered over the years who helped me deepen my understanding of this subject. Some of my favourite people are librarians, and I depended on them extensively to help me with my research. I particularly want to thank Tyana Grundig, Michele Melady, and the entire staff of the CBC Reference Library in Toronto for their expert assistance. Thanks also to Brenda Carroll of the CBC Image Research Library, as well as Elizabeth Seitz and the staff at the University of Regina Archives, the University of Winnipeg Library, the Archives of Ontario, and Library and Archives Canada. My manuscript would have been considerably weaker without some sound advice along the way from many people. I owe a particular debt of gratitude to my friend, Hope Kamin, who also happens to be one of the best editors in the country.

It isn't possible to do a project like this without support from family. I rely on conversations with my children, David, Mark, and Michelle, to gain better insights into all kinds of subjects, and investigative journalism is one of them. When you have children with expertise in the law, philosophy, and the arts, it would be foolish not to take advantage of free consultations. Finally, this book could not have been written without the unqualified support of my lifelong partner and wife, Harriet Zaidman. Her advice, encouragement, editorial suggestions, critiques, and assorted assisted-living techniques, all helped me complete the task. Her influence is present throughout the book. Thank you.

Chapter 1

Bringing Down the Government

Every government is run by liars and nothing they say should be believed.

I.F. Stone[1]

It is every reporter's secret, and sometimes not so secret, desire. A brown paper envelope arrives in the office. Inside, there is a document implicating the highest political forces in the land with wrongdoing. The document becomes the smoking gun in an investigation that creates political turmoil across the country. Cover-ups are stripped away and the truth is finally revealed. The government, incapable of withstanding the onslaught of publicity, falls.

On 5 April 2001, *National Post* reporter Andrew McIntosh received the proverbial envelope. It came in the regular mail delivery at the newspaper's Ottawa bureau. The envelope had his name on it, but it bore no return address. Inside was a loan-authorization document from the Business Development Bank of Canada. McIntosh scanned the papers and found a reference, in the footnotes, to a company owned by the prime minister, Jean Chrétien. It suggested a secret relationship that had never before been disclosed. Over the previous 18 months, McIntosh had pounded away at a series of stories involving Chrétien's private dealings near Shawinigan, Quebec. There had been allegations of favouritism, political interference, illegal lobbying, financial handouts to unsavoury characters, and a host of other suspicious activities. The scandal had already been dubbed Shawinigate. Now, if the contents of the envelope were legitimate, the story would move to an even higher ethical and legal plane. McIntosh immediately flew to Toronto where he consulted with his bosses and the newspaper's lawyer. There was a sense of intense urgency and excitement. Everybody examining the document felt the resulting exposure could have dire consequences for the political career of the prime minister.[2]

Ever since Watergate, bringing down the government has become the gold standard for many investigative journalists. It's an extension of the watchdog role many journalistic organizations assign themselves, a function steeped in Enlightenment ideals. By bringing errors, problems, and scandals to light, the media keep government in check. If the scandal becomes so odious that the public loses confidence in its elected leaders, it's only natural that a minister or the government itself should step aside, though no mainstream editorial boards would go so far as to invoke John Locke's 'right to revolution' as a remedy.[3] In some news organizations, political journalists are encouraged to think of themselves as the Opposition. They are asked to scrutinize the decisions and actions of elected officials and senior bureaucrats. Frequently, the research interests of opposition members and journalists coincide, and there is often sharing of information. Journalists typically assess the success of their investigations on the basis of the results. If a story results in the calling of an inquiry, or the resignation of a minister, or the fall of a government, the news organization will be seen to have succeeded.

Is there a moral dimension to this journalistic impulse? Scholars generally agree there is, but there is less consensus on its exact character. David Protess argues that such work represents a journalism of outrage. 'Investigative journalists *intend* to provoke outrage in their reports of malfeasance. Their work is validated when citizens respond by demanding change from their leaders. Similarly, corrective policy actions provide official legitimacy to an investigative story. Investigative reporters find personal satisfaction in doing stories that lead to civic betterment.'[4] Many journalists follow a 'mobilization model' by attempting to change public opinion through their exposés, then mobilizing the same public to become agents of change.[5] But if society expresses indifference to an investigative report, it often deflates the crusading spirit of the journalist. James Ettema and Theodore Glasser say the stories of investigative journalists call attention to the breakdown of social systems. 'In this way investigative journalists are custodians of public conscience.'[6] At the same time, the authors point out an apparent paradox: by acting as custodians of conscience, are the journalists violating their objectivity, and going beyond merely observing and reporting facts?[7] Many Canadian journalists have weighed the question and determined that any subjectivity in choosing topics of investigation does not colour the objective methodology that is always required in conducting the inquiry. As examples in this chapter show, although motivations were rooted in the historic role of holding governments to account, there may also have been specific partisan objectives on the part of some journalists or institutions. But in no case did that appear to interfere with the quality of the legwork.

Governments frequently interpret journalistic scrutiny as partisan, accusing the reporters of working hand-in-hand with opposition parties to discredit them. Investigative journalism in the political arena is inherently oppositional, and it isn't uncommon for the government of the day to feel besieged by aggressive reporters. John Zaritsky was in the Toronto *Globe and Mail* newsroom when Bill Davis and his Progressive Conservatives won an overwhelming majority in the 1971 Ontario election, capturing 78 of 117 seats. 'I want all of you to understand that we are now the official Opposition in this province', managing editor Clark Davey told reporters that evening. Zaritsky took the instruction to heart, undertaking rigorous investigations of suspicious land deals and conflicts of interest that ultimately forced the resignations of two key cabinet ministers. In retrospect, he was happy with the result both journalistically and politically. 'I was unabashedly a devotee and admirer of Stephen Lewis, the NDP leader, and I was rabidly anti-Tory. I was out to get whatever I could on his government.'[8] Still, Zaritsky never let his political leanings affect the quality or accuracy of his work. The reporting was solid, it was honoured with a National Newspaper Award, and Zaritsky's lasting satisfaction was journalistic rather than political.[9] 'I still remain proud of the fact that as a result of those stories the Davis government brought in conflict-of-interest legislation and took steps to clean up the process.'[10] Despite the scandals, the Davis administration survived and remained in power until 1985.

There was a different outcome in Manitoba, when CBC Radio reporter Curt Petrovich began investigating dirty tricks in the 1995 provincial election. The story had circulated years earlier, but was never properly investigated. The Progressive Conservative government of Gary Filmon was seeking re-election in 1995, and it desperately wanted to unseat NDP candidates in key ridings. Some senior Conservatives hatched an unlikely scheme. They would create a phony aboriginal party, run three candidates in swing ridings, and hope the native candidates would steal enough votes from the NDP so that the Tories could squeak through. Those were the cynical origins of the Independent Native Voice Party. Conservative party activists covertly provided strategy and funds to the candidates. In the end, the scheme ended in failure as the NDP captured all three ridings. But Filmon's Conservatives won the election, and they dismissed a brief flurry of suggestions that they had anything to do with the aboriginal party. The story dropped from public view.

Three years later, Petrovich picked up the trail once more. He was being encouraged by a disaffected Conservative to look further into the issue, but without first-hand testimony from the aboriginal candidates themselves, it would be hard to prove anything. Persistent legwork finally paid off as Petrovich located one of the candidates, Darryl Sutherland, and convinced him to talk. Sutherland, who had a grade 6 education and had never even voted in a provincial or federal election, described how he had been approached to run for office.[11] He had been promised a $5,000 campaign fund that could be used for meals and expenses, and a vehicle to drive during the election. The bizarre story of a vote-splitting scheme went national in June 1998, and the provincial government was in crisis.[12] Further revelations forced Filmon's hand, and he called for a commission of inquiry. In the end, the scandal implicated many high-ranking Tories in the province, including the premier's principal secretary and the Treasury Board secretary.[13] Millionaire Tory businessmen were part of the scheme as well, secretly writing cheques to support the native candidates in denominations low enough to come under the radar of mandatory reporting requirements. In his final report, the inquiry commissioner, Justice Alfred Monnin, was scathing in his assessment of the explanations he had heard in testimony: 'In all my years on the bench, I never encountered as many liars in one proceeding as I did during this inquiry.'[14]

Filmon fought back by accusing Petrovich of bias. He said the reporter had supplied Sutherland's phone number to the NDP, suggesting they engaged in a joint, partisan effort. 'If the CBC has an ombudsman, they should be looking at that action and saying: Is that fair journalism?' Filmon said.[15] It turned out the NDP had asked Petrovich for the phone number, and he merely passed the message along to Sutherland. Filmon never officially complained to the CBC Ombudsman, and Petrovich's reporting was fully endorsed by his management. In 1999, he earned a Michener award for meritorious public service journalism, with the judges praising the 'dogged pursuit' he displayed in tracking down the story.[16] Although Filmon was never personally implicated in the vote-rigging scheme, his party's credibility was badly bruised. Many analysts attributed his loss in the 1999 provincial election to the scandal. If any single factor could be said to have brought down his government, it was Petrovich's investigative reporting.

By the time McIntosh had received his brown paper envelope, the Shawinigate affair had passed through many stages. It had been one of McIntosh's main pre-occupations since joining the *National Post*, and his skilful investigative work kept producing new and more troubling sidebars to the controversy. Throughout 1999, he filed 10 stories that looked intensively at the prime minister's ownership of a Quebec golf club and the subsequent events surrounding the entrepreneurs who took control of related businesses. But the impact of the stories, which were complex and difficult to follow, was questionable. The Liberal Party comfortably won its third majority in November 2000, and Shawinigate didn't seem to be a major factor in the campaign. Now, with the possibility of further documented revelations, it appeared the situation could turn. Before examining the controversy that followed McIntosh's surprise mail delivery, it's instructive to consider how the Shawinigate affair unfolded. In many respects, it offers a textbook example of a modern-day investigative journalist's methodology.

McIntosh was born in Montreal and developed an early fascination with newspapers, engendered by his parents. 'My mother would read the paper back to front, which is sometimes how I read it, because I often find the most interesting stuff way back inside the paper. I liked the idea of communicating by writing. We played "town" in the basement of my house, and I published the paper in town. I wanted to be a newspaper guy.'[17] After high school he enrolled in Concordia's journalism program, and began selling freelance articles to the *Globe and Mail*. He noticed there were many young journalists in the marketplace competing for attention, but few willing to write business stories. So he began specifically pitching ideas to the business section. He got summer stints at the Montreal *Gazette* and then the *Globe*, soaking up reporting skills however he could. McIntosh benefited from experiences and methodologies of senior reporters, and he had no hesitation asking people like Victor Malarek, Peter Moon, Jock Ferguson, and Graham Fraser for tips on how to find information. At 22, he got his first taste of political reporting covering the Quebec election of 1985. He did so well the *Globe* offered him a full-time job.

McIntosh was influenced by a statement Jacques Parizeau, then Quebec finance minister, had made to the press gallery in Quebec City. 'When I want to know what's being said in Quebec City, I read you guys. But when I want to know what's being done in Quebec, I read the *Globe and Mail*'s Report on Business.' It reinforced his belief that the real stories were to be found in tracking where the money goes, who receives it, and what they spend it on. Over the next four years at the *Globe*, he applied that method to finding stories in the business and political world. During a stint covering politics in Ottawa, McIntosh followed a money trail in the construction of a new prison. Up to $1 million had been spent on a site in Quebec, when the location was arbitrarily switched to Prime Minister Brian Mulroney's riding. In a foreshadowing of stories to come, McIntosh relied on an unnamed senior government source who told him the decision came on direct orders from the prime minister.[18]

In 1989, McIntosh was recruited to join an investigative reporting team at the Montreal *Gazette*. It was a chance to broaden his range of stories and spend time doing more intensive digging. He also learned new techniques from his more experienced team members, William Marsden, and Rod Macdonell. Marsden taught him the power of chronologies, a technique John Sawatsky and other investigative reporters of the 1970s had developed. 'I think Marsden more than anyone else taught me how to prepare for an interview, that you don't just wing it. You need to have a plan, you've got to have your material organized and know what you need.' McIntosh benefited from the trial and error of reporters who had gone before him, gradually accumulating all the key investigative methods and adopting a systematic approach to his research. McIntosh, Marsden, and Carolyn Adolph worked on an exhaustive, 10-part report into the 1992 shootings of four people at Concordia University. Over a number of months, the three reporters laboriously compiled their research and constructed a chronology of the troubled life of Professor Valery Fabrikant. The result was a dramatic exploration into the psyche of a man, and how he came to take the lives of four of his colleagues.[19] When budget concerns led to the dismantling of the investigative team, McIntosh returned to business reporting and continued to accumulate a network of sources that would routinely provide him with exclusive stories for the newspaper.

While at the *Gazette* in 1995, McIntosh spotted a brief news item buried in the business section of *La Presse*. It said Jean Chrétien had sold his shares in the Grand-Mère Golf Club, located in his St. Maurice riding, to a golf division of the Delta Hotel chain. McIntosh was intrigued. Firstly, it was not widely known that Chrétien had an ownership position in a golf club. Secondly, he found it odd that a large hotel chain would buy a minority interest in an out-of-the-way golf club. Busy with other stories, he filed it away for a future inquiry. The chance came three years later, in August 1998, when he began work for the *National Post*. It was one of five stories he pitched in his first meeting with editor Ken Whyte. The *Post* was set to begin publication in October, and Whyte was eager for political stories with impact. He told McIntosh to spend a week or two checking into the story, and they would assess where to go from there.[20]

McIntosh embarked on an inquiry that, in terms of its methodology, amounted to a handbook for investigative journalism. Here are the various steps he took:

- First, he consulted secondary sources from publicly available records and books, determining that Jean Chrétien and two associates paid $1.25 million to buy the golf course from pulp and paper giant Consolidated Bathurst in 1988.
- Next, he traced the origin of the news story that had piqued his interest, finding that it was the result of a press release issued by Montreal public relations company Groupe Everest (which would later be implicated in the federal sponsorship scandal.) The story said Delta's new golf division had paid a fair market price for Chrétien's shares before he became prime minister.

McIntosh subsequently learned that Delta was not the purchaser of the shares and never had a golf division.

- Federal and Quebec corporate searches gave him ownership details about Chrétien's original purchase. Quebec court records threw further light on the business affairs of the golf course. That's how he discovered the purchase also gave Chrétien and his partners the assets, goodwill, and ongoing business of the Grand-Mère Inn, located adjacent to the golf club.

- Land title searches of the inn showed it had been bought by Yvon Duhaime, a Shawinigan businessman. A mortgage deed told him the inn had received a $615,000 loan from the Business Development Bank of Canada, a federal Crown corporation, in September 1997, and another $50,000 from a federally funded regional economic development group.

- After amassing all the relevant public documents on the properties and businesses involved, McIntosh began a series of research interviews with area residents. He learned Duhaime had a suspicious history. McIntosh checked Duhaime's criminal history on a Quebec court database, and discovered he had a record for repeat drunk driving, assault, and uttering death threats. He also found Duhaime had a history of failing to pay income taxes and other financial obligations.

- Wondering why the Business Development Bank would give such a large loan to a man with a chequered past and history of financial troubles, he filed an Access to Information request with the bank. Though the request was denied, he learned from the bank that applicants are forced to disclose criminal records.

- In an interview with the head of Delta Hotels at the time of Chrétien's supposed sale, McIntosh learned that the 1993 deal had never been consummated. This appeared to indicate Chrétien still had an ownership position in the golf course.[21]

The initial arrangement to spend a couple weeks on the story turned into several months of investigation. McIntosh was peering into the private business affairs of the prime minister in a way no journalist had done before. There were some tantalizing questions. Did Chrétien still own his share of the golf course, despite his claims (and a press release) to the contrary? Did Chrétien intervene to help Yvon Duhaime, who had bought the inn from the prime minister and his partners, secure federal funding? There was no smoking gun, but enough material to put the issues before the public. He began writing a series of stories in January 1999. In retrospect, McIntosh thought he could have done more digging before he began publishing.[22] But as articles started to appear, more information came to light. McIntosh developed some confidential sources who began feeding him details, which he used to do further public record checks and interviews. A source told him the prime minister had joked about having to make many phone calls to get Duhaime his loans. He learned that aides to Chrétien attended meetings at which Duhaime's application was discussed. Companies in Chrétien's riding that did business with the golf course, and with an unpaid aide of Chrétien's, were later awarded more than $4 million in federal job-creation grants and loans. McIntosh also discovered that another hotelier in Chrétien's riding got $1.5 million in federal grants and loans, with the prime minister's help, even though he had defrauded business partners and misappropriated close to $1 million in Belgium.

At the same time, the federal government was trying to manage a growing crisis at Human Resources Development Canada. Allegations of mismanagement in the department's $1 billion jobs-grant program were confirmed in an internal audit. Auditor General Denis Desautels found breaches of authority, improper payments, and poor monitoring. The *Post* also added up all the various federal job-creation grants that had gone to Chrétien's riding since 1996, and found the total was more than Ottawa had spent in all of Manitoba, Alberta, and Saskatchewan during the same period.

The most potentially damaging story for the prime minister came in the middle of the 2000 election campaign. Despite previous firm denials from the Prime Minister's Office, McIntosh reported that Chrétien had repeatedly called the president of the Business Development Bank, urging him to grant a loan to Duhaime. He used confidential, unnamed sources and documents as evidence. Confronted on the campaign trail with the story, Chrétien admitted it. But he said it was his duty as an MP to help a constituent. 'You call who you know . . . it's the normal operation', he told reporters.[23] The federal ethics counselor said Chrétien's actions broke no rules, because no guidelines on such behaviour existed, though future policies made it clear that similar calls from ministers would not be permitted.

National Post editors, who were initially disappointed at the lack of concrete evidence of wrongdoing, grew happier with each new revelation. The newspaper was a creation of press baron Conrad Black, whose right-wing views encouraged editors to view themselves as part of the opposition to the Liberal government. Partisan politics were of no concern to McIntosh, who exercised thorough objectivity as he relentlessly dug into greater and greater detail. 'People were under the impression that Conrad Black wound me up and sent me out as some sort of attack dog', McIntosh said. 'But it was not their idea to do this story. It was my idea.'[24] Still, the stories were being repeatedly used by the opposition parties to denounce the Liberals, and gave fodder to *Post* columnists and editorialists who were focused on promoting the movement to unite the right-wing political forces in Canada. Black and Chrétien had never been on good speaking terms, but the prime minister called him about half a dozen times to complain about the unrelenting stories. One of the calls came at 3 a.m. when Black was in Europe. 'I thought we hammered it a little too hard, and beyond a certain point I had some sympathy for Chrétien', Black is quoted as saying in Chris Cobb's book on the *National Post*. 'He was hypocritical and corrupt, of course, but he had a right not to be harassed on the point every single day with all the Shawinigan stuff. Of course it has never been properly examined what went on. In a proper two-party system I think Chrétien would have been out. . . .'[25]

If some editors at the *Post* thought it had the potential to bring down the government, their views changed with the results of the 2000 election. Shawinigate didn't play much of a factor as the Liberals swept back to power. It's not clear how many people took the time to read the complex stories. And many media outlets ignored McIntosh's stories at first. This was partly due to the typical, competitive shunning by rival media organizations of investigative stories, especially stories that rely on unnamed sources. Others were convinced that the *Post* was just on a campaign to get the prime minister. 'Parliamentary press gallery reporters initially ignored my stories. . . . It seemed as though most gallery members hoped that the upstart *National Post* would move on to something else.'[26] McIntosh said the obstinacy of other journalists meant it took the press gallery far too long to discover that the federal job-creation grant story was a major scandal. But even inside the *National Post*, there was an admission that the complexity of the Shawinigate issue worked against it. 'I'm sure most people still don't understand it, and that was always the problem', said Ken Whyte. 'It was too complicated.'[27]

In the first year of his investigation, McIntosh had conducted more than 200 interviews, reviewed thousands of pages of government documents, and conducted hundreds of land-title, corporate, and courthouse searches. He didn't let the election results stop his work. If previous patterns were any indication, a counter-attack of some sort was to be expected. It came in an unusual form, in the wake of the brown paper envelope's arrival on McIntosh's desk. The document was from the Business Development Bank, outlining the loan to Duhaime. In the footnotes was a reference to a debt owed by Duhaime to JAC Consultants, Chrétien's family holding company. The amount was small, $23,040, but if legitimate, the document showed a financial link between Chrétien and the man he was trying to help get a federal loan. McIntosh confronted Duhaime, who replied: 'You're not going to turn Canada upside down over $23,040, are you?'

While the *Post* was still debating whether to go with the story, Quebec bailiffs raided the home of the former president of the Business Development Bank, François Beaudoin, trying to determine if he was the source of the leak, and documents were filed in support of the searches, including the letter McIntosh had received. That made the story available to all media. The development bank and the Prime Minister's Office both claimed the document was a forgery. The denials were enough to mute the controversy over the latest Shawinigate revelation. But if Chrétien felt he was on the hotseat over the revelations, McIntosh was soon to come under equally intense pressure. The RCMP asked him to hand over the original document so it could perform forensic tests, with a view to finding the source. Leaking a bank document was an offence, and police wanted to solve it. McIntosh refused. He soon learned the identity of the source who had provided him with the seemingly smoking gun. Eventually, the RCMP secured a warrant and assistance order to seize the document. The *Post* appealed, and, for nearly two years, McIntosh wondered whether he would be compelled to identify his confidential source.

The substance of the original investigation receded and a sideshow became the principal focus of the parties. McIntosh wondered why the RCMP went to so much trouble to get the document. 'It was never just about $23,000. It was about so much more. It was about gross abuse of power. . . . It was about trying to silence and crush those who dare question and expose what was clearly wrong.'[28] In the appeal to the Ontario Superior Court of Justice, McIntosh and the *Post* argued the necessity of confidential sources for investigative journalism to flourish. They cited examples of how confidential sources had helped to uncover important stories. The *Globe and Mail* and the CBC intervened on behalf of the *Post* in the case. In an affidavit that was more than 100 pages long, McIntosh was completely transparent in how he had researched the Shawinigate stories, and how he had cultivated his sources. He even explained the steps he took to protect leaked documents, such as retyping the information into a computer file and storing the original in a secure location. McIntosh was determined not just to protect the person who gave him the development bank document, but to uphold the right of all journalists to grant confidentiality to sources. When a judgment on the case was reserved, he endured a worrisome wait. Every day after he got home from work, his children would ask whether the decision had come.

McIntosh had cause to worry. A negative decision would mean not just forfeiture of the document, but could also lead to a court process during which McIntosh would be forced to identify sources. He was determined not to do so, and he knew that meant the possibility of going to jail. Although jailing of journalists in Canada for refusal to name sources is rare, it happened at least three times in the twentieth century. The first was in 1914, when W.R. McCurdy of the *Halifax Herald* was called before Nova Scotia's House of Assembly and asked to identify the author of an anonymous letter to the editor that had accused government members of corruption. He refused, and the legislature sentenced him to jail for 48 hours. Eighty years later, a cameraman for a Hull, Quebec television station refused to name a source at the preliminary hearing of a policeman charged with assault and obstruction of justice. He was sentenced to three days in jail for contempt.[29] The most serious case happened in 1969, when CBC researcher John N. Smith appeared before a fire commissioner's inquiry into Montreal-area bombings. Smith, who worked for the weekly current affairs program *The Way It Is*, had tape-recorded an interview with an alleged member of the FLQ. The inquiry wanted him to testify, but Smith refused, citing his need to protect confidential information. He was held in contempt and sentenced to spend seven days amid the rats and filthy conditions in Montreal's Bordeaux jail.[30]

When the McIntosh decision finally did come, on 21 January 2004, Justice Mary Lou Benotto quashed the search warrant and assistance order. In the process, she issued a landmark ruling that clarified the importance of confidential sources for investigative journalism in Canada.

> Sources want confidentiality for a variety of reasons. They may, themselves, be breaching a duty of confidentiality. They may have stolen the information. They may fear economic reprisals. They may lose their jobs. They may fear for their safety. They may fear for the safety of their families.
>
> The Crown argues that the actions of these sources should not be encouraged. I disagree. If employee confidentiality were to trump conscience, there

would be a licence for corporations, governments, and other employees to operate without accountability. . . .

If the journalist-informant relationship is undermined, society as a whole is
affected. It is through confidential sources that matters of great public importance are made known. As corporate and public power increase, the ability of the
average citizen to affect his or her world depends upon the information disseminated by the press. To deprive the media of an important tool in the gathering
of news would affect society as a whole. The relationship is one that should be
fostered. . . .

Freedom of expression is a cornerstone of our society. The ability of the public to know what its elected leaders are doing is fundamental to a democracy. We
rely on the news media to provide us with this information. The expectation that
a source will remain confidential is often the very reason people feel free to go to
the press. Often the more explosive the story is, the greater the risk to the informant if he or she is exposed. Reputations, livelihoods, and security may be at stake.
Without confidentiality the press would not receive some information. Protection
of the confidentiality serves the interests of the informant. In serving the interests
of the informant, the interests of society are served to an even greater degree.[31]

On the very same day, in an irony no fiction writer could have credibly scripted,
RCMP raided the home of *Ottawa Citizen* reporter Juliet O'Neill, looking for leaked
documents she had used in a story about Maher Arar, the Canadian who had been
deported to Syria and tortured. But the day belonged to McIntosh, who finally felt
vindicated in a battle that pitted him against formidable forces. Jean Chrétien had
retired as prime minister a month earlier. Shawinigate was a major embarrassment in
his 40-year career in Parliament, but it wasn't a fatal blow. In the end, the affair may be
remembered more for how the reporting was done, and how a fundamental principle
of investigative work finally gained recognition in the Canadian courts.

McIntosh's Shawinigate revelations were creating additional work for *Globe and Mail*
journalist Daniel Leblanc in 1999. As a rookie reporter in the *Globe*'s Ottawa bureau,
Leblanc tried to play catch-up with McIntosh, while also covering other daily news
stories from Parliament Hill. But, one day, he came up with an original story idea in an
unlikely place. From his home in Hull, Leblanc noticed an unusual figure looming in
the distance. It was an 11-storey-high hot-air balloon in the shape of a Mountie on a
horse, making an appearance at a nearby Gatineau festival. The balloon was making its
rounds at events around the country, having been launched as part of the force's 125th
anniversary. Leblanc sensed something strange. The RCMP was in a financial crisis at the
time, and was clamouring for more money. Questions were being asked in Parliament
about why investigations were being cut short for lack of funds. With such a financial
situation, how could the force be spending money on giant balloons?

Back at work, he decided to find out more about the issue. He filed access to
information requests with the RCMP and Public Works, trying to get as much

information as possible about the cost of the balloon. The request was filed 28 September and was met with delays and suggestions that records weren't available. Leblanc pressed for more details. On 17 December, the government released a small bit of information about the balloon, but it was enough to produce a front-page story in the *Globe* on 31 December. In an edition of the paper devoted to the dawning of the new millennium, an Ottawa story with a touch of humour appeared below the fold. Leblanc reported that the balloon had been built in England at a cost of about $100,000, but the government had paid $324,000 to rent it for 11 months. An Ottawa-based marketing firm owned the balloon. Leblanc checked, and sure enough the firm turned out to be a contributor to the Liberal Party. That's as far as the story went, and it likely succeeded in producing a chuckle or two for readers as they prepared to celebrate the coming of Y2K. But in the corridors of power in Ottawa, there was far less laughter. Leblanc had touched the surface of a potential political quagmire. In fact, the story would be the beginning of a process that would ultimately put an end to the Liberal Party's grip on power in Canada.

Born in Ottawa, Leblanc had a good grasp of the city's political culture. His parents were public servants, and while studying political science in university he spent a few months working in the office of Liberal MP Denis Paradis. He was struck by the rivalry between federal and Quebec politicians, and their non-stop competition for visibility. The 1995 Quebec sovereignty referendum was a defining moment in these relationships, and Leblanc couldn't help but notice Ottawa's efforts in the months following the narrow federalist victory to boost Canada's image in Quebec. The Canadian flag suddenly seemed to be everywhere in Quebec. By 1995 he decided he wanted to be a journalist, and enrolled in Carleton University's journalism program. His best practical experience came as a research assistant to the *Globe and Mail's* Edward Greenspon, who was working on a book at the time with Anthony Wilson-Smith. In October 1998, when the *Globe* was creating a new position in Ottawa, Greenspon asked Leblanc if he was interested. He jumped at the chance to put his knowledge of politics and journalism to work.[32]

The story of the hot-air balloon might have been a one-off affair about a quirky piece of federal spending, but Leblanc sensed there was more. The desire to publicize Canada in Quebec may have led to more excesses. Then, he received an anonymous phone call from a federal bureaucrat in response to the story, telling him to continue digging. There was one further contact, but Leblanc never knew the tipster's name or any significant details of what he should be probing. It spurred him to keep going. On 11 January 2000, he filed a further access request with the federal public works department. It asked for 'all records detailing the sponsorship budget within Public Works, since the 1994-1995 fiscal year. The records would include, without being limited to, the events that received federal money such as festivals, hot-air balloons and the airing of commercials.' Subsequent testimony would show that Leblanc's request threw senior officials in the department into a panic. The human resources jobs-grant scandal was in full swing, and no one had yet probed the details of the sponsorship program, which officials realized might prove embarrassing to government. In fact, the entire sponsorship program was a subterranean effort that was largely unknown to the public. It had begun as early as 1994, when the advertising section of Public Works began spending money on events that would publicize the federal government. It accelerated after the Quebec referendum, when Ottawa decided it needed to have maximum visibility in Quebec. But the advertising section, under the directorship of Chuck Guité, turned to outside agencies with strong Liberal connections to conduct most of the business. An internal audit in 1996 showed problems in how the program was being run, and the lack of controls when it came to overseeing billings and the awarding of contracts. The audit had never been made public, nor had government acted on its recommendations.

Unknown to Leblanc, an internal power struggle was taking place over his access request. Anita Lloyd, the department's access coordinator, made her bosses aware of Leblanc's request. They labeled it officially as 'interesting', the departmental euphemism for requests that had the potential to embarrass the minister or cause some level of political grief. While departmental officials were pulling together records to satisfy the request, Lloyd received an unusual order from her superiors. She was to interpret the request as if it had not used the word 'budget' in its wording. In this way, the department could release a more limited list of expenditures that related just to specific events. Sponsorship dollars that had flowed to non-event matters could be excluded, and these were the ones that had the most potential for embarrassment. Lloyd offered to call Leblanc and clarify exactly what he wanted, and whether he would be content with this interpretation. Her bosses told her not to do that.

But Lloyd, who had worked as an access officer since 1988, didn't follow orders so readily. 'I felt that if I did, then I would be misleading the applicant and he would not be receiving all of the information that he had requested and he may think that I was indeed doing that. In fact, I thought it wasn't legal and I thought it wasn't ethical', she told a commission of inquiry.[33] Lloyd consulted a lawyer on three different occasions about her dilemma, and finally refused to sign off on the idea of providing Leblanc with an edited list. Leblanc's original request was fulfilled. Lloyd would eventually be deluged with nearly 500 access requests from the media dealing with the sponsorship program.

Leblanc's access request provoked more than just consternation amongst access officers in the Public Works department. The minister, Alfonso Gagliano, ordered another audit of the sponsorship program, even though departmental officials hadn't acted on the recommendations of the 1996 review. Not surprisingly, the new audit found similar problems. Gagliano would later tell a public inquiry he ordered a moratorium on disbursements from the program after hearing the audit's findings in September. But inquiry commissioner John Gomery was skeptical, noting that monies began flowing again in November.

By early June of 2000, Leblanc had written four stories on the sponsorship program, but was running out of fresh information. 'I had no other avenues to follow, no leads to chase. In fact, I had no specific intention of pursuing the matter further—until that phone call.'[34] The call, on 1 June, was from an anonymous female whistle-blower. She alleged some advertising companies were overcharging for work and sending kickbacks to the Liberal Party. She told Leblanc about Jacques Corriveau, a long-time friend of Jean Chrétien who eventually became known as one of the key figures in the sponsorship scandal. The woman identified herself only as MaChouette, or 'my dear', and Leblanc kept in touch with her by e-mail for the next two years. He eventually figured out who she was, but carefully protected her identity as she fed him important details from the inside.[35]

In August 2000, Leblanc and reporter Campbell Clark revealed a Montreal company that employed Gagliano's son had won subcontracting sponsorship work. Unnamed Liberal Party sources in Montreal and Ottawa were quoted as saying there was uneasiness in the party over the company. Like Shawinigate, it was a complicated story and difficult to follow. The story's importance emerged gradually. Through 2001, there were stories raising more and more questions about the program. The *Globe* reported on a $615,000 federal contract to a Montreal company that essentially required it to evaluate its own work. Another story told of a fund that was set aside to sponsor unforeseen cultural and sporting events, many of which were in the ridings of Gagliano and Prime Minister Chrétien.

But the piece that seemed to turn the tide came in March 2002. 'The Chrétien government has paid a company with close Liberal ties a total of $550,000 to produce a report of which no trace can be found', Leblanc and Clark reported. The report had been requested under Access to Information nearly two years earlier, but Ottawa finally admitted it didn't have the document. Neither did Groupaction Marketing of Montreal, which was supposed to have produced it. What's more, the newspaper showed Groupaction to be a major contributor to the Liberals. No one could ignore the story any longer. The auditor general was asked to look into the matter, and in less than two months Sheila Fraser made public her blunt assessment. Senior civil servants 'broke just about every rule in the book' when handing out contracts to Groupaction. She said there was an appalling lack of documentation surrounding the program, making it difficult to determine accountability. She recommended a full-scale audit and an RCMP investigation.

While those investigations proceeded, Leblanc and Clark continued to produce more revelations: outrageous billings, nepotism, political patronage, and suspected fraud. By the time Fraser's full report was tabled in February 2004, the extent of the problem was largely known. In his first act as prime minister, Paul Martin ordered a public inquiry into the scandal. Though he won a narrow minority victory in June, Martin lost significant support in Quebec and struggled to contain the damage of the sponsorship story. The inquiry hearings, which began in September, were widely seen as fatally damaging Liberal Party chances to hang onto power. Gomery found clear evidence of political involvement in the scandal, which included gross overcharging, inflated commissions, kickbacks, and illegal contributions. He also pointed to the 'reluctance, for fear of reprisal, by virtually all public servants to go against the will of a manager who was circumventing established policies and who had access to senior political officials'.[36] Some of the key perpetrators faced criminal charges. But for the

Liberals, the main consequence was the January 2006 election, when they went down to defeat and turned over the reins of power to the Conservatives for the first time in 13 years.

The idea that the media should act as a watchdog, a fourth estate, or a counterweight to government, is rooted in Enlightenment ideals. Many media organizations claim to speak on behalf of the people, watching government closely, and pouncing when they detect corruption or wrongdoing. Just how loudly the watchdog barks, though, is based on a variety of factors. In numerous cases, the rhetoric of the publishers and news directors exceeds the reality. Legislative and parliamentary reporters are routinely fed trial-balloon 'scoops' to boost their egos, invited into the comfortable corridors of power, and corrupted with small courtesies and favours. Flattering and co-opting the press gallery is an important aim for politicians, and the effortless movement of many political reporters into public relations jobs for the people they formerly covered is evidence of the tactic's success. It is far easier to be handed the details of an announcement a day before its official release, and thereby score a supposed 'exclusive', than to spend weeks or months digging into matters of genuine public importance. The journalists described in this chapter chose the route of investigation and independent inquiry, hoping to provoke outrage with their findings.

Andrew McIntosh's stories raised serious questions about practices by the highest politician in the land, but the prime minister managed to survive the storm. Daniel Leblanc's curiosity about a hot-air balloon, on the other hand, may have started a chain reaction that eventually brought down a government. 'It's always a bigger issue than just one story or one factor', Leblanc believes.[37] No one can say with certainty what the determining factor was for the complex string of events that led to the scandal. But it appears to be as clear an example as any of how investigative reporting can unravel secrets that go right to the heart of a government's credibility.

Chapter 2

Pioneers

If the government is acting wrongly, it ought to be checked. Censure of government causes inquiry and produces discontent among the people, and this discontent is the only means known to me of removing the defects of a vicious government and inducing the rulers to remedy the abuses. Thus the press, by its power of censure, is the best safeguard of the interests of mankind.

William Lyon Mackenzie[1]

Tucked away in a handful of Canadian libraries are copies of an obscure and largely forgotten newspaper. The *Welland Canal*, published in 1835, doesn't register in any history of Canadian journalism or newspapers. Yet its columns contain something akin to a modern-day exposé, a scathing attack on the corruption and outright fraud perpetrated by the directors of a semi-public corporation. Facts are marshaled to prove conclusively that the canal company's books had been cooked with false entries, erasures, and deliberate fraud. The company's owner is accused of lavish expenses, a charge documented with precise details of the beer, gin, and cigars he improperly billed on his expense accounts. There are stories of shady land transactions, stock manipulation, and practices that would send modern forensic accountants into a tizzy of excitement. In all, the newspaper establishes beyond any doubt its claim of a 'systematic series of efforts to cover dishonesty and embezzlement'.[2] The sole writer, publisher, and distributor of the *Welland Canal* newspaper was William Lyon Mackenzie, arguably Canada's first true investigative journalist.

Mackenzie, of course, has a secure place in Canadian history for his many other accomplishments. He was the first mayor of Toronto, a strident critic of Upper Canada's Family Compact, and ultimately the leader of the 1837 rebellion. But Mackenzie was also a pioneering journalist who concentrated on investigating the world around him. Even after his military defeat in 1837 and subsequent banishment from Canada, he continued his uncompromising journalism, always paying attention to his unique brand of truth seeking.[3]

Before Mackenzie stepped foot in Canada in 1820, a muckraking tradition had already been established—a tradition he would soon take to a new level by infusing it with a more rigorous method and a consistent search for facts. Elements of oppositional journalism were evident even as the earliest colonial printers tried to survive by currying favour with government. In a pattern that would be repeated often in the future,

American influences figured prominently in Canadian journalism, leading directly to the first instances of the muckraking impulse. Republican ideas were swirling south of the border, and journalists were active in denouncing colonial subjugation. All of this set the stage for the arrival in Nova Scotia of a 16-year-old printer's apprentice, Isaiah Thomas, who precipitated the first significant clash between journalists and government authorities.

Thomas was hired by Anthony Henry, proprietor of Canada's first newspaper, the *Halifax Gazette*. The paper, which began publication quietly in 1752, was always careful to pay respect to colonial authorities. That changed in 1765 when Thomas arrived from Boston, a hotbed of republican ideology.[4] The teenager quickly discovered that Henry, while good-natured and pleasant, was lazy and not particularly skilled. This gave Thomas a far greater hand in editorial decision making than he could have expected. It also led to the appearance in the *Gazette* of articles criticizing the Stamp Act, a piece of colonial legislation that slapped a tax on many forms of printed matter. Throughout the North American colonies, the Act was a flashpoint for opposition to British authority.

The first time a negative article appeared in the *Gazette*, colonial authorities summoned Henry to explain himself. He pleaded ignorance, claiming he had never even seen the article. The next time, he said he had been sick, apologizing profusely in the process. But the colonial secretary by now correctly assessed the situation and demanded that the young journeyman Thomas be called to account. Thomas himself recounted what took place when he reported for questioning by Secretary Richard Bulkeley.

Q. Why came you here?
A. Because I was sent for.
Q. What is your name?
A. Isaiah Thomas.
Q. Are you the young New Englandman who prints for Henry?
A. Yes, sir.
Q. How dare you publish in the *Gazette* that the people of Nova Scotia are displeased with the stamp act?
A. I thought it was true.
Q. You had no right to think so. If you publish any thing more of such stuff, you shall be punished. You may go; but remember, you are not in New England.
A. I will, sir.[5]

Not long afterwards, Thomas drew inspiration from an edition of the *Pennsylvania Journal* to decorate the *Gazette* with artwork mocking the Stamp Act. All of this was becoming decidedly irksome for Secretary Bulkeley. Henry was stripped of his government patronage, and the newspaper ceased publication for a few months. A new, more careful and subservient editor took over the newspaper, and Thomas returned to the US. Henry went on to establish, albeit briefly, the first Canadian newspaper to be completely free of government patronage.[6] The entire incident sounded the first note in Canada of journalistic opposition to government authority.

While Thomas was advocating American republicanism in Canada on a freelance basis, Fleury Mesplet did so officially. Born in France, Mesplet was a printer who travelled first to England and then to Philadelphia. With the outbreak of the American Revolution, republicans formed a strategy of convincing the people of Quebec to join in the attack against Britain. This became all the more urgent after American forces captured Montreal in November 1775. Mesplet was dispatched by the second Continental Congress to set up shop in Montreal and convince the local population to support the American Revolution.[7] By the time he arrived, the British were in the process of recapturing the city, but Mesplet was undeterred. Prior to the British conquest, New France had an official policy banning printing and newspapers. Now the field was open for Mesplet to become the city's first printer, and, on 3 June 1778, he published Montreal's first newspaper, *La Gazette litteraire, pour la ville et district de Montreal.*

Together with his editor Valentin Jautard, Mesplet advocated a philosophy inspired by Voltaire and the French *philosophes*, the eighteenth-century group of French Enlightenment intellectuals. Voltaire was perhaps the most journalistically inclined of the philosophes, according to Herbert Altschull.[8] Voltaire instructed both historians and journalists to write about histories of men rather than histories of kings, and concentrate more on current events than ancient times. He disseminated the ideas of Locke widely, adding a French revolutionary fervour to them. He also began to hint at a more rigorous methodology for journalism, born out of his skeptical stance and devotion to science. He advised writers not to believe anything that hadn't been proved, and to accept facts that could be demonstrated only with 'the greatest and most recognized probability'.[9]

In the newly conquered territory of British North America, this kind of aggressive journalistic stance did not win favourable reviews from local authority. When Mesplet's newspaper denounced decisions of a local judge in 1779, the colonial governor acted. Mesplet and Jautard were arrested, the newspaper was suspended, and any hint of oppositional journalism was silenced. They stayed in custody for more than three years, but that didn't deter them from continuing their journalism. They eventually founded the Montreal *Gazette* in 1785. Soon after, it was the stirrings of the French Revolution that began to inspire Mesplet's journalism.[10]

Isaiah Thomas and Fleury Mesplet embodied Enlightenment ideals. Both were excited by developments in America and sought to spread such ideas further. The Enlightenment encouraged people to reject blind allegiance to religion and authority, ushering in an era of seeking truth from facts. In the field of science, this led to important discoveries about how the world operated. In the social sciences, it encouraged free inquiry. Thomas and Mesplet were not investigative journalists by any definition. They had no developed journalistic methodology, and no consistent approach to discovering facts that would describe their surrounding social reality. But they exhibited the first, early indications of the muckraker's modus operandi: skepticism of authority, and the courage to call the powerful to account.

By the early nineteenth century, Canadian muckraking began to mushroom in earnest. Economic conditions paved the way for individual entrepreneurs to make their living through printing, and many of the publishers sided with the burgeoning merchant class that felt suppressed by colonialism. Editors everywhere began criticizing the tight financial oligarchies and compacts that held sway throughout the colonies. Journalists became instrumental in spreading the call for reform and responsible government. And government authorities were not shy about retaliating.

The first four decades of the nineteenth century saw an unprecedented attack on journalists and editors. Criminal charges, jailings, intimidation, and physical attacks were all part of the arsenal. This was a period of warfare between the various family compacts and cliques, on the one hand, and anti-colonial reformers and revolutionaries, on the other. In Upper and Lower Canada, and in the Maritime provinces, the clash was fiercest on the journalistic front.[11] This was hardly surprising, as many of the pro-reform editors were simultaneously politicians, agitating for responsible government in legislatures as well as in print.

In Lower Canada, repression was swift and generally ruthless. Governor James Craig suppressed the anti-colonial *Le Canadien* and jailed its editors, Pierre Bédard and François Blanchet, in 1810. Over the next three decades, many more met the same fate. Jocelyn Waller of the *Canadian Spectator* was arrested and charged with libel in 1827, only to grow ill and die while the case was still pending. Ludger Duvernay was jailed four times and forced into exile for his oppositional journalism. Étienne Parent, Daniel Tracey, and many other journalists were similarly persecuted.

In Upper Canada, it was largely the same story. An early precedent was set in 1819, when Bartemas Ferguson, publisher of the *Niagara Spectator*, was charged with seditious libel. He had reprinted an article by agrarian radical Robert Gourlay that was critical of colonial administrators. Ferguson was slapped with an 18-month sentence, a fine of £50, and a provision that he stand in the pillory for one hour a day during the first month of his sentence. While the pillory portion of the sentence was later commuted, the point was clearly driven home. Gourlay himself was exiled for his activities.

Even the most off-hand comments could land journalists in trouble. Francis Collins, writing in the pages of the *Canadian Freeman*, called Attorney General John Beverley Robinson a 'native malignancy'. Robinson himself laid a charge of libel, and Collins was sentenced to a year in jail together with a fine.[12]

Printers and journalists in the Maritimes paid an onerous price for voicing pleas of reform. Anthony Holland, godson of the *Halifax Gazette*'s Anthony Henry, started the first Halifax newspaper to advocate for reform in 1813. Despite his cautious approach in the pages of the *Acadian Recorder*, Holland was castigated and forced to apologize for offending colonial authorities with his writings. William Wilkie was not so accommodating. He published a 21-page pamphlet in 1820 accusing Halifax magistrates of corruption. Charged with criminal libel, Wilkie was convicted in five minutes and sentenced to two years of hard labour.

Government accusations of malicious intent and criminal libel were common against Maritime journalists, but public opinion often sided with the editors. James

Hazard of the *PEI Register* was acquitted of his charges, and John Hooper of the *Saint John British Colonist* escaped largely unscathed. In 1835, two cases demonstrated how difficult it was becoming for colonial powers to keep their muckraking critics in check. Robert Parsons of the *Newfoundland Patriot* wrote an article critical of Chief Justice Henry Boulton. Boulton retaliated by citing him for contempt, fining him £50, and sentencing him to jail for three months. But Parsons had his supporters, and they made their views known clearly, from a 5,000-name petition to a threat they would tear down the courthouse. Parsons was freed, and his fine repaid.[13]

The more renowned case of the same year occurred in Halifax. On New Year's Day, the *Novascotian* printed a letter to the publisher, Joseph Howe. Signed simply 'The People', it began with a condemnation typical for its time:

> In a young and poor country, where the sons of rich and favoured families alone receive education at the public expence—where the many must toil to support the extortions and exactions of a few; where the hard earnings of the people are lavished on an Aristocracy, who repay their ill timed generosity with contempt and insult; it requires no ordinary nerve in men of moderate circumstances and humble pretensions to stand forward and boldly protest against measures which are fast working the ruin of the Province.

Muckraking by way of letters to the editor was common at the time. Written by George Thompson, one of Howe's friends, the letter went on to denounce the magistrates who controlled the local government in Halifax. It accused magistrates and police of illegally taking more than £30,000 from the pockets of the people. The magistrates bypassed the anonymous author and went after Howe directly, charging him with 'seditiously contriving, devising, and intending to stir up and incite discontent and sedition among His Majesty's subjects'. The prosecution expected a repeat of the Wilkie affair, but they underestimated the future premier of Nova Scotia. No apologies or excuses were forthcoming. In his six-and-a-quarter-hour address to the jury, Howe called the magistrates 'the most negligent and imbecile, if not the most reprehensible body, that ever mismanaged a people's affairs. . . . They may expect much from the result of this trial; but before I have done with them, I hope to convince them that they, and not I, are the real criminals here.'[14]

Howe's trial echoed an American case of exactly one century earlier. New York printer John Peter Zenger had criticized the corrupt administration of the colonial governor in the pages of his *New York Weekly Journal*. He was arrested and charged with seditious libel. In 1735, a jury acquitted Zenger, the first tangible victory for journalistic freedom in the American colonies. If nothing else, it demonstrated that a jury could be convinced of a just cause, in spite of the letter of the law or the admonitions of presiding judges. In Howe's trial, the jury was treated to impassioned oratorical flourishes:

Will you permit the sacred fire of liberty, brought by your fathers from the venerable temples of Britain, to be quenched and trodden out on the simple altars they have raised? Your verdict will be the most important in its consequences ever delivered before this tribunal; and I conjure you to judge me by the principles of English law, and to leave an unshackled press as a legacy to your children. . . . Yes, gentlemen, come what will, while I live, Nova Scotia shall have the blessing of an open and unshackled press.[15]

The jury acquitted Howe in 10 minutes. A number of magistrates resigned, and Howe rightly proclaimed the verdict a victory for press freedom. How lasting a victory is open to question. Howe's successor at the *Novascotian* was imprisoned for not paying damages following a series of Tory libel suits.

It was freedom to editorialize that most of the early muckrakers were fighting to win. Some, like Gourlay, used innovative methods to find out what grievances people had.[16] But for the most part, they paid little attention to investigating how political structures and institutions actually worked. They were generally content with denunciations and polemic. When facts were not close at hand, a ringing editorial could still be written.

William Lyon Mackenzie was different. He was just as fiery in his polemics as his fellow reformer journalists, but his exposés often had a factual underpinning the others lacked. When he wasn't agitating against the Family Compact, he was studying how it worked. And like any honest researcher, he would question his partisan loyalties when facts got in the way of his presuppositions.

Born in Dundee, Scotland in 1795, Mackenzie was exposed to a unique blend of Enlightenment influences—Scottish Highland, British radical, and European. He started reading voraciously at age 11, and in the next few years he claimed to have consumed 957 books on subjects ranging from divinity and history to drama and agriculture. Gambling and drinking were a part of his late teens and early 20s, but he made a fresh start when he sailed for Canada in 1820.[17]

Mackenzie worked briefly on the Lachine Canal, did occasional newspaper freelancing, but concentrated mainly on his duties as a partner in a hardware and general merchandise shop in Dundas, Upper Canada. His love of books continued, and the store also served as a circulating library. All the while he read, observed, and grew increasingly impatient in his work. He felt he needed to make a contribution to his new society, and journalism seemed the best route. He moved to Queenston in 1824 and established the *Colonial Advocate* newspaper.

The first issue of his paper, dated 18 May, made it abundantly clear where Mackenzie stood:

Our foreign commerce, confined and shackled as it is, and as it has been, is entirely in the hands of the British capitalists. . . . We earnestly desire to see established, throughout Upper and Lower Canada, New Brunswick and Nova Scotia, efficient societies for the improvement of arts and Manufactures. . . .

We will never flatter power, nor become the assassins of private character. . . .
It is the system we condemn, and few numbers shall go forth until we make ourselves distinctly understood on this head.[18]

Later, Mackenzie offered a fuller explanation for his motivation in starting the newspaper:

I had long seen the country in the hands of a few shrewd, crafty, covetous men,
under whose management one of the most lovely and desirable sections of
America remained a comparative desert. The most obvious public improvements
were stayed; dissension was created among classes; citizens were banished and
imprisoned in defiance of all law; the people had been long forbidden, under
severe pains and penalties, from meeting anywhere to petition for justice; large
estates were wrested from their owners in utter contempt of even the forms of
the courts . . . a sordid band of land-jobbers grasped the soil as their patrimony,
and with a few leading officials, who divided the public revenue among
themselves, formed 'the family compact' and were the avowed enemies of
common schools, of civil and religious liberty, of all legislative or other checks to
their own will. . . . At one-and-twenty I might have united with them, but chose
rather to join the oppressed, nor have I ever regretted that choice, or wavered
from the object of my early pursuit.[19]

While denying he was a radical reformer or a disloyal subject, Mackenzie plainly stated
he would be a critic of the colonial administration. But editorializing against systemic
abuses was only one part of the mission. Mackenzie was intent on finding out how the
Family Compact dominated society, and exposing its flaws for everyone to see. An early
indication of how he approached his journalistic methodology came in 1822, even
before he had taken up newspaper work full-time.

Mackenzie described a business trip he took to Youngstown, New York, across from
the British Fort George. He noticed a merchant loading a couple of two-horse sleighs with
large white boxes. Mackenzie surmised they were filled with tea, though at the time, it was
illegal to import tea from the US to Canada. He observed the sleighs travelling down the
ice road to the Canadian shore, past a group of Canadian soldiers who took no action.
Later, he saw the sleigh-drivers leaving Fort George and heading further into Upper
Canada. Mackenzie's aim in relating the story was to expose how arbitrary regulations
could be nullified by public opinion and actions. But his reportage took nothing for
granted. The soldiers, he said, were not bribed to turn a blind eye, 'for I afterwards
inquired particularly as to that fact'.[20] As to where the tea eventually ended up, Mackenzie
wrote: 'I have been credibly informed the shop-keeping establishment of the then custom-
house officer did not lack a supply of the scarce and valuable commodity. . . .'[21] At the
end, Mackenzie was careful to say that he never opened the packages himself, so couldn't
be completely certain it was tea. The anecdote was meant to illustrate a political point,
not to level accusations at individual smugglers. No incident at all was required for

Mackenzie to rail against colonial importation policies. But the attention to determining specific facts foreshadowed a more modern journalistic methodology.

While Mackenzie didn't stick to his early pledge never to attack individuals, he kept his keen investigator's eye on the workings of the system. He dissected the interconnections of the Family Compact, showing how they used personal and social connections to assist each other and oppress the rest of society. He delved into the inner workings of the Canada Company, illustrating how large profits were being diverted to private hands through the sale of land. He analyzed the banks, and the Bank of Upper Canada in particular, demonstrating how they were not acting in the best interests of the people. He published exposés of government corruption, misuse of public funds,

William Lyon Mackenzie, Canada's first investigative journalist. (Archives of Ontario, S 2123)

investigations into the treatment of blacks in America and Upper Canada, even critiques of the lack of police in York. Attorney General Robinson, on first reading the *Colonial Advocate*, didn't take long to form a judgment: 'Another reptile of the Gourlay breed has sprung up among us. What vermin.'[22]

Mackenzie's investigative impulse strengthened after he was elected to the Legislative Assembly in 1828. He became one of the assembly's most active members, presiding over committees into such matters as the price of postage, the condition of roads, bribery of election officials, conditions in jails, and corruption of government contractors. Having the power to compel witnesses to testify was a boon to the crusading journalist, who used his political position to boost his journalistic work, and vice versa. Like many of his fellow reformer editors, Mackenzie was subjected to a variety of attacks. In 1826, a group of Tories with connections to senior colonial figures trashed his printing office in York and threw his type into the lake. Undeterred, he sued for damages and won. A few years later, he foiled a murder attempt. Mackenzie was repeatedly charged with libel, repeatedly expelled from the Legislative Assembly, and repeatedly re-elected by his constituents.

Mackenzie took a wide interest in many subjects, and never missed an opportunity to expose an injustice. He was offended by slavery in America, and on seeing a parade in New York, wrote that he hoped 'the day may soon come, in which the task-master shall no more dare to lift his whip to the unhappy African; and in which man shall cease to possess the power to buy, and sell, and torture his fellow-man.'[23] He railed against prison conditions in Upper Canada, the cost of letters to England, the state of roads, the outright bribery that characterized electioneering. The banks were a prime target for his investigative skills and his condemnation. It is the farmers, the millers, and the labourers who produce wealth, not the banks, he argued. 'In exhibiting the sources of wealth, I do not forget the important share of labour performed by woman', he said.[24]

In 1832, during a trip to Britain, Mackenzie met with William Cobbett, whom many assumed was one of his chief role models. Cobbett, after all, had set up the muckraking *Cobbett's Weekly Political Register* where he denounced government corruption and unjust legislation. As one of the earliest investigative British journalists, Cobbett printed numerous exposés that put him squarely into conflict with the authorities. In 1810, he was sentenced to two years in jail for his muckraking defence of militiamen who were flogged for protesting unjust treatment. Cobbett, like Mackenzie, wrote about conditions affecting ordinary people, and was not afraid to leave his study to find out what was really going on in the world.[25]

But Mackenzie's assessment of this early journalistic icon was blunt. While praising him for his celebrated and formidable work, and admiring his social goals, Mackenzie reported that Cobbett 'is not very scrupulous as to the means of bringing about this great good'. He accused Cobbett of adopting the maxim of 'all's fair in politics' and thereby issuing statements 'not always so correct as they might be'. He added: 'Mr Cobbett's manner is kind and prepossessing but I think he does not bear contradictions so well as some men of less genius and power of mind.'[26] The great man had great ideals, but in Mackenzie's assessment, his methodology was lacking.

The clearest example of Mackenzie's skill at investigative work was his handling of the Welland Canal issue. Mackenzie considered himself an expert in canals, having worked in the field on both sides of the Atlantic. And for years he kept a close eye on the Welland Canal Company, which used public and private funds in its gigantic construction work. In 1835, the Legislative Assembly named Mackenzie as one of the company's directors. Mackenzie had often predicted that shareholders would suffer serious losses. Canal president William Hamilton Merritt tried unsuccessfully to block Mackenzie's appointment to the board. Confirmed in his new role, Mackenzie immediately left for the Niagara peninsula to investigate the company's operations, promising to report his findings back to the assembly.

The result was a lightning-quick example of journalistic muckraking. Mackenzie, who had already given up editorship of the *Colonial Advocate* to concentrate on politics, decided to publish his findings immediately. He single-handedly wrote the *Welland Canal*, a weekly newspaper, with the first issue dated 16 December 1835. 'This newspaper will be published every Wednesday by the Editor and Proprietor, at his office in York Street. The whole edition will be distributed, post-paid, gratis.' Mackenzie explained that he couldn't wait for the legislature to reconvene, and the publication of the newspaper was the most convenient and immediate way of getting out the news. No stranger to libel, Mackenzie admitted the risks. 'The parties blamed will have the advantage, too, of the courts of justice, if I have overstepped the limits of truth, for I have assumed whole responsibility, without seeking the shelter of that privilege which always attends the publication of a parliamentary report.'[27]

Mackenzie's detailed report was a damning indictment of the company and its leaders, whom he condemned as 'a knot of speculators undeserving of the confidence of the country'. He audited the accounts of 1832 and 1833 in detail, finding false entries, suspicious erasures, outright fraudulent practices, favouritism, and systematic dishonesty and embezzlement. Mackenzie detailed violations, large and small, going back to the inception of the company. Three editions of the *Welland Canal* newspaper were published, and anyone reading them would have little reason to challenge Mackenzie's conclusions. As with many muckraking exposés that would follow, the canal stories did not elicit the kind of sweeping legislative reforms Mackenzie would have liked. And as expected, he was sued for libel, eventually being ordered to pay a fine of two shillings.

As we have seen in this chapter, the ideas of the British and French Enlightenment had an effect on early Canadian journalistic expression. American revolutionary sentiment also spread north, engendering a republican spirit in some writers. These ideas surfaced in a nineteenth-century radical press that fought colonial authoritarianism, and advocated for responsible government. Repression was the usual response from the preservers of the status quo. A muckraking tradition became established in Canada, but polemic was the principal method of work. Yet even in the eighteenth century, Voltaire was urging a more scientific approach to gathering and assessing information. William Lyon Mackenzie took up that challenge.

Unlike his modern investigative counterparts, Mackenzie had a decided advantage. As a politician and director of the Welland Canal, he had complete access to the books.

He had no need to rely on access to information requests or government whistle-blowers. But when it came to laying bare a fundamental injustice, his instinct was to take the journalistic route of exposure. And he didn't rely solely on rhetoric or political invective to make his case. His smoking guns were the facts.[28]

Investigating Corporate Canada

'A picture is worth a thousand words, and the picture presented by the 28 charts in today's Report on Business is pretty clear.' Douglas Goold, editor of the *Globe and Mail's* Report on Business, was describing his newspaper's unique investigation into Canadian mergers and acquisitions, and how it revealed evidence of widespread illegal trading. The charts showed the movements in stock prices of a select number of companies that had been swallowed up by larger outfits in the previous year. A team of journalists did an exhaustive analysis of business mergers between July 1998 and July 1999, finding extraordinary run-ups in prices before the public had learned anything about the deals. The analysis was clear: secret information had produced huge profits for a small circle of insiders, leaving small investors in the cold.

Unlike the inquiry into the Welland Canal, the *Globe's* investigation didn't have Mackenzie's advantage: It had no special access to private company books or ledgers. But its methodology was every bit as precise, deriving facts from the numbers themselves and inviting readers to draw conclusions based on the findings. 'More than half of this country's biggest deals were preceded by a substantial run-up in stock prices before the public ever heard a word. It's clear someone was talking,' the newspaper concluded. 'So how many charges have regulators laid? None.'

The *Globe* outlined its methodology in detail. It described how it received a list of Canadian mergers from an investment-banking firm late in the summer of 1999, and then pared it down to deals worth more than $150 million. Hostile and unsolicited takeovers were examined separately, since fewer people would be party to those discussions and the takeover firm would have a greater interest in maintaining secrecy. The *Globe* then spent two months analyzing the remaining mergers, focusing on the target companies. It found the share price of nearly half the firms rose more than 25 per cent in the four months leading up to the announcement of the deal. In a substantial number of cases, the run-up was more than 50 per cent. Mysterious price increases were especially evident in the days just before the press release or news conference heralding the merger or acquisition.

'Left unchecked, illegal insider trading threatens the integrity of our capital markets system', University of Toronto finance professor Michael Berkowitz told the newspaper. 'The problem is, because of its very nature, we have no idea how widespread it is.' The *Globe's* week-long series, which began 18 October 1999, won a National Newspaper Award for business reporting.

Chapter 3

To the Modern Era

All men are honest men when they are well watched, and human nature in all ages and climes needs watching.

George Brown[1]

The idea of a watchdog press seemed broken by the end of the 1830s. In the great struggle between Tory and Reform forces, the status quo prevailed. The smashing of the rebellions of 1837–38 brought Canada's first period of sustained muckraking to an end. Mackenzie fled to the United States, and other Reformers were jailed, executed, or exiled. Muckraking journalism went into a period of hibernation.

Newspapers, meanwhile, were on the verge of profound change. The era of the editor-entrepreneur single-handedly running a small, opinionated broadsheet was beginning to end. Technological advances were speeding the transmission of news, first by stagecoaches and steamships and then by railways. By the 1840s, Americans were constructing an experimental telegraph line between Washington and Baltimore, and the telegraph era soon followed.[2] News could suddenly be dispatched quickly over vast distances. The laying of the Atlantic cable in the 1860s made European news more immediate, eliminating the need to send reporters racing out to sea to greet ships bearing outdated reports. The industrial revolution also sparked innovations in press technology and papermaking. Entrepreneurs began to understand that newspapers could be profitable enterprises, though it would be several decades yet before rising literacy and a more developed advertising culture would push journalism into the modern business era.

The radical colonial journalists had sparked an abiding interest in politics, and politicians of all stripes realized the power of the press in swaying opinion. In the period between the establishment of responsible government and Confederation, many newspapers were directly controlled by political interests. George Brown of the *Globe* typified the era, as did the various Tory efforts to counter his rising influence. But the journalism of these newspapers, for the most part, lacked the concerted probing and challenging of the status quo that characterized the early nineteenth-century radical editors. While there were occasional exposés and disclosures, most editors were inspired by partisan warfare, aiming their guns at specific political enemies. Brown's chief biographer, noting the *Globe*'s occasional forays into muckraking journalism, makes the point clearly: 'Reformation of the prisoner, liberation of the slave—these were strong enthusiasms for George Brown. But first, last, and always, he was a political journalist and a fervent Reform partisan.'[3]

Another revolution was occurring in Western journalism at the time. It centred on methodology. The trends began developing around mid-century in Britain, the US, and ultimately Canada. 'A distinction emerged between those writing the editorials in the office and those gathering news in the field', according to British historian Hugo de Burgh. 'The report became differentiated from the analysis, as it is today; feature articles appeared, distinct from either, and included what we now call "human interest"; "hard" news was distinguished from "soft" news; literary journalism was introduced; the interview was invented; newspapers campaigned.'[4]

Investigative journalism, as Mackenzie discovered, was not really possible without the tools to derive the truth from facts. And facts cannot usually be uncovered while pontificating on partisan politics in the comfort of a secluded office. You have to go into the real world, or at least send correspondents there, to inquire, observe, interview, and discover. The very act of interviewing others was not firmly enshrined in Western journalistic practice until mid-century. Nor was the simple act of sending reporters to events with notebooks and pencils in hand. 'The journalistic method is the pursuit of independently verifiable facts about current events through enterprise, observation, and investigation', says Mitchell Stephens.[5] Journalism eventually evolved from the mere recording of official notices and transcription of legislative debates to the need for legwork, interviewing, and reporting. But pursuing independently verifiable facts remains a challenging objective, one that continues to separate mere reporting of opinion and comments from investigative work.

Some of the first writers to adopt a more modern reportorial methodology were not journalists at all, but nineteenth-century European novelists and intellectuals. Dickens, Zola, Hugo, and Dostoyevsky all paid attention to first-hand observation of the conditions of ordinary people. They were intent on analyzing the ravages of the industrial revolution on the poor, and knew that direct contact would provide a richness of detail and authenticity of dialogue.[6] These and other European intellectuals disseminated some of their writings through newspapers, which popularized the notion that facts could be gleaned through analysis of objective conditions. For his part, Horace Greeley of the *New York Tribune* turned to Karl Marx as one of his European correspondents, relying on his analysis of economic and social trends to inform American readers.

The rise of the penny press produced sporadic instances of investigative journalism, though it was limited in scope and more often designed to titillate than inform. Selling newspapers for a penny brought journalism to a far wider audience, and gave some entrepreneurs the chance to break free from political ties. The process began in both Britain and the US in the 1830s, but was slower coming to Canada. By 1869, the *Montreal Star* unveiled its penny enterprise with the aim of appealing to the working class. Others followed, including *La Presse*, the *Toronto Telegram*, the *Toronto Star*, and papers throughout Ontario.[7] From a commercial point of view, publishers were aiming to recreate the success of James Gordon Bennett, who managed to boost circulation of the *New York Herald* above 40,000 within two years of introducing his populist paper. The formula was straightforward: shorter, snappier news items; livelier, sensationalist writing; and a heavy dose of local news.

One of the most successful of the penny-press practitioners was John Ross Robertson, who launched the *Toronto Telegram* in 1876. A staunch Conservative and Orangeman, he was less interested in challenging the status quo and holding the federal government to account than he was in boosting circulation by stirring passions about more local concerns. He took aim at city hall, notifying local officials that the *Telegram* would not be slow to expose and denounce, and that no mercy would be shown.[8] The newspaper began investigating civic contracts, printing details for the public to view. Conflicts of interest among aldermen were exposed, as was malpractice in the issuing of licenses. The newspaper investigated the water commission, forcing meetings to be held in public for the first time. Under the headline 'The Canadian Bastille', the *Telegram* described instances of inhumane treatment and torture at Central Prison in Toronto. Echoing the exposés of tight Family Compact connections and shenanigans, Robertson accused city councilors of looking out for themselves and their friends. 'They lobby a contract through the council for a friend on the understanding that the friend shall purchase all his material from the alderman, or aldermen, who procure him the contract.'[9]

The muckraking and populist style brought the *Telegram* a healthy circulation and was one of the factors in making Robertson a millionaire. Other publishers took notice and emulated the *Telegram*'s method. But the muckraking aspect was a tactic, and it never became a sustained force. As Robertson himself observed, a newspaper 'is published to make money, and its educational influence is merely an incident in the business of making money'.[10] Conservative Prime Minister John A. Macdonald never had much to fear from individual reporters. Newspapers loyal to the Liberal cause were more intent on fighting Macdonald through their editorials, and not inclined to invest the resources needed to expose the underlying Ottawa reality. The Pacific Scandal, in which Macdonald and other cabinet ministers solicited funds from railway promoters for their electoral needs, was exposed by Liberal politicians, not by enterprising journalists. Liberal-friendly newspapers were then provided damaging evidence to print, but it was all generated at the political level. The major newspaper publishers, for all their talk of representing the people's interests, were big entrepreneurs who craved maximum circulation and who often had overriding partisan, political agendas.

Arising alongside the popular press movement were the labour papers, most of them small and short-lived. Spawned by a more radicalized working class and rising trade unionism, these newspapers professed support for labour and took up its cause exclusively. Editorially, this meant fighting for shorter working hours, improved conditions, equality of women in the workplace, universal suffrage, and higher wages. Journalistically, it sometimes involved muckraking exposés of oppressive workplaces. William Rowe, editor of the Hamilton-based *Palladium of Labor*, published details of injuries on the job in an effort to highlight inadequate working conditions. He introduced what historian Ron Verzuh says may have been the first attempt at muckraking in a Canadian labour journal by hiring an unnamed investigator to probe conditions in cotton mills. As a result, the newspaper reported 'children as young as nine and ten years of age are kept at work for 12 hours each day'.[11]

Many similar newspapers sprung up around the country, including the *Labor Advocate*, the *Montreal Echo*, the *Industrial Banner* in London, and the *People's Voice* in Winnipeg. Unlike the major dailies, these newspapers agitated for thoroughgoing change in social structures. Some openly espoused socialist solutions. All the while, they probed actual conditions in factories and workplaces. Some were content merely to editorialize, while others sought facts from actual experiences.[12] One of the most skilled journalists in this regard was Thomas Phillips Thompson, who wrote for several labour papers and was active in radical politics as a reformer and later as a socialist. Before writing a column for the *Palladium of Labor* and later editing the *Labor Advocate*, Thompson worked as a reporter for more mainstream publications.[12] At the *Globe*, he was asked to produce stories on the cotton industry as part of the newspaper's examination of tariffs and John A. Macdonald's National Policy in 1882. His nine-part series was a solid example of investigative reporting, incorporating interviews and first-hand observations. He wrote about child labour, poor working standards, and appalling living conditions at cotton mills. 'A Cornwall landlord tells me of 13 mill families living together in a tenement of about 24 by 30 feet,' he wrote, and quoted a Hochelaga resident as saying: 'The mill operatives generally work and live like slaves.'[14] He reported seeing workers as young as nine years old, even quoting the president of the Coaticook Mill as saying many employees are not more than 10.[15] Work days last from 12 to 14 hours, with compulsory additional work not uncommon. Thompson even had a modern-day appreciation of the environmental and workplace hazards at the mills. 'The ever-roaring carding machines, spinning frames and looms, are constantly throwing off fibrous particles of cotton, which are inhaled in large quantities, no matter how clean the mill may be kept.'[16] Thompson wrote with a sense of passion that prefigured similar accounts of sweatshops and textile mills in the following century. 'The social mill grinds harshly, and there are many poor lives crushed by the juggernaut of progress,' he said.[17]

Alongside the investigations of labour journalists were some early Canadian works of sociology. Most notably, Canadian businessman Herbert Ames exposed squalid living conditions in his 1897 book *The City Below the Hill*. Analyzing working-class districts of Montreal, he found low wages, overcrowded housing, grinding poverty, hunger, and disease. His exposé was one of the most illuminating pieces of Canadian investigative work to emerge in the latter part of the nineteenth century.

The turn of the century spawned an extraordinary movement that defined investigative journalism for the next half century and beyond. For the most part, the movement swept the United States, but had only faint echoes in Canada. It became known as muckraking, a term coined by US President Theodore Roosevelt, who compared crusading journalists to a character in John Bunyan's *Pilgrim's Progress*, 'the man who could look no way but downward with the muck-rake in his hands; who would neither look up nor regard the crown he was offered, but continued to rake to himself the filth on the floor.'[18]

Muckraking resulted from a collision of factors specific to American social and economic conditions of the time. Rapid industrialization had created a ruthless and unfettered commercial atmosphere. Masses of immigrants were thrown into American cities and factories and left to fend for themselves with little or no regulation. The gap between rich and poor was immense, and large sections of the middle class began to feel alienated. The Progressive movement arose in response to these trends, with the aim of instituting reform. Initially an adjunct to the movement, the muckrakers often went beyond moderate reforms to suggest more wide-ranging solutions.

Meanwhile, American magazines were assuming a more populist approach. S.S. McClure was a pioneer in this regard, starting *McClure's Magazine* in 1893 with the idea of producing a cheaper, mass-circulation periodical. By the end of the nineteenth century, at 10 cents an issue, *McClure's* had circulation of around 400,000. And he encouraged his writers to tackle hard-hitting exposés, guessing that his readers would embrace the concept.

The first example of the new muckraking movement is generally considered to be 'Tweed Days in St. Louis', a *McClure's* article by Lincoln Steffens that appeared on 2 October 1902. It was one of a series of local government exposés that Steffens eventually collected and published as *The Shame of the Cities*. In a way, Steffens was building on previous penny-press exposés of local corruption, but his sustained and exhaustive research took it to a higher level. The next month, *McClure's* followed up with the first in a series of 19 groundbreaking articles on the history of the Standard Oil Company. They were written by Ida Tarbell, who had already gained popular acclaim for her *McClure's* series on Abraham Lincoln.[19]

Tarbell's methodology signalled a further development in investigative journalism, and one that had a marked effect on muckrakers who came later. Her aim was to find out everything she could about how trusts worked, and Standard Oil proved the ideal example. In explaining why she chose the company as her target, Tarbell explained:

> Its vast profits have led its officers into various allied interests, such as railroads, shipping, gas, copper, iron, steel, as well as into banks and trust companies, and to the acquiring and solidifying of these interests it has applied the methods used in building up the Oil Trust. It has led in the struggle against legislation directed against combinations. Its power in state and Federal government, in the press, in the college, in the pulpit, is generally recognized. The perfection of the organi-zation of the Standard, the ability and daring with which it has carried out its projects, make it the pre-eminent trust of the world—the one whose story is best fitted to illuminate the subject of combinations of capital.[20]

And there was another, very practical consideration. Voluminous material existed on the company, much of it in the archives of state and federal bodies that had investigated Standard Oil over the years for restraint of trade and kickbacks to the railroad industry.

This provided substantial documentary evidence about the company and its controlling Rockefeller family, which Tarbell supplemented with interviews and analysis of court and financial records. Tarbell made it clear she was more interested in getting at the complete truth than writing a polemic.

> When the work was first announced in the fall of 1901, the Standard Oil Company, or perhaps I should say officers of the company, courteously offered to give me all the assistance in their power, an offer of which I have freely taken advantage. In accepting assistance from Standard men as from independents I distinctly stated that I wanted facts, and that I reserved the right to use them according to my own judgment of their meaning, that my object was to learn more perfectly what was actually done—not to learn what my informants thought of what had been done.[21]

Soon *Collier's*, *Cosmopolitan*, and other American magazines filled their pages with muckraking articles. Steffens had led the way with exposés of local government, and David Graham Phillips took aim at federal politicians with his 'Treason of the Senate'. Ray Stannard Baker wrote about railroad and financial corruption, and produced a pioneering series on racial discrimination and poverty among African Americans. Other writers attacked the quackery of patent medicines, fraud in the insurance industry, the shocking rate of workplace injuries, and all other forms of social injustice. These were not merely denunciations. Chemists were hired to test the suspected patent medicines, and labour-intensive research went into the exposés. Most of the stories were written in a breathless, entertaining fashion that appealed to masses of readers. Here is how Phillips defended the title of his article on the Senate:

> The treason of the Senate! Treason is a strong word, but not too strong, rather too weak, to characterize the situation in which the Senate is the eager, resourceful, indefatigable agent of interests as hostile to the American people as any invading army could be, and vastly more dangerous: interests that manipulate the prosperity produced by all, so that it heaps up riches for the few; interests whose growth and power can only mean the degradation of the people, of the educated into sycophants, of the masses toward serfdom. . . . The Senators are not elected by the people; they are elected by the 'interests'.[22]

And when it came to opening the first of a series of articles on patent medicine fraud, Samuel Hopkins Adams had no trouble hooking his readers with the following:

> Gullible America will spend this year some seventy-five millions of dollars in the purchase of patent medicines. In consideration of this sum it will swallow huge quantities of alcohol, an appalling amount of opiates and narcotics, a wide assortment of varied drugs ranging from powerful and dangerous heart depressants to insidious liver stimulants; and, far in excess of all other

ingredients, undiluted fraud. For fraud, exploited by the skilfulest of advertising bunco men, is the basis of the trade.[23]

Perhaps the most influential of the early muckraking efforts was Upton Sinclair's exposé of the meat-packing industry. Commissioned to do a series of articles by the socialist magazine *Appeal to Reason*, Sinclair immersed himself in the world of the Chicago meat plants. He eventually used the form of a novel to publish his results. *The Jungle*, initially rejected by several publishers, became a sensation throughout America and around the world. It told the story of Jurgis Rudkus, a young Lithuanian immigrant, who confronts the harsh realities of capitalism in his new country. It exposed not only the horrendous working and living conditions of immigrant labourers, but also the dangerous and filthy habits of the meat-packing industry.

The American muckraking movement led to a series of legislative reforms, including passage of the Pure Food and Drug Act. Tarbell's research undoubtedly had an effect on the eventual anti-trust actions against Standard Oil. In the early years of the century, mass circulation magazines discovered the value of muckraking journalism in their marketing efforts. The genre had turned into a means of generating profits, and investigative journalism was being treated like a commodity. But the subversive nature of many of the articles couldn't peaceably co-exist with the powerful financial interests that controlled the magazines. By 1912, the process began to ebb. Many of the writers gravitated to the Democratic or Progressive parties, while others, like Sinclair, concentrated on socialist politics. Libel suits also encouraged magazines to curtail the activity, as did overt pressure from advertisers. By the First World War, the muckraking era in America was over.[24]

In Canada, meanwhile, there did not seem to be any significant reflection of the US muckraking movement. Canadian magazines had not yet entered the mass-circulation era, and were generally overwhelmed by American competition. John Bayne Maclean, who would eventually become one of Canada's most successful magazine entrepreneurs, was certainly aware of the American trend. He met and maintained a relationship with McClure, but clearly didn't embrace the idea that a literature of exposure would work in Canada. While his American counterparts were pillorying industry and the excesses of big business, Maclean founded *Canadian Machinery and Manufacturing News* in 1905, followed by the *Financial Post* in 1907. And in his *Business Magazine* of 1905, predecessor to *Maclean's*, the first original article extolled the success of Senator George Fulford, who made his fortune hawking a dubious patent medicine called 'Pink Pills for Pale People'.[25]

It was left to newspapers to do what little muckraking work would appear in Canada during this period. Most of these were scattered, localized efforts. In Calgary, the eclectic, satirical *Eye-Opener* took aim at local corruption and scandal. Editor Bob Edwards had no allegiance to any part of the establishment. He delighted in skewering politicians, business people, and corrupt practices wherever he could find them. The *Toronto Star* made some efforts at exposé journalism as well. Joseph Atkinson had taken the helm in 1899, and tried moving the paper in a populist direction, identifying more closely with working people and immigrants. Editorially, the *Star* pushed a social democratic agenda that included support for pensions, unemployment insurance, and public ownership of utilities, and a more robust respect for labour rights than the Tory *Telegram* was exhibiting. Famous for its crusades, the *Star* devoted extraordinary coverage in 1905 to a scandal in the plumbing industry that involved kickbacks, inflated prices, and unnecessarily high costs to builders. When the exposé led to criminal charges, the *Star* provided blanket front-page coverage of the trial, boasting that, 'The facts elicited corroborated what The *Star* has already given to its readers regarding the methods of the (plumbers') association.'[26] The episode led to an ongoing campaign against combines of all kinds. When Prime Minister Mackenzie King finally introduced anti-combines legislation in 1910, he credited the *Star*'s pressure.[27]

Perhaps the most tangible manifestation of the American muckraking movement in Canada came in 1914, when a socialist book publisher in Chicago released *A History of Canadian Wealth* by Gustavus Myers. The *Toronto Star* took note of the book immediately, quoting extensively from it under a news story headlined: 'How Canada's Wealth is Now Centralized.'[28] But the story made no mention of who the mysterious Myers was, or why such a book would be published in Chicago. In fact, Myers was an integral part of the American muckraking trend, though he disdained some of its more sensationalist aspects. US historian Louis Filler calls him the movement's historian, more so than Tarbell, Steffens, or Baker.[29]

Born in 1872, Myers worked as a reporter with the *Philadelphia Record*, then as a feature writer in New York. He was politically active in New York's Social Reform Club, and soon began delving into historical research. In 1900, he published *A History of Public Franchises in New York City*, and followed it soon after with *The History of Tammany Hall*. He became fascinated with how America's rich had accumulated their fortunes. 'While the other muckrakers captured popular attention with articles on trusts, insurance, labour trouble, impure food, and other national scandals, Myers patiently turned pages of old books, magazines, and newspapers to learn the true history of capitalism in America', says Filler.[30] The result was his unique *History of the Great American Fortunes*.

Myers drew a distinction between his work and the more sensationalistic muckrakers, whose 'superficial effusions and tirades' were 'based upon a lack of understanding of the propelling forces of society. . . . They give no explanation of the fundamental laws and movements of the present system, which have resulted in these vast fortunes; nor is there the least glimmering of a scientific interpretation of a succession of states and tendencies from which these men of great wealth have emerged . . . the natural, logical outcome of a system based upon factors the inevitable result of which is the utter despoilment of the many for the benefit of a few.'[31] In between research on his books, Myers did work on other muckraking projects, including the 'Treason of the Senate.' It's not entirely clear why Myers, who was so heavily involved in American research and politics, decided to devote attention to Canada. It may simply be that he was disappointed no one had bothered to write a genuine muckraking analysis of the country.

Although long ago it was recognized that they who control the means by which a dependent class must live, control the livelihood and conditions of that class, yet it is not inordinately astonishing that thus far no economic work tracing the sources of these accumulations of private wealth in Canada has preceded these present volumes.[32]

One reason, he suggests, is that histories and social explanations 'have been absurdly and erroneously made to revolve around personalities instead of social and economic forces'. Myers said he had to dig laboriously into Canadian archives, and tediously explore masses of official documents to conduct his research. 'That many, if not most of them, have never heretofore been consulted is a striking commentary upon the character of conventional, so-called history', he said, not immodestly. His work was not unlike Mackenzie's, and it underlined once again a crucial method for the investigative journalist or historian: checking the public record. Myers showed that the raw information for his exposé was neither hidden nor covered up, but available to anyone who put work into finding and synthesizing it.

Though written as a history, Myers' work is filled with muckraking gems and exposures, the first being that fewer than 50 men were estimated to control $4 billion, or more than one-third of Canada's material wealth as expressed in railways, banks, factories, mines, land, and other resources. He painted a picture of brutality, fraud, and murder in describing how aboriginal people were swindled during the fur trade. Using company documents and official federal committee reports, he documented stock watering, shortweighting, and other corporate malfeasance by the Hudson Bay Company. He showed how the clergy were complicit in fraud when it came to granting land reserves. Then, in the era of railway expansion, he demonstrated how politicians enriched themselves with grants and kickbacks, and through directly granting themselves favourable treatment as speculators. By the end of the book, Canadian readers might have wondered whether a fanciful agenda had produced such an unending litany of fraud and abuse. But every statement was meticulously documented, with references to verifiable sources. In a review of his book, the *New York Times* slammed Myers as a muckraker who believed the masses are poor because of their unwillingness to imitate the vices of the rich. Yet even the critical reviewer admitted: 'This is said without disparagement of the apparent effort of Mr Myers to be accurate. His facts are not denied, but his inferences from them will not be admitted generally. All he says may be true, and yet there are other offsetting facts which compensate for the blemishes disclosed.'[33]

'This American Socialist', wrote historian Stanley Ryerson, 'was, in fact, our first social historian.' Still, *A History of Canadian Wealth* remained an obscure and largely forgotten work until it was published in Canada for the first time in 1972. From there, it found its way into reading lists, university bookstores, and the hands of a new generation of Canadian muckrakers who were eager to take an alternative and more challenging view of the country's history and power structures.

The brief historical survey in this chapter illustrates a number of themes that recur in later years. Technological changes gave journalists the tools to do a better job of finding out facts, and refinements in reporting methods also aided the process. The rise of the penny press produced, in some instances, a journalism of exposure that demonstrated elements of modern-day investigative work. But the institutional framework in which this work arose wasn't conducive to a thoroughgoing journalism of holding powerful interests to account, in the way William Lyon Mackenzie had done. Rising from the margins were labour newspapers that produced certain types of exposés, though the genre doesn't seem to have influenced mainstream Canadian newspapers and magazines. The Canadian magazine industry also appears to have remained aloof from the wave of muckraking that swept the United States at the turn of the century. Although sporadic attempts at investigative analysis of Canadian history and social structures took place, in the form of works by Gustavus Myers and Herbert Ames, they were limited in scope and influence. Even political upheavals that shook the credibility of existing governments, such as the Pacific Scandal, do not seem to have been initiated by an inquiring media. The watchdog press was barely stirring.

Muckraking with Mass Appeal

The populist, muckraking tone is evident from the very first sentence of the book. 'Sitting in a plush chair in the dark dining room of a Toronto hotel, eating a lunch of fresh trout, the wealthy investor makes no bones about it: he doesn't pay income tax. Nor do his friends, he says. Why should they? The Canadian tax system provides plenty of opportunity for them to avoid tax, making any tax payment almost like a voluntary contribution.' Linda McQuaig goes on to detail how the rich benefit from Canada's tax system, and how any vision of a progressive, graduated income tax regime is an illusion. It's an engaging blend of history, analysis, investigative journalism, and polemic, reminiscent of Lincoln Steffens, David Graham Phillips, and Gustavus Myers. Even the title of her 1987 book conjures up the Progressive-era muckrakers of a century earlier: *Behind Closed Doors, How the Rich Won Control of Canada's Tax System and Ended Up Richer*.

McQuaig honed her investigative instincts at *Maclean's* and the *Globe and Mail*, then turned to more wide-ranging inquiries in book form. Her exposé of the tax system became the first in a series of bestselling books. They all followed a pattern of challenging conventional wisdom and targeting the cosy cliques of the rich and powerful. The power of the books didn't always derive from the unearthing of reams of new or previously unknown information. Instead, it was the weaving of lesser-known facts into a chatty and provocative tale that drew people's attention. 'I take a lot of the stuff that's known to a small group of experts, information that contradicts popular perceptions, and I put it in readable form so ordinary people can have access to it.'[34]

She returned to the *Globe* after writing the tax book, staying just long enough to expose a major scandal in Ontario government circles and pick up a National Newspaper Award for her efforts. But daily journalism has its limitations, and she continued her book work. Soon the business lobby and the free-trade pact became the topic of an exposé, followed by an examination of the threat to Canada's social welfare system. Other works took issue with prevailing neo-liberal conceptions of the deficit, along with exposés of corporate greed. Then she showed how the quest for oil drove US forces to attack Iraq and threaten world security. But it was the 1987 tax analysis that set her muckraking career in motion, making McQuaig one of the most persistent and articulate critics of the Canadian establishment.

Chapter 4

Bigger and Better Scoops

What I learned about journalism (at the *Toronto Telegram*) was that it was a suspect craft, dominated by hypocrisy, exaggeration, and fakery. At the Tely, we
toadied to advertisers, eschewed investigative reporting, slanted our stories
gleefully to fit the party line (Conservative) and to appeal to the one man who
counted—the publisher, John F. Bassett.

Walter Stewart[1]

Walter Stewart's reminiscences about his early days at the *Telegram*, where he began his career in 1953, are not as exaggerated as they might seem. Mainstream Canadian journalism was docile at mid-century. Aggressive, challenging stories were nowhere to be found. It was an era in both Canada and the US of lapdog journalism, in the phrase of American political scientist Larry Sabato.[2] Many Canadian dailies were in the hands of colourful entrepreneurs who were eager to attract advertisers, boost their local business communities, and generally ensure that no one rocked the boat. Rapid commercialization of the press from 1890–1920 turned newspapers into profit centres. 'Dependence on advertising revenues caused publishers to turn news into a commodity designed to attract readers, who in turn were sold on advertisers' products, thus completing the commercialization of the press and turning it into an industry like any other', says historian Minko Sotiron.[3]

Two world wars had a profound effect on the relationships between government, powerful institutions, and the press. Challenging authority at times of war was seen as unpatriotic. Dissent was suppressed in a variety of ways, and exposés of government could be viewed as aiding the enemy. In the post-war reconstruction phases, there was pressure to support the effort to achieve maximum prosperity. Watchdogs were not wanted.[4]

Canada was hardly scandal-free, but the media were not instrumental when it came to exposure. Newspapers played no role, for instance, in discovering that Beauharnois Power was bribing politicians to ensure permission was granted for a hydro project in Quebec. And even after it had been revealed in the early 1930s that federal Liberals received huge kickbacks from the company, there was no sustained press crusade to discover further details. The whole affair blew over quickly, and the Liberals suffered no lasting damage. While there were occasional media exposés, they were sporadic and often bore the imprint of having been leaked for partisan political purposes. Some of those scoops were written by George Drew, who worked for *Maclean's*, en route to his successful political career. In 1931, he published an exposé of armament makers, and on the eve of World War II he showed how a Canadian manufacturer had received a suspicious and untendered government contract for Bren light machine guns. The Bren gun scandal eventually led to changes in the way federal contracts were awarded, and Drew, a future Ontario Tory premier and federal Conservative leader, undoubtedly enjoyed the discomfort it caused Liberal Prime Minister Mackenzie King.[5]

As in the latter part of the nineteenth century, the alternative media provided examples of investigative work. Radical and communist papers occasionally delved into the workings of specific mines, factories, and other workplaces. There were also scattered attempts to update the historical and economic analysis Gustavus Myers had begun. Radical media in the US contributed some muckraking work. In 1934, *New Masses* magazine sent a New York social worker to West Virginia to investigate rumours of deaths on a massive tunnel project. The result was an exposé the next year of an undocumented industrial tragedy.[6] Perhaps the most interesting American muckraking of the period, though, was the work of disaffected mainstream journalist George Seldes. Feeling frustrated at the *Chicago Tribune*, he quit to become an independent journalist, writing exposés his former bosses wouldn't print. He wrote analytic stories on the Catholic Church, the world armaments industry, and on fascism. In 1940, he founded *In Fact*, an independent newsletter that built a circulation of about 175,000. He delighted in telling stories he claimed were being suppressed in the mainstream press, and crusaded particularly against tobacco and its cancer-causing qualities.[7] I.F. Stone, Ralph Nader, and other maverick American writers followed in his footsteps, but Canada had no equivalent crusader.

By the time Clark Davey arrived at the *Globe and Mail* in 1951, he came to a quick conclusion. 'There wasn't a lot of enterprise reporting being done at the *Globe*. There wasn't a lot of enterprise reporting being done anywhere.'[8] He encountered an Ottawa press gallery where reporters, instead of acting as an unofficial opposition, often chose political sides and displayed partisanship in their coverage. An American journalist, Louis B. Seltzer, was also identifying problems with the press corps in Washington. He said political reporters were being fed information that was tailor-made to fit the needs of the federal agencies involved. Such attitudes bred indifference and negligence, and he said the absence of more challenging media was disgraceful.[9] Davey, who went on to become the *Globe*'s managing editor, began to detect some changes in the 1950s, but they were slow in coming.

One came oddly at the same newspaper Walter Stewart accused of hypocrisy and fakery, the *Toronto Telegram*. Judith Robinson, daughter of the newspaper's long-time editor 'Black Jack' Robinson, broke a story in 1953 that had significant repercussions in Ottawa. She accused Harvey Lunam, a Regina contractor, of supplying Liberal MP Austin Dewar with seven personal cheques at the same time Lunam's company was being awarded federal building contracts. 'I discovered these cheques while investigating the circumstances under which the Harvey Lunam Construction Co. later defaulted on its Dominion Government contracts and left sub-contractors holding the bag for more than $230,000', she wrote.[10] Robinson's story made it appear kickbacks were being paid. Pictures of the suspicious cheques accompanied the story.

Dewar came fighting back the next day, saying he had paid Lunam back, and showing that the two had exchanged cheques at different times over a number of years to help one another out financially. What it appears they were doing was taking advantage of the time lag in cheques clearing to transact business, a sharp practice that produced short-term profits, but not a crime. Although Robinson's story made it sound as if she had conducted an exhaustive, independent investigation, the MP at the centre of the controversy had a different explanation for the origin of the scoop: dirty Tory tricks. 'John Diefenbaker hasn't got the intestinal fortitude to suggest to me that I have done anything wrong, so he and the other Tories hide behind the skirts of a woman and try to smear me through a newspaper', he told the *Toronto Star*.[11] The Commons was in an uproar for the next few days, with Tories calling for blood and Dewar sticking to his story.

Finally, Prime Minister Louis St. Laurent entered the fray, calling the cheque exchange an abuse. Even though no kickbacks were proved, and Lunam had won all his contracts as the lowest bidder, the appearance of the affair was too costly for the government. Dewar resigned his seat, a week after the original article appeared. It was the first resignation of its kind in more than 20 years, and most significantly, it had been triggered by a media report.

Robinson's story seems odd by modern standards. It contained no comment from either Lunam or Dewar, and gave no indication of how the reporter got access to the private banking documents. That didn't stop the Toronto Men's Press Club from awarding it the 1953 National Newspaper Award for spot news reporting. And in the combative Toronto newspaper landscape, even the competition realized something new had taken place. A *Globe and Mail* editorial entitled 'For Good Work Well Done' highlighted its significance:

> It is now five years since the National Newspaper Awards were established. An analysis of the awards year by year suggests a growing realization of the purpose of the prizes, which is to improve the general level of newspaper work in Canada. But this year there has been a valuable precedent set in the award for spot news reporting to Miss Judith Robinson of the Telegram. While Miss Robinson is a columnist, her work in this instance was in the fine tradition of vigorous, hard-hitting news gathering, which the awards have tended to ignore until now. . . . There has been a marked absence of controversial material in the prize lists. . . . The Men's Press Club has broadened the field of the contest and has given appropriate, if belated, recognition to one of the primary functions of the press. This is a healthy innovation, indeed.[12]

In the end, Robinson's story was a relatively minor affair involving a small-time contractor and a backbench MP, but it caused a stir in Parliament, and it led to a resignation. The National Newspaper Awards did not yet have a category for enterprise or investigative reporting, but even so it made sense to consider this an instance of spot news. Robinson was almost certainly tipped off to the story, as Dewar alleged, and handed all the material in a neat package. In the world of the mainstream press, this was a monumental scoop, and if anyone was bothering to think about investigative journalism in those circles, it was in the context of finding bigger and better scoops.

But the mainstream was not ready to embrace a new age of muckraking quite yet. In 1953, the same year Robinson published her exclusive story, a young Ron Haggart came to Toronto looking for work. Haggart had emerged from university journalism and the *Vancouver Sun* with a tool-kit of investigative skills, and was eager to apply them in a bigger market. *Telegram* editor J. Douglas MacFarlane offered him a three-week trial, asking him to look into three hot topics of the day, including the way private clubs operated in the city. Haggart went to work, promptly exposing a Bay Street private club as nothing more than an open bar that was skirting the law. What he didn't know was that the club was the favourite watering hole for *Telegram* staff. Haggart was let go after his three-week stint.[13]

Over at the *Globe and Mail*, which had eloquently defended hard-hitting news gathering, the reality sometimes conflicted with the rhetoric. Harold Greer, one of the paper's most aggressive and analytical reporters, spent months in the early 1960s investigating police corruption and police complicity in the running of gambling clubs. He had built a significant body of evidence, but the newspaper's libel lawyer advised against publication. Management agreed. Greer was enraged and quit the newspaper. He resurfaced soon afterwards, at the beginning of 1962, on the staff of provincial Liberal leader John Wintermeyer, who promptly suggested that professional gamblers might be receiving protection from police and public authorities. That triggered a Royal Commission on Crime. Although its findings were inconclusive, the whole episode led the *Globe* to wonder about how it had handled the story.

'A sordid side of life in staid Ontario had been revealed and instinctive doubt of complacent establishments remained', said former *Globe* editor Richard Doyle. 'Among the players at the Globe, the urge to scratch the surface of "well enough" was now entrenched and credit for that had to be shared by Harold Greer.'[14]

The tendency to dig beneath the surface was never widespread in this period, but it did flare up in the work of several reporters over the years. Frank Drea's series in 1960 on the exploitation of immigrant workers in the building of Toronto's subway system had significant impact, leading to changes in provincial labour laws. Drea, who eventually converted his profile into a political career with the Ontario Conservatives, started an Action Line column in the *Toronto Telegram* in 1965. It afforded some of the earliest examples of aggressive consumer reporting, as he championed the cause of ordinary readers. Pierre Berton took on some similar battles in his *Toronto Star* column, beginning in 1958.

Perhaps the most insightful and enterprising of the reporters during this period was Haggart, whose sense of injustice and desire to hold the powerful to account produced many probing articles and columns. His civic-affairs column for the *Toronto Star* in the 1960s routinely skewered the hypocrisy and lack of credentials of various applicants for favours at city hall. But even Haggart was mainly concerned with commentary, and the impulse generally in newspapers of the time was for the quick exclusive, and not extensive investigation. Though the idea of a socially responsible press was beginning to take hold on a theoretical level at this time, it was slow to translate into an aggressive strain of journalism that used forensic skills as its methodology.

An interesting exception to that trend was a cluster of projects concerning wrongful convictions. It was rare for court cases to be re-examined in the media, especially those that had exhausted all levels of appeal. But a debate surrounding capital punishment in the late 1950s and early 1960s focused attention on convicts who were sentenced to die. An increasing number of politicians, social activists, and journalists began reflecting on English jurist William Blackstone's renowned admonition: 'It is better that ten guilty persons escape than one innocent suffer.'[15]

The conviction and execution of Wilbert Coffin triggered a number of journalistic investigations. Coffin was hanged at Montreal's Bordeaux jail in February 1956 for the killing of an American hunter in the Gaspé three years earlier. The bodies of three hunters from Pennsylvania were found in a forest, and the Quebec government came under intense pressure to solve the case. Even US Secretary of State John Foster Dulles had demanded quick action. Coffin, a prospector, was arrested and convicted of one of the murders, even though no weapon was ever found and there was nothing tangible linking him to the crime. Doubts persisted about his guilt, especially since many felt the government of Maurice Duplessis was trying to appease US authorities and protect the tourism industry. *Toronto Star* reporter J.E. Belliveau took great interest in the case, unearthing many important facts and gathering together his findings in a June 1956 book. Belliveau believed Coffin was innocent, and joined a committee to reinvestigate all aspects of the case. The publicity drew the interest of the Court of Last Resort, an American group founded by novelist Erle Stanley Gardner that tried to reopen cases of wrongful convictions. The *Star* capitalized on Belliveau's work by showing him working side-by-side with distinguished lawyers and academics on the Coffin file. It used Belliveau's journalism as a marketing tool to boost circulation, touting him as an 'ace newsman' who 'digs deep for facts that make headlines'.[16]

Journalist and future Canadian senator Jacques Hébert was also fascinated by the Coffin case, using it to unleash the full force of his muckraking skills. Unlike Belliveau, Hébert had a pronounced political motivation for looking into the story. Hébert had used his journal *Vrai* to expose corruption and excesses of the Duplessis regime, and he wrote a number of articles blaming the government for Coffin's execution. He too wrote a book, published in 1958, proclaiming Coffin's innocence. The issue simmered for years, with occasional revelations but no real smoking guns to prove one way or another whether Coffin had been involved. Then, in 1963, Hébert wrote a second book called *J'accuse les assassins de Coffin*. It was a scathing attack on the justice system under Duplessis and a bold attempt to reopen the case. Hébert had travelled across North America, interviewing a hundred people in his search for fresh clues. While Belliveau had carefully marshaled evidence and tried to present a sober analysis of the case, Hébert sprinkled his narrative with sweeping and vitriolic denunciations. He said the police were hell-bent on framing Coffin, the prosecutors were only interested in their personal glory, and the judge was unenlightened and biased. 'The slightest trail that led to any other suspect but Coffin was systematically covered up', he wrote. Even Coffin's lawyer came in for criticism, with Hébert denouncing 'the blunders, the stupidity, the incompetence, and the unbelievable inefficiency' of his work, adding that 'even a mediocre lawyer with the slightest amount of common sense could have saved Coffin.'[17]

Hébert's charges were so shocking that the authorities were forced to act. The Quebec government called a royal commission in direct response to the book. After hearing from more than 200 witnesses, it decisively upheld the original conviction in its 1964 report. Hébert denounced the process as a 'ludicrous inquiry in which the commission's only investigators were precisely those persons implicated in the Coffin case from the start'.[18] In fact, the commission spent much of its time trying to discredit the very journalists who had brought the case to the public's attention. Commissioner Roger Brossard used his final report to defend the integrity of Quebec's judicial system and vilify any journalist who dared question it. 'The Coffin affair began modestly in the dark dens of newspapers and press agencies looking for sensational news, and in the too impulsive imagination of journalists to whom "news" is more important than accuracy or truth', said Brossard, who recommended stronger libel laws to keep the press in check.[19] He reserved his strongest criticism for Hébert's book, which he said was steeped in a sea of falsehoods, inaccuracies, and slanders. The Quebec government wanted revenge, and it prosecuted Hébert for contempt of court. He was found guilty and handed a $3,000 fine, along with a sentence of 30 days in jail. He served just three days before securing bail pending an appeal. Hébert's friend and legal adviser, future prime minister Pierre Trudeau, eventually helped overturn the conviction. The Coffin case, meanwhile, has never been resolved. Coffin had consistently maintained his innocence, and many still believe he was wrongly convicted.

An execution at Toronto's Don Jail in December 1962 spurred more journalistic inquiries into wrongful convictions. Betty Lee of the *Globe and Mail* wrote a series in 1963 about the Arthur Lucas case. Lucas was an American who had been convicted in Toronto of murdering an FBI informant. The Crown had spared little effort in its prosecution, spending nearly $40,000 while the Legal Aid counsel for Lucas had access to $1,500. Working with leads supplied by Toronto lawyer Walter Williston, Lee wrote six meticulously researched stories reviewing the case and calling key points of evidence into question. The *Globe* billed her first piece as 'an investigative report', and editor Richard Doyle later said she accomplished something that was seldom done: 'review a trial her own paper had neglected when it was before the courts'.[20] As in the Coffin case, Lee's articles could only result in setting the historical record straight. There was no possibility of reversing the sentence. 'I do not criticize the fairness of any judge who heard the case', said Williston. 'But against capital punishment I have this indictment: that even when a man is tried by a judge of much experience, and an appeal is heard by jurists of great learning, it is still possible for him to be put to death for a crime he did not commit.'[21] Though Lee's stories didn't lead to a reopening of the case, the series had lasting impact. Lucas and Ronald Turpin, who were hanged on the same day, were the last people ever to be executed in Canada.

While Lee and Hébert were trying to show that justice was not infallible in Canada, a Toronto writer and mother of four was painstakingly collecting evidence in what would become the country's longest-lasting and most renowned wrongful conviction controversy. Isabel LeBourdais, born in 1909, earned her living as a public relations officer for the registered nurses' association in Ontario. But her passion was social justice, and she had spent her life fighting for the underdog and championing progressive causes. She had been active in the peace movement and the Co-operative Commonwealth Federation, and was a vocal advocate for decriminalizing abortion. In 1960, she read about the case of a 14-year-old Ontario boy who had been convicted of murder the year before. Steven Truscott was found guilty of murdering 12-year-old Lynne Harper in 1959 and was sentenced to die. The federal cabinet commuted his sentence, but Truscott exhausted all his appeals and faced a lifetime in prison. LeBourdais, who had a teenage son of her own, felt compelled to look into the case. Even if Truscott had committed the crime, she believed he needed psychiatric help rather than imprisonment. But once she began examining the facts, her assessments were more urgent. 'I came to the conclusion that this was not a sick boy who needed treatment but a normal boy who was innocent. Once I had made that discovery, I decided that I could never drop it until I had had the injustice redressed.'[22]

Her dogged pursuit of the truth would continue for the next six years as LeBourdais carried out one of the most exhaustive independent analyses of a Canadian conviction. She ordered the trial transcripts and read them several times, a process most writers and journalists typically didn't bother with before then. In more than 2,000 pages of testimony, she discovered a prosecution built entirely on circumstantial evidence and a theory that had Truscott committing the murder in an improbable half-hour window. It would have been physically impossible for him to have committed the crime in that time frame, she concluded. She also saw instances of witnesses changing their evidence or providing contradictory testimony on the stand. LeBourdais interviewed every key individual involved in the case. She talked to all the jurors in the original trial. She found evidence that tended to point to Truscott's innocence, evidence that was overlooked. She pinpointed flaws in the Crown's logic, and questioned the propriety of the judge's charge to the jury.

As she was compiling her research, LeBourdais tried to publish her initial findings. She was an experienced writer and had contributed stories to *Chatelaine*, *Saturday Night*, *Canadian Home Journal*, and many other magazines. But she had no luck getting editors interested in her story. *Chatelaine* read and rejected the proposal. *Star Weekly* sat on the idea for four months without responding. All the while, she kept researching. Eventually, LeBourdais concluded she had enough material for a book. She caught the interest of McClelland and Stewart, and by 1963 she had completed a third draft. The publisher thought some passages were too strident, and after taking the manuscript to lawyers, began having second thoughts. After prolonged negotiations, LeBourdais decided not to make any further changes, and broke off talks. She submitted it to five different publishers who all turned it down, citing legal concerns. It seemed no one had the courage to print her story.

Early in 1965, LeBourdais decided to write to Ludovic Kennedy, the British author who had written *Ten Rillington Place*. It told the story of a man who was hanged for a murder that had been committed by someone else. Kennedy encouraged her to approach his own publisher in London, Victor Gollancz. She did, and he immediately agreed to take on the project. Gollancz, a socialist and humanitarian who advocated the abolition of capital punishment, said: 'This is the kind of book for which my firm exists.'[23] Ironically, when he sought a publisher for the Canadian rights, McClelland and Stewart finally agreed to sign on. Her book was published in March 1966 as *The Trial of Steven Truscott*. 'Steven was a fourteen-year-old boy, like yours and mine', she wrote. 'Some man with a very sick mind raped and strangled the young girl that night. No one ever asked whether Steven had the sickness of the strangler and the rapist. No one really cared about that. Steven was charged, prosecuted, and convicted. Every witness, every clue, every fact that did not support a case against him was overlooked or ignored from the hour the body of Lynne Harper was found.'[24] She called for a royal commission to investigate every aspect of the Truscott case.

The book's impact was seismic. The first printing of 15,000 copies sold out in a week. Readers snapped up all the copies of two further printings that month. In the first 10 days after the book came out, LeBourdais did more than 30 radio and television interviews. Parliament immediately began discussing the case. Opposition leader John Diefenbaker adopted her call and demanded a royal commission. He said the government needed to conduct a paragraph-by-paragraph analysis of her work. Prime Minister Lester Pearson said he had taken a personal interest in the case and promised quick action. Behind the scenes, though, efforts were being made to discredit LeBourdais. Truscott's original trial judge, Ronald Ferguson, was clearly inspired by the Quebec government's assault on Jacques Hébert. In a letter to then justice minister Pierre Trudeau, Ferguson called the book 'a thoroughly dishonest piece of writing, and I regard it as my duty to draw the matter to your attention and to say that in my view, she ought to be prosecuted for public mischief.'[25] The tide of public opinion, however, was squarely on the side of LeBourdais and not sympathetic to a judge who had sentenced a 14-year-old boy to die.

A month after the book appeared, the government referred the Truscott case to the Supreme Court. But Truscott's time had not yet arrived. He had been silent at his original trial, but took the opportunity to testify at the Supreme Court. Still, in 1967, the court decided he didn't deserve a new trial. Two years later he was paroled, and the case lay dormant for the next three decades until he re-emerged to tell his story to CBC Television's *the fifth estate*. The CBC built on the work of LeBourdais and uncovered new evidence, renewing calls for Truscott to be exonerated.[26] By the time LeBourdais died in 2003, at the age of 93, Canadians were still debating the case and Truscott was continuing the fight to clear his name. (In its review of the case, the Ontario Court of Appeal unanimously acquitted him of the Harper murder on 28 August 2007.) LeBourdais, along with

Belliveau, Hébert, and Lee, had all contributed to a growing public sentiment that eventually forced government to abolish capital punishment in Canada. And the meticulous investigative work LeBourdais had produced would both instruct and inspire other journalists over the years, to the benefit of Donald Marshall, Guy-Paul Morin, David Milgaard, James Driskell, and other wrongly convicted Canadians.

In the era of bigger and better scoops, no newspaper reporter had greater claim to supremacy than Robert Reguly. Born in Fort William in 1931, he fought forest fires and cut lumber in the Northern Ontario bush, eventually taking a job as a timber scaler. A love of reading encouraged him to study journalism, so he enrolled at the University of Western Ontario when he was 20. After newspaper jobs in Winnipeg, Timmins, and Sudbury, he eventually joined the *Vancouver Province*, where his tough, aggressive style landed him some major scoops. One of the most notable was a scandal involving BC's former forestry minister, who had disappeared after allegations of involvement with bribery. Reguly convinced an oil company to show him the ex-minister's credit information, allowing him to trace his movements all the way to San Francisco. It was an early example of Reguly's unique ability to find missing people, a technique that eventually earned him the reputation of being Canada's leading investigative reporter.[27]

Reguly joined the *Toronto Star* in 1959, working the rewrite desk and serving a stint at the Parliamentary Press Gallery in Ottawa. It was the year of the St. Lawrence Seaway opening, and the *Star* decided it needed a shipping reporter. Reguly worked the beat,

Isabel LeBourdais spent six years investigating Steven Truscott's murder conviction. (Courtesy of Julien LeBourdais)

getting to know the major players in the industry. It would serve him well when he confronted one of Canada's most mysterious stories of missing persons, the case of Hal Banks. Banks, an Iowa-born ex-convict, had come to Canada at the invitation of the federal government and shipping companies to root out Communist influence in the Canadian Seamen's Union. He organized and ran the Seafarers' International Union of Canada in a dictatorial fashion, employing bribery and strong-arm tactics to quash all opposition. In 1964, he was sentenced to prison for conspiring to assault a rival union leader, and also faced perjury charges. But in July of that year, he suddenly disappeared, and an embarrassed federal government and RCMP said they had no idea where he was.

Sightings of Banks would reach the *Star* newsroom periodically. The paper's labour reporter got tips that he had been seen in Puerto Rico, Miami, New Orleans, New York, San Francisco, and San Diego. Questions were asked in Parliament, but no leads were apparent. Finally, the *Star*'s managing editor, aware that his former shipping reporter had known Banks, dropped by Reguly's desk to see if he could locate the missing man. It turned out to be simpler than he expected. Reguly visited the SIU headquarters in Brooklyn, mingling with the seamen in the basement bar, and then visited the rival National Maritime Union. He was provided a list of possible locations to find Banks, and at the third stop, he spotted a white Cadillac with Quebec licence plates. At the beginning of October, in a story the *Star* trumpeted as a world copyright, Reguly spun a Runyonesque first-person account of his journalistic coup in Brooklyn.

I found Hal Banks yesterday—sitting all alone on a union yacht docked in Mill basin here, the familiar cigarette clenched in his teeth.

Later, I got slugged for my troubles and chased by four SIU goons but got away with the help of a dedicated and quick-thinking cab driver.

It took only two hours to locate Banks, 55, though police of two countries have been searching since July when he vanished from Montreal.

Realizing his story of stumbling across Banks might be denied and ridiculed, Reguly found a $5 camera in a nearby store and was back an hour after his initial sighting to take a picture.

At my approach Banks ducked into the boat and several guards charged at me. One of them managed to hit me on the head with something, causing a small gash.

I ran down six-lane Flatbush Ave., dodging traffic with four goons in hot pursuit.[28]

Over the years, different accounts have emerged on how the *Star* was able to find Banks so quickly. For his part, Reguly says it was simply common sense. 'It's my theory that people on the lam go home, that is, to where they have friends and protection. It was very simple. You had to start somewhere, and where else would you start? Why wouldn't anybody just go to the SIU headquarters?' Though the American government ultimately refused to extradite Banks, Reguly's reputation took a great leap forward.

Not quite so simple, but even more explosive, was Reguly's coup in tracking down Gerda Munsinger. It became the ultimate Cold War scandal, with equal parts political intrigue and sexual escapade. Ottawa was thrown into a state of frenzy in 1966 when the Liberal justice minister revealed that Munsinger, an East German prostitute and potential security threat, had slept with cabinet ministers in the previous Conservative government of John Diefenbaker. The scandal had been hushed up for years, but in light of Britain's Profumo affair, in which a cabinet minister slept with a woman who also had a relationship with the Soviet naval attaché, the media took it up with vigour. Initial reports suggested Munsinger was dead, and there was confusion about her exact name. Reguly chased down leads in Montreal, hunting through telephone directories to find an old apartment address. Working with *Star* reporter Robert MacKenzie, he determined the trail led to Munich. Within hours of getting off the plane, Reguly was interviewing the woman that dozens of reporters had been trying to find.

'*Star* Man Finds Gerda Munsinger' screamed the 144-point headline on 11 March 1966. 'In a chintzy apartment in Munich, the girl at the centre of Ottawa's sex-spy scandal talks of life in Canada—and two cabinet ministers she knew', the paper boasted. Reguly's story documented her affair with Pierre Sevigny, Diefenbaker's associate minister of national defence. She still wore the gold September birthstone ring Sevigny had given her, and she acknowledged knowing a second Conservative cabinet minister 'very well'. It was another world copyright for Reguly, whose picture ran just below Munsinger's on the front page. Once again, his first-person account described how he added up the clues that led to her door.

The Munsinger case cemented Reguly's reputation as the reporter who could get the big scoop. And the *Star* wasn't shy about trumpeting his abilities. The newspaper began referring to him as 'Canada's best-known investigative reporter'. He was given increasingly important assignments, and often pitched in when sources needed to be chased for big stories. When reports of bribery were floating around Toronto City Hall in 1968, Reguly was called back from his post as Washington bureau chief to nail down the story. His aggressive reporting led to many more exclusives during stints as a foreign correspondent. After presidential candidate Bobby Kennedy was shot by Sirhan Sirhan in 1968, Reguly broke away from the pack of reporters and took a taxi to Pasadena where he interviewed the assassin's mother, brother, and employer. He was proud of his ability to get people to talk.

Like many reporters of his generation, Reguly dislikes the term 'investigative reporter'. There were no overarching agendas guiding his work, only a moral sense of right and wrong and a desire to carry out any assignment thrown at him. His only methodology was straightforward legwork, enhanced when needed by the technique of flattering sources, buying them drinks, or offering the occasional financial inducement. He lived for the scoop. It brought him extraordinary fame. But as we will see later, the desire for bigger and better scoops would eventually be responsible for ending his career.

The journalism Walter Stewart observed in the 1950s may have seemed suspect, hypocritical, and beholden to advertisers and bombastic owners, but there were hints of impending change during this era. Individual practitioners were sprouting here and there, applying techniques that went beyond the lazy stringing together of official quotes that passed for objective journalism. Reporters like Robert Reguly showed how journalistic success could be achieved with application of technique and hard-nosed inquiry. While the renewed concept of a socially responsible press was circulating in academic circles, there was no specific scheme for applying the idea to the working media. Mainstream media organizations appeared to recognize the practice of vigorous, hard-hitting journalism when they saw it, but for the most part were shy about actually doing it. A cluster of high-profile stories dealing with apparent wrongful convictions was instructive for many journalists, as it demonstrated the necessity of doing exhaustive research on a single topic. But it wasn't immediately obvious that journalists who did these kinds of stories were reaping any rewards. Jacques Hébert ran afoul of the law in his pursuit of the Coffin case, and Isabel LeBourdais suffered years of rejection as she tried to interest publishers in her Steven Truscott tale. The journalists who chronicled instances of wrongful convictions were clearly motivated by a sense of outrage, and a strong desire to see justice done. In Alasdair MacIntyre's analysis, they were demonstrating virtues of justice, courage, and truthfulness through applying standards of excellence in their social practice of inquiring journalism, despite pressures from either their own institutions or external forces.[29] For the most part, though, it was the scoop that held sway. The modern era of the politically powerful exposé was on its way.

Exonerating the Innocent: The Journalist as Detective

On a brutally cold January morning in 1969, a knife-wielding man viciously assaulted and murdered Saskatoon nursing assistant Gail Miller. In a city that had witnessed just one homicide in the previous two years, the incident caused a sensation, but police had few clues and almost no hard evidence. Under intense pressure to solve the crime, they eventually charged 16-year-old David Milgaard. The teenager was simply passing through town at the time and had no involvement in the murder, but Saskatchewan's justice system convicted and sentenced him to life in prison. That's where he might have stayed, were it not for the efforts of his crusading mother and a number of determined Winnipeg journalists.

Joyce Milgaard worked tirelessly to exonerate her son, and along the way she enlisted the help of Peter Carlyle-Gordge, Manitoba correspondent for *Maclean's* magazine. In the 1980s, Gordge helped track down some of the original trial witnesses and dug up new information. But justice officials weren't paying much attention. After 20 years, Milgaard's appeals finally began receiving significant publicity when Dan Lett of the *Winnipeg Free Press* got involved. Lett reexamined evidence at the trial, interviewed key witnesses, and wrote a number of crucial stories questioning the original conviction. The publicity led to an anonymous tip. Someone suggested another man, Larry Fisher, might be responsible for the murder. It appeared he had been involved in similar attacks on women in Regina.

Journalists at CBC Manitoba began investigating, and found some startling evidence. Fisher's crimes had not been in Regina, but in Saskatoon. In June 1990, the CBC reported that Fisher had committed four sexual assaults in Saskatoon, three of them shortly before Miller's murder and one a year after. The modus operandi was often the same, and matched the way Miller was attacked. At least two of Fisher's victims had lived in Miller's neighbourhood. The CBC mapped the homes and workplaces of the victims, and found that some could easily have taken the same bus as Gail Miller had every day. They discovered Fisher had a pattern of stalking women on buses or at bus stops. What's more, Fisher lived in the basement suite of the very same house Milgaard had been visiting in Saskatoon.

From all appearances, police and justice officials had overlooked the most obvious suspect in the murder. Media interest in the Milgaard case exploded. The CBC's *fifth estate* convinced Fisher, a convicted rapist, to give an interview, in which he denied all wrongdoing. Despite the evidence, the federal justice minister moved slowly and reluctantly in responding to Milgaard's pleas. But the Supreme Court of Canada eventually decided that Milgaard's conviction should not stand, and in 1992 he was set free. Investigative journalism continued to probe the case, with David Roberts of the *Globe and Mail* raising questions about how Saskatchewan police and justice officials handled the affair. Years later, DNA evidence completely exonerated Milgaard, and pointed the finger firmly at Fisher, who was tried and convicted of murdering Miller. After spending 23 years behind bars for a murder he didn't commit, Milgaard eventually collected a $10 million compensation settlement. And the journalists involved had the satisfaction of having helped correct one of the most serious errors the Canadian justice system could have made.

Chapter 5

The Public Broadcasters

'Good evening. Tonight *See It Now* devotes its entire half hour to a report on Senator Joseph R. McCarthy, told mainly in his own words and pictures.'

It was 9 March 1954 and Edward R. Murrow was beginning his famous salvo against the menace of McCarthyism. The renowned CBS journalist had put together a devastating portrait of the red-baiting senator from Wisconsin. Using clips of McCarthy himself, Murrow showed a badgering, bombastic figure who displayed an arrogant disregard for the truth as he tried to implicate people in Communist conspiracies. Not far away, a young Canadian journalist was paying attention. Douglas Leiterman was at Harvard University, in the midst of a Nieman fellowship that was exposing him to all the modern currents in American journalism. Leiterman was a newspaperman, and it hadn't occurred to him that the brand new medium of television could be a forum for aggressive reporting. As the words and images unfolded on Murrow's CBS broadcast, there was a palpable impact, not only on American politics but also on the minds of a future generation of television journalists on both sides of the border. Leiterman was hooked.

> This is no time for men who oppose Senator McCarthy's methods to keep silent, or for those who approve. We can deny our heritage and our history, but we cannot escape responsibility for the result. . . . The actions of the junior senator from Wisconsin have caused alarm and dismay among allies abroad and given considerable comfort to our enemies, and whose fault is that? Not really his, he didn't create this situation of fear, he merely exploited it and rather successfully. Cassius was right. 'The fault, dear Brutus, is not in our stars, but in ourselves.' Good night, and good luck.[1]

Leiterman was one of the Young Turks at the *Vancouver Province* in the early 1950s, working under the tutelage of Torchy Anderson, Ross Munro, and Sid Scott, all of whom would send their reporters looking for scoops whenever they had the manpower and the money to spare.[2] He didn't fit the average reporter profile of the time, having studied economics, political science, and law as he was working the night desk. Anderson encouraged him to apply for the Nieman journalism award, and in 1953 he packed his bags for a year-long session of seminars and intellectual debate.

At Harvard, he came into contact with some maverick journalists who were rebelling against the malaise of timid and official journalism. One of his Nieman classmates was Robert Emmett Hoyt, a Washington reporter for the Knight newspaper chain. Hoyt specialized in exposing corruption in city government, national politics, and social behaviour. In their Nieman group, Hoyt usually asked the toughest questions, always in a soft, deceptively respectful voice. Much like I.F. Stone, his distrust of officialdom and orthodoxy led him to seek other paths to the truth. Another classmate was Alvin Davis, an aggressive reporter and city editor for the *New York Post*, who also upheld the banner of skeptical inquiry.

Leiterman's experiences left him convinced that in-depth, no-holds-barred reporting was indispensable to a functioning democracy. He also developed a keen sense of outrage. 'As a police reporter, business reporter, and general-assignment writer I came to see all the suffering and misery which was not part of my own life. And I came to believe that much of it could be avoided, and that society could take steps in our country to lead its members to happier and more worthwhile lives. . . . Out of it all, almost imperceptibly, I began to develop a sense of the power of the press and a modest sense of mission. Wrongdoing could be exposed.'[3]

Back at the *Vancouver Province*, Leiterman was assigned to take the pulse of Europe a decade after VE Day. He rented a motorcycle and travelled thousands of kilometres through 12 countries, faking mechanical trouble to get into East Germany and sneaking into Yugoslavia through Greece.[4] In 1956 and 1957, he toured a dozen Asian countries and produced a 36-piece series called *Window on Asia*. As a correspondent for the Southam News parliamentary bureau, Leiterman joined the ranks of a minority of journalists who attempted to go beyond daily reporting. His tenacity made him stand out, and brought him to the notice of CBC producers who were busy building a new current affairs program that was experimenting with the kinds of journalism Leiterman wanted to practise. He joined the CBC in November 1957, and on his first day Patrick Watson took him to lunch and convinced him that the new medium was a good way to engineer social change. It was the beginning of a new relationship that would have significant impact both on innovative television programming and investigative journalism in Canada.

Television was still in its infancy in Canada, but public broadcasting had been firmly established since the creation of the CBC in 1936. Just as the newspaper industry was completing its transition to commercialization in the years following World War I, government was grappling with a fledgling radio market that was dominated by American stations. The Canadian Radio League became an advocate for a public broadcasting system, with one of its founders, Graham Spry, declaring that, 'It is a choice between the State and the United States.'[5] Spry saw informational exchanges as crucial to the health of a dynamic society, and he wasn't willing to let the free market decide how such interactions would work in the new field of broadcasting. 'Here is a majestic instrument of national unity and national culture', he said. 'Its potentialities are too great, its influence and significance are too vast, to be left to the petty purposes of selling cakes of soap.'[6] By the 1950s, with CBC television beginning to take shape, public service continued to be regarded as crucial. Policy makers saw television, in part, 'as a pedagogic service with public affairs programming as its cornerstone'.[7] This was the landscape Leiterman entered when he joined the public broadcaster in 1957.

Leiterman became a story editor for *Close-Up*, a program the CBC itself described as 'one of the most ambitious newsgathering enterprises to date in Canadian television'.[8] Though it was conceived as a broadcast equivalent of *Life* magazine, *Close-Up* experimented with many forms of journalism, including investigative work. 'The planners of the program say it will be more concerned with a comprehensive presentation of human problems than with a simple reporting of the facts', said a CBC Press Service announcement in advance of the 6 October 1957 start date.[9] 'Where controversy or crisis exists or when news needs the added clarification of a searching look, *Close-Up* will go after comment from the persons principally involved.' The idea that something more than conventional news reporting was needed to get to the truth of situations wasn't entirely obvious at the time. Everyone knew the difference between a newspaper and a magazine, and the additional context that longer-form journalism could provide. However, the team assembled by the CBC to produce *Close-Up* wanted to take the distinction a step further—much further, in fact, than the guiding principle of the CBC's news service, established in 1941, which proclaimed a mission to present 'all the significant news of the day's happenings in Canada and abroad factually, without bias or distortion, without tendentious comment, and in a clear and unambiguous style'.[10]

The on-air team was drawn from the pool of Canada's best-known media personalities. J. Frank Willis, one of the most familiar voices on Canadian radio, made his TV debut as host and editor-on-the-air. Other contributors included Pierre Berton, then managing editor of *Maclean's*; Blair Fraser, *Maclean's* Ottawa editor; Jack Webster, the West Coast's controversial print-and-radio reporter; clergyman and author Charles Templeton; and CBC personalities Elaine Grand and Percy Saltzman.

But it was the editorial board members, all of them younger than 35, who shaped the program and gave it its unique posture. Watson, the youthful academic turned television producer in CBC's public affairs department, was the co-producer. George Ronald, former city editor of the *Brantford Expositor* and Washington correspondent for Canadian Press, and Ron Krantz, CBC's national assignment editor, rounded out the team. And the leader of the board was CBC wunderkind Ross McLean.

At 32, McLean was already a hardened veteran of early broadcasting in Canada. He had joined the CBC in 1948 and became one of three pioneering television producers when the service began on 8 September 1952.[11] He created many of the CBC's first television programs, and by the time *Close-Up* aired he had 1,739 individual television episodes under his belt. With his trademark horn-rimmed glasses, McLean had a shy and reserved manner, but a towering presence. He attributed his success to a literary flair inherited from his grandmother, and he drew inspiration from an eighth birthday gift of a toy microphone.[12] But his real success derived from a well developed sense of public service, and a fearlessness when it came to challenging established authority. His constant question to staff was: 'How will it serve the audience?'[13]

McLean's biggest success to date had been *Tabloid*, the CBC's answer to *Today* on NBC. It began as a supper-hour program in 1953 and ran for 10 years. It presented what is now a familiar blend of news, interviews, weather reports, chat among hosts, and entertainment. McLean was shrewd when it came to using celebrity to build an audience, and he had an intuitive understanding of the need to present information in an engaging way. His motto for *Tabloid* was 'Facts with Fun'. He had a knack for spotting talent and was responsible for introducing some of Canada's earliest broadcast celebrities, both men and women, to the screen. He was never afraid to experiment with the medium. The viewers responded, and at its height the show drew an audience of 250,000 in Toronto alone.

Tabloid's menu of light entertainment didn't mean the show was devoid of controversy. In 1956 a viewer, Dr E.E. Robbins of Montreal, sent a letter critical of the program to McLean, who responded by presenting the letter on air, and encouraging viewers to offer their own response to Robbins. To assist, the doctor's address and phone number were broadcast. The doctor said he was flooded with telephone calls and visits from angry *Tabloid* viewers, including one woman who told him to drop dead. When people weren't calling, they were ringing his doorbell. Two unsolicited chickens were delivered to his home. Robbins sued, and eventually won $3,000 in damages. CBC management, meanwhile, went into damage control. CBC's Ontario chief suspended McLean for 'a grave error of judgment and good taste', transferring him to another assignment. McLean swiftly apologized, and soon the tempest subsided. It became a curious episode in his career, but a signal of more controversy to come.[14]

While *Tabloid* established Ross McLean's reputation as a populist programmer, *Close-Up* was an entirely different creation, a genuine newsmagazine with ambitious and daring intentions. Though the BBC's *Panorama* was arguably the oldest television newsmagazine, *Close-Up* paved the way for the genre in North America. McLean undoubtedly drew inspiration from Murrow's programs as well, both *See It Now* and the interview-based *Person to Person*, and Mike Wallace's tough interviewing style on ABC was also an influence. But the resulting blend was unique, and the program dabbled in pioneering forms of investigative broadcast journalism.

In its first year, *Close-Up* sent reporters travelling 400,000 kilometres around the world, interviewing everyone from Somerset Maugham and Ann Landers to Robert Service and Brigitte Bardot. Later, it would air an exclusive television interview with Fidel Castro, well before the downfall of Cuban dictator Fulgencio Batista. The program had a sweeping range of interests, delving into homosexuality, mixed marriages, unwed motherhood, Italian communism, Spanish bullfights—everything McLean felt could entertain as it informed. With an uncommonly generous $20,000 weekly budget, the show's producers and reporters had ample room to explore anything of interest. They weren't above staging stunts to make a point or draw an audience. In one episode, producers investigated marketing trends and the new practice of 'subliminal projection'. To demonstrate the technique, the program flashed subliminal messages during the 30-minute show, and then visited a Winnipeg man and his family to determine whether they were aware of any hidden messages. In another episode, the program staged a mock bank robbery to dramatize an increasing crime wave in Toronto.[15]

Even critics who were skeptical at the outset came to recognize there was something different about the program. Trent Frayne, writing in the *Globe and Mail*, called the program coy and esoteric in its early stages, but said the turning point came when it took a probing look at US Vice-President Richard Nixon. 'Like the CBC (news department), they had been refused the cooperation of Nixon and his Washington staff. Unlike the CBC, they dropped in there. *Close-Up* neatly flew a camera crew to Nixon's west-coast birthplace and talked to his family, school teachers, and early political opponents. Another crew rounded up Washington insiders.' For Frayne, it was probing journalism that scooped the American networks on their home ground.[16]

Some of the program items seemed like forerunners to more contemporary broadcast magazine investigations. In April 1958, *Close-Up* showed hidden-camera footage of would-be American immigrants to Canada being interviewed in the Chicago office of the Canadian Department of Citizenship and Immigration. The Americans expressed their views of life in the US, why they wanted to leave, and what their expectations were of Canada. It was a remarkable, unvarnished performance by real people who didn't know the camera was rolling. The film was arranged in advance with the Canadian government, and shown only after the interviewees gave their consent. But it revealed a new television technique aimed at capturing authentic reactions and information.[17] That same summer, the program aired an investigation of the Mafia that included interviews with former members of organized crime families. Charles Templeton flew to Rome to interview a variety of Mafiosi, including one of mobster Lucky Luciano's former lieutenants.

Leiterman thrived in the environment, using his analytical skills in a new medium to reach a wide audience. One of his first projects was a portrait of Louis St. Laurent, a film McLean called astonishing, and one that provided 'insight into the man that has been curiously lacking in Canadians' conception of him all along'.[18] Leiterman's growing understanding of television was evident in his hour-long exploration of BC's Sons of Freedom Doukhobors. The religious sect was embroiled in controversy, and some of its more radical members engaged in arson and bombings to protest heavy-handed government repression of their rights. Among others, Leiterman interviewed Bill Markin, a 68-year-old Freedomite who explained the bombing exploits that sent him to jail for 10 years. The film gave context and texture to a story that had been covered mostly superficially to that point, and it took viewers to a place they hadn't been before. Patrick Watson was exploring similar territory when he made the first-ever documentary inside a maximum-security prison in Canada.

Taking viewers to strange and forbidden places did not always sit well with CBC management. An item on homosexuality stirred controversy, and another on unemployment drew government charges that the man *Close-Up* featured as a victim had been paid by the CBC and had actually turned down job offers. Just months after *Close-Up* first went to air, CBC manager Marcel Ouimet was complaining internally about the show's choice of stories and treatments. He said he hoped the producers would never lose sight of their obligation to present balanced comments.[19]

By its second year, *Close-Up* was drawing more than 1.3 million viewers. Other media were now paying close attention, and tried to deflate some of the program's bigger scoops. The most celebrated example came to be known as the Shady Lady Affair. In May 1960, the program featured a silhouette interview with an anonymous woman claiming to be 'the other woman' in divorce cases. Canada's divorce laws at the time required proof of adultery, and this sensational interview featured a 25-year-old woman claiming to work for $100 a night manufacturing phony evidence so clients could file for divorce. Seated on a bed, she told interviewer June Callwood she would accompany men to hotels, partially undress, and stage a make-believe adulterous encounter so that courts could be supplied with so-called evidence. Even before the program was shown, protests were raised in the Senate about the propriety of the broadcast, and government officials thought the whole matter warranted further investigation. The Ontario Provincial Police began sifting through 8,000 files of women who were co-respondents in divorce cases over the previous few years to see if they could identify the woman in the shadows. Newspaper reporters worked feverishly to try to do the same.

On 5 July, the *Toronto Telegram* splashed its entire front page with a giant scoop of its own: The Shady Lady Tells All—CBC TV Divorce Show 'Phony'. The newspaper interviewed Joan Johnson, also known as Joan Campbell, who said she fabricated her story in the CBC interview. What's more, she said the CBC paid her $150 to do the interview. No mention was made of how much the *Telegram* paid for her stunning reversal. It was a major embarrassment for McLean, but the CBC said it had done nothing unethical and defended the larger story about the inadequacy of Canada's divorce laws. The story served up a feeding frenzy for Canadian newspapers and politicians. In the end, it was little more than a commentary about the dodgy credibility of one woman, but it also showed the inherent risks in aggressive journalism. McLean learned a useful lesson about how to do such stories in the future, but he paid a significant price for it. His relationship with CBC management soon soured to the point where he felt the need to leave. When the program he had created finally folded in 1963, McLean was wistful: '*Close-Up* is dead, followed to its grave, as I shall probably be to mine, by the Shady Lady.'[20]

Close-Up played a significant role in the development of two important features of investigative work: the intensive, aggressive research into a single subject that was so often ignored by daily reporters, and the accountability interview. Television was a unique medium for the interview, as it revealed information, not just in the content of the answers, but in the manner that people responded. Murrow and Wallace recognized the power of the interview in the American television context, as did René Lévesque in his Radio-Canada current affairs program *Point de mire*. But the producers in CBC's English television department developed the process further. Patrick Watson considered the focused accountability interview to be a crucial element in the investigative work of the era.[21] Leiterman argued that it was important for interviewers to adopt a devil's-advocate posture for truth to begin to emerge. And both were acutely aware that an aggressive interview often made for compelling television. 'In the late fifties', said

Ross McLean, one of the CBC's *pioneering television journalists, created some early forms of investigative journalism.* (CBC *Still Photo Collection*)

Watson, 'I began to realize that careful, thoughtful, reasonable discussion was not what held viewers to the screen. It was vigorous dispute and strong images that did the trick. . . . And a kind of formulation or principle began to emerge. I said to myself, "This is not an information medium. It is . . . *theatre*. It may be dealing with factual information and opinion about current events, but when it works it works because it engages the viewer emotionally in the way a play does. . . ."'[22]

Watson moved to Ottawa in September 1960 to put his theories more fully into practice. He began to produce *Inqui'ry*, a look at national political issues that featured hard-hitting interviews. Topics ranged from income tax and national defence to censorship and Quebec separatism. Davidson Dunton, the CBC's first chairman and the president of Carleton University, was the program's first host, followed by academic Laurier Lapierre and broadcaster Warner Troyer. Leiterman, meanwhile, left *Close-Up* soon afterwards to concentrate on documentary filmmaking. He had come to the medium as a complete newcomer and swiftly turned into one of its visionaries. More than 100 *Close-Up* episodes convinced him that cinéma-vérité techniques were crucial in illuminating the underlying reality of his subject matter. Over the next few years, his prolific work included a number of powerful documentaries that ran under the CBC's *Background, Intertel,* and *Document* series.

Some of Leiterman's most memorable work in this period revolved around race relations in the US. CBC had commissioned a documentary called *One More River* for *Intertel,* a consortium of international broadcasters. Leiterman's co-director was fellow CBC employee and his future wife, Beryl Fox, and his brother Richard was cameraman. Before he even began filming, Leiterman produced an outline of the film suggesting there had been significant progress in the state of American race relations in recent years. He pointed to the US Supreme Court ruling in 1954 that struck down school segregation as unconstitutional. His outline was based on published reports, but, as he began investigating further and travelling in the South, a different picture emerged. His preconceived notions dashed, he continued the research and put together a portrait of American blacks still struggling to gain any semblance of equality.

Leiterman filmed in nine states, always looking for opportunities to let the camera capture reality rather than relying on interviews with experts. Fox was shown walking down the street with a black man in Charlotte, North Carolina as crowds gathered to stare. They were denied entrance to a whites-only theatre. It was all filmed by a camera hidden in a moving vehicle. Later, the crew was assailed as they filmed a group of black children being denied entrance to a lunch counter. In addition to the hidden-camera work, Leiterman and Fox secured extraordinary access to images that had rarely been filmed before, including a Ku Klux Klan grand dragon on a Georgia farm.

The film was controversial, and CBC management initially decided it wouldn't be shown. Leiterman refused to make changes and take management suggestions to insert what they considered more moderate and mainstream views into the piece. After some delay and further negotiating, the film was broadcast, though some members of the international consortium also refused to show it. Leiterman was not completely surprised at the controversy, since there had been previous indications of CBC sensitivity to *Intertel* projects. In 1961, for instance, the corporation suppressed a documentary thought favourable to Fidel Castro called *Cuba, Si.* CBC executives killed the already completed hour-long piece because they feared it would offend American viewers by showing popular support for Castro in Cuba.[23]

In spite of the delay, *One More River* became a critical success, eventually winning the first prestigious Wilderness Award. Maurice Wiggin, critic for the *London Sunday Times,* named it the best of the *Intertel* offerings. 'It was technique that made *One More River* great', he said. 'Mr Leiterman stripped away and discarded those ancient and wearisome props, the filtering factors, the intermediaries—the "television personalities"—who most arrogantly presume to stand between us, the viewers, and the light of direct experience.'[24] Wiggin said this was television's most important and perhaps only original contribution, the one thing no other medium could properly do.

Leiterman's techniques and views of cinema-verité brought a unique version of reality to Canadian television screens in the early 1960s, opening up possibilities of doing investigative journalism in entirely new ways. They also caused consternation in many circles. A *Globe and Mail* editorial titled 'The Eve of '84' warned of a Big Brother society emerging if tight controls weren't placed on the indiscriminate use of cameras and microphones.[25] While sticking to his methodology, Leiterman agreed that his new techniques were capable of both enlightenment and harm. The new producer and cameraman, capable of recording reality like never before, were also increasing the potential for mischief, he said. 'He (the television journalist) must set his own standards of decency and integrity, because he has the raw material of human frailty in his hands. . . . The creepy-peepy cameras put a new premium on the old-fashioned virtues of judgment and responsibility. Privacy will be much more invaded and conversations more often overheard.'[26]

Though they were living in different cities and involved in separate projects, Watson and Leiterman kept in touch. They would routinely critique each other's work, and muse about the possibility of creating a current affairs program that could truly reach a mass audience. For all its successes, *Close-Up* never approached the gigantic ratings numbers of the American dramas and variety shows. Watson and Leiterman were confident a new program combining all the best elements of their previous work could achieve the aim. And they were also observing developments around the world in public affairs television. After a rocky start in 1953, the BBC's *Panorama* continued to grow in popularity as it experimented with different current affairs models. Granada Television took a more aggressive approach when it launched *World in Action* in 1963. Unlike the studio-based *Panorama*, it devoted each half-hour episode to a single issue, using mobile field production and close-up photography in a style Leiterman was also advocating. Its first editor, Tim Hewat, 'operated on the assumption that few viewers would willingly subject themselves to 30 minutes of "current affairs" unless grabbed by their lapels. . . . Hewat's achievement was that he created a mass audience for what had till then seemed a preserve of elites.'[27] By 1967, it had added a specific 'Investigation Bureau' and set out to do groundbreaking investigative work. The Australians, wanting a *Panorama*-style program of their own, created *Four Corners* in 1961. It was destined to become the Australian Broadcasting Corporation's flagship investigative program.

There was another major influence on the Canadian producers, this time from a less likely source. In November 1962, the BBC began airing a satirical program called *That Was the Week That Was*. The live, Saturday night program opened each time with a song by Millicent Martin, recapping the week's big stories. The rest of the show included skits, interviews, and lampoons. There was no intensive research, and often no discernible journalism in many of the segments. Instead, humour and satire were applied to current affairs, often with devastating effect. The host of *TW3*, David Frost, became an instant celebrity as audiences mushroomed with each passing week. The outbreak of the Profumo affair was a gift to the producers, with the sex scandal offering endless satiric possibilities. The program was a national sensation for two years until the BBC killed it, worried that it would exercise undue influence in an election year.

By 1963, Leiterman and Watson were starting to get specific about what a new program might look like. They screened hours and hours of *TW3*. According to Watson, '. . . while the rock and centre of what we intended was solid journalism, documentary, straight reporting, intense interviews, we also felt that cheeky, outrageous satire would do a lot to win the affection and trust of our audiences.'[28] The program they eventually created owed much to *TW3*, from its satiric posture to its opening song and to its very name. But the Canadians managed to weave a number of strands into a completely unique tapestry. They called their creation *This Hour has Seven Days*.

Each weekly episode had a budget of $31,850, making it the best-financed public affairs show the CBC had produced. Leiterman and Watson, who each received a modest annual salary of $16,400, put together a talented team of broadcast and print journalists.[29] They deliberately looked for the kind of people who could move beyond the mentality of the two-minute news story, people who had the desire and ability to delve more deeply into their subject matter.

Historians have had difficulty pinpointing the exact moment when the term 'investigative journalism' came into common usage. As we have seen, there were sporadic references as early as 1952 in the US, but no systematic naming of a new genre. In his *Evolution of American Investigative Journalism*, James Aucoin points to 1962, when John Hohenberg, curator of the Pulitzer Prizes, drew a distinction between exposure journalism and routine reporting in reviewing the previous year's entries. Hohenberg labeled the exposure stories 'investigatory', which Aucoin says is perhaps the first published attempt to name the practice.[30] And in Canada, one of the earliest references to the genre is the one enunciated in Watson and Leiterman's 1963 program design, which they called a manifesto. It called for the program to have a specific format that would include the following:

1. A Film Report: The mainstay of the magazine will be the film report with live links covering in energetic style the significant current affairs of the week.
2. An Investigative Report: Using special camera techniques we will probe honesty and hypocrisy. . . . By encouraging leads from our viewers, and inviting their alertness, we will provide a kind of TV ombudsman to draw attention to public wrongs and encourage remedial action.
3. A Hot Seat would be a tough encounter with a prominent guest who is hot in the news and prepared to be grilled.[31]

Seven Days went on the air at 10 p.m. on Sunday, 4 October 1964 and began its well documented journey to become the most-watched program in Canadian current affairs history. It wasted no time deflating the pomposity of Canada's various elites. In its tone and content, it tried to remedy what Leiterman and his colleagues thought was the main defect of typical CBC current affairs programming: 'it still tends to be awfully considerate of the Establishment, of our various establishments, to take for granted that they are working pretty well. But a lot of people out there feel they are outside the system, that they're getting screwed by the system and by the establishments. They don't trust politicians, or police, or industry. They need something on television that gives them more of a voice.'[32]

Though *Seven Days* staff could hardly be described as a band of revolutionaries, they were getting close scrutiny by government agencies charged with rooting out subversion.

An RCMP Security Service memo dated 6 November 1964 dealing with Communist activities within Canada reads: 'Attached are a number of CBC internal information bulletins and articles from the *CBC Times* pertaining to some of the new fall series which it is expected will come to our attention.' Later, referring to Leiterman and Watson, the memo says: 'Their backgrounds have been with *Document, Close-Up*, and *Inquiry* series, which shows have occasionally come to our attention in the past.' In a later memo, dated 18 February 1966, the Security Service writes: '. . . it could be shown that certain programs and personnel are perhaps somewhat strenuously progressive.'[33]

Investigative journalism on *Seven Days* appeared in various forms: field reports, accountability interviews, consumer advocacy items, and in-depth documentaries. There were stories about car safety, inequities in the justice system, overuse of drugs, capital punishment, links between smoking and cancer, clubbing of baby seals, and many other intensively researched topics. Before he could make any breakthroughs on network television in the US, Ralph Nader appeared on *Seven Days*, relentlessly grilling an engineer from American Motors about why he didn't consider padded dashboards a mandatory safety measure. The program took up the cause of a low-level federal administrator in the North who had lost his job for unauthorized diversion of funds, even though the money was being used to improve housing for aboriginal people. It was a signal to viewers that the program would play an ombudsman's role, and it sparked many to call the program with further story ideas.

One of the most celebrated investigative stories concerned Ontario farmer Fred Fawcett, who stopped paying taxes to protest his township's refusal to build an access road. After a confrontation with tax assessors, he was arrested and eventually declared mentally incompetent. He wound up in the Penetanguishene Hospital for the Criminally Insane, and had been there four years when the media began investigating his case. *Seven Days* wasn't the first media organization to take note of the case, but it came up with an innovative way to skirt the bureaucratic refusal of authorities to allow Fawcett to be interviewed. A crew accompanied his sister on a visit to the institution, smuggling camera equipment in picnic baskets to his room. A very sane-looking Fawcett appeared on the program, articulately protesting his treatment. Two weeks later, Ontario Premier John Robarts announced that Fawcett's case would be reviewed, and he was released soon afterwards.[34]

Some of the most outstanding examples of enterprising journalism came in the form of the hour-long documentaries that ran every fourth week in the *Seven Days* slot, under the *Document* series title. The most talented contributor on this front was Beryl Fox, who had worked on *One More River* and followed it up with *Summer in Mississippi*, which traced the story of three civil-rights workers who had been murdered there. Fox was born into a working class, socialist family in Winnipeg's north end. She dropped out of high school, worked in factories, eventually going back to university and then landing a job with the CBC as a script assistant. Her talents were quickly rewarded, and she became one of the corporation's most innovative filmmakers.

Fox and cameraman Erik Durschmied went to Vietnam in 1965 at a time when mainstream media outlets were still applauding American intervention in Indochina.

She set out to show how the war was affecting both the American soldiers and the Vietnamese peasantry. The result was a raw portrait called *Mills of the Gods*. It sketched a picture of Vietnam that hadn't yet emerged in the media. Footage showed American soldiers snapping trophy photos with enemy corpses, and standing by as their South Vietnamese comrades tortured prisoners of war. In the film's most searing scene, Durschmied is in the right-hand seat of a Skyraider aircraft as an American pilot drops napalm on villages below. 'That was an outstanding target', the pilot exults. 'We can see the people running everywhere; it was fantastic.' The film had a dramatic impact on Canadian and, ultimately, British and American attitudes to the war. Despite the novelty of having a woman do a documentary in Vietnam (the *Globe and Mail* called her 'a neat young blonde' while the *Toronto Star* noted she was 'petite and pretty'), the film was widely praised. Fox would end up returning to Vietnam twice more in the next three years to continue her documentary work.

Beryl Fox in Vietnam, shooting her documentary Mills of the Gods. (CBC *Still Photo Collection*)

At the same time that *Seven Days* was doing groundbreaking journalism, it was also serving up doses of sensationalism. Producers thought it would be a good idea, for instance, to schedule an interview with American Nazi leader George Lincoln Rockwell, much to the dismay of Jewish organizations who picketed the CBC. It allowed some critics to question what the program's mission really was. Ron Haggart, writing in the *Toronto Star*, wondered what was so bold about interviewing a Nazi. 'The responsibility of journalism to find out, to find out some more, and to find out still more, is too important, and too seldom carried out, to have talent frittered away on this smudgy sensationalism.'[35]

The program's hot seat also served to stoke controversy. From the very beginning, there were complaints about unfair editing. While some of the interviews served to unearth new information, others seemed more designed for their theatrical effect. In interviewing cabinet minister Mitchell Sharp, host Laurier Lapierre kicked things off by stating, 'The affairs of this country are in a hell of a mess', then waited for Sharp to react. After a particularly contentious interview with John Diefenbaker, a senior CBC official released a statement in response to the complaints about the way he was treated. 'So far, this program has had its good interviews and some bad ones. I would agree that some of these have been marred by the quality and manner of the questioning. The Corporation is aware of this and has endeavoured to make *This Hour* a program which measures up to CBC standards.'[36]

How the corporation tried to make the program measure up is well documented in the furious memos that flew between CBC managers about the show's form and content. 'Would you please be good enough to refuse permission for the use of the write-in gimmick which has been used on occasion in *Seven Days*', wrote vice-president H.G. Walker to W.H. Hogg, director of news and public affairs.[37] Walker didn't appreciate calls for the public to take action and send letters to politicians based on what they had seen on the show. Walker also didn't approve of the ombudsman role the program took on, arguing that it was 'a precarious business to always champion the underdog'.[38]

Before long, CBC managers were compiling lists of errors the program had made and supposedly needless controversies it had stoked. One such document, drawn up for a vice-president, was entitled a 'Master List' of 'On Air Items which were Controversial or Against Policy'. One complaint was that a picture of a rope was shown in an item about capital punishment. Another was that Laurier Lapierre had displayed undue emotion in a piece about Steven Truscott. The memo chides Patrick Watson for using the phrase 'you guys in Parliament' when questioning cabinet minister Judy LaMarsh. Tellingly, there is criticism of singer Dinah Christie's lyrics in a song about US policy in Vietnam. The memo notes: 'This is just one example of a long series of straight and light items which made fun of or criticized the US involvement in Vietnam. These skits do not appear to contravene any specific corporation policy, but they are in bad taste.'[39]

Despite the happy conclusion of the Fred Fawcett case, which seemed to reward the program for upholding a just cause, the corporation was upset with the way cameras were sneaked into the hospital. Vice-president Walker called it 'a pure and simple case of subterfuge and deception, which is not acceptable'.[40] The displeasure went straight to the top of the CBC. President Alphonse Ouimet said: 'The fact of non-identification as CBC staff and the concealment of the camera equipment were the objectionable aspects, as far as the corporation is concerned.' When the entire matter and all aspects of *Seven Days* controversies were discussed in parliamentary hearings, Leiterman gave a far more nuanced analysis of the Fawcett affair, and one that represents CBC policy today: 'It would be very dangerous and wrong if this kind of practice were employed in very many cases. But it does seem to me that in certain cases, which are carefully discussed with supervisors, it may be permissible.'[41]

Reeves Haggan, the CBC's general supervisor of public affairs, served as a buffer between senior management and the program's producers. In a letter to his boss in February 1966, Haggan expressed hope that the program would continue the following year. It's clear he was summing up points they had discussed earlier in the day, and Haggan seemed intent on finding a way to satisfy senior management that the program's perceived faults could be successfully addressed. He mentioned three contemplated revisions to the show: '(a) elimination of all prurient and sleazy items; (b) lessening of satire combined with application of higher standards in this field; (c) confining investigative reporting to matters of substance with careful and thorough research and insistence upon accuracy and fairness.'[42]

But *Seven Days* could not be saved. After two seasons, 50 episodes, and more than 400 items, the show was killed. Leiterman was fired, Watson and Haggan resigned, and the entire team was dispersed, even though the program was drawing a record audience of 3.2 million in its second year. Not even a broad campaign waged by CBC staff, celebrity supporters, and outside pressure groups could convince CBC management to give in. The decision nearly spawned a walkout at the corporation, and a group of CBC employees in the Prairie region sent a condemnatory telegram to the president, saying, '. . . we are convinced that there has been and continues to be a long series of attempts to limit the freedom of controversial broadcasting by the CBC and to undermine the authority of its program personnel.'[43] Even early critics of the program saw that something had been lost with its demise. Ron Haggart, writing in the *Toronto Star*, said the show had produced 'a journalism in which the journalists themselves decide, what are the issues of concern and importance, a journalism in which the issues are established not by the politicians, but by those who watch them with pencil and film'. Haggart saw the program as a turning point, not just in television production, but also for North American journalism generally. 'It will be impossible now to retreat from the standards of inquisitive and skeptical journalism for which they stood as symbols.'[44]

The CBC had eliminated the most innovative current affairs program it had ever created, but American broadcasters were intrigued by the experiment. Jack Gould of the *New York Times* wrote that the program proved 'there is no doubt the Canadians are journalistically adventurous in a way that does them proud'. Noting the CBC tradition of being much less timid than the American networks, Gould called the show lively and engrossing. 'The show enjoys finding weak links in the accepted order of things and its "hot seat" for guests is now a minor Canadian institution. American TV news coverage might be stimulated if it was similarly inclined to get out the needle; it certainly makes for different viewing.'[45]

NBC screened hours of the program, but ultimately decided the content was too adventurous to copy. Leiterman, meanwhile, had joined CBS in New York, and smuggled a few off-air film recordings of the program to show his new bosses. While they liked much of what they saw, CBS executives couldn't accept having skits, songs, or satire in a current affairs program. The Edward Murrow tradition didn't even permit background music in current affairs items, so the liberties taken by *Seven Days* seemed too sensational. But CBS wanted to create a new magazine program, and they asked Leiterman to write a detailed planning document. It became the basis for high-level discussions on what the new show should look like and who should produce it. 'Since I was a new boy at the network it was decided that a hotshot news producer, Don Hewitt, would get the job. I was invited to work with Don but I chose instead to stay with CBS Reports and do hour-long documentaries', said Leiterman.[46] When *60 Minutes* began its inaugural season on CBS in 1968, the Canadian influence was clear to everyone. 'It'll look familiar to Canadians because it has roughly the same format we've been used to for several seasons in our own magazine-type pub-affairs shows', said Bob Blackburn in the *Toronto Telegram*.[47] And Patrick Scott of the *Toronto Star*, while praising the American program, couldn't help commenting that for Canadians 'this sort of programming is old hat'.[48]

Leiterman's early days at CBS were rewarding. His salary tripled, he had generous budgets and deadlines, and he settled into a comfortable life producing films for bosses who were supportive.

> I really had it made and figured I'd spend the next few decades there—until the day I screened a doc called *From Harlem to Sugar Hill*. The president of CBS News (a transplanted corporate lawyer who rode his limo in to work daily from the same part of Connecticut from which I rode the train) sat in the back row of the darkened studio and left half way though. My film was about the middle-class blacks, and the film found that they were not quite the happy, successful, and fully accepted contributors to the American dream that the CBS News president had expected me to see. He shelved our year's work then and there. Making the film, I'd become deeply concerned by the chasm of prejudice which still separated black people from full participation in American life. I felt that I had made an honest film and could not continue working for CBS if they would not air it, so I resigned.[49]

Leiterman's tenure with CBS lasted less than two years. And in Canada, upstart CTV quickly filled the void created by the cancellation of *Seven Days*. The network launched its own newsmagazine, *W5*, in the same Sunday night timeslot on 11 September 1966. Former CBC UN correspondent Peter Reilly was the show's executive producer and host, and he was eager to pick up where *Seven Days* had left off. 'I operate on the theory that we should oppose the government', he proclaimed, criticizing the Ottawa press gallery in the process for being 'such a bunch of sniveling sycophants' who felt the prime minister could do no wrong.[50]

The program was an unabashed imitation of *Seven Days*, starting with a satirical song and complete with its own hot-seat interview of a cabinet minister. This time it was print journalists Charles Lynch and Doug Fisher going after the patient Mitchell Sharp, followed by Reilly himself badgering separatist MP Gilles Grégoire. Despite Reilly's earlier assurance that 'there'll be no sensation for its own sake' on the program, the first edition featured a self-styled exposé on how a recent mass-shooting incident in Texas could happen in Canada. A sniper had climbed to the top of the University of Texas Tower in Austin and opened fire, killing more than a dozen people. *W5* sent Robert Kemp, a 15-year-old *Telegram* copy boy, to an army supply store where he bought an 8mm Mauser rifle with a telescope. He concealed it in a newspaper and carried it to the top floor of Toronto City Hall, and proceeded to point it at pedestrians. Whether the segment displayed anything of public value was left for viewers to decide, but for CTV it illustrated a new approach to current affairs.

The CBC had invented a new grammar for newsmagazine shows, and CTV adopted it, clearly hoping the mass audiences would follow. The gruff and talented Reilly wanted to put unreasonable laws to the test, champion the underdog, and expose injustices. He had a reporter smuggle a tape recorder into the Don Jail to interview a mentally ill young man who had been the victim of delayed justice. There was an item investigating cruelty to horses in the industry set up to harvest pregnant mares' urine for pharmaceutical purposes, a story that would continue to be controversial for decades to come. Another segment examined how the US-Canada Auto Pact would affect prices. Though not as well financed as *Seven Days*, the program attracted talented journalists over the years and aired some memorable investigations. It tracked down jury members of a hanged murderer to question them about the conviction, and it unleashed renowned scoop-hunters such as Frank Drea to chase exclusives. In the realm of innovative programming, it was often years ahead of its time. One segment in 1967, called 'Lifeboat', set up its own version of reality-TV by placing eight people adrift, metaphorically, with enough food for only two. The passengers voted to see who would be kicked off the boat.[51]

The formula was good enough to make *W5* an enduring success for CTV and one of the longest-lasting programs of its kind anywhere. Though it achieved healthy audiences early on and broke occasional investigative stories, *W5* seemed to lack the intellectual depth of *Seven Days*. With just two producers, two story editors, and four researchers, there was a limit on how much actual investigation it could do. Reilly himself didn't last long at the program. After just 13 weeks with CTV, he quit in a dispute with network bigwig John Bassett, publisher of the *Telegram* and head of CFTO-TV. The argument centred on Reilly's refusal to share a story with the *Telegram*, but Bassett's threat to yank the show from his station or change its time slot made Reilly realize he was in for extended fighting over editorial control. Reilly chose the Four Seasons hotel as the venue for his abdication, a site familiar for *Seven Days* press conferences and rally cries. But there were no issues of government interference or censorship this time, only a dust-up between a gruff newsman and a blustery media tycoon. If this was history repeating itself, there was a little more farce than tragedy involved.

At the CBC, meanwhile, a period of malaise set in. To appease viewers who were angry at the cancellation of *Seven Days*, the corporation announced a replacement program that was eventually called *Sunday*. Ironically, it hired Daryl Duke to be the show's executive producer, even though he had directed one of the more controversial *Seven Days* episodes involving a topless San Francisco disco dancer. Eager to appease the younger generation of viewers *Seven Days* had attracted, Duke spared no rhetoric in describing his program. '*Sunday* is a show which will run the gamut of human experience, mixing raw journalism with the emotional audience involvement of a medieval bearpit or bullfighting arena. With *Sunday* I hope to give a mind-expanding, full view of life, a view which has all the intensity and chaotic clarity of an LSD trip. In short, I am trying to approach a format which, in its ultimate form, could provide the first experience in psychedelic television.'[52]

Despite the overblown publicity, *Sunday* was just another public affairs program, generating the kind of controversy the CBC could manage. 'The men Ouimet appointed as head of current affairs well understood that a return to the *Seven Days* brand of journalism would not be tolerated or funded', Leiterman says. 'Everyone left in current affairs knew they had to keep their heads down to keep their jobs.' *Sunday* lasted five months before being cancelled.

Watson was more charitable in his assessment of CBC's attempts following *Seven Days*, but it is clear the corporation was struggling to regain the audience's trust. In the fall of 1967, Ross McLean was brought back to lead a large team that attempted to re-create the magic formula once again. *The Way It Is* lasted two seasons, and produced some memorable segments. Watson himself appeared on the program in its second year as a co-host, and Leiterman was commissioned to produce an investigation into air safety. But television was moving into a different era, with colour broadcasting and enhanced production values on everyone's minds. The fight between CTV and CBC for the Sunday night newsmagazine audience was fierce, and while there were occasional forays into probing, investigative work, the genre wasn't seen as the most direct path to the highest ratings. 'I am willing to swear off consistent earnestness', McLean said at the time.[53] Leiterman, an astute observer of the scene from both inside and out, looked back at those days with a blunt assessment of the state of affairs. 'The climate at the CBC for most of a decade was utterly hostile to journalistic innovation.'

No analysis of Canadian journalism can fail to take into account the role played by public broadcasting. Unlike the United States, which allowed private interests to take control of the airwaves as radio developed in the 1920s, Canada chose a route that blended public and private interests. With the creation of the CBC in 1936, a public sphere of discourse and communication was established. By its very nature it was distinct from the private broadcasters, and it created unique programming. As television developed in the 1950s, public affairs programming assumed particular

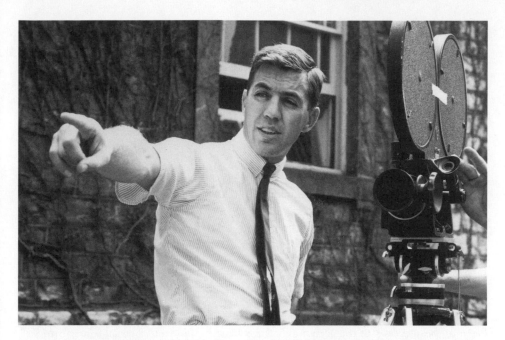

Douglas Leiterman used investigative techniques in his groundbreaking documentary and current affairs work. (CBC Still Photo Collection)

importance. Factual programs were seen as critical in educating and informing the public about matters of importance. Some of Canada's television pioneers fused these public-service values with a knack for entertainment, devising programs that captured people's attention and allowed them to think critically about their country and the world. When it came to the most aggressive versions of the public affairs programs, producers devised new techniques to research and gather information. Intensive research into single topics, as opposed to the superficial treatment of news items common in newspaper coverage of the day, produced many important stories. Taking advantage of the unique characteristics of television, producers also used accountability interviews, hidden recordings, and cinéma-vérité techniques to create investigative reports. This made a substantial contribution to the development of investigative journalistic methodology in Canada at a time when the genre had not yet entered into mainstream usage. And while some of the practitioners had been influenced by trends in the United States in the 1950s, the new work done by the public broadcasters in turn played a role in guiding future American developments. The ultimate clash between the public affairs producers, on the one hand, and CBC management and the government, on the other, provides further insight into the dynamic between institutions and practitioners. As we will see, public broadcasting continued to play an important, but by no means exclusive role in developing investigative journalism in later years.

Chapter 6

Out of the Mainstream

Some issues may be deeply troubling to millions of ordinary people, but unless the issues find some established vehicle for expression they will be ignored by most journalists of both the spoken and the printed word. The US television networks, for all their technical brilliance and financial power, are still operating largely within the limitations of 'official' journalism.

Ron Haggart[1]

Despite the successes of the early public broadcasting pioneers, official journalism still held sway in the mid-1960s in Canada, as it did in the United States. The efforts of various independent writers and journalist mavericks weren't enough to spark a full-fledged outbreak of investigative journalism in the mainstream. The report of a special Senate Committee on Mass Media in Canada didn't mince words when analyzing the state of newspapers in 1970. It decried the kind of newspaper that seldom extended its journalistic enterprise beyond coverage of the local trout festival. Such newspapers rarely annoyed the powerful in their news pages, and they used editorials mostly for Chamber of Commerce boosterism. 'It is our sad impression that a great many, if not most Canadian newspapers fall into this classification', the report said.[2] But the gathering social conditions were providing a foundation for media to break free from their official constraints. They needed a nudge, and it came from the alternative press.

In the US, there were increasing signs that public confidence in government was eroding. Although public opinion polls from the late 1950s showed people generally trusted government, the trend was beginning to reverse by the middle of the next decade.[3] The seeds for the reversal in confidence were sown early in the new decade. The US administration was caught in a series of lies, beginning with President Dwight Eisenhower's claim that the American U-2 spy plane was merely a research aircraft. When the Soviets, who had shot the plane down over their territory in 1960, produced the pilot along with his admission of espionage, the administration acknowledged its deception. Public exposure of lies relating to the Bay of Pigs invasion in Cuba further weakened the government's credibility. A White House press gallery that generally shielded the administration from full disclosure was suddenly under pressure to test presidential statements for their truthfulness.

America's escalating involvement in Vietnam led to the spinning of a far more elaborate web of lies, though complete exposure of the truth would come much later.

When glimpses of the reality surfaced from time to time, official reaction was swift and often severe. In August 1965, CBS correspondent Morley Safer reported on the burning of Vietnamese village Cam Ne by the Marines. He showed American troops systematically torching every house in the village with flamethrowers, matches, even Zippo cigarette lighters. Safer said afterwards the Marine Corps 'went into Red Alert, denying everything, saying that a couple of the houses were burned by collateral damage from artillery or something. It was just blatant bullshit, and that's an example of what really drove me crazy in Vietnam. I mean, if you're going to lie, tell a good one.'[4] Later Safer learned President Lyndon Johnson had called the president of CBS directly to condemn the report, and the Pentagon pressured the network to replace him, while the Marines banned him from the areas they controlled in Vietnam.

It was a similar story the next year when Harrison Salisbury of the *New York Times* wrote a series of articles from North Vietnam, documenting civilian deaths from US bombing missions, even as the White House was denying any such casualties. The administration ratcheted up the pressure once more. Even though the Pulitzer Prize jury voted to give Salisbury the award for his series in 1967, an advisory board bowed to political pressure and vetoed the decision. And when James Cameron filed dispatches critical of US actions directly from North Vietnam to the *London Evening Standard* and the *New York Times*, a smear campaign was launched to discredit him. *Time* magazine called him 'a conduit for the North Vietnamese Communists'.[5] Cameron had documented his visit on film, and the BBC acquired the footage, only to suppress it as 'unacceptable in the current circumstances'. All of these strident reactions to the glimmers of truth emerging from Vietnam served to make the mainstream press hesitant at a time when aggressive inquiry was needed.

But for society generally, Vietnam was becoming a flashpoint. Skepticism and then open opposition to the war infused many aspects of culture throughout the US, Canada, and other countries. Anti-war sentiment fuelled the activism of the youth and student movement. It put millions of people into motion, and a variety of other social movements accelerated as a result. Mainstream media didn't react quickly to the new times, according to David Protess, 'preferring to cover reactively the overt turmoil rather than risking to uncover its hidden dimensions'.[6] It was principally the alternative press that began to give expression to the new sentiment. And the early developments in the US served as models to Canadian journalists who were eager to express similar views.

Editorial opposition to America's involvement in Vietnam began very early in the alternative press. The left-wing and communist press took up the cause immediately, and soon others joined. In 1954, the *Catholic Worker* questioned what the US was doing in Indochina, and began denouncing the immorality of American actions. *I.F. Stone's Weekly, Liberation*, and the *Village Voice* added to the chorus through the 1950s and into the 1960s. But the greatest impact came from the correspondents who gathered facts on the ground, much as Beryl Fox had done with her Vietnam documentary for the CBC. One of the most influential was Wilfred Burchett, the controversial Australian correspondent who wrote for the *National Guardian*. His series of stories revealed new details about American defeats at Bien Hoa, Loc Ninh, and Binh Gia, contradicting the one-sided picture painted by US military spin doctors.

Burchett's documented reports sparked others to delve into facts surrounding Vietnam, and perhaps the most influential of all the American alternative publications to do so was *Ramparts*. The San Francisco magazine began as a Catholic literary journal in 1962, but was transformed into a slick muckraking magazine by mid-decade. In July 1965, it published a seminal investigative piece called 'The Vietnam Lobby', by Robert Scheer and Warren Hinckle. It meticulously documented 'the history of a small and enthusiastic group of people—including a cardinal, an ex-Austrian Socialist leader, and a CIA agent—who maneuvered the Eisenhower administration and the American press into supporting the rootless, unpopular, and hopeless regime of a despot'.[7] This investigative work, which relied on publicly available documents to weave a tale of deliberate American duplicity, was followed in February 1966 by an insider exposé. Master Sergeant Donald Duncan, who had just left the US army after 10 years service, blew the whistle on what his comrades were doing in Vietnam. He wrote about torture, killing of prisoners, and assassinations. Titled 'I Quit—Memoirs of a Special Forces Hero', Duncan's presentation was a devastating indictment of American military operations in Vietnam. 'The whole thing was a lie', Duncan wrote. 'We weren't preserving freedom in South Vietnam. There was no freedom to preserve.'[8]

Ramparts didn't confine its exposés to Vietnam. It uncovered new information about the Kennedy assassination, the CIA's involvement in Che Guevara's execution, US President Lyndon Johnson's business connections, clandestine activities on US campuses, police persecution of the radical Black Panthers, and dozens of other controversial issues. There were routine, sensational accounts, including a report by William Turner called 'I was a burglar, wiretapper, bugger and spy for the F.B.I'. At a time when a host of underground newspapers and magazines began publishing across America, many of them low budget, ragtag affairs, *Ramparts* used glossy paper and an attractive layout to appeal to students, the intelligentsia, and the middle class. Its content was sometimes scorned but more often matched by the mainstream media. Its stable of writers included both icons of the New Left and talented investigative reporters who worked outside the mainstream, including Seymour Hersh.

The investigative reporting of *Ramparts* and other publications provided a model for journalists who were ready to break free from mainstream shackles. And the objective conditions of the 1960s were providing a receptive audience, as Michael Schudson discovered when he researched his social history of American newspapers.

Several journalists I interviewed in 1977 recalled that young reporters recruited to journalism in the 1960s frequently covered the civil rights movement and the antiwar movement. Young people, more likely to fit into the youth culture of casual manners and language, open sexuality, and rock music, covered the campuses and social movements and were influenced by them. They often felt uncomfortable in their reportorial roles, almost as if they were agents of "straight" society spying on a subversive culture. They found themselves sympathetic to the ideas and values of the people they wrote about and increasingly skeptical, uneasy, or outraged at the transformation of their stories between copy desk and printed page.[9]

Some newspapers began to see the appeal of finding facts instead of simply regurgitating official statements. *Newsday* in New York started the first US mainstream newspaper investigative team in February 1967, devoting three reporters, an editor, and a secretary-researcher to produce at least three major reports a year.[10] It was under the direction of Robert Greene, a 38-year-old reporter who had been a staff investigator for the US Senate Rackets Committee, and the New York City Anti-Crime Committee. The same year AP created a special assignment team to move beyond conventional reporting. And the *Boston Globe* set up a 'Spotlight' team, modeled on *Newsday*'s, in 1970.

But the trend was slow to take hold. Mainstream media were hesitant to abandon their peculiar brand of objectivity, which focused more on heeding sources deemed reliable and official than on painting an objective picture of underlying realities. Investigative work by local reporters in the US often failed to get national attention.

Nothing illustrates this timidity better than Seymour Hersh's inability to find a major media outlet willing to publish his 1969 exposé of the My Lai massacre in Vietnam. Hersh was a former Associated Press reporter who was writing a book about defence spending when he got a call from a lawyer with a tip: Vietnamese civilians had been killed by an American soldier. Hersh began an urgent investigation that quickly turned up the story of Lieutenant William Calley and the mass slaughter of men, women, and children in My Lai by the Charlie Company crew. Confirmation came directly from Calley's lawyer, a former judge in the court of military appeals. Hersh used a tested technique, suggesting to the lawyer that Calley had been charged with killing a large number of civilians, only to be corrected with the actual number from an official document. Later he tracked down Ron Ridenhour, a former GI who had gathered first-hand evidence of the killings. It added up to a compelling story of an American war crime and a cover-up. But *Life* and *Look* magazines both balked at running the piece. A small Washington foundation called the Fund for Investigative Journalism helped bankroll the research, and Hersh turned to an alternative agency, the little-known Dispatch News Service, to distribute the story at $100 to any taker. David Obst, Hersh's friend and neighbour, ran the news service and peddled the story to more than 30 newspapers.[11]

On 13 November 1969, Hersh's story hit the newsstands, and investigative journalism entered a new phase in America.

> Lieutenant William L. Calley, Jr., 26, is a mild-mannered, boyish-looking Vietnam combat veteran with the nickname 'Rusty'. The Army says he deliberately murdered at least 109 Vietnamese civilians during a search-and-destroy mission in March, 1968, in a Viet Cong stronghold known as 'Pinkville'.

Suddenly the alternative had gone mainstream. This was not anti-war muckraking and editorializing; it was a careful and meticulous indictment of American brutality and lawlessness. Facts were piled upon a foundation of other facts, all of them soberly corroborated, inviting readers to draw logical conclusions about the conduct of US troops.

The same social forces sweeping across America were being felt north of the border, and young people were usually in the forefront. Journalists at Canadian University Press vowed to become agents of social change, and some initial investigative work began appearing in campus newspapers. Although the 1960s demonstrated some early broadcasting forays into investigative work, the mainstream print media lagged. It fell once again to the alternative media to set an example, and to provide a forum for disaffected conventional journalists.

Canada already had a radical alternative journalistic tradition, but it had never delved deeply into investigative work. The *Canadian Forum* was sympathetic to the left and eager to challenge the status quo, but its primary focus was art, literature, and poetry. Communist publications such as *Masses* and *New Frontier* in the 1930s promoted socialist realism, anti-fascism, peace, and support for the working class. But apart from detailed historical analyses of the type provided by Stanley Ryerson, there were few intensive investigations into the inner workings of specific institutions or corporations. By the 1960s, as alternatives to the old-style Communist parties were springing up, New Left publications engaged mainly in ideological battles.

Still, some muckraking seeds were being sown. When Cy Gonick left the north end of Winnipeg to attend the University of California at Berkeley in the 1950s, he was thrown into the cauldron of progressive politics. His involvement with *Root and Branch*, one of America's incipient New Left journals, put him into contact with Robert Scheer and other journalists who would eventually transform *Ramparts*. Back in Canada in 1963, he founded *Canadian Dimension* magazine, 'the product of the post-nuclear generation of leftish thinkers', according to its introductory editorial.[12] It played an important role in acting as a forum for alternative ideas, and encouraged independent inquiry unrestricted by corporate or mainstream interests. It didn't herald a mushrooming of investigative inquiry immediately, but it provided a foundation for others to build on.

The publication in the 1960s of the *LA Free Press* spawned an era of underground newspapers and magazines across North America, designed specifically to appeal to youth and students. The Ottawa-based *Canadian Free Press* was among the first to emulate the trend in 1967, and soon dozens more sprang up across the country. Most were devoted to drug culture, rock and roll, and student activism, but there were occasional forays into investigative work. In the Maritimes, a more serious strain of alternative publication appeared. Two English teachers in New Brunswick started *The Mysterious East* in 1969, hoping to emulate *Ramparts*. The first issue featured an article on water pollution, and later items dealt with political corruption and corporate monopoly. Soon the monthly had a circulation of 5,000. 'We saw ourselves as a corrective for a press that had fallen away from what we considered its duties to be', said one of the founders, Silver Donald Cameron.[13]

A curious blend of radical politics, mainstream journalistic experience, and social activism led to one of the most successful alternative newspapers in the country, the *4th Estate*. It was the brainchild of Frank Fillmore and his son, Nick. Frank's father, Roscoe, was a legendary Maritime radical. He was a founder of both the Socialist Party and the Communist Party of Canada, and went to the Soviet Union soon after the October revolution to support the Bolshevik cause. 'I learned a lot of my feelings and instincts from him as a teenager', said grandson Nick. 'He was always reading interesting publications. Wilfred Burchett was a journalist that he read. And the red thing was always there. When I was a boy our house was raided in the middle of the night, I was taken out of bed in the backyard while the RCMP raided the house. I had that kind of environment.'[14]

Journalism ran parallel to politics in the family. Frank engaged in muckraking work at the *Dartmouth Free Press*. One of his exposés led to the elimination of the practice of jailing debtors in the province. He developed some traditional investigative techniques, becoming familiar with company searches, tax investigations, and complex corporation probes. Nick, meanwhile, spent a number of years working for different Maritime newspapers, eventually joining Canadian Press. It was an unremarkable career in many ways until, he says, there was a maturation of his political views and journalistic skills that led father and son to create their own newspaper.

The first version to come out in 1968 was called *The People*, an echo of the famous letter that got Joseph Howe into trouble 133 years earlier. An investigation of housing conditions in the black slums in and around Halifax was well received. The edition of more than 3,000 sold out, and the Fillmores realized they had touched a nerve in the community. Reborn the next year as the *4th Estate*, the newspaper combined aggressive reporting with social activism, packaging it in a professional format that posed a real threat to the mainstream *Halifax Chronicle-Herald*. At its height, circulation climbed to 14,000. The newspaper was a million-dollar business with a staff of six to eight people, a solid advertising base, and the ability to attract a range of writers. Even the Senate Committee on Mass Media took note of the newspaper's success, commenting that the city's two daily newspapers were not only consistently scooped by the alternative upstart but 'appear reluctant to publish anything that might embarrass the government'.[15]

Looking back, Fillmore doesn't remember calling the work investigative reporting or thinking about it in that way. Yet it involved a vigorous examination of the social realities in Halifax, and it focused on an active discovery of facts. In that respect, it went far beyond many other alternative or underground publications of the time, which largely contented themselves with denunciations and editorializing. The newspaper routinely uncovered major stories, such as its investigation into cost over-runs at the heavy water plant in Glace Bay, which triggered questions the next day in the House of Commons. It also probed the performance of individual politicians at the legislature and published regular report cards. But Nick Fillmore says the most important stories were the ones that merged journalistic inquiry with social activism.

'One thing that was shocking was that we discovered poor people living in the slum of north end Halifax were paying more money per square foot for renting an apartment than people living in the south end, which was the rich end of town', he said.

We put a little box in the paper and if you felt you were being treated badly by your landlord you could contact us. We had a qualified building inspector who would go look at your property, and then we would decide among ourselves whether this person was getting ripped off or not. We would call up the landlord and say look, you've got one or two choices, you can make improvements to this property or you can read about yourselves in next week's paper. It was as simple as that. Eighty or ninety per cent of the time improvements were made. This was considered rather scandalous in a conservative community like Halifax, but we brought a lot of improvements in housing to black people and poor people at the time.[16]

Fillmore discovered bad conditions at the local school for the blind. Not content with merely exposing the situation, he helped found a blind-rights action movement. He also played a hand in forming the Nova Scotia tenants' association, the provincial public housing association, and the Nova Scotia union of civil liberties. 'These were people's movements. We covered them and we reported on them, and gave them a voice.' The newspaper's influence didn't go unrecognized in the corridors of power. Premier Gerald Regan solicited Fillmore's support for his plan to take over a privately owned power company and make it a Crown corporation. It was a move Fillmore supported philosophically, and he had no discomfort collaborating with the government to achieve its aim.

Early on, there was a split between father and son, and Frank began publishing the rival *Scotian Journalist* with its own muckraking approach. Nick and his wife continued to build the *4th Estate*, tilting at the establishment while playing by mainstream rules when it benefited the business. A bid to get national advertising succeeded in scoring an account with the Sobey's grocery chain, a lucrative contract that ended summarily after the newspaper published a story critical of the firm. The threat of damaging lawsuits also had an effect on the business side of the venture. Fillmore finally decided to leave the newspaper in 1976, and it ended its run the next year.

On a national level, the most successful of the era's muckraking publications was *The Last Post*. It was founded by a group of disillusioned mainstream journalists who were imbued with the excitement and passion of the late 1960s political scene in Montreal, and who all felt frustrated in trying to break from their employers' conventional restraints. The mood was summed up by Drummond Burgess, a Montreal *Gazette* reporter, who felt no inhibitions about trashing his own newspaper and others like it. 'No straight newspaper is going to rock the boat', he said. 'Its purposes are . . . to control the thinking about news, and the access to news . . . to defend the games the system plays to justify itself and keep itself in power . . . and to warn the establishment of restlessness among the natives that has to be either bought off, talked off, or repressed.'[17]

Fellow *Gazette* reporters Nick auf der Maur and Mark Starowicz had similar feelings. They were keenly aware of how nervous the establishment was at the slightest sign of alternative thinking or dissent. They didn't know it at the time, but the RCMP Security Service was carefully monitoring all kinds of journalistic activity for hints of subversion. In auf der Maur's case, there is a revealing notation in RCMP files about a panel interview he conducted for the CBC in Montreal on 23 April 1969. It was a feature marking the anniversary of the takeover of government in Greece by a military junta. An RCMP analyst assigned to watch the broadcast concluded: 'These persons (the panelists) were unanimous in their condemnation of the recent Greek government and its deficit of democracy in Greece, but no mention was made of Communism in any form. No pro-junta views were expressed on this program.' The analyst said it amounted to free TV time for the left-wing Greek community, with none for the government.[18] There would have undoubtedly been similar scrutiny of Starowicz, who conducted a month-long investigation into intimidation and threats by the Greek Embassy against dissidents in Canada. His exposé in June 1969 reported on some of the 70 documented incidents of harassment. The RCMP Security Service, which kept an active tab on Communists, journalists, student radicals, and activists of all kinds, wasn't shy about dropping hints to employers about potential troublemakers in their ranks.

Starowicz had run into trouble with *Gazette* management. He had started at the newspaper as a 17-year-old copy boy earning $32.50 a week, and graduated to reporter, working evenings, weekends, and summers while he finished university.[19] The venerable English daily tried to cover the city with 17 reporters, and Starowicz was one of only three who could speak French. In 1967, he was assigned to follow René Lévesque for a week and do a profile on the politician as he headed to a key Liberal Party conference in the city. Another *Gazette* reporter, Claude Hénault, was to do the same with Lévesque's Liberal Party nemesis, Eric Kierans. Fifteen minutes before deadline, Hénault's piece was nowhere to be found, so Starowicz's detailed profile was splashed across the entire top half of the op-ed page. Lévesque crowed that even the normally hostile *Gazette* supported his pro-sovereignty views. And when Starowicz wrote a lively account the following month of the founding of Lévesque's Mouvement Souveraineté-Association, which the newspaper promptly buried deep inside its pages, *Gazette* management had had enough. They told Starowicz not to do enterprise work, and assigned him to minor features. The breaking point came when he was told to cover the Santa Claus Parade, and promptly led it off with a dig at Eaton's, one of the paper's major advertisers. Soon after, he was told his services were no longer required.[20]

Starowicz, auf der Maur, and Burgess talked frequently about their frustrations with the mainstream press. It led to an animated discussion one evening at The Bistro on Mountain Street in Montreal, which included fellow journalists Robert Chodos and Patrick McFadden. At the end of the evening, the idea for *The Last Post* was born, and the first issue hit the newsstands in December 1969.

'*The Last Post* was created by a group of journalists, photographers, and cartoonists across the country to unearth and publicize facts which are omitted, ignored, or obscured by the commercial press', the magazine announced to its readers.[21] The first issue took direct aim at conventional Canadian publications, such as *Star Weekly*, *Maclean's*, and *Canadian*, pointing to their feature articles about fashion, scuba diving, hockey players, and other lifestyle topics, and mockingly congratulating the magazines for 'hitting them where it really hurts'. The editorial co-operative named Burgess, Peter Allnutt, and Terry Mosher as members, and future issues featured some of the people who would become top investigative journalists of the following decade: John Zaritsky, Brian McKenna, Starowicz, and others. They were the Young Turks of the Canadian journalistic establishment, free of their old-style employers, and happily writing the articles they felt the mainstream wouldn't allow.

A feature article in the first issue dealt with chemical- and biological-warfare research in Canada. Richard Liskeard, billed as a freelance writer based in Vancouver, gathered available records and evidence to paint a picture of the Defence Research Establishment in Suffield, Alberta. 'Here, since the spring of 1941, in laboratories and in the field, Canada has tested and perfected nerve gases, asphyxiating chemicals, and strains of viruses that are judged most effective against people, cattle, food supplies, and vegetation. Here Canada, a minor military power, made the big league.'[22] It was a detailed examination of an issue that the mainstream had not considered terribly important. Liskeard was clearly influenced by Seymour Hersh, who had written a book about American use of chemical and biological warfare. The article noted that Canadian research had borne fruit for the US forces in Vietnam.

The muckraking tone of the first issue shone through in its handling of corporate news. An article on Brascan, the Canadian natural resources giant, and its activities in South America suggested that 'if the lid can be kept on Brazilian democracy for a few more years, Brascan will be home free, with the wealth it has taken from Brazil spread around the world'. And an analysis of government support for the Ford corporation noted that a federal cabinet minister had close ties to the company, even as Ottawa was forgiving $75 million in duties Ford owed to the treasury. By the fourth issue, the founders were giving readers more insight into the production process. Each issue cost about $2,000 to produce, they said. 'Nobody gets paid . . . we're a rather loose co-operative spanning several cities, and some people with salaries help meet office and equipment expenses.' Readers were offered the option of buying a subscription in perpetuity for $50.[23] But perpetuity was a vague concept, especially when it came to the frequent birth and death of publications in the 1960s.

By 1970, the political situation in Quebec was maturing. The independence movement was accelerating, and many student activists and underground press writers joined the sovereigntist ranks. Other radicals, disillusioned by the Moscow-influenced Communist party and inspired by developments in China, founded the Communist Party of Canada (Marxist-Leninist). The press of these and other political movements concentrated on denunciations of the status quo and continuous ideological debate, veering occasionally into specific investigative work, particularly when it came to examining certain companies or aspects of the economy. At the National Film Board, Denys Arcand shot a documentary examination of the exploitation of textile workers in Quebec. While *On est au cotton* depicted the harsh conditions of workers and their suffering at the hands of their bosses, it also highlighted the domination of Quebec industry by American interests. The Canadian Textile Industry said the film promoted class warfare, and the NFB banned it for six years, along with two other films it deemed too controversial.[24]

At publications like *The Last Post*, meanwhile, there was no ideological cohesion. Starowicz said editors sometimes discussed common positions on issues, but deliberately avoided affiliations with political movements. The invoking of the War Measures Act in October 1970 galvanized them into a common stance of defiance, and *The Last Post* assumed the role of a news service, disseminating information from Quebec to other alternative publications across the country.

For Brian McKenna, the War Measures Act was a watershed as well. He had joined the *Montreal Star* in 1967, imbued with the belief that he could be an agent of social change at a mainstream newspaper. Everything he did on the job was an attempt to advance that ideal in some way. And he felt supported in the cause when Frank Walker joined the paper in 1968 as editor-in-chief. Suddenly the staid, conservative *Montreal Star* decided it wouldn't be an English newspaper publishing in Quebec, but a Quebec newspaper publishing in English. The orientation changed, and Walker turned to young people for a new perspective. McKenna became one of 'Walker's boys', a group of young and aggressive reporters who had free rein to report the tumultuous events of the day as they saw them. McKenna worked the night shift, which allowed him to cover the excitement on the streets at the time. 'Every night there's another demonstration, the nationalist movement is catching fire, the Vietnam war is in full inferno, the protests in the streets were on nightly, and there's a smell of revolution in the air. All these things together made Montreal an exciting place to begin a career in journalism.'[25]

But the October Crisis of 1970 changed everything. Demonstrations turned into a double kidnapping, murder, and armed troops in the streets. 'The attempt at a quiet revolution at the *Star* came to a crashing end', said McKenna. Stories that challenged the establishment or the status quo would be spiked. McKenna would often hear the phrase that would accompany the shelving of a story, an admonition that the piece didn't find favour in the eyes of 'the powers that be'. Complicating life for McKenna was his participation in a successful union organizing drive. Suddenly management was not as enamoured with youthful enthusiasm as it had once been. McKenna turned to *The Last Post* to get some of his spiked stories into print, but he gradually began considering other options. Soon he landed at CBC in Montreal, where an aggressive recruitment drive was assembling journalists like Brian Stewart, Mark Phillips, Don Murray, and Nick auf der Maur.

Eventually many of *The Last Post* writers gravitated back to the mainstream as well, bringing a renewed investigative edge with them. Starowicz tried balancing both worlds for a time, holding down a reporting job at the *Toronto Star* while filing stories under a pseudonym for *The Last Post*. In fact, the paper's supposed Vancouver stringer, Richard Liskeard, turned out to be Starowicz himself. He happened to be on assignment in New Liskeard, Ontario when he was filing his chemical-biological warfare story, and borrowed the town's name. By the sixth issue, Richard Liskeard was listed as a member of the magazine's editorial collective. But his double life wouldn't last long. A Starowicz story that the *Star* had spiked ended up in *The Last Post*, albeit re-written. Editors noticed, and Starowicz was fired. Shut out of mainstream Montreal circles, and now fired from the country's largest newspaper, Starowicz was despondent. He launched a grievance through his union, only to abandon it some months later.[26] But CBC producer and talent scout Margaret Lyons invited him to join the public broadcaster, and he became one of its most creative and dynamic producers. Though he continued contributing to *The Last Post* for a number of years afterwards, he was less constrained at the CBC, and more able to do the kind of journalism he felt needed doing. It led to

Mark Starowicz moved from the mainstream to the alternative press and back to the mainstream.
(CBC Still Photo Collection)

the creation of organizational structures at *As It Happens, Sunday Morning*, and ultimately *The Journal* that fostered aggressive and inquisitive journalism, and periodic exposés ranking alongside the best examples of Canadian investigative work.

Journalism researcher Mark Feldstein has suggested a unifying theory to explain the ebb and flow in muckraking activity over the years. 'Investigative reporting reaches a critical mass when both its supply (stimulated by new technologies and media competition) and its demand (by an aroused public hungry for exposés in times of turmoil) is high', he says, referring to the American context.[27] Feldstein warns that his 'muckraking model' shouldn't be misconstrued as a reductionist attempt to explain away all the complexities of journalism history and development. Yet it appears to offer interesting insights into the Canadian landscape in the 1960s and 1970s. The social forces of the 1960s were putting large numbers of people into motion. Confidence in government and establishment institutions was being shaken on many fronts. The public was growing increasingly skeptical about political leadership. Though Vietnam was an American military involvement, anti-war sentiment had significant impact in Canada and gave rise to mass demonstrations and protests. One part of Feldstein's model, the demand for investigative journalism, was clearly present. As the next chapter will show, the supply side was about to be satisfied as well. All it needed was a gentle push to get going, and the alternative media played a critical role in providing the momentum.

Investigative Journalism Outside the Mainstream

Alex Roslin knew he had a good story when he discovered a pattern of unpublicized dumping of toxic metals and other residue into the Great Lakes. What he found especially surprising was that even the most dedicated environmentalists who spent their time monitoring the lakes had no idea the practice was going on. Roslin, a Montreal journalist, published his findings in Toronto's *NOW* magazine in May 2005. The research was thorough and the evidence compelling. Roslin even had former senior shipping officials confirming the facts and confessing that they had always felt uncomfortable doing it. *This Magazine* provided Roslin some additional financial help from its fledgling investigative journalism fund, and he published a more detailed version of the story in the magazine's September-October 2005 edition. A frequent contributor to non-mainstream publications, Roslin confirmed once again the importance of alternative publications in disseminating original investigative journalism.

The practice Roslin publicized is known as cargo sweeping, and he showed that it was routine for the 130 vessels that traverse the Great Lakes. It involves dumping the old residue from cargo holds into the water before filling up with a new shipment. The residue can consist of iron ore, nickel, copper, zinc, lead, and other toxic metals. Evidence showed the discharges were potentially harmful to aquatic life, wetlands, and marshes. The effect of sustained dumping might have devastating consequences for the entire Great Lakes eco-system. What's more, the practice seemed to violate a number of laws on both sides of the border, and a 1978 International Maritime Organization accord, signed by 119 countries, prohibited cargo sweeping in any inland waters. But Canada had never signed the agreement, and shipping companies in the US lobbied the American government to vary the terms of the accord to allow inland dumping, so long as it was a prescribed distance offshore. The net effect was the continued accumulation of tonnes of garbage at the bottom of the lakes.

Roslin's story came from his detailed research into the activities of Canada Steamship Lines, one of the companies responsible for the dumping. He spoke to three former chief engineers with the company who not only confirmed what was going on, but also said the cargo was generally dumped either at night or during times when no other ships or aircraft were nearby. After exposing the problem, Roslin offered a possible solution. Off-loading the debris on shore, while adding to the shipping companies' expenses, was an alternative. Even the former company officials thought it was a feasible idea. Though Roslin's stories hadn't appeared in the large national newspapers or broadcast outlets, the impact of the research reached the House of Commons and gave further ammunition to efforts by environmental groups to clean up the Great Lakes.

Chapter 7

In Watergate's Wake

Never believe anything until it is officially denied.
Claud Cockburn, Irish muckraker[1]

By the early 1970s, the objective conditions were ripe for an explosion of investigative journalism. A spark was needed to ignite the genre in the mainstream. That spark arrived on 17 June 1972, when five men were arrested while trying to bug the offices of the Democratic National Committee in Washington's Watergate complex.

Aggressive reporting had already made a significant reappearance in the US mainstream. Despite his initial inability to be published, Seymour Hersh was honoured with a Pulitzer Prize in 1970 for his My Lai reporting, and the *New York Times* used former State Department employee Daniel Ellsberg's disclosures to break the Pentagon Papers story. Teams of diligent reporters were being assembled in a handful of newspapers to do more intensive investigations, but official Washington media circles were still slow to react. 'Standards of investigative reporting fell on their ass in Watergate', according to Hersh, 'particularly when it came to sources or finding sources. If it weren't for those two guys in Washington (Bob Woodward and Carl Bernstein) we probably would have passed over it. I think that even in Washington an awful lot of reporters are content to be stenographers.'[2]

There is an ongoing debate about how critical reporters were in uncovering key elements of the Watergate scandal. Some argue that congressional committees and government investigative staff performed the heaviest lifting.[3] But it's undeniable that in the early going, Woodward and Bernstein were in the forefront of pursuing the story. The *Washington Post* published more than 200 pieces on Watergate in the six months following the initial break-in. When Congress and the courts became involved, the media frenzy accelerated. The *New York Times* assigned Hersh to the beat, and he often published several stories a week in an effort to scoop the *Post*. More reporters joined in, and President Richard Nixon had to expand the number of journalists on his self-described 'enemies list'.

Woodward and Bernstein used no particularly innovative methodology in their work. They were young, aggressive, and hard working in their pursuit of sources, and their newspaper's management encouraged them with resources and prominent play of their stories. By recruiting W. Mark Felt, former deputy director of the FBI, as their secret 'Deep Throat' source, they were able to break important elements of the story far earlier than others could. In February 1973, the Senate created the Select Committee on Presidential Campaign Activities, and the newly re-elected president came under increasing scrutiny. With each new report of illegality and cover-up, Nixon's administration weakened and Woodward and Bernstein's reputation rose. Far before Nixon's resignation in 1974, Americans were coming to believe that all kinds of scandals were possible right inside the highest office of their government. The publication of *All the President's Men*, and the subsequent Hollywood glamourization of 'Woodstein', brought investigative reporting to a plateau not seen in America since the turn-of-the-century muckraking era. By 1974, *Time* magazine was reporting that journalism schools across the United States were being inundated with applications, with 'would-be Woodwards and Bernsteins queuing up for the nation's 213 undergraduate and graduate journalism programs'.[4] At Columbia University's Graduate School of Journalism, for instance, applications for the 128 places doubled two years in a row to nearly 2,000.

Media competition led to new teams of investigative journalists at newspapers and broadcast outlets, and to more extensive work by reporters who were already in the field. At the *Chicago Tribune*, the investigative team spent months looking into voter fraud in the 1972 primary elections. Reporter William Mullen got a job at the Chicago Board of Election Commissioners, where he saw hundreds of suspicious signatures on ballot applications. The team investigated for months before printing the series, which earned a Pulitzer Prize in 1973, alongside the *Washington Post*'s award for its Watergate reporting. That same year, the Pulitzers also honoured newspapers for investigations into financial irregularities at Boy's Town, Nebraska, and for the disclosure of Senator Thomas Eagleton's history of psychiatric therapy, leading to his withdrawal as a Democratic vice-presidential candidate. At *Newsday*, Bob Greene and his investigative team were travelling to Turkey, interviewing hundreds of sources and eventually printing an exhaustive inquiry into the heroin trade. In 1974, no fewer than five of the Pulitzers went to investigative projects, leading *Time* to declare it a 'Year of the Muckrakers'.[5]

The idea that muckraking journalism could topple a president gave impetus to many reporters. Corruption and other forms of wrongdoing became the targets. Some looked for it in high places, others set their sights lower. But a different strain of investigative work was also taking hold in this era. It concentrated on an intensive examination of systems and structures, much in the way Gustavus Myers and other muckraking journalists had done. In 1974, Tom Miller spent a year investigating the coal industry and wrote a series entitled 'Who Owns West Virginia' in the *Huntington Herald-Dispatch*. He followed it with another called 'Who Owns West Virginia Media'. The most sustained form of this kind of reporting came from *Philadelphia Inquirer* reporters Donald Barlett and James Steele. They carried out investigations of various industries, social institutions, and government agencies, always looking for how they worked and how they affected people. While others were chasing corrupt officials and trails of political scandal, they concentrated on gaining a deeper understanding of society. 'We don't see ourselves as righting wrongs, but merely looking at complicated public issues for patterns that haven't been seen before', Steele said.[6]

The explosion of investigative work across the US inevitably made its way into Canada. By 1972, the National Newspaper Awards decided it needed an Enterprise Reporting category. David Crane of the *Toronto Star* won the first year it was offered for an examination of the planned northern gas pipeline and how it would affect both the Arctic environment and the lives and culture of aboriginal people. The story made no effort to emulate the large-scale investigative efforts of the American teams, but by veering from the daily news agenda and providing critical analysis of an important issue, it stood out. At the *Montreal Star*, meanwhile, an aggressive young reporter was drawing inspiration more from his own life experience than American models to produce some enterprising journalism. Victor Malarek was a product of foster homes and Montreal's juvenile care system. After brushes with the law as a teenager, he signed on as a copy boy with *Weekend Magazine*, graduating to junior police reporter with the *Star*. He quickly turned to what he knew best, the city's juvenile court process, and began writing original stories about inadequate conditions and failings in the system. His exposé in 1972 of suicides in Centre Berthelet, a boys' jail north of Montreal, led to a provincial inquiry. It also launched Malarek's career as a street-smart journalist whose passion to hold institutions to account helped him break dozens of major stories over the years for the *Globe and Mail*, the CBC, and CTV.

Enterprise work at the CBC assumed a different form, as attempts were being made to combine investigative reporting with consumer issues. Jock Ferguson, an aggressive television producer who had met Ralph Nader while in Washington, designed a program concept and became the show's first producer. The CBC's public relations department knew it had a populist product when it announced the new program. 'It's goodbye to bad guys at the *Marketplace*, CBC-TV's new weekly series designed to inform and protect harassed Canadian consumers in this age of spiraling prices, questionable sales practices, and insidious small print on iron-clad contracts.'[7] The show debuted at 10 p.m. on 5 October 1972, with stories about the rapid rise of food prices across Canada, retailer and processor profits, and an examination of magazine and encyclopedia sales. The following week featured an investigative report on school bus safety. There were some aggressive stories in the program's early days. In one case, the program hired a special investigator to pose as a customer at an Ontario food store that was promising high quality meat at discount prices. *Marketplace* became a popular current affairs show, but Ferguson's overly aggressive posture got him fired after the first season, the beginning of a rocky relationship he would have with the CBC over the next few years. The wounds of *Seven Days* and all the failed attempts to replace it were still with the CBC, and the corporation remained cautious in its approach to challenging journalism. By January of 1974, the *Toronto Star*'s television critic was labeling the program 'functional but dull'.[8]

A more daring attempt by the CBC to program journalism that challenged the status quo came in the form of *Ombudsman*, which took to the air on 6 January 1974. The corporation believed it would serve as the television equivalent to various newspaper columns that had pioneered the idea of fighting for the little guy. It would be 'a social service, responding to the problems of the individual, particularly those problems that are caused or aggravated by bureaucracy'.[9] What the corporation didn't foresee was that the program would inevitably delve into major investigative work as it tried to get to the bottom of complaints, eventually widening its scope from individual issues to systemic social problems. The immediate inspiration for the program came from the Netherlands, where a similar show had been playing since 1969 to giant audiences. The host of the Dutch show grew so popular he eventually became the country's Secretary of State. The CBC chose Robert Cooper, a dynamic Montreal lawyer and McGill University lecturer, as its show's host. At 28, he had already built a reputation as a special counsel for Quebec's police commission on organized crime. And as a former drama student and organizer of a free storefront legal advice clinic, he seemed ideally suited to the job.

With his drooping brown mustache, high-pitched voice, and horn-rimmed glasses, Cooper became an instant if unlikely TV star. He doggedly pursued justice for the people who came forward, uncovering the facts of their cases and grilling the unfortunate government bureaucrats or ministers who were responsible. The program was first conceived as a half-hour every second Sunday night at 10:30 p.m., but by the fall it increased in frequency. A lawyer headed a team of 15 researchers to look into viewer complaints. The idea was not just to create television programming, but also to intervene on behalf of the complainants and help them solve their cases, even if it resulted in no publicity. Only four provincial governments actually had ombudsmen at the time, so the program succeeded in serving as a central outlet for complaints. In its seven-year run, the program received 60,000 letters, intervened in about 18,000 cases, and showed 250 of them on the air.[10]

'We're using the media for social change in a way that has not been done before', Cooper said. 'We're taking it one step beyond the documentary form, which exposes abuses. We want to expose them and then correct them on air.'[11] The canvas was so broad, it allowed Cooper to examine a huge array of issues. He fought individual workers' compensation and unemployment insurance cases; he challenged inequities in funding for mentally ill children in Ontario; he questioned why hit-and-run victims didn't get compensation when they were injured by uninsured drivers; he advocated for BC farm workers, cab owners in Yellowknife who were battling a monopoly, an unwed Regina mother who was denied welfare benefits after enrolling in university, and workers who were left with nothing when their company went bankrupt. He even took up the cause of Canadian Football League quarterbacks who were contesting the designated import rule.

As an outsider, Cooper felt less constrained than regular corporation staff about what his CBC bosses wanted from the show. Two months into the program's run, it featured the story of Winston Upshall, who had signed a contract with his employer and then discovered he had to work untold overtime hours without a premium, and was not eligible for unemployment insurance benefits. Upshall was a camera operator, and his employer was the CBC. Cooper convinced CBC president Laurent Picard to appear on the show, and a vigorous explanation of the company's policies was offered. Still, Cooper insisted an injustice had been done to Upshall, and Picard said he would

Robert Cooper (right), host of CBC's Ombudsman *program, speaks with US consumer advocate Ralph Nader. (*CBC *Still Photo Collection)*

address the situation. The program, Cooper told him, would keep in touch to see that he had.

This was a minor brush fire between Cooper and CBC brass, but more serious ones were on the horizon. Like Jock Ferguson, Cooper would eventually come into conflict with CBC management. But in the immediate post-Watergate era, the show's popularity demonstrated a significant public desire for serious journalistic investigation into systemic social problems.

If CBC Television was unsure of how far to take its investigative offerings, the public broadcaster's radio service often appeared less hesitant. Mark Starowicz's *As it Happens* program commissioned an investigation into lead contamination in 1974. Story editor Max Allen put together a hard-hitting documentary that accused two Toronto smelters of poisoning the environment. Evidence was offered to show how companies used their own hired guns as experts to discredit opponents of the contamination, and the provincial government was also accused of complicity in the process. In an effort to gain publicity, the CBC made advance copies of the program's transcript available to journalists. Blair Kirby of the *Globe and Mail* wrote a small piece on the day the item was set to air, calling it the most thorough investigation to date on the lead contamination issue. He called it 'a definitive and terrifying show, and investigative journalism at its best'.[12]

The advance publicity succeeded in alerting potential listeners to the 7 p.m. broadcast, but it also attracted attention the CBC didn't anticipate. Lawyers for Canada Metal Co. and Toronto Refiners and Smelters Ltd. raced to the courthouse and secured an ex-parte injunction. An articling student, dispatched to the CBC's Studio F in Toronto, arrived 15 minutes before the program was set to air, and served Starowicz with the injunction. It prohibited the documentary from stating that the smelters had bought misleadingly favourable medical evidence, and that they had deliberately concealed evidence from medical experts. Allen performed some quick edits, inserting bleeps to replace the contentious portions. Over the censored parts, host Harry Brown read the terms of the injunction. It was an unusual and remarkable broadcast that only succeeded in drawing far more attention to the documentary than would otherwise have been the case. The entire, uncut version of the piece had already been broadcast to the Maritimes.

The injunction was subsequently lifted, but the CBC was slapped with a contempt citation for revealing too much of what the original court prohibition had to say. And defamation actions dragged on for years, with the CBC eventually agreeing to a small settlement to end a $14 million lawsuit.[13] Watergate may have turned its journalistic purveyors into heroes in the US, but in Canada, there was no easy road to success for investigative reporters.

Woodward and Bernstein were more than just distant iconic figures for Henry Aubin, the Montreal reporter who created some of the decade's best investigative journalism. He was working in the *Washington Post* newsroom alongside Bernstein when Woodward was trying to graduate from a suburban weekly to the *Post*'s staff. But the metro editor was resistant, and there were no immediate job openings. Then, Aubin decided to leave the newspaper on Labour Day, 1971, taking a year-long break from journalism to move with his wife to Morocco. It created an opening that Woodward filled. Without it, Aubin jokes, Watergate might never have become what it did.[14]

Born in New Jersey in 1942 to parents of Huguenot origin, Aubin graduated from Harvard and decided he wanted to be a writer. Fiction was on his mind, but his father pushed him in a more practical direction. He took a job with the *Philadelphia Bulletin* in 1965, and quickly became a young Washington correspondent for the newspaper. His editors paid attention to the anti-war activists of the era, and Aubin became the only mainstream American reporter to cover the peace movement on a full-time basis. The assignment actually offered Aubin the opportunity to do some early investigative work. His city editor, suspicious that anti-war activism was being fuelled by communism and nefarious forces, wanted him to infiltrate the movement. Aubin felt it wasn't ethically justified, and refused.

But the idea of doing challenging, research-intensive journalism was forged early for Aubin. He remembers a formative moment in 1968 while attending a Washington journalism seminar with Nick Kotz, a *Des Moines Register* reporter who had won a Pulitzer Prize for exposing unsanitary conditions in meat-packing plants. Kotz talked about the benefits of activist reporting, and it was a message that stayed with Aubin. During his year at the *Washington Post*, he worked on a number of in-depth features and did a three-month investigation with another reporter into the health system. But Aubin was growing tired of the Washington scene. Having worked at the highest levels of American newspaper journalism early, he didn't harbour ambitions of climbing ever-higher career ladders. When he returned from his year abroad, Aubin successfully applied for jobs at a number of smaller newspapers. He eventually took a position at the *Gazette* in Montreal in June 1973.

Aubin began as a general assignment reporter, but his analytic skills led him to probe most issues far more deeply than same-day turnaround journalism could accommodate. His city editor approached him one day with a story about how his wife was complaining about the rapid rise of the price of bread. Could Aubin find out why, the editor wondered. Two days later, the reporter came back and said the story was far bigger than just the cost of bread. Aubin spent three months investigating food prices, uncovering evidence about the oligopolies that controlled different foods. He was the first to write extensively about John McDougald, head of Argus Corporation, who controlled Dominion supermarkets, Massey-Ferguson, and other major Canadian companies. His series showed how supermarkets arranged their shelves and aisles to encourage maximum purchases, and how they used psychological techniques to increase sales volume. Aubin's stories blended investigative reporting, explanation, and analysis in a form of storytelling that made for populist reading. His efforts were rewarded with the second National Newspaper Award in the Enterprise category.[15] Later, he spent five more months on follow-up food industry stories, this time winning a national business-writing award.

By the end of 1974, Aubin was in a position to choose his own projects. Still, there was a price to pay for the kind of work he did. When his city editor asked him what long-form piece he wanted to do next, Aubin was unsure. The oil industry was an obvious choice, with everyone concerned about energy cartels and high oil prices. 'I'd just finished an 11-week probe of another industry and shuddered at the thought of another long period of research. Other reporters in the office, saddled with routine daily articles, look at you cross-eyed because they think you're not pulling your oar, or so you imagine. Your wife and kids look at you like a stranger because you're never home.'[16] Aubin eventually realized that if he was going to take on the hard work and anxiety of another major investigation, it needed to be something that would break completely new ground. He wanted a project that would uncover an area no one had even thought of examining before.

He found it in the idea to study Montreal itself. He wanted to know who made the decisions about the transformations Montreal was undergoing at the hands of developers. He was curious about who owned the key portions of his adopted city, and how municipal officials served their interests. Just as Tom Miller had deconstructed the ownership patterns of West Virginia, Aubin wanted to find the real brokers in his city. Who, in effect, owned Montreal?

What began as a two-month project eventually mushroomed into 18 months of research. Aubin visited six countries, interviewed more than 400 people, and spent countless hours studying municipal, provincial, and federal property and corporate records. The result was a 15-part series at the end of 1976, later expanded into a book called *City for Sale*. 'I had naively assumed that indigenous interests—wealthy Montrealers—basically owned the city, with foreigners through their investments being on the periphery of power.' Instead, he found a trail that led beyond Quebec and Canada to shadowy dummy companies around the world. In one case, a middle-class stucco home at the end of a quiet street in Schaan, Liechtenstein was shown to be headquarters for a company owning six major high-rise apartment buildings in Montreal. Aubin knocked on the door of 236 Kirchstrasse, and the 71-year-old resident who was listed as president and director of many of the companies insisted he didn't know who the real owners were.

It added up to a pattern of anonymous, unaccountable ownership in Montreal. The Montreal municipal power structure, Aubin said, is 'little more than a collection of local yokels acting as agents and intermediaries for these much larger global interests'. Aubin showed what was happening in Montreal to be representative of a much larger pattern. 'The story is really about many, perhaps most, cities in the West. Many of the interests active in leveling neighbourhoods and building forests of high-rises in Montreal are . . . the same interests active in scores of other major cities—whether it be Calgary, New York, Los Angeles, Atlanta, Paris, Brussels, Rome, Casablanca, Melbourne, or Johannesburg. They include the biggest interests in the world, bigger even than the oil companies, which in many cases they own.'[17]

Aubin's series wasn't a mere catalogue of property ownership records. During the course of his research, he discovered some startling trends. The flight of Italian capital, for instance, was shown to be turning Montreal into an international haven for illegal money. The cause, in part, was an open-door policy towards foreign property investments by different levels of government. Aubin sketched a portrait of financial empires such as the House of Rothschild, the Bronfmans, and foreign-owned powerhouses like Genstar. He revealed that the biggest landlord in the city was the Roman Catholic Church, and after combing through thousands of computerized land records, he published for the first time a list of the church's major real-estate holdings.

Given the explosive findings and originality of the work, Aubin thought the *Gazette* would embrace the project with delight. Instead, as the research progressed, management grew less supportive. 'They were never able to say they didn't want to publish it', Aubin says. 'It dragged on and on. They showed no enthusiasm, hoping I would quit.' The *Gazette* was very much the newspaper of the Montreal English establishment at the time, and Aubin saw that as the problem. 'It was not a series that the Montreal establishment would welcome. It questioned the establishment.' Aubin remembers protracted meetings with management, trying to convince them of the value of the work. One meeting with the managing editor left him so discouraged he vomited into the wastebasket. But he persevered. 'It took all the political cunning I had to get it into the paper.'[18] When it came time to submit it for a National Newspaper Award, Aubin learned from the managing editor's secretary that all the newspaper's entries had gone out in the mail, except for his. So he photocopied the series and sent if off by himself. When the winners were announced, and he was again given the Enterprise prize for his work, his managing

editor was the first to bound into his office, pumping his hand and offering congratu-
lations, as if he had championed the series all along.

Aubin saw the *Gazette*'s attitude as symptomatic of the climate in the country at the
time. Even though Watergate had catapulted investigative work into the mainstream,
there were limits, as Jock Ferguson and Robert Cooper had discovered. 'Management
was leery of doing investigative work. It didn't want lawsuits, it didn't want to rock the
boat.'[19] Part of the reason was a legitimate fear, Aubin believed, of mistakes and sloppy
research. The explosion in the genre led to 'wanabee investigative journalism' that didn't
meet rigorous standards. Still, while newspapers were anxious for recognition and
journalistic awards, many were mindful not to disturb unduly their establishment
patrons.

City for Sale went beyond describing the problem and offered some solutions. Aubin
suggested beefing up existing disclosure laws for companies to engender better
corporate accountability, and also recommended stiffer pollution laws to crack down on
offenders. He urged better urban planning, and suggested members of pension plans
get more active in finding out how their monies were being invested. He even hinted
that the repatriation of Canada's constitution would have to happen before real progress
could be made in stemming foreign influence on the country's affairs. But Aubin's
understanding of the power he had uncovered made him cautious. 'Most laws will not
work. Legislation cannot really undo the ways of international capital. Such capital will,
when its managers put their mind to it, generally find ways to override or circumvent
laws. . . . Power in shaping Montreal is held by people, whether foreign or domestic,

Henry Aubin (left), author of City for Sale, *exposed the secrets of land ownership in Montreal.
(Penelope Aubin)*

who are faceless. Being unknown, they can exercise power without accountability. They are powerful largely by default, by the abnegation of power by the community itself. Their power is waiting there to be shared.'[20]

The French edition of *City for Sale* quickly became the No. 1 non-fiction best-seller across Quebec, and it drew wide attention everywhere. 'The seemingly endless research of public, corporate, and land records—required to unmask a city's invisible landlords—is a valuable public service', said a reviewer at Aubin's old newspaper, the *Washington Post*. 'Aubin's work offers a blueprint for other tireless truth-seekers, and it raises some searching questions.'[21] Yet Aubin's own newspaper refused to review *City for Sale* until six months after its launch—when the book's acclaim in North America and Europe shamed it into doing so.

Watergate's legacy remains a lively topic of debate among journalists and researchers. Few deny, though, the inspiration it provided to media outlets and individual journalists around the world. The idea that two lowly reporters could affect an institution as powerful as the US presidency resonated in newsrooms everywhere. As we have seen, it encouraged other journalists to do probing work of their own. It also helped to turn investigative journalism into a commodity. Major mainstream newspapers, in some cases the same ones that Canada's Senate committee had criticized for being docile, began seeing the potential commercial advantage in publishing muckraking work. That led to inevitable conflicts between institutions eager to boost sales and audience, on the one hand, and journalists who were trying to hold powerful, vested interests to account. Eventually, it encouraged Canadian journalists to band together and take measures to improve the practice of investigative work into their own hands, free of constraints imposed by their institutions. In the meantime, the 1970s saw an explosion of various forms and varieties of investigative work, as the next chapters reveal. Mark Feldstein's supply-and-demand model appears to have reached equilibrium in this decade, producing a volume of investigative work that has yet to be surpassed.

Health Canada's Deep Throat

Sig Gerber, executive producer of CBC's *Marketplace*, noticed a brown paper envelope in his mail slot one spring morning in 1989. Inside were confidential documents from the federal health department, detailing concerns about the controversial Meme breast implant. More than 12,000 Canadian women had already been given the implant, a polyurethane foam-covered artificial breast manufactured by Bristol-Myers Squibb. But there were problems. The foam had disintegrated in some women's bodies, and there was a fear the implants were releasing cancer-causing chemicals.

Gerber's program had been investigating the issue for weeks, and had made contact with a health department insider. Research chemist Pierre Blais told them about a secret meeting of government scientists that had raised serious concerns about the implants, though the government took no measures to stop sales. Blais himself wrote a memo questioning the continued distribution of the product, only to be asked by a superior to rewrite it and revise his conclusions. It was an explosive allegation of a government cover-up, but Gerber refused to go with the story until he had conclusive proof. The brown paper envelope provided the missing link: minutes of the scientists' meeting and the two versions of the Blais memo. On 28 March 1989, *Marketplace* broke the story.

Marketplace went to extraordinary lengths to protect Blais, but the government had a good idea who was responsible for the leak. Blais, 49, was told to clean out his desk and was escorted from his office. He fought his dismissal and was eventually reinstated, but quit soon afterwards in disillusionment. The government continued to defend the safety of the implants. That didn't change until April 1991, when the US manufacturer voluntarily pulled them from the market around the world. New American studies had shown the implants released a chemical called TDA, a potentially cancer-causing agent. As a result, the Canadian health department finally asked doctors to stop using the implant.

Blais went on to work as an independent consultant, often criticizing government for its lax oversight of medical implants and devices. *Marketplace* continued to track the issue. In a 2003 story, it found problems in medical devices ranging from malfunctioning heart valves to an artificial lens for the eye that clouded over. It also uncovered Health Canada documents that showed the government's approval process sometimes allowed faulty devices to be sold before they were properly tested.

Chapter 8

Robbers and Cops

The commission of a crime justifies fascinating violations of privacy. . . . In fact, criminals and their victims, even given the heavy-handedness of most crime coverage, may be the most fully-drawn characters in the news.

Mitchell Stephens[1]

On a spring evening in 1973, a tanned, well-dressed young man walked into the offices of *Le Devoir* on Montreal's Sainte-Sacrement Street and asked to see Jean-Pierre Charbonneau, the newspaper's crime reporter. As he approached Charbonneau's desk, the man pulled out a gun and began firing at close range. Charbonneau dove for cover, but not before he had been hit in the forearm. In the ensuing confusion, the gunman raced from the building and escaped in a getaway car. Charbonneau was taken to St. Luc Hospital where doctors examined him and pronounced he was in satisfactory condition, and lucky to be alive.

'He was a punk', Charbonneau told reporters at the time, 'a little dark-complexioned guy wearing white gloves and sunglasses.'[2] The punk turned out to be Tony Mucci, an 18-year-old aspiring member of the Montreal Mafia. A year later, Mucci was acting as a bodyguard for Paolo Violi, the second-most powerful Mafia figure in Quebec, when Charbonneau spotted him on the street. Police arrested Mucci, and after a plea bargain, he was sentenced to eight years in prison. For Charbonneau, it was a sober introduction to the world of crime reporting. 'I've been in this two years', he said after the shooting, 'and I've already been warned a couple times.'

At 23, Charbonneau was a veteran of the crime scene. He had graduated with a degree in criminology, and spent a summer at *La Presse* working with the newspaper's top crime reporter, Michel Auger, who introduced him to many of his police sources. In 1971, he wrote a series of stories for *Le Devoir* on municipal corruption in St. Leonard. The next year, he investigated shady dealings involving the future director of the Montreal Metro police force. Both stories triggered public inquiries, and Charbonneau began working on a book about organized crime in the province. He was the fastest-rising star in the Montreal world of crime journalism.

Charbonneau, who went on to a career in provincial politics as a Parti Québécois MNA and president of the Quebec National Assembly, had no illusions about why criminals didn't like his work. He sided squarely with the police, relying on them for information and assistance. Faced with a choice between cops and robbers,

Charbonneau believed it to be foolish for journalists to remain impartial. 'If you are an investigative reporter in this field, if you want information about organized crime, you can have sources in the mob, or you can have sources in the police department. And you can't play both sides. So I decided at that time to choose my side, and I preferred to get my information from the police.'[3] The choice gave him access to secret intelligence information and the fruits of investigations he could never have assembled by himself. For Charbonneau, the role of investigative reporter was similar to that of a detective, with a crucial exception. Police investigators could place bugs, wiretap phones, hire informants, and amass detailed secret intelligence. By allying himself with the police, he gained access to all that information.

Charbonneau was part of a new generation of reporters who were working a very familiar beat. Crime reporting is as old as journalism itself. As early as the sixteenth century, publications in France and England were routinely printing articles about murders and sensational crimes. When the penny press began making its appearance in Britain and the United States, crime reporting became institutionalized as a staple of everyday coverage. No matter how news was defined, editors recognized the sheer entertainment factor that accompanied stories about police and criminals. It allowed writers to delve into the private and seedy sides of individuals at a time when similar reporting about politicians, business people, or other members of society was unknown. The opening of courts to journalistic coverage accelerated this process.[4] When Canadian penny papers began publishing, they too embraced the genre. As time progressed, few newspapers could afford to be without a police or courts reporter. An analysis of newspaper content for several editions in 1899 showed that nearly 18 per cent of *La Presse*'s front page was devoted to crime and violence.[5] In the coming decades, there would be publications geared entirely to the exploits of criminals and police.

The stereotypical cop reporter was someone who befriended officers, hung around the station, and was rewarded with scoops. No analytical or investigative skills were required to win favour with the city editor, only an ability to maintain good relationships with the people who fed you stories. The situation was summed up by Jocko Thomas, the legendary *Toronto Star* reporter who spent 60 years on the crime beat. 'Investigative reporting wasn't my usual work. I didn't have any particular liking for it, and I had never been very successful in breaking a story that meant that kind of meticulous reporting.'[6] On his retirement in 1989, after serving the insatiable appetites of 43 different city editors over the years, he was rewarded with a gold badge and honourary membership in the Metropolitan Toronto Police Association and police pensioners' association.[7]

Small time crooks made for endless streams of copy on the police beat, but organized crime posed a bigger challenge. By the early 1970s, Canadians were becoming more curious about the existence of Mafia operations in their country. The revelations of Mafia informant Joe Valachi in the 1960s led to widespread awareness of Mafia activities in the US, and the 1972 release of *The Godfather* movie brought the subject under mass scrutiny. The public appetite for such stories was particularly high in Quebec, where two inquiries had been set up to look into mob connections in the construction industry and organized crime in general. Something more than the traditional reporting from police headquarters was needed to get an understanding of the criminal networks. With his unique skills and training, Charbonneau was well positioned to satisfy the demand.

Charbonneau was three months into his assignment of covering the Quebec commission on organized crime when he was shot. The incident didn't deter him. He had already decided to write a book about the subject, and was confident that his police sources would provide him the necessary information. Quebec police had planted a bug in the milk cooler at Paolo Violi's headquarters, providing them with detailed information about the inner workings of the Quebec Mafia. This information made its way to the crime probe and Charbonneau's newspaper articles. When his book, *The Canadian Connection*, appeared in 1976, it provided a detailed and comprehensive picture of the history of the Mafia and the worldwide narcotics trade. Charbonneau later became a consultant to the very same crime commission he had covered.

Charbonneau's work was based entirely on his police sources, and on his belief that a detached view of the crime scene wasn't possible or desirable. It's difficult to determine, therefore, whether the story he tells approximates the truth or the version police wanted him to hear. Charbonneau readily acknowledged his position in the introduction to his book. 'Certain people, and especially those prejudiced against the police, will no doubt complain that this account is incomplete and biased. It is! . . . and it could not have been otherwise. Thanks to exceptional cooperation of RCMP authorities, I had almost unrestricted access to the archives of the Narcotics Squad. This historical reconstruction was made with the help of material from the archives, and with the testimony of police officers who conducted the investigations. Certainly, police files must be read with caution. They can only shed a partial light on what lives and stirs in the criminal world, even though they often contain the personal accounts of informers and key witnesses. Only those who inhabit the underworld can describe its real face, and for obvious reasons, such people rarely choose to speak openly and frankly about it.'[8]

As a compendium of the information police had gathered about the Quebec underworld, *The Canadian Connection* was well crafted. But if there were any examples of grandstanding or incompetence on the part of Montreal narcotics officers, it wouldn't be found in Charbonneau's writings. He described the patience, devotion, determination, and sacrifice on the part of the squad, and defended them from criticism. 'It takes intelligence, finesse, and wiliness to penetrate the secrets of the great narcotics networks. In that respect, the agents of the Royal Canadian Mounted Police, particularly those in Montreal, have acquired a professionalism over the years which today, it must be said, makes them the envy of more celebrated police forces around the world.'[9] Charbonneau made clear there were no conditions attached to his cooperation with the federal agents, though he agreed to keep some information confidential and he modified some details to respect arrangements police had with their informants. He also asked two lawyers to study his manuscript in advance and suggest changes: the former prosecutor for the narcotics squad, and the assistant chief prosecutor for the crime commission.[10]

The proliferation of profitable local television news programs in the 1970s, first in the United States and then in Canada, increased the demand for crime coverage. Dramatic, on-the-scene coverage of crime became a staple for the 'Eyewitness' and 'Action News' formats of many local stations, leading to the well-known ethos of 'if it bleeds it leads'.[11] The enduring popularity of police and legal television dramas only fed the public appetite for such news. While some newspapers and television stations limited their coverage to the daily briefings of police departments and the random crimes of big cities, others tried to dig deeper. At the CBC in Montreal, there was a desire to document the world of organized crime in a detailed way. To present a rounded picture, it was felt that the criminal mind needed to be explored more fully. Brian McKenna, who had left the *Montreal Star* to join the CBC in 1973, hired Michel Auger to help with the research. Auger used his contacts to collect information from both police and criminal elements. In one case, a former bank robber who had just been released from jail was persuaded to talk about his craft. But the most ambitious idea was to use a hidden camera to document the real life of a Mafia don. McKenna decided to construct a day in the life of a crime boss, and he chose Vincent Cotroni as his subject.

Cotroni was the undisputed Mafia leader in Montreal, but he remained a shadowy figure. The Cotroni family came to Quebec from Calabria in 1924, and Vincent embarked on a career as a wrestler. He also came into steady conflict with the law, but was often acquitted or let off with lenient sentences. By the 1950s, his stature as an underworld leader had grown. Montreal became an important centre for American mobsters, and Cotroni forged links with the New York Bonanno family. Still, he preferred a low profile, and filed a million-dollar lawsuit against *Maclean's* magazine for suggesting he was the Montreal Godfather. He preferred to be known as a successful businessman.

McKenna's idea was to film Cotroni without the mobster's knowledge, and it worked. 'We thought that trailing major Mafiosos would be complicated, but the reality was rather amusing', says Auger. 'Our work couldn't have been easier. In fact, Mr Vic, as some called him, had poor eyesight, which made him very cautious at the wheel of his late-model Cadillac. So it was almost child's play to follow and film him with a camera hidden in a plain pickup.'[12]

It was one of McKenna's first major projects for the CBC, and it had enormous impact. The resulting film, called *Settling Accounts*, won the CBC's Anik award. Although it was shown in Montreal, there was some reluctance to release it nationally, because the CBC network was already working on an ambitious project of its own on organized crime—a project that would turn into one of the most original and daring examples of investigative journalism in the decade.

> Good evening, I'm Warner Troyer. What you are about to see tonight is not a set of pretty pictures. It is the first of two programs on organized crime in Canada. . . . Some of the images are brutal; some of the language is offensive . . . and many of the implications of what you will see may be disturbing. But these are all qualities of the world of organized crime as it exists here in Canada with its close ties to the United States and other areas of the world.

This program, and the one tomorrow night, are the result of two-and-a-half years of investigative television journalism by a team headed by producers William Macadam and Martyn Burke. In order to provide you with a look at just who are the leaders of the organized crime world in Canada . . . and how they gain their power and their fortunes, it was often necessary to employ unusual filming techniques. Hidden cameras, concealed microphones, and night lens equipment were frequently the only means of accomplishing the task. It was decided on several occasions to sacrifice technical quality simply in order to bring the faces of organized crime onto your home screen.

After that tantalizing introduction, CBC viewers on 12 June 1977 were shown 90 minutes of a program called *Connections: An Investigation into Organized Crime in Canada*. The next evening, a second 90-minute edition was broadcast. For the first time, a succession of mobsters, Mafiosi, loan sharks, and contract killers appeared on Canadian television. There were images of Paul Volpe, Johnny Papalia, Natale and Jimmy Luppino, and other gangsters. Viewers were shown the Godfather of Montreal, the old Don of organized crime in southern Ontario, and the leader of the Vancouver Mafia. Research explained how organized gangs had infiltrated key segments of Canadian society. A gang leader spoke on camera about revenge killings and partici-pating in murders for which he was never charged. The program even claimed the Mafia attempted to penetrate the inner circles of Canadian politics. 'A small and determined group of criminals is now capable of subverting virtually every one of our institutions', the program solemnly warned.

The presentation was meant to be sensational, and it worked. Newspapers dropped their traditional animosity over being scooped, lavishing praise on the series. 'With a daring that most Canadian newspapers have so far avoided for fear of lawsuits, the CBC special, *Connections*, fired at its targets from coast to coast—and fired with deadly aim', said the *Toronto Star*.[13] 'Thanks to a powerful exercise in television journalism, the myth of a virgin Canada untouched by the ravages of organized crime has been blown to bits', said the *Ottawa Citizen*.[14] The *Vancouver Province* felt the series warranted comment in a lead editorial. 'The CBC television programs this week documenting the extent of organized crime in this country, with names and precise information that show deep, concrete research, indicate what can be done by a public broadcasting service when it has the will, focus, and commitment to do it. Indeed, the CBC revelations stand as a reproach to both the private broadcasting systems and the newspapers which have failed in their public duty as watchdogs of the public interest. The same information could have been obtained by them but they either couldn't or wouldn't look for it.'[15]

The stories caused an uproar in the House of Commons and in legislatures across the country. Opposition leader Joe Clark called for a royal commission on organized crime. British Columbia's attorney general said he wanted all provinces to unite to fight the criminal threats. US law enforcement agencies were requesting the programs for use as training films. Although no official audience figures were ever reported, it seemed millions of Canadians had watched the programs and were talking about them.

While the CBC was being credited for groundbreaking investigative work, *Connections* was largely the handiwork of a private production company and two men with very little journalistic experience, William Macadam and James Dubro. Both brought unique skills and life experiences to the project, and a sense that the traditional conventions of television need not apply. They were supported by a dynamic CBC executive who was eager to sponsor investigative work, Peter Herrndorf. And they benefited from the craftsmanship of producers Martyn Burke and Richard Nielsen to create an effective finished product.

Macadam travelled an unlikely path to his success as a muckraker. His father was Sir Ivison Macadam, the initial Director-General of the Royal Institute of International Affairs in the UK. His mother, Lady Caroline, came from a long line of American politicians, and had worked for Henry Stimson, secretary of state in the administration of US President Herbert Hoover. After he graduated from Eton, his sense of adventure led him to Canada, where he began working in the logging camps along the BC coast. At 26, he started a charter bush-flying operation.

Steeped in political discussions from an early age, Macadam couldn't resist taking part in Canadian politics. He became the youngest ever vice-president of the Progressive Conservative Party at 24, and ran for Parliament unsuccessfully in 1965. He was involved in organizing the 1967 PC leadership convention, and then took charge of Robert Stanfield's election campaign of 1968. After working in the Opposition leader's office for a number of years, Macadam began to think back to earlier influences in his life. He had long admired the work of Edward R. Murrow, who was a family friend. And he had paid attention to the excitement generated by *Seven Days*. Suddenly, he decided to take a radical turn. 'I felt I could do a lot more in television than in public life.'[16]

Macadam founded a company called Norfolk Communications, and began pitching ideas to the CBC. He wanted to take on the most difficult projects possible. Early on, he profiled motorcycle gangs in Ottawa, a subject no one had captured on television before. He had no qualms about approaching gang members and asking for interviews, an indication of the fearlessness that would prove invaluable for the *Connections* series. The documentary earned him just $150 and airplay only in Ottawa, but it was proof that he could succeed in his new career. Looking to research more ideas for even bigger pitches to the CBC, Macadam called a friend he had met at a party, Jim Dubro. It was the beginning of a complex and sometimes strained relationship that nonetheless produced a material advance in the methodology of Canadian investigative journalism.

Dubro had graduated from Boston University with a BA, magna cum laude, in classical civilization and English literature. He earned his MA at Columbia, where his thesis explored 'Dr Johnson's Biographical Theory (from *The Rambler* and *The Idler*) and his Life of Richard Savage.' He took further courses at Harvard, where he also assisted professors in preparing research proposals, and acted as a research assistant to the dean of education. Dubro honed his organizational skills while working as a fund-raiser at Harvard, where he built a cross-indexed file system on foundations and individuals who were targeted for potential donations. Macadam got him excited at the prospect of big television projects. Dubro put his PhD aspirations aside and became head of research for Norfolk Communications.[17]

Dubro put together a list of story ideas for Macadam, one of them triggered by a passing reference in a *Ramparts* article to a secret agency called the Communications Branch of the National Research Council (CBNRC). *Ramparts* had interviewed a former analyst with the top-secret National Security Agency, the US body that collected electronic intelligence from phone calls and other transmissions. The story made a single mention of a Canadian agency that, apart from a similar passing mention in the *New York Times* 12 years earlier, was essentially unknown in the country.[18] Macadam and Dubro proposed a documentary on CIA and intelligence activities in Canada and the US. The CBC commissioned the project in the spring of 1973, and the research began.

'This major story was a result of scholarly research—a painstaking look at all material published on intelligence for the past 20 years', Dubro said. 'It is through carefully reading articles and books on the subject at hand that much of the sensational information will emerge, as well as the best interview subjects.'[19] Dubro believed that whether the research subject was top-level espionage or sixteenth-century poetry, the techniques were essentially the same. The first step was an exhaustive reading of the literature on the subject, paying special attention to the footnotes and bibliographies. 'Once you have cross-referenced and listed the footnote references and bibliographies, you begin to have a pretty clear idea of who the authorities are and what evidence they have to support what they are saying. Then you go to those sources and do the same, locating their sources and references and cross-indexing them. Before long you find yourself dealing with the same basic, raw data used by the authorities you have been reading. Then you are in a position to interpret their conclusions and draw some conclusions of your own. . . . Acknowledgements in books are particularly useful.'[20] Even spy novels proved helpful. Dubro found one novelist, a former CIA officer, willing to talk about valuable inside information.

As an academic, Dubro realized the pitfalls in following the scholarly approach too slavishly. 'Scholars are full of information that can lead you down a false path', he said. That's why it was crucial to supplement the background research with interviews. While 90 per cent of a journalistic project might be found in documents and public records, people have to be tapped for the remaining crucial piece of the puzzle, and for advice on how to access all the documents in the first place.

The result of all the research was broadcast on 9 January 1974 as *The Fifth Estate— The Espionage Establishment*. It described Canada's worldwide activities on the espionage front, featuring a former US State Department official who claimed the DEW radar line in the north was used to snoop on communications in the Soviet Union. The program delved into the history of the CIA and National Security Agency in the US, pointing out how the Americans and their allies divided responsibilities to allow them to monitor communications widely. The biggest revelations came in the form of specific details about CBNRC. The program showed how the secretive branch operated as a listening post for communications intelligence, both in Canada and abroad. It also used hidden filming to dramatize the secretive world of intelligence. Dubro staked out the home of the RCMP's chief liaison with the CIA in Virginia. And using a technique that would become more commonplace as the decade progressed, the program showed hidden camera footage of CBNRC director Kevin O'Neill getting into his car in suburban Ottawa. After the broadcast, O'Neill claimed the program was inaccurate, but refused to elaborate. 'If you're an official in the government, and you're engaged in classified work, you can't comment on it.'[21]

Former prime minister John Diefenbaker declared the program 'the most amazing I've seen in years', and Prime Minister Pierre Trudeau was badgered in the House of Commons about the revelations.[22] Trudeau acknowledged that the government collected information on Canadian soil, but said he wasn't aware of any operations abroad. Neither Trudeau nor his ministers could point to specific inaccuracies in the broadcast. Outside the House, the prime minister was just as coy as his intelligence officials. 'I don't want to comment on questions of security. It's much too delicate. The danger is you will drag out confidences from me and I'll say things that I regret.'[23]

The show's careful research and ultimate impact were not lost on Peter Herrndorf, who was appointed head of CBC's current affairs department in the spring of 1974. He wanted Norfolk to do another project, and asked Macadam for a list of ideas. But months went by before the CBC would commit. Finally, in December of that year, Herrndorf commissioned Norfolk to prepare a research report on one of Macadam's story proposals—organized crime in Canada. He agreed to pay $15,500 for the research, and would decide later if it warranted development into a film.[24]

Dubro plunged into the job with the same academic approach he had used for the espionage project. He began with a wide literature search, building an inventory of names and contacts for follow-up interviews. Although much had been written and publicized about organized criminal activity in Quebec, including the steady stream of revelations from the province's crime probe, there was little information about the rest of the country. In fact, many government officials and academics were adamant that organized criminal networks did not really exist in Canada. In a Toronto speech some time earlier, Ontario's attorney-general had declared: 'I want to assure you that there is no such monolithic criminal group here in Metro that, on the Godfather pattern, controls an area of criminal activity.'[25] It was a quote the producers would gleefully include in their eventual broadcast, side by side with clear evidence to the contrary.

Macadam and Dubro decided they needed to talk to all the key people identified in the early research, from academics to law enforcement officers to justice experts. They travelled the country, conducting research interviews and gathering material. It was all catalogued and cross-indexed. Each interview led to another lead, and the list of contacts grew. They hired Jean-Pierre Charbonneau and Michel Auger to provide information about the Quebec scene, and tried to derive information from every reporter who had tackled the organized crime beat. They were trying to build a profile of the individuals and families that controlled criminal activity in Canada, and to see how the groups connected. It was broad research, with no preconceived notions of what they would find. They were also not encumbered by any strict deadlines, though the patience of the CBC at various times throughout the project would wear thin.

The research took them to New York and Washington. Macadam and Dubro knew what many journalists quickly discover on the crime beat: American officials are often far more open than their Canadian counterparts. They made important connections with Drug Enforcement Administration officials who were eager to supply information about Canadian suspects. Within three months, they had amassed so much material they hired a full-time file clerk.

A key decision, taken early, was that criminals themselves would have to be interviewed extensively for the series. Most crime reporters simply never bothered, finding it far easier to deal exclusively with the police. Macadam knew from his motorcycle-gang film that it could be done, and he had no hesitation trying. He saw no reason to start anywhere but the top. In the spring of 1975, he called the lawyer for Paul Volpe, a notorious Toronto mobster, who agreed to pass the request along. Macadam then called Volpe himself. The conversation was recorded.

After identifying himself, Macadam said he was doing research for a documentary about organized crime.

'Yeah . . . so?' Volpe replied.

'Well, uh, I've been told . . . uh, there have been a lot of allegations that you are a pretty big man in organized crime.'

'What organized crime? I'm just a businessman.'

'Well, uh, if you're just a businessman, how would it be if we had lunch together and we could go over some of these allegations people have been making?'

'Sure, okay, where do you wanna do it?'[26]

Macadam was masterful in his treatment of sources, often playing the role of a confused and clueless producer who was asking dumb questions and needed guidance to get his story straight. He projected a vaguely sympathetic tone with mobsters he would interview, charming them into continuing the conversations and providing increasingly more information. The meeting with Volpe produced valuable details that Macadam and Dubro didn't have. Volpe acknowledged his connections to the Luppino Mafia family in Toronto and Hamilton, and mentioned that he had been a partner in a Haitian casino with Vito de Filippo, a member of the New York Bonanno family. It was the beginning of a strange relationship between the two men, eventually producing a dramatic segment in the documentary called *Portrait of a Mobster*. It also confirmed the importance of a cardinal principle in investigative work, the necessity of approaching the targets of investigation for information.

Macadam and Dubro became obsessed with the research. Though he was getting just $200 a week for his efforts, Dubro worked day and night. Macadam quickly expended the CBC contract monies and began pouring in funds of his own. Finally, in October 1975, they presented a 54-page research report to the CBC, filled with names, Mafia connections, and potentially explosive stories. 'Our research has led us to believe that organized crime is far more serious a threat today than it is generally understood to be. It has already gone a long way in infiltrating almost every segment of our society in Canada, including businesses and high government office. We consider it a cancer in advanced stage of development and a cause for very serious national alarm . . .'[27] It sounded like an overblown pitch, but the details in the research backed up the allegations. CBC money managers, surprised at the scope of the expenses before any shooting had even begun, were worried. But Herrndorf pressed forward, assigning experienced producer Martyn Burke to co-produce the project and allocating a generous $80,000 budget for shooting, which was scheduled to begin the following February.

Even as filming progressed, the research continued. By the end, Dubro had compiled 32 index-card file drawers containing 35,000 names. Each was cross-referenced with notations that pointed to supporting photos, exhibits, documents, and tapes. In the pre-computer era, it constituted a massive database that rivaled information banks held by law enforcement agencies. The sensitivity of the information necessitated precautions. Access to the production company's offices was limited, and staff had to sign secrecy agreements. The entire project became known as *Connections*, but the clandestine nature of the work meant that, too, was kept quiet. The response to inquiries at the CBC and beyond, was that the production team was working on a program called *Commerce*.

Macadam and Dubro realized they would have to use surreptitious means as a tool to get closer to the truth. 'We felt to expose criminals we had to have a certain arsenal, and we worked with lawyers to figure out what that arsenal would be.'[28] It meant hidden cameras and microphones, night lenses originally developed for use in Vietnam, and body packs with miniaturized recording equipment. A beat-up van with smoked-glass windows became the principal means for getting hidden-camera footage. Fictitious business names and phone numbers were placed on magnetic plates on the van so the vehicle wouldn't draw suspicion. Producers used walkie-talkies to keep in touch with the camera operator.

Seven Days had occasionally resorted to hidden cameras, but never on a scale like this. Some in the CBC were opposed to the idea, especially since Macadam and Dubro were not experienced journalists. But Herrndorf thought it was crucial to capture the story properly. 'You're not going to get organized crime figures in the studio to come on air and do a conventional interview', Herrndorf said.

> We were using a great deal of surveillance journalism, and these techniques had historically not been used much in Canada. The understanding I had with the unit was that I had to approve the kind of techniques that they used in the show. I did approve all of it. The distinction we made was that in all those cases where there was very little doubt that somebody was an active participant in organized crime, we would go along with those surveillance techniques. When there was some real question about whether somebody was essentially an innocent bystander, we tended to be much more cautious.[29]

Caution was not always the watchword as the *Connections* team pursued its quarry. To capture part of a segment on loan-sharking, Macadam fitted himself with a body pack and walked into the Toronto office of David McGoran, a known associate of Paul Volpe. He was accompanied by his cameraman, and McGoran quickly ushered them into a back office. Macadam identified himself as a CBC producer and asked questions directly related to loan-sharking. Even as his hidden tape recorder was rolling, he assured McGoran it wasn't for publication. Suddenly, McGoran asked: 'Are you wired up? You got a tape thing on you?' Macadam denied it, but McGoran slipped his hand along Macadam's sweater and felt the microphone. McGoran angrily ordered them out of his office, and Macadam was relieved that nothing more deadly occurred.

'The worst part of my day was getting into my car and starting it, wondering whether it would blow up or not', Macadam recalled. 'After about three months, all that went away. The only power the mob has is fear. I felt if the Mafia or organized crime came after us, every journalist in the country, and the police forces, would have zeroed in on them. It would have been the craziest thing possible for anyone to do to attack us. I felt that as long as we had a camera we would be pretty safe.'[30]

An American journalist who was probing organized crime in Arizona about the same time was not so lucky. Don Bolles was an investigative reporter with the *Arizona Republic*, and had broken many stories about local corruption and mob activity. A source called him to a meeting in a downtown Phoenix hotel in June 1976. He was supposed to provide information on land fraud involving organized crime. When the source didn't show up, Bolles returned to his car and turned the ignition. A bomb went off, injuring him severely. Bolles died of his injuries 11 days after the bombing. The focus of the American journalistic community then turned to Phoenix, and reporters from across the US travelled to Arizona to complete the investigation into organized crime that Bolles had begun.

Over the first few months of 1976, the *Connections* crew shot footage in Toronto, Hamilton, Guelph, Montreal, New York, Detroit, Buffalo, Miami, Vancouver, and San Francisco. By April, they asked the CBC for an additional $24,000. It soon became routine to request additional funds. More than 50 hours of film were shot, and much of the material was explosive. But the sweep of the story was so huge that the team was finding it difficult to focus. Deadlines passed, and Herrndorf eventually assigned Richard Nielsen, an experienced independent producer, to come in and re-focus the work. He crafted the material into 14 separate magazine segments, and the team settled on presenting the material in two 90-minute packages. When all the costs were totalled, the series came in at $500,000, not all of it paid by the CBC. Macadam said he financed a significant portion of the project with his own funds.

Despite all the tribulations, Herrndorf was pleased with the finished stories. '*Connections* was either going to be a huge success, or it was going to be the Mirabel of investigative journalism', he said, referring to the 1975 airport project outside Montreal that was massively over-budget and just as massively under-utilized. 'We were very lucky that we ended up getting something as powerful and as penetrating as it was. It did an incredibly important job, sensitizing Canadians, businesses, and individual consumers to the fact there was real organized crime in Canada, that it was happening in Montreal and Toronto and Vancouver. They did a terrific job. We got a very important story.'[31] And there was a desire for more. The CBC commissioned a second series of *Connections*, triggering even more research and culminating in three-and-a-half additional hours of programming on 26–28 March 1979.

'The last time we were passive observers. This time we have become more active participants', said producer Martyn Burke.[32] It was Burke's understated way of saying that the techniques the team used became more aggressive and controversial.

They recruited Paddy Calabrese, a former member of the Buffalo-based Magaddino crime family, to help. Calabrese had become a government informer years earlier and was in the federal witness-protection program. They asked Calabrese to call Joe Romano in Vancouver and set up a meeting. Romano was a known Mafia member, and the *Connections* team wanted to see if Romano would participate in a fake scheme they had concocted to buy stolen securities. So elaborate was the set-up that Calabrese actually placed his first telephone call from a known mob location in California, designed to give Romano the comfort of thinking that he wasn't being set up by law enforcement officers.

When the meeting took place in Vancouver, hidden cameras captured the entire conversation, including Romano's plans for laundering the securities. He also boasted of his connections in society, which included contacts with a British Columbia judge. It was the kind of sting operation police themselves might not have been able to pull off, as it smacked of entrapment. Calabrese was also used a second time, this time in Toronto, to see how Mafia members would react to his proposal that he move millions of dirty dollars out of Italy.

The *Connections* team also engaged in trading information with police, a practice that would become controversial among investigative journalists in later years. Dubro said they would occasionally allow police to look at surveillance footage they had gathered, or share intelligence about connections they had drawn in their research. The Ontario Provincial Police assigned Constable Al Robinson to work with them, as he did with a select number of other crime reporters in the province. Macadam had seen political reporters do the same thing in Ottawa during the '60s, gathering tidbits about one party and then offering it to a rival party in return for some other nuggets of information. The practice wasn't a concern at the time; it was simply seen as another tool to get closer to the truth. 'We didn't have to answer to any standards in those days', Dubro said.[33]

They did have to answer to lawyers and the laws of libel, but Dubro said that didn't turn out to be as big an obstacle as they originally imagined. 'The lawyers, of course, balked at first at putting all this on the air. But we overwhelmed the lawyers with so much documentation and detail that they had to relent on most of the material. On the most dicey material, such as naming "respectable" associates of mobsters, the CBC brass courageously overrode the lawyers on journalistic grounds and risked the many lawsuits they knew would ensue.'[34] Lawsuits did ensue, but not nearly as many as originally suspected. Some small suits involving misidentification of minor characters were resolved with apologies and out-of-court settlements.[35] The most serious challenge came from Conservative MP John Reynolds, who said he had been unfairly linked with organized crime figures on the West Coast. Seven years after the original broadcast, just as the lawsuit was set to go to trial, a settlement was reached. Reynolds got no money, but the CBC agreed never to show disputed portions of the *Connections* series again.[36]

Macadam went on to do a film in the United States about the KGB, but he soured on investigative work soon afterwards. The reality of serious work is that budgets cannot always expand to fund the research that needs to be done. 'You don't know what will reap rewards and what won't. That makes all the accountants frightfully nervous. It's such a difficult genre. I got out of it. People weren't willing to put up the funds for it.'[37] Dubro, meanwhile, continued to hone his organized crime expertise, contributing to more films and writing a series of books on the subject. For Herrndorf, the expense of the project in the end was worthwhile, and the series also helped CBC graduate to a more sophisticated level of work. 'One of the consequences of the series (and other CBC programming of the '70s) was that the CBC set up its journalistic policies document flowing out of that', Herrndorf said, referring to the code of standards that continues to govern CBC work.[38] And for most people who took part in the *Connections* series, there is a belief that a similar project could not be done today, given its expense, the controversial nature of the methodology, and the fact that 'the CBC is a little more risk averse.'[39]

In the world of cops and robbers, journalists have not always trained their sights on the criminals. With increasing frequency in the post-Watergate era, it was the police who became the subjects of journalistic investigation. That's what was on *Globe and Mail* managing editor Clark Davey's mind when he approached star reporter Gerald McAuliffe in the spring of 1974 with an idea.

Davey had read the *Chicago Tribune*'s series on police brutality the previous fall. It was an exhaustive probe into the practices of Chicago's police force, documenting horrifying cases of abuse. The newspaper's investigative team, fresh from its Pulitzer-Prize-winning probe into voter fraud, looked at more than 500 allegations of brutality. From those, 37 were chosen for intensive inquiry. Reporters spent five months attempting to verify the accuracy of complaints. Lie detector tests were used to corroborate information. The multi-part series drew national attention, and it achieved tangible results. Three police officers were indicted, and police brutality investigations were transferred to a civilian review board.

Although similar allegations dogged police departments across North America, they rarely surfaced publicly. There are generally no independent witnesses to police brutality, and departments routinely investigate alleged acts of impropriety themselves. Toronto too had its share of police brutality allegations. Davey asked McAuliffe to see what he could find out.[40]

If anyone could get to the bottom of the story, it was McAuliffe, one of the most persistent diggers in Canadian journalism. Born in 1939, he was one of nine kids in a struggling Toronto family. McAuliffe got his start at the age of 20 at a small Cobourg radio station, earning $55 a week. He proceeded through a succession of Ontario newspapers, building up a real-world knowledge that made up for his limited grade 8 education. He would forge friendly relationships with government clerks, and study the intricacies of the municipal code in his spare time. When he needed to do a title search, he would get a lawyer to show him how. McAuliffe would see angles to stories that others didn't. And once he was onto a story, he wouldn't let go. 'Gerry was a hustler, a character out of Damon Runyon', said Davey. 'He was an absolute ferret. When he got his teeth into someone's flank, they were going to give him what he wanted before he was done.'[41]

McAuliffe's investigative instincts began to blossom in 1964, when he started working at the *Hamilton Spectator* under managing editor Denis Harvey. He learned from a confidential source that an elderly woman had died in a local hospital as a result of medical incompetence, and he found the local coroner had covered it up by omitting relevant information from the death certificate. Next, he exposed fraudulent dealings inside the city's land assessment office. Eventually he headed a four-member team that examined the sale of farmland in and around Hamilton. In a series called *The Land Grabbers*, he documented suspicious transactions, including one instance of a company buying land under 32 different names. McAuliffe's stories in Hamilton and throughout his 35-year journalistic career triggered a dozen public inquiries, royal commissions, select committees of the legislature, and, in one case, a major inquest.

But it was McAuliffe's work on police stories that often had the greatest impact. He had a knack for uncovering police wrongdoing, and a strong belief that the people society vested with so much power needed to be held to account. His working experience in small-town Ontario had exposed him to routine corruption. 'I saw the inner workings of a corrupt police department. I saw cops perjure themselves on many occasions. And most of the people who were victimized were poor people', he said.[42] McAuliffe had a tendency to see issues in black and white terms. When it came to police, the slightest hint of wrongdoing set him on the chase.

A good example at the *Spectator* was the case of George Clinton Duke, a millionaire businessman with an extensive criminal record. Duke had been the leader of a notorious Depression-era gang of jewel thieves in upstate New York, until he was finally arrested and sentenced to 30 years. After serving part of his sentence, he was deported to Canada, where he started a prosperous lawnmower business near Hamilton. He led an extravagant lifestyle, maintaining relationships both with Canadian Mafia members and officials of the Ontario Provincial Police. His garden parties were well attended by police officers, including the OPP commissioner. And there was a recurring pattern of driving and impairment charges against Duke that were routinely and mysteriously dismissed.[43] Despite his criminal past, the OPP issued Duke a gun license and allowed him to keep an arsenal at home, including a machine gun that he occasionally mounted on his golf cart so he could shoot birds on his estate.

McAuliffe found out about an incident in which Duke had pointed a gun at a woman, threatening her life. When police refused to lay charges, she filed a private prosecution. The case was shunted to family court where there was little chance of publicity. McAuliffe exposed the story, along with the attempts to cover it up. It triggered a commission of inquiry, and the story mushroomed into a full-scale scandal.

While more revelations came to light and politicians entered the debate, McAuliffe was paying a price for his exposé. Police began targeting him, using intimidation and occasionally physical force.

'Here I was pregnant with our third one when the Duke (commission of inquiry) started', said Bonnie, McAuliffe's wife. 'We'd get calls that would threaten to kidnap the kids, they'd threaten to firebomb the house, and my attitude was "screw you". I think in part Gerry has been able to do what he did because he never had to worry about me and the kids not going along with what he did. I loved his job. I had been raised to believe if it isn't right, you fix it.'[44] On one occasion, the McAuliffes were at the Hamilton press club when Bonnie became suspicious that Gerry was in the bathroom for too long. She sent someone to look for him, and he found McAuliffe being assaulted by on-duty police detectives. They wanted him to reveal his sources and tell them where he was getting all his information. Then, a man later identified as a mob courier told McAuliffe he would end up in Hamilton harbour if he continued to implicate police in the Duke affair. The harassment became routine, and something McAuliffe and his family accepted as a cost of doing the kind of work he did.

When the *Globe and Mail* decided to build a modest investigative unit in 1972, its first distinct team, McAuliffe got the phone call. A small office behind city desk was set aside for their use, with heavy padlocks and an iron bar securing the information inside two steel cases. McAuliffe shared an office with Hugh Winsor, and at various times Peter Moon and John Zaritsky contributed investigative stories. In practice, very little team reporting took place. Instead, each reporter was given sufficient time to break individual stories. McAuliffe quickly wrote a series of front-page exposés on corruption and mismanagement at the Ontario Workman's Compensation Board, leading to the dismissal of the chairman and a legislative inquiry. He exposed corruption in the tender process for the new Ontario Hydro building, and did a series of stories on violence and mob activity in the construction industry.

When Davey approached him with the idea of looking into hints of police brutality in Toronto, McAuliffe didn't need much convincing. He began working his sources, building a file of alleged incidents. Given the nature of the story and the clout of the police force, the *Globe* knew it had to tread carefully. 'Of all the investigative projects the paper undertook, none was approached with more caution and concern than McAuliffe's probe of brutality as practised by the Metropolitan Toronto Police Force', according to Richard Doyle, the newspaper's editor.[45] 'To plant seeds of doubt about Toronto's finest would be seen as sabotage and worse.' The *Globe* decided to use the same methodology the *Chicago Tribune* had employed, hiring a polygraph expert to conduct lie detector tests on complainants before using their stories. After five months of investigation, McAuliffe's 10-part series began running on 15 October 1974.

Like a prosecutor outlining his case at the start of a trial, McAuliffe laid out the highlights of what was to come in his series. It would be a tale of terrifying abuse and torture at the hands of police. Of the 20 complainants McAuliffe had chosen for intensive investigation, none failed a polygraph test outright. But three turned in inconclusive tests, so their stories weren't reported. Nine separate cases would be presented, he wrote, buttressed by medical records and polygraph results.

A 19-year-old says he was beaten, handcuffed, stripped, and blindfolded. Then a spring-type 'claw' was clamped on his nose, then his penis, to force him to make a confession. 'He (the policeman) didn't open the claw to remove it', the young man told the *Globe and Mail*. 'He pulled it off and cut my penis. Then a door opened and a police officer looked in. He said, 'Oh you are using the claw', laughed and left the room.

Another case involves a teenage male who says he was stripped in a back room of a police station, stood naked in front of an air conditioner operating full blast, then doused with cold water.

Another suspect says a detective took his service revolver, cocked the hammer and pressed it to the suspect's forehead threatening to shoot. The same man claims that another detective forced a fistful of sawdust into his mouth.[46]

As the *Globe* expected, there were some vocal negative calls and threats to cancel subscriptions. Pro-police elements in various media jumped to the defence of the force, accusing the newspaper of tarnishing the reputation of all officers because of the actions of a few bad apples. The harassment McAuliffe had experienced in Hamilton continued in Toronto. Even before the series began, McAuliffe came under pressure. There was an attempt to entrap him. He was approached by a man who offered to sell him a colour television set—an expensive item at the time—for just $25. And the TV would be free if McAuliffe could get others at the *Globe* to buy more sets. The man turned out to be a courier for the mob. After the series began, the tension increased. 'I would go to work in the morning with a Metro police intelligence squad car sitting outside the front of the house, following me into work.'[47] McAuliffe knew that a genuine police undercover operation would never reveal itself so openly. Intimidation was the real purpose. Meanwhile, more overt threats came over the phone. 'This son of a bitch would call and tell me what time the boys would go to school, what they were wearing, what their birth dates were', recalled Bonnie. 'I made my kids with heads like swivels. The games in the car were: look out the window, how many people in the car, does the man have a hat, does the man have a moustache. That's how programmed I made my kids. I wasn't going to have them grow up and be afraid of their shadows because of what Gerry did. I said nobody's going to intimidate my family.'

By the third day of the series, the provincial government announced a public inquiry. At first, it seemed the Ontario police commission would be involved, but further pressure forced a broad, independent inquiry headed by an Ontario judge. The police fought back. In November, they took out an ad in Toronto newspapers, urging people to cut out and return a coupon in support of the force. Some 13,000 people responded. A convenience store staged a 'Cops are Tops' campaign. There were organized efforts to barrage the newspaper with complaints. The *Globe* was forced to run a story reporting that 80 per cent of all calls and letters it received on the series had been supportive of the police. If the newspaper knew it was unleashing a whirlwind, it couldn't have known where it would ultimately lead. The final outcome wouldn't become clear until the public inquiry reported its findings.

That day didn't come until 18 months later, when the inquiry reported evidence of excessive force in half a dozen complaints it had investigated. The judge suggested police had lied in a number of the cases. No charges could be laid under the Police Act, because the six-month statute of limitations had long since passed. But McAuliffe and the *Globe* felt vindicated. It had been the first major exposé of a large police force in Canada, and it appeared in the country's pre-eminent mainstream newspaper despite pressures on both editors and the reporter. It would set the stage for a more thoroughgoing exposé into dirty tricks and wrongdoing by Canadian police, this time on a national stage.

Historian Mitchell Stephens, in describing instances of crime reporting in sixteenth-century England and France, clearly sets out the motivations of the editors. 'The journalists who were feeding the early printing presses learned what all journalists have learned: that crime news is prime news.'[48] With the rise of television, and particularly local North American newscasts, crime reporting became more frequent and visually graphic.[49] In the Canadian context of the 1970s, crime reporting provided some important examples of investigative reporting and new use of methodologies. While Canadian editors also realized the appeal of crime news, some decided to delve deeply into the subject. Jean-Pierre Charbonneau painted a detailed picture of the Mafia and organized crime in Quebec, but his sources were admittedly one-sided and limited. His

Gerald McAuliffe (on telephone) with Paul Murphy at the Hamilton Spectator. *(Courtesy of Gerald McAuliffe)*

close contacts with police and justice officials provided inside information and details that normally would never be publicized. Other journalists tried exploring the topic from more than a single source's point of view. They also used the new technologies offered by television to capture realities of organized crime that had never been seen before. The team that produced the *Connections* series for the CBC contributed to the development of investigative journalism methodology in Canada by intensively studying the issue with the tools of academic inquiry. Through the use of hidden cameras and microphones, sting operations, and other forms of aggressive inquiry, they attempted to get closer to the truth of the situation. Their work raised ethical concerns about invasion of privacy, entrapment, and intrusive inquiry, all of which led to a further refinement of journalistic standards and practices in the CBC. With crime news seen as a profitable journalistic commodity, other Canadian media delved into the topic as well. In some cases, such as Gerald McAuliffe's series for the *Globe and Mail*, the target became police themselves and their excesses. This too led to the development of new journalistic techniques, and an appreciation of the dangers inherent in pursuing the very people who were paid to uphold justice. The methodologies used in the 1970s to cover both police and criminals offered important lessons to the next wave of Canadian investigative journalists.

Canada's Biggest Mass Murder

Kim Bolan had been on the job just six days as a *Vancouver Sun* reporter when the Indian army attacked the Golden Temple, the Sikh religion's holiest shrine, in 1984. The government wanted to dislodge militants who were agitating for a separate Sikh homeland. The consequences of the attack would be felt across India and Canada for years, and Bolan became not just a chronicler of the story but a player in many of the sub-plots. For Canadians, the conflict in India was brought home tragically when Air India Flight 182 was bombed in June 1985, killing 329 people. Most of the victims were Canadians of Indian origin. Bolan was called into the newsroom on the day of the bombing. The young Vancouver reporter would spend much of the next two decades literally risking her life to discover the truth about what happened.

In 2005, Bolan chronicled her efforts in a book called *Loss of Faith: How the Air India Bombers Got Away with Murder*. It was her objective, she said, to connect the dots on a multitude of news stories she and others had produced over the years. She was a junior reporter on the day the bombing occurred, but her contacts and experience grew as she continued to develop leads about the case. She travelled to India four times over the years, and developed key contacts throughout the Indo-Canadian community. Her stories about fundamentalist separatists in the Sikh community, and their possible connections to the bombing, made her a target for intimidation and attacks. She received death threats, and was told her name was on a hit list. The seriousness of the threats became clear to everyone after the murder of fellow journalist Tara Singh Hayer in 1998. While Bolan continued working, the newspaper paid for her family to leave the country for a week. When they returned, her two young sons were no longer permitted to answer the phone or the door. The following year, threats became so pronounced that Bolan was advised to leave her home and live under full-time security protection. All the while, she continued to report new perspectives on the investigation.

When charges were eventually laid against three men for the Air India bombing, Bolan believed the story might soon come to an end. But one man had his charges reduced to manslaughter, while the others were ultimately acquitted. Bolan's book highlights the evidence the trial judge ought to have considered, but didn't. In the end, she concluded that the families of the victims were justified in having lost faith in the justice system. 'Canada failed to protect the innocent, to punish the guilty, and to bring out the truth.'[50]

Chapter 9

Newsmagazine Wars

A news organization's comfort level with investigative reporting is a litmus test, of sorts, of how seriously it undertakes its obligation to inform the public. A newsroom that doesn't dig deep for some of its news is saying, in effect, that all the important news is at or near the surface. This, of course, defies logic and common sense as surely as it fails our citizenry.

Gene Roberts, former managing editor, the *New York Times*[1]

Appearing on his own radio network in June 1973, CBC president Laurent Picard was ambushed by a provocative question. It came from Douglas Leiterman, former producer of *This Hour Has Seven Days*. Could the president name a single CBC reporter specializing in investigative journalism, Leiterman asked. Picard couldn't offer a name. For the CBC, once the standard bearer of challenging journalism, it was an embarrassing moment.[2]

Over at CTV, there was no similar malaise. Though budgets and staff were smaller, CTV programs offered some individual examples of investigative journalism that had impact. Jack McGaw was producing populist programs that exposed filthy food practices and polluting cars.[3] A series of hour-long investigations called *CTV Inquiry* used tests to break original stories. McGaw tested the exhaust of cars and found half of the newer vehicles didn't meet pollution standards. Turning his attention to politics, he oversaw production of a program that looked into Canada's wiretap laws. At the time, there were still instances where placing a wiretap could be considered legal. CTV did just that, in the caucus room of the NDP on Parliament Hill.[4] The bug was discovered, but the resulting program made its point forcefully.[5]

CTV's biggest star in the field of probing, enterprise work was Michael Maclear, the British-born journalist who had emigrated to Canada in 1954 and spent years as a foreign correspondent. Maclear's reports on *W5* were always powerful and credible. In the program's season opener for 1973, Maclear showed how Canadian airline pilots were being forced to work up to 16 hours per day, four days in a row. He compared it to similar practices in Britain, and revealed that Canadian pilots were ready to strike over the issue. Maclear's reporting was one of the factors keeping *W5* ahead of its Sunday night CBC competition, and CTV thought it could leverage his success even further by giving him his own show. In the fall of 1974, he began writing, producing, and hosting his self-named program *Maclear*. The first edition was an exposé of so-called psychic surgeons in the Philippines, charlatans who claimed they could perform surgeries without cutting the skin. Thousands of tourists, including Canadians, fell for the scam. Maclear filmed the practice, in which surgeons pretended to reach into the abdomens of patients to perform the surgery. In one case, some bloodstaining occurred on a patient's clothes. Maclear took the clothing to a Toronto police laboratory to have it tested, and it turned out to be pig's blood. He suggested it might be from a hidden fingertip capsule used by the phony surgeons to add to the effect. Another Maclear program in his first season exposed British military abuses in Northern Ireland, showing how they employed concentration camps and secret trials. Maclear went on to produce 60 episodes over three years, usually drawing more than a million viewers a night.[6]

CTV appeared to be winning the prime-time, public affairs program wars. Since the death of *Seven Days* in 1966, the CBC had tried repeatedly to find the right successor, but nothing took hold. Different attempts were made at Sunday night programs, but the life span of each was no more than a year or two. Peter Herrndorf, appointed head of current affairs in 1974, set out to change the situation for the CBC. He was well positioned to do the job. Starting at the CBC in Winnipeg in 1964, he had progressed through the ranks until ending up as one of the senior producers of *The Way It Is* under

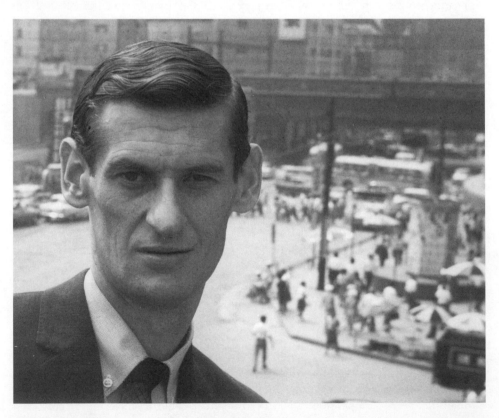

Michael Maclear worked as a foreign correspondent for CBC before doing populist and high-impact investigative work for CTV in the 1970s. (CBC Still Photo Collection)

Ross McLean. Recognizing Herrndorf might be destined for significant accomplishments, the CBC funded his way to Harvard where he earned his MBA. At 34, he took on the task of rebuilding the CBC into the cultural powerhouse he knew it could be. And one of the key areas he felt the corporation needed to dominate was investigative journalism.

Herrndorf had admired the gutsiness and originality of *Seven Days*, but he also drew inspiration from the early CBS experiments in the US. He had seen *Biography of a Bookie Joint*, a documentary that exposed gambling problems in the US by putting hidden cameras across from a shop in Boston and staking it out for weeks, getting pictures of people patronizing the betting parlour. Producer Jay McMullen had even placed a camera inside a small box to capture pictures of actual betting. In another documentary, McMullen opened his own company and began ordering restricted pills from drug suppliers across the US to show how easy the process was. Herrndorf was struck by the research and hard work that went into the productions. While his main objective was to create a major, popular magazine program that could last 10 years or more, he wanted investigative work to be an integral component.[7]

'We wanted a program that would put us on the map from a journalistic point of view, that could do the big, important stories without slavishly following the news. We thought one of the things that could really separate us from everyone else was long-form journalism. Investigative journalism was a part of that. And the kind of investigative journalism I was interested in and brought to current affairs in the mid-1970s was journalism that was built around weeks and months of not very glamorous slogging.'[8] To do it, Herrndorf realized there would have to be a significant commitment of resources, and a recruiting drive to bring the right kind of people to the job. His first task was to write the program bible.

Herrndorf summed up his thinking in the founding document when he set out the program's goal: 'To produce a weekly current affairs magazine whose journalism is distinguished, professional, aggressive, candid, and iconoclastic . . . whose subject matter is wide-ranging and provocative . . . and which is consistently interesting and entertaining to a large and broadly based audience.'[9] The document made it clear the new program would not be a derivative of *Seven Days*. As for the show's characteristics, Herrndorf suggested the magazine should concentrate on film production and not be tied to a studio; it should be topical but not a slave to the week's front page headlines; it should avoid a traditional preoccupation with politics and politicians; and it should shun the superficial or highly impressionistic treatment of stories. He wanted stories that 'tell us something about the way power and influence is exercised . . . and about the way decision making (both public and private) really takes place in Canada, stories that expose individuals, companies, and institutions who are involved in illegal or irresponsible activities, that examine public policy or governmental behaviour in a critical way.' At the same time, he wanted offbeat and humorous aspects of Canadian life, and a deliberate attempt to balance its harder, investigative stories with softer material, particularly stories concentrating on interesting Canadian personalities.[10]

The bible was specific. He wanted a 10 per cent share of the audience by Christmas of the first season, rising to 12 to 14 per cent by spring. And he aimed to spend a substantial amount of money, $51,000 per week, to achieve it. After setting out the roles and responsibilities of the staff on the new show, Herrndorf produced an extraordinary list of 140 potential producers, story editors, and performers for the program. It contained virtually everyone doing important journalism in the country at the time, both inside the CBC and elsewhere.[11] A major recruiting drive got underway.

Herrndorf assembled an effective mix of people to lead the program. He chose Glenn Sarty as the executive producer, recognizing that a seasoned television professional would be needed to guide the process. Sarty had been with the CBC for two decades, and most recently had run the afternoon program *Take 30*. Herrndorf invited Ron Haggart to be one of the senior producers, considering him one of the great newspaper journalists in the country. Haggart had gone from the *Star* to the *Telegram* and then to a stint with CITY-TV news before accepting the CBC offer. And the second senior producer was Robin Taylor, a talented journalist Herrndorf had first met in Winnipeg a decade earlier. Taylor's previous assignment had been running the CBC Newfoundland supper-hour program.

With an airdate of September 1975 looming, staff had to be hired quickly. Herrndorf wanted the top investigative talent he could find, and he was able to attract five people he was confident would deliver the kinds of stories that would set the agenda: Gerald McAuliffe, Philip Mathias, and Joe MacAnthony from the newspaper world, and John Zaritsky and Brian McKenna of the CBC. 'It was the first time in the CBC we had that kind of talent and resources, dedicated to going after major stories', said Herrndorf. Together with the *Connections* project, Herrndorf saw it as a whole new era of investigative reporting at the corporation. 'For me, if I had had a set of heroes in journalism, it had to do with the people who did that slogging to break the really important story, the story that exposed corruption, that exposed influence-peddling, that exposed abuses in hospitals or the school system. I think all of us felt that was the essence of great journalism, and the CBC hadn't been doing much of it.'[12]

Mathias would bring a wealth of business reporting expertise to the program. Born in Britain, he earned a chemistry degree and landed work as a supply teacher before trying his hand at journalism with a variety of trade publications. While labouring away at magazines such as *Tin and its Uses, World Crops*, and *Manufacturing Chemist and Perfumer*, he gained insights into the business world. He moved to Canada in 1964 and was hired two years later by the *Financial Post*, where he quickly established a reputation as a tenacious digger. A business deal in Manitoba caught his attention. In 1966, the provincial government announced a $100 million pulp-and-paper project at The Pas that would create 4,000 new jobs. Oddly, it was also proclaimed that the Swiss and German investors in the project did not want to be named. Mathias unearthed information about the Churchill Forest Industries deal that would eventually expose it as a massive international fraud.[13] He looked at a variety of similar projects in other provinces, exposing suspicious dealings by governments desperate for economic development. Once the *Post* saw what he could do, editor Paul Deacon gave him the time and resources to conduct further business investigations. Mathias credits that support with his success at exposing flawed business projects in a number of provinces. Surrounded by reporters with technical expertise, he became a persistent investigator at a time when boosterism characterized most business reporting in mainstream newspapers. He was motivated by a strongly defined sense of right and wrong, and was driven to expose wrongdoing by a sense of moral outrage.[14]

MacAnthony had also established a reputation as a disturber of the status quo, though it had cost him dearly. The Irish-born journalist worked at Dublin's *Sunday Independent* newspaper in the 1970s when his editor, Conor O'Brien, asked him to look into a venerable national institution, the Irish Hospitals Sweepstakes. Since 1930, the lottery had been a fundraising mechanism for Irish hospitals. Though lotteries were illegal in the US and Canada, many tickets were clandestinely sold, often with the tacit approval of authorities, as it was assumed proceeds were going to a good cause. MacAnthony spent a year investigating, travelling to North America and uncovering a tale of corruption, graft, payoffs, and cronyism. He found the hospitals were getting less than 10 per cent of the ticket proceeds, but middlemen were raking in fortunes. Ireland's richest family was one of the chief beneficiaries. The story ran in January 1973, leaving all of Ireland astonished. It was the first time anything negative had been written about the sweepstakes. Even though MacAnthony was later considered one of the early practitioners of investigative journalism in Ireland, the country wasn't quite ready for his brand of reporting. Powerful institutional forces came down heavily on MacAnthony and his editor for daring to expose such a bedrock national icon. When ownership of the newspaper changed, MacAnthony suddenly found himself without any support. The reporter lost his merit pay and started getting signals that his days at the newspaper were numbered. His chances at finding another job in Ireland were slim. MacAnthony had done some freelance work for CBC's *Take 30*, and its host, Adrienne Clarkson, suggested he could try his luck in Canada. MacAnthony came in the fall of 1974, and was soon doing in-depth research for the CBC.

Herrndorf arranged for some familiar faces to host the program. He elevated Clarkson from a decade of afternoon programming to be the highest-profile host, along with veteran journalists Warner Troyer and Peter Reilly. Troyer would be gone after the first year and Reilly died in the second, but Clarkson went on to do 200 shows in the next eight years. All that remained to be determined was a program name, and just three weeks before its initial airdate the CBC finally decided on *the fifth estate*, a reference to the electronic media and its place in society. Not everyone was instantly impressed. Ross McLean, the pioneering television producer, wasn't initially convinced it would work. 'The result struck me as a program manicured to within an inch of its life. I was also encumbered by my strange reservations about Clarkson as a broadcaster. I even resented the lower-case affectation of its name.'[15]

But McLean and many other skeptics began to change their opinions as the program went to air for the first time, on 16 September 1975. The lead story, called 'Death at 100 Below', was the result of McAuliffe's enterprise. It told the story of an air disaster a year earlier that left 32 people dead in a crash near Rae Point, Northwest Territories. It revealed startling new information about how the crash occurred, and raised questions about irregularities in the ensuing inquest. For Clarkson, it was an archetypal story, uncovering new information, challenging authority, and showcasing the plight of the victims. From a journalistic point of view, it resulted in a home run, as it triggered a front-page story in that day's *Globe and Mail*. And as a piece of watchable television, it also succeeded. A survivor was shown in his hospital bed, explaining how he tried to save other passengers. Just as the tight shot widened to reveal his bandaged hands, he talked emotionally about how people tried desperately to put out flames with their bare hands.

If the segment was a taste of work to come, it also became an example of the inherent dangers in investigative work. The coroner at the inquest into the crash felt his reputation had been damaged by the broadcast, and he launched a lawsuit. More than three years later he won his case in court, collecting $5,000 in damages.

Over the next two years the program produced some groundbreaking investigative documentaries. McKenna examined the growing scandal over the 1976 Montreal Olympic games, a story that uncovered embarrassing information about senior city officials and contractors.[16] Mathias spent six months investigating and exposing the corrupt practices at the Vancouver Stock Exchange, regarded by many as the most poorly regulated exchange on the continent. He analyzed about 1,000 stocks that were traded on the exchange over two years, finding evidence of infiltration by corrupt elements. The hour-long documentary was later used as a training film by securities regulators in the US.[17] And Joe MacAnthony broke some important new elements of the escalating scandal over wrongdoing at the RCMP security service. The program also used the tools of television technology to aid in its investigations. In one of its segments, it surreptitiously recorded recruiting efforts by the Moonies, the fanatical followers of Sun Myung Moon's Unification Church, and it routinely sent hosts into aggressive pursuit of accountability interviews.

The program developed an interest in the inner workings of big business, trying to probe an area that daily newspapers did not consistently examine critically. It examined a proposed investment in Chile by Noranda Mines, and took a challenging look at Canada's sugar-refining industry. McAuliffe provided the research for a piece in December 1976 called 'Citizen McCain'. It examined the New Brunswick food processing giant and found the McCain family had received millions over the years in government grants and loan guarantees. The story looked critically at the government assistance, and featured a polite but confrontational exchange between Clarkson and Harrison McCain.[18] It was the kind of television many politicians and businessmen weren't used to seeing. New Brunswick Premier Richard Hatfield criticized the program, and Conservative MP Fred McCain, a relative, proposed a motion in the House of Commons to reprimand all those who had been involved in the story's production.[19]

The fifth estate's audience success was making CTV nervous. Michael Maclear was appointed head of current affairs for CTV in 1977, and he immediately suggested *W5* might be cancelled or changed significantly. By the fall, the name was dropped in favour of *CTV Reports*. But the program's profile continued to decline. Maclear left CTV in 1978, and in the next fall season, *W5*'s old name re-appeared. *The fifth estate* had every reason to be pleased about its success, but there were underlying tensions among staff. Some of the newspaper reporters recruited to the program were finding it difficult to adapt to the new medium. A few felt the hosts were grabbing all the credit for stories that would normally bear their bylines. Others believed the nature of the medium didn't allow for a full exploration of complex issues. 'The investigative format is defeated by television', MacAnthony said. 'You have to boil so much down to fit in the time slot. Some say journalism is the accumulation of significant detail; that's exactly what television can't offer.'[20] McAuliffe was also growing impatient with Sarty's constant pre-occupation with the entertainment value of the items. By 1977, he was accusing the program of growing too soft. Haggart, meanwhile, recognized that having three scandals in the program every week would prove to be tedious. Exposés were important and producers wanted at least one a week, but there had to be a mix. Haggart preferred to characterize all of the program's content as 'original reporting', whether it was investigative or descriptive of a social situation. 'Print journalists tend to forget that TV is an emotional medium, not one for dissemination of facts or encyclopedic dissertations', Sarty said.[21] The conflicts led McAuliffe to resign from the program, but he said in retrospect that he might have made a better transition to television had he worked a stint in the news department first.

The creative tension was magnified by media scrutiny of McAuliffe's resignation and subsequent unhappiness among staff. Robin Taylor addressed the issue in a memo to employees in the spring of 1978: 'Let me start by confessing that I have never believed that "morale," in the normal way the word is understood, has ever been all that high on *the fifth estate*. The fierce competition, the rivalries, the pressures, and the decisions handed down by senior production people have from time to time caused some glorious rows and created some burning resentments.' More important than personality conflicts, in Taylor's mind, was the criticism that the program had not been producing as much investigative journalism as it should. He listed some of the traditional stories the program had aired that everyone would consider investigative, but then went on to suggest staff not be overly narrow in defining the genre. 'Because they have not uncovered corruption, or been carried on the front pages of the Toronto newspapers, a great many of the stories seem to have been deprived of the accolade "investigative" even though they have required just as much investigation (and sometimes more) than many of the items listed above.'[22]

Taylor was acknowledging the television reality that required producers to serve up entertainment along with information. Though *the fifth estate* adopted its magazine format largely from *60 Minutes*, it resisted the temptation to indulge in celebrity profiles or strict personality stories. The program's graphic image of a filing cabinet stuffed with folders signaled to viewers it was a show with serious intentions. But Sarty knew that sensitive, human stories could capture an audience. Some of the program's most watched items were documentaries by John Kastner, such as those on women struggling with cancer, and on people who had to undergo cranial surgery to correct deformities. Despite Taylor's vigorous defence of the program, he himself was calling for more hard-edged stories in a production meeting the following year.[23]

Though the program had to produce compelling content, it developed a rigorous methodology to ensure its journalism was accurate. Robin Taylor called it a courageous but a cautious program. 'Our credo always was—you had to have the proof.'[24] Sarty, Taylor, and Haggart, or Cabinet as staff called them, would attend all the screenings of items in production and offer comments. They would call in CBC lawyers when necessary. Even before an idea was approved for shooting, Haggart would grill researchers and producers on their facts, challenging them to get the little things in their stories right, just as much as the major points. He had a famous credo: if everyone knows something to be true, it is usually wrong. He was the editorial conscience of the program, and staff continued to revere him long after he left. Even though the very first *fifth estate* program ended in a losing lawsuit, Haggart was proud that in his 13 years with the show, there were only two others that went to trial. One resulted in a win, and one a further loss.

Lawsuits weren't the only challenge to the *fifth estate*'s aggressive style of journalism. The business community was angered by the increased scrutiny and what it considered a bias. More than 20 companies and business associations decided to fight back. In 1978, they formed a group called the Ad Hoc Committee for Improved Business Reporting. Members included many of Canada's largest corporations, such as Royal Bank, CNR, Canadian Pacific, General Foods, Inco, McCain Foods, Redpath Industries, Seagrams, Bell, and others. A number of business associations representing bankers, manufacturers, advertisers, and retailers also joined. The committee prepared briefs and made appearances before regulatory bodies, challenging what it considered the CBC's lack of objectivity and anti-business bias.

In a brief called 'A Resumé for the CBC', the committee lambasted the corporation for ignoring its own policies when it came to dealing with business issues and companies. It warned the corporation that the attitude would lead to poor relations with the community. 'There currently exists a spirit of guarded and reluctant cooperation in the private sector with most requests for information or interviews made by the CBC. In fact—and most unfortunately—a number of companies now have a strict policy of non–co-operation with the CBC. The same policies and attitudes are not apparent for other media in Canada, including CTV. The CBC must already be aware that it is the only medium in Canada to earn this dubious distinction.'[25]

The committee listed six specific grievances, all of them containing what it felt was bias and a violation of the corporation's own policies. Half the examples were taken from *fifth estate* stories. It denounced the program's Noranda segment, which had featured criticism of the company's decision to invest in Chile, a country that had recently fallen into the hands of a military junta. It reserved its greatest objection to a comment by host Eric Malling, who had said at the conclusion of the piece: 'The appalling presumption of that guy from Noranda, now that the country is run by a bunch of bandits in their country. Of course, when it was a democratically elected government under Allende, that didn't represent the people at all. Why do we let these guys out?'

The committee also criticized the program's documentary on the sugar-refining industry, accusing Malling of changing the wording and tonal inflection of a question in a retaping of his questions. And it was vitriolic in its condemnation of 'Citizen

McCain', calling it 'an excellent example of lack of balanced journalism'. Interviews that favoured McCain were edited to show the company in a negative light, and McCain's critics were accepted and unchallenged, it said. It also objected to the use of the term 'corporate welfare' to describe government assistance the company had received.

Haggart wrote a spirited defence to the accusations, picking apart the inaccuracies in the committee's brief and refuting the allegations of bias. The Noranda story was correct, and the accusations of tampering with clips on the sugar piece were wrong, he said. On the McCain's story, he fought back with vigour. 'There is no doubt there was a great deal in the program McCain's profoundly wishes had been left unsaid. The program was an examination of the expenditure of public money, $10 million in direct grants (more than the annual budget of the CBC television current affairs department) plus much more public money at risk in loan guarantees. No one had ever reported these figures before. As a recipient of public money, we examined McCain's record in the fields of plant safety, labour relations, foreign acquisitions, producer relations, vertical integration, corporate concentration, and political relations. This was original reporting of the highest standard . . . this is tough, frank, accurate journalism.'[26]

Haggart's only concession came in response to the complaint about Malling's comment on the Noranda situation, which had even come under fire from a former director-general of the BBC. He said Malling's language was inelegant and excessively curt and abrupt, and it failed to fulfill the program's standards of clear, forceful, educated English. But Haggart could not stomach apologizing for a comment that characterized the Pinochet regime in Chile as a bunch of bandits. He said the intent and intellectual content of Malling's remark would have fallen within CBC's policy guideline that permits background and explanation, had it been phrased in a more refined way.

The pressure didn't come as a surprise to Herrndorf. He saw a pattern developing at *the fifth estate* of being tough on big businesses and corporate practices, and more sympathetic to individual entrepreneurs. 'To some degree, they were ahead of their time. Fifteen years later it became evident there was a fair amount of corporate abuse in terms of practices.' By 1979, when Herrndorf became a network vice-president, he faced regular pressures from corporations that were unhappy with coverage. The complaints took two forms. Most directly, there were threats to pull advertising from the network if a particular story moved forward. At a more sophisticated level, there might be a content analysis attempting to show bias on the part of a program or producer. For Herrndorf, the complaints were confirmation that the CBC was a major player with considerable influence in the discourse of the country. 'The trick for the CBC was to listen, take note of anything that seemed to make sense, and largely ignore any attempts to pressure it.'[27]

That was not always a simple task, since CBC executives were sensitive to the kind of lobbying that could have an impact on their political masters. While Herrndorf was building a new capacity for investigative work, he realized the process was making some of his superiors very nervous. 'A succession of CBC presidents found it difficult to deal with. Al Johnson (president from 1975 to 1982) often found it difficult to deal with the whole notion of investigative reporting.' Herrndorf pointed to the research Philip

Bob McKeown, Adrienne Clarkson, and Eric Malling, hosts of the fifth estate *in the early 1980s.* (CBC *Still Photo Collection*)

Mathias conducted into the allegations of sexual abuse by former Nova Scotia Premier Gerald Regan. Weeks of digging into the story made its way back to the CBC brass, and the story never made it to air. It took another 15 years for the program finally to look into the issue, complete with an examination into whether there was interference in the journalistic process in the first place.

One of the stranger events in the early history of *the fifth estate* was the effort by the CBC's own merchandising department to produce a book about the program. This came as a surprise to staff members, who learned about it through a memo from Sarty in March 1981. The unlikely author chosen for the task was Stephen Godfrey, a dance critic for the *Globe and Mail*. Sarty asked all employees to give him the benefit of their memories and memorabilia. In the meantime, CBC Enterprises proceeded to publicize the project in advance, assigning it a self-aggrandizing title: *fifth estate: the Award-Winning Current Affairs Show that Doesn't Just Report the News—It Makes the News*. More than 2,000 advance orders came in.

The idea of self-promotion on such a scale seemed odd to the program's team of professional skeptics. Their suspicion turned to dismay when they saw the first draft of the book. After wide consultations with program leaders and hosts, Godfrey was sent back to try again. His next version didn't change their opinions. No one wanted to see the book in anything resembling the form Godfrey had produced. Quietly, the project simply went away. A small piece by William French in the *Globe and Mail* said Godfrey had reportedly received $10,000 for his efforts, but was told the work wasn't needed. And part of the settlement stipulated he wasn't to talk about it. French coyly suggested the whole affair was a perfect topic for a *fifth estate* investigation.[28]

The episode remained clouded in mystery both inside the CBC and beyond. The idea that the CBC's premiere investigative program would somehow suppress a journalistic account of its own history struck many as ironic and unusual. Eric Malling kept the first draft of Godfrey's book, along with many of the internal memos that flew back and forth about it in 1981 and 1982. After his death in 1998, his papers were deposited at the University of Regina's archives. Explanations about the mysterious disappearance of the book, which continued to be advertised on some online bookstores, are contained in Malling's records.

Godfrey approached the task as a journalist, interviewing many of the people on staff and some who had since left the program. He wasn't interested in hagiography. Instead, he tried to explore some of the conflicts and controversies the program had encountered over the years. For the most part, it was a highly laudatory account, almost fawning in parts. But he was also critical in some areas, and downright nasty when it came to one or two incidents in the program's history. By allowing the key program staff to vet the script, Godfrey was in the uncomfortable position most journalists seek to avoid—submitting to pre-publication review. The results were predictable. Everyone had a complaint. Some were trivial; others were substantive. Many were vicious.

Malling said the book was flat, difficult to read, incomprehensible in parts, and filled with factual errors. He accused Godfrey of 'making a goulash' of his quotes. He was also offended by Godfrey's statement that *fifth estate* producers actually write the scripts. Malling thought Godfrey should have said that producers '*may* write the script'. It was clear the topic was a sensitive one for Malling who, like all the hosts, came into each project usually after considerable research and production planning had already taken place. In practice, producers often drafted initial copies of scripts, and sometimes crafted final ones. Each host worked differently, and some had more journalistic involvement than others. 'I appreciate and commend SG's efforts to show how important the producer is to our show and to individual items, but I resent him crediting the producer with all decisions throughout his discussion of the items.'[29]

Malling had his lawyer look at the manuscript, particularly in light of a lawsuit the program and Malling were facing at the time. The suit, among other things, complained about harassment. Malling's lawyer said passages of the book painted him as an aggressive and even pushy investigative questioner, which 'could lead to all kinds of cross-examination of Mr Malling which we would prefer to avoid'. He also objected to the book's discussion of clandestine filming, stakeouts, and hidden cameras as part of the program's techniques. Godfrey had offered the opinion that even the most innocent victim would appear guilty when confronted without warning by a camera. The less the plaintiffs know about how the program actually worked, Malling's lawyer said, the easier it would be to defend the action. As a result, he recommended deleting 13 entire pages from the book.

Adrienne Clarkson was just as dismissive as Malling, accusing Godfrey of not understanding or liking television. She said his draft was tedious and banal, and misquoted her. 'Even the compliments in this book are off-key, more tuned to confirming stereotype than to meting just praise. The kind of compliments dished out here aren't the type that ring true; they're thrown out like gobs of candy floss.' Clarkson's greatest venom was reserved for Godfrey's analysis of the 'Citizen McCain' item of 1976. In his first draft, Godfrey called it 'one of the most flawed of *the fifth estate* stories'. He accused the program of misleading the McCains about the nature of the story, and taking quotes out of context. 'It hit hard in all directions, and rarely found its target. . . . Like all *fifth estate* stories, the facts it presented were scrupulously researched. But they were obscured by the omissions and innuendos that were scattered through the story.' Godfrey said the item 'seemed more of an attack on modern capitalism than on one of its prime exponents'.[30] Even though the language was toned down in the second draft, at the insistence of program producers, it remained critical of the supposed flaws in the piece.

'I gave a lot of blood on that item', Clarkson said in her memo, adding that she couldn't stand by and allow Godfrey to vilify it. She insisted the McCain story was an important one that broke new ground. 'The strident tone of this chapter may not owe everything to objective critical analysis', Clarkson said. 'Harrison McCain and the writer's father, Senator John Godfrey, have both been long connected as Liberal Party bag men and friends. Enough said.'

The most damning indictment of Godfrey's book came from Haggart, whose typically elegant prose was spiced with indignant barbs. Bill Morgan, CBC's head of current affairs, met with Haggart on 15 December 1981 and asked him to prepare a briefing paper on the book. Two days later, Haggart delivered a six-page, single-spaced document that must surely have put an end to the project immediately. He reiterated and reinforced the other criticisms from the unit about factual errors and misquotes, noting that Godfrey didn't use a tape recorder for any of his interviews. He then launched into a frontal attack on Godfrey that would have outraged the writer if the document had ever become public.

Stephen Godfrey is not an accomplished reporter. . . . Stephen Godfrey is a pedestrian, flat, and unimaginative writer. . . . Stephen Godfrey's command of the cliché is absolute. . . . Stephen Godfrey has absolutely no concept of defamation or the law of libel. . . . The author has absolutely no sense of history, no sense of the history of broadcasting. . . . Stephen Godfrey is lost, completely and hopelessly lost, in the technology of broadcasting. . . . Stephen Godfrey is both confused and intellectually dishonest. . . . The only cogent case I have heard for the immediate publication of this book is that it would be embarrassing to delay it and might subject the CBC to criticism. This position makes the assumption that a bureaucratic enterprise, once undertaken, proceeds by the force of its own momentum, regardless of its worth. This may well be an acceptable way to plan an invasion of Gallipoli or of Dieppe, but it is not the proper way to publish a book.[31]

Haggart recommended the CBC pay Godfrey an additional 25 per cent of his fee to sign a new contract that would bring in a different writer. Godfrey could then have a joint byline or no byline, at his option. But all the criticism put an end to the deal, and the CBC braced for any hint that the whole fiasco could go public. Nine months later, Haggart wrote a confidential memo to Morgan with the warning that the *Globe* would likely be writing about the book deal soon. He prepared a response, part of which read: 'The book was not killed; it was suspended. The CBC owns the material and may try again with a more experienced author. It still may be able to do so at a modest profit.'

No book on *the fifth estate* was ever published.

Still, no additional self-promotion was needed to safeguard the program from losing its reputation of producing high-quality investigative work. In the early 1980s, it drew huge audiences with items about the assassination of John F. Kennedy and an exposé of how nature programs captured dramatic animal footage by faking scenes. And arguably the most celebrated item in the program's history was a documentary produced by John Zaritsky called 'Just Another Missing Kid'.

Zaritsky told the story of 19-year-old Eric Wilson of Ottawa, who took his Volkswagen van on the road in 1978 for a summer school course in Boulder, Colorado. Somewhere in Nebraska, he lost contact with his family, and they never heard from him again. They soon began receiving his credit card slips with forged signatures on them. Police agencies in the US were of no help in locating Eric, so his father and brother began investigating on their own. They hired a private eye, and the facts began to emerge. Wilson's van turned up in Maine, driven by career criminal Raymond Hatch. But law enforcement authorities felt they didn't have enough to charge him with Wilson's disappearance. Only after persistent work was the family able to show that Hatch and an accomplice had kidnapped and murdered Wilson. He was eventually charged with second-degree murder.[32]

The facts were woven into a dramatic detective story, with the family members as heroes battling an indifferent legal bureaucracy. Zaritsky had honed his investigative skills with the *Hamilton Spectator* and the *Globe and Mail*, but in a few short years with the CBC he had mastered the art of making documentaries. The result was a film that drew critical praise when it was broadcast on *the fifth estate*, and wider acclaim when it was released in theatres in the US. It went on to become the only CBC current affairs documentary ever to win an Academy Award, and it spawned an American made-for-TV movie called *Into Thin Air*.

Compared to Zaritsky's Oscar-winning film, *the fifth estate*'s 'Tainted Tuna' documentary was a workman-like piece of television. But it had phenomenal impact, demonstrating the program's power in affecting public policy. In September 1985, Eric Malling reported on the trouble Star-Kist Tuna was having with federal fisheries inspectors. Two years earlier, inspectors began rejecting cans of tuna coming from the company's New Brunswick plant. Although the fish was not dangerous to human health, inspectors felt some of the cans were tainted by decomposition and other defects. A power struggle ensued between the company and the fisheries inspectors. Star-Kist lobbied New Brunswick Premier Richard Hatfield to intervene, even threatening to close its 400-worker plant.

Hatfield appealed to John Fraser, fisheries minister in the government of Brian Mulroney. Fraser determined there were different opinions about the state of the tuna in question. He overruled his own inspectors, gave the benefit of doubt to the company, and released one million cans of tuna his own department had declared unfit because of decomposition. A calm but persistent Malling grilled Fraser about his decision, suggesting the minister might want to fire his own inspectors if he didn't trust their judgment. He even accused Fraser of 'knuckling under' to the pressure exercised by Hatfield. Fraser appeared abrasive and arrogant in the interview. 'What else is a minister supposed to do', he demanded of Malling. 'This isn't political interference. That's just the ordinary way you try to run a country.'[33]

If this were just another political controversy, it might have blown over in a day or two. But it involved tuna, a staple for many Canadians, and viewers couldn't stomach the idea of a politician deciding what they could eat when his own inspectors had declared the product unfit. Parliament was in an uproar the next day. Opposition leader John Turner borrowed liberally from Malling's own terminology in denouncing the fisheries minister: 'Get that tuna off the Canadian shelves. You knuckled under to Premier Hatfield. You put politics before the health of this country.'[34] Fraser gamely tried to defend his decision, but the heat was too intense. Two days after the broadcast, he reversed his action and ordered the million cans of tuna recalled. Still, he wasn't making any apologies. 'I regret very much that the consequences of a television program put a lot of Canadians in a state of anxiety', he said, adding that he was still eating the tuna in question.[35]

The recall didn't end the controversy. The opposition demanded to know when Mulroney learned of the decision to approve the tainted fish. Even though Fraser had indicated the Prime Minister's Office was aware of the decision, Mulroney distanced himself from the whole affair, saying it was 'pretty damned obvious' the tuna should never have been released to supermarkets. That comment decided Fraser's fate. He resigned from cabinet a few days later, and Mulroney himself offered to step down if anyone could prove he knew about the scandal before the CBC broadcast. No one ever did, but Tunagate, as the media dubbed it, hounded Mulroney for months. When the prime minister attended a playoff baseball game in Toronto soon afterwards, fans chanted: 'Tuna. Tuna.'

It was a triumphant result for Malling, whose unique approach and charming style had driven the success of many *fifth estate* stories since he first joined the program in its second season. But he would soon begin to worry about the program's ability to sustain its momentum. By 1988, he felt the show looked dated. 'It lacks energy. It rarely makes news. It seems to have lost the edge', he wrote in an internal analysis.[36] Malling noted that the program had lost 100,000 viewers in the previous two years, though still registering an impressive 1.4 million. But he lamented that the sharp and energetic people who used to make a real effort to watch the show no longer did so, and he even quoted the mother of fellow host Bob McKeown as saying: 'Your show doesn't seem to be as interesting as it used to be.'

Malling came to the conclusion the program wasn't doing enough investigative journalism. His content analysis seemed to bear out the judgment. In the program's third season, three-quarters of all the stories had dealt with public issues or investigative reports. There were a similar number in the fourth season. But that had changed significantly a decade later. 'In the past year we did nine investigative items (out of 65) . . . most of them pretty feeble as that category goes.' Instead, he said the program was focusing too heavily on stories dealing with disease and crime. 'They are always easy stories, but surely not our bread and butter . . . *fifth estate* was not created to broadcast a steady diet of tabloid-type stories. The reputation of *the fifth estate* is as an investigative program.'[37] Malling's 26-page analysis suggested sweeping changes, from the way stories were selected and presented to the manner in which staff development and program budgeting were conducted.

Management recognized that the program needed to strengthen its roots, and a year later Kelly Crichton was hired as executive producer. But Malling remained restless, and he was soon lobbying for a new program he wanted to call *Edges*. He felt traditional current affairs programs should be exposing, not confirming, conventional wisdom. It was a contrarian approach that he would soon take over to CTV and a rebranded *W5 with Eric Malling*.

The era of Malling, Ron Haggart, and Robin Taylor had ended, and Crichton began building a new team to take the show into the 1990s. CBC news veteran David Nayman became senior producer. The program retained its reputation as a natural home for the country's most talented investigative journalists. Linden MacIntyre joined the program as a host, and despite their lack of television experience, Crichton also brought newspaper reporters Victor Malarek and Stevie Cameron on board. Though Cameron had made a successful career of exposing political patronage, and loved her job at the *Globe and Mail*, she couldn't resist making the jump to *the fifth estate*. From Thames Television, Crichton also hired the talented Neil Docherty, who produced a series of provocative documentaries including the Emmy-award winning 'To Sell a War', which exposed the Kuwaiti royal family's public relations campaign to sell Americans on the 1991 war against Iraq. Docherty's film, 'The Trouble with Evan', was a groundbreaking glimpse into the life of an ordinary family and the continuous stream of verbal abuse heaped on an 11-year-old boy. It was a unique form of inquiry into a seemingly mundane reality, using surveillance cameras with the approval of the subjects. In the end, it captured a terrifying picture of parents abusing their child, with statements like: 'I would like to lock you up in a cage and let everybody look at you like you're an animal.' Docherty continued to produce acclaimed documentaries for *the fifth estate*, often co-producing them with PBS newsmagazine *Frontline* and other international broadcasters and newspapers.

Under executive producer David Studer, who succeeded Crichton, *the fifth estate* continued to broadcast detailed investigative journalism, from exposés of government corruption to inquiries into flaws in Canada's justice system. Over the years, audience fragmentation and the huge growth of specialty channels led to fewer viewers and increased competition from different genres of American programming. A continuous debate raged about what the right mix of programming ought to be for programs like *the fifth estate*. Some considered public policy investigations to be crucial to its mandate, no matter how difficult it was to find dramatic characters and illustrative storylines, while others favoured topics that more easily lent themselves to entertaining storytelling. The program's original bible suggested the show should be prepared to spend an average of three weeks on most of its stories, and up to seven or eight weeks on a major story. In fact, some complex *fifth estate* investigations have taken a year or more, a process not always appreciated by some CBC managers who demanded a more tangible return on resource investment.

Perhaps the most cogent analysis of the program's mandate came in an internal document prepared by CBC management in 1993 for the CBC's board of directors. At a time when cuts to the CBC's budget were the order of the day, the document compared production costs for *the fifth estate* and CTV's *W5*. The numbers showed 32 staff for the CBC program compared to 22 for CTV's, but in the bottom-line cost per 1,000 viewers, the totals were roughly equal. The accompanying notes to the board made it clear that the two programs, while superficially similar, were very different in some important ways. The principal distinction between the two shows, it said, is *the fifth estate*'s concentration on investigative journalism, 'by far the most difficult and demanding form of journalism'. While it acknowledged that CTV did some investigative work, it said *the fifth estate*'s primary focus was a tighter one.

'In both its own view and that of its audience, *the fifth estate* is first and foremost an original investigative program which deals with the use and abuse of power in our society, seeing as its mandate the critical examination of cases in which something has gone wrong with the system.'[38] How this analysis played out at the board of directors meetings isn't known. But *the fifth estate* has continued to be the cornerstone of CBC's current affairs programming, just as Peter Herrndorf had envisioned in 1975.

W5, meanwhile, remains the longest-running program of its kind in Canada. CTV executive Robert Hurst attributes the success to its adaptability. The program, now called *W-FIVE*, went through several format and time slot changes over the years. Hurst says: 'The problem with TV public affairs programs that die is they become disconnected from

Victor Malarek's career in investigative journalism included work at the Montreal Star, Globe and Mail, CBC, *and* CTV. *(CBC Still Photo Collection)*

their viewers; whereas every few years *W-FIVE* has gone through a remake, a reenergization and a review of its place in Canadian television public affairs and documentary work.'[39] Executive producer Malcolm Fox, who joined the program in 1983, believes *W-FIVE* is more focused in its approach than *the fifth estate*. 'The key word for us is: How relevant is this to Canadians? Are we going to get a million bums in the seats to watch this?' Even though the program has been moved into different time slots over the years, it manages to retain a large audience with its populist fare.

The early efforts of those in public broadcasting to create challenging journalism were dealt a blow by CBC management's decision to cancel *This Hour Has Seven Days* in 1966. The struggle was a classic case of conflict between an institution reluctant to disturb the status quo and a group of journalists who were intent on improving their social practice, in this case the practice of vigorous journalism that held government and powerful interests to account. The cancellation left bitter feelings for years, and dampened the enthusiasm of many CBC producers. Even as the CBC retreated, the private networks recognized a commercial opportunity. CTV created *W5* in the same year as *Seven Days* died, and it remained successful over the years. The hour-long magazine program appeared to be a valuable genre, and CTV was eager to exploit its revenue potential. The CBC's experimentation served as an inspiration to CBS as well, which created *60 Minutes* in 1968. By the early 1970s, as the success of alternative media exposés was influencing more investigative work in the mainstream, the CBC still appeared stalled.

The situation changed in 1975, when Peter Herrndorf created a program that included investigative journalism as a key component. The work processes and methodologies established by *the fifth estate* were unique in Canada, and it brought television investigative journalism to a more professional plateau. Institutional and external challenges remained. On the one hand, powerful corporate forces complained that the program was biased against them, while internal pressures to promote entertainment values and draw large audiences were always present. CTV continued to recognize that the genre had commercial appeal, and has restructured *W5* many times in a successful effort to retain its popularity. While Canadian newsmagazine programs have generally avoided the celebrity journalism common in the US, CTV has put more emphasis on inspirational and populist stories. With each passing year, the portion of CBC Television's budget that comes from advertising and other non-governmental funds increases, inevitably introducing more private sector values into programming decisions. In recent years, *the fifth estate* has focused on hour-long dramatic tales that embody 'movie of the week' storytelling qualities. For producers whose inclination is to research investigative projects no matter what the entertainment potential, the challenges are significant. The competitive need on the part of both public and private networks to gain a large audience share means crucial but non-visual investigations often do not get commissioned. For instance, *W-FIVE*'s Malcolm Fox says it is unlikely he would have pursued a topic as important, but difficult to tell, as the sponsorship scandal. 'Will a million people watch? That's the question we ask. This is private TV, and we're in the business of selling ads.'[40]

Investigative Reporting and Mass Appeal

When *W-FIVE* began investigating the safety record of U-Haul trucks in 2005, program producers weren't surprised to find problems. After all, Ontario Provincial Police had seen routine safety failures at their roadside checks over the years. Between 2002 and 2004, police had checked 220 U-Haul trucks. Nearly half the trucks failed safety inspections. The Ontario Safety League found similar results, prompting the province's transportation ministry to check nearly 700 trucks from 14 rental companies. U-Haul's failure rate was four times the industry average. There were motorists across Ontario who had individual horror stories about their rentals. 'But does U-Haul have a poor safety record across the country?' asked Victor Malarek in the October 2005 broadcast. '*W-FIVE* took the case on the road to find out.'

With 1,500 locations across the country, U-Haul was the largest moving-vehicle rental company in Canada. *W-FIVE* conducted a simple test. The program rented vehicles in four different provinces, and then took them for independent safety checks. Four vans were tested in Vancouver, and all four failed the test. Vehicles did not measure up to provincial safety standards. The problems ranged from defective lights and batteries to leaky brakes and bad steering. One truck even needed to be boosted when it was at the shop. The pattern repeated itself in other cities. There were four more tests in Montreal, and four more failures. Four vans were rented in Toronto, and they also failed. So did the single van that was rented in Calgary. In total, of 13 vans the program tested, not a single vehicle passed the minimum standard required in its province of origin. The average age of the vehicles tested was 15 years, and each had more than 200,000 kilometres on the odometer.

The program interviewed a former U-Haul employee in silhouette. She said the company never made safety a priority. Malarek confronted U-Haul's Canadian district vice-president with the results. 'You've got to be lucky, I mean really lucky nobody's been killed or seriously hurt on the roads', Malarek said. 'You're right, you know', replied Claude Boucher. 'We're not proud of our safety record.' For Malarek and the *W-FIVE* team, it was a prototypical segment— straightforward and populist storytelling designed to be of interest to thousands of Canadians. U-Haul has since claimed to have put hundreds of new vehicles on the road, closed down problematic dealerships, and addressed other safety concerns. But subsequent investigations, by *W-FIVE* and other media outlets, have continued to highlight problems with the company's road safety record.

Chapter 10

Dirty Tricks

I sought (what Galsworthy) called 'the significant trifle'—the bit of dialogue, the overlooked fact, the buried observation, which illuminated the realities of the situation.

I.F. Stone[1]

Deep in the clandestine bureaucracy of the RCMP's Security Service, in the middle of 1975, an alarm bell was ringing. A troublesome and potentially perilous American phenomenon was spreading to Canada, and the Mounties were ready to respond.

'As in the case of the US, there is a growing trend in Canada towards investigative reporting', said the Security Service internal memorandum, stamped Secret. 'No doubt this trend in Canada has been given impetus by exposure in the US press of the so-called Pentagon Papers and the Watergate scandal.'[2] The author wasn't merely lamenting the rise of a more aggressive form of reporting in both countries. The concern was more practical. 'The purpose of this paper is to provide some comments regarding the exposure of methods and techniques of the intelligence community as a result of pressure by the media. . . . Regardless of what may be the motivation behind the media exposés, whether the motivation be ideological, anti-establishment, or professional ambition on the part of the reporter, the result is the same. At the very least, such publicity must sensitize individuals and groups of security interests to our methods and techniques; this makes the role of monitoring them increasingly more difficult.'

The author of the memo could not have been more prescient. Around the same time it was being circulated in RCMP ranks, a *Vancouver Sun* journalist was moving to Ottawa to take up a new posting as parliamentary reporter. He would soon be digging into the very methods and techniques the Security Service desperately wanted to keep under wraps. In the end, his work would lead to some of the most startling and controversial revelations in the history of Canadian journalism, setting off a process that culminated in the dismantling and reorganization of the Security Service itself.

In many respects, John Sawatsky is the most pre-eminent investigative journalist Canada has produced. In his penchant for going after stories the rest of the media weren't adequately covering, he tackled topics other reporters would have considered impossible to crack. His newspaper articles and subsequent books about the RCMP and Canada's spy-watchers provided a window into Canada's most secretive agency. His book on lobbying in Ottawa highlighted details of the lucrative and sometimes insidious relationships between business and government. And his research work into Prime Minister Brian Mulroney was a textbook example of an investigative biography that presented fresh insights into the country's most powerful politician.

All the while, Sawatsky developed a methodology of investigative work that tried to put research on a more scientific footing. His ideas about organization and classification of material, along with the mindset he brought to approaching sources, were important factors in his success at ferreting out information. Most importantly, he became a student of the mechanics and linguistics of the interview. He demonstrated, in both theory and practice, that the specific sequencing and wording of questions was crucial in providing the highest quality of journalistic information.

Sawatsky was born into a large Mennonite family in Winkler, Manitoba in 1948. In 1936, his parents began having children every even-numbered year, and John was the seventh of eight. His father had given up farming to open a photo studio and then a car dealership, but the harsh Manitoba winters encouraged the family to look west. A severe snowstorm that stranded Sawatsky and his parents in a car between snowdrifts for several hours was the breaking point. They moved to Abbotsford, BC in 1956 where his father established a raspberry farm. John was sent to a private Mennonite school.[3]

He wasn't a stellar student. Sawatsky initially failed grade 12 English, and his marks were barely good enough to qualify for a university system that was lowering entrance requirements and throwing its doors open for all students. One of his principal passions in high school was politics, and Sawatsky became an avid follower of news and radio open-line shows. He was ambitious and knew he wanted to go to the city, but wasn't sure yet what career path to follow. Journalism was not yet even a consideration. The lack of focus and his quixotic nature extended to his choice of university as well. He took the bus to Vancouver with the aim of registering for university, went to West Hastings Street and whimsically decided to take the first bus that came, no matter which direction it took him. An eastbound bus would take him to Simon Fraser University, a westbound one to the University of British Columbia. The first bus went east, so Sawatsky registered at Simon Fraser, and he credits the chance occurrence with setting him on a career in journalism.[4]

But the path was far from direct. Sawatsky quickly ran out of money, and began living in his van in the university parking lot. After three months, security guards banished him from the lot, so he moved to the forest south of the university. This went on for four months until municipal officials finally declared his arrangement a fire hazard, ordering him out of the bush. Around the same time, Sawatsky learned that members of student council were assigned offices. So he ran in a by-election in the spring of 1970, promptly won, and lived for the next few months in his office.

It was at his very first council meeting that a kind of epiphany occurred. Sawatsky looked over to the press table where he saw one lonely reporter for *The Peak*, Simon Fraser's student newspaper. 'I just remember that was the moment it hit, I'm sitting at the wrong table, I shouldn't be here, I should be over there.'[5] Sawatsky was drinking in the freedom and new ideas Simon Fraser offered. He headed to the library every day to read newspapers from across North America. He had a desire to make a contribution to society, and journalism seemed like a route to accomplish it. His exuberance led him to join *The Peak* without bothering to leave student council. He even covered a council meeting himself once, playing the role of newsmaker and journalist simultaneously. But it was a penchant for digging out new information that drove his work. Soon he became the newspaper's most widely read columnist. Students would get their tabloid, turn to the back page, and see what Sawatsky's column had exposed.

One of his biggest scoops involved the head of Simon Fraser's education department. Sawatsky discovered he had secretly taken another appointment at the University of Washington in Seattle, arranging his schedule so that he could be in the US Tuesdays and Thursdays and back at Simon Fraser the rest of the week. A long-distance call from Vancouver to Seattle was costly at the time, so Sawatsky had to clear the expense before going ahead. But when the story was published, it was a genuine scandal. The culprit was removed from his position, and the power of Sawatsky's pen was recognized both by students and staff.

Even more popular with students was Sawatsky's muckraking examination of library fines. Like many universities, Simon Fraser would withhold student marks and delay graduation if fines were not paid. Sawatsky wondered what the penalty was for faculty who didn't settle their fines, and found out there was none. He went further, managing to get a copy of the computer printouts of all outstanding fines. On the list were several departmental chairs, some deans, and the university's vice-president. Sawatsky published the list, and basked in the outrage that followed. The university senate held a special investigation and hearings, eventually changing the lending system to allow patrons to keep books until another lender requested them.

As he drew closer to graduating, it seemed natural for Sawatsky to look for a career in journalism. While at *The Peak*, he had taken one of his exclusive stories to the *Vancouver Sun*, and became the newspaper's part-time Simon Fraser reporter. Early in 1973, he joined full time. And he quickly realized that despite his university reputation, he needed to improve his skills. 'I don't think I had a method back then. I didn't even have a concept of journalism. That came later. I'm not a natural writer. I have a lousy memory. I'm not quick-witted. Quite the opposite. All the natural tools that you should have, I didn't have.'[6]

His first realization was that daily journalism had a narrow, 24-hour outlook. Stories were pitched, researched, written, and published all within a day, and the next morning the process began all over again with a clean slate. Few reporters had the drive or the opportunity to go beyond the daily cycle. Sawatsky wanted to track developments over time, and build up an expertise that could enhance his reporting. His first victory on that front was to secure a drawer in a newsroom filing cabinet where he could keep notes. The second was to assign himself a beat so that he could move beyond the superficiality of covering stories every day with no grounding in the intricacies of the subject matter. He decided he would cover the energy beat, a fortuitous choice in a year when oil prices and energy generally would become one of the biggest topics in the news.

Sawatsky's other central insight was into the methodology of reporting. 'I'd come back from stories, and I simply didn't know what the story was. Too much had happened. I spent all my efforts taking notes. I couldn't write fast enough. I couldn't decipher my notes. My handwriting was lousy.' The solution was simple, but Sawatsky believes he was the first print reporter in Vancouver to begin using a tape recorder consistently for interviews. His first was a cheap one that failed at a critical time. Then he invested in a $200 Sony recorder, a considerable expense for the thrifty reporter who was only making $125 a week at the time. But he never regretted the purchase, and it changed his outlook on journalism. He believes it allowed him to break stories that other reporters missed. And it also gave him insight into his own skills at approaching and questioning sources, a process that he would refine later in his career.

Energy continued to dominate the headlines when Dave Barrett's NDP government created the BC Petroleum Corporation as the sole Crown agency buying all the natural gas in the province. Sawatsky believed in the concept of public control, and when the agency approached him with the offer of a job, he took it, becoming the corporation's research coordinator. It was a heady time, and it thrust him into the highest echelons of power in the province. He worked closely with the corporation's chief, who in turn was a confidante to the premier, and he would often be involved in briefings at Barrett's office. But the lure of public service through journalism remained stronger. Sawatsky didn't feel the same kind of excitement he did when uncovering an important story. After nine months, he returned to the *Sun*. In retrospect, Sawatsky didn't regret taking the job, because he knew that journalists always wonder what life is like on the other side of the press table. He briefly scratched the itch, and it was gone.

The *Sun* assigned Sawatsky to Parliament Hill, and in the summer of 1975 he headed to Ottawa, happy to be able to put his love of politics and his political science degree to good use. He found a press gallery whose members rarely left the Hill or dug beneath the stories being served up daily by official sources. The *Sun* was expanding its bureau and didn't rely on him for daily coverage, so he had the freedom to look around for meatier stories. He found one in the sale of a Canadian CANDU nuclear reactor to Argentina, and a government cover-up over how high the costs might go. Then, he turned his attention to an institution that was beginning to come under increasing scrutiny, the RCMP. There were criticisms about how the force was investigating a bribery scandal involving a Montreal senator and a company trying to extend its lease for an airport retail shop. And there was a tantalizing hint of a more serious scandal: illegal break-ins by the police.

The unraveling of the RCMP's reputation began with an accident in the summer of 1974. A man was caught planting a bomb at the home of a Montreal supermarket executive. In fact, the bomb had gone off prematurely in the man's hand, causing painful but not life-threatening injuries. Police arrested him and found he was no ordinary suspect. The bomber turned out to be Constable Robert Samson, a member of the RCMP's clandestine Security Service. It appeared he was moonlighting as an agent for a Quebec Mafia boss. By the time his case went to trial, in March 1976, Samson was getting more talkative than his RCMP bosses would have liked. The bombing, likely a freelance effort to discredit a militant strike by supermarket workers, was one matter, but he said he had done far worse things while employed at the RCMP. He mentioned, specifically, an illegal break-in at the offices of a left-wing Montreal group to steal some of their documents and files.

The incident he described occurred in October 1972, just four months after the Watergate break-in. It had been an illegal operation coordinated by the RCMP, the Quebec Provincial Police, and the Montreal municipal police. The target of the break-in, the Agence de Presse Libre du Québec (APLQ), realized police must have been involved because robbers had taken documents but left money and other valuables behind. The group called a press conference to accuse police of wrongdoing, but the media paid virtually no attention. Even when Samson referred to it in his court case, there was just momentary media interest. 'It was written off as a few overzealous policemen exceeding their mandate. A few days later the matter was dropped', Sawatsky later wrote.[7]

But Sawatsky's work was just beginning. He began his inquiry broadly, trying to find out how the RCMP worked and what its history was. 'I knew nothing about the Mounties. I didn't know the difference between a corporal and a colonel. The first thing I did was to go to the Library of Parliament and looked up stuff.' He came across the Royal Commission on Security, which had published a report in 1969. Half way through the hundreds of numbered paragraphs was a statement that made him sit up and take notice. 'It said that it's inevitable a security service will break the spirit of the law if not the letter of the law. It never occurred to me at that time that it could happen in the RCMP. That report was published in 1969; news stories were written, but no one had picked up on that. I said to myself: they're saying there's illegal activity here; I'm going to find it.'

Even so, he tried to approach his investigation with no preconceived notions. He went to the RCMP directly, but they refused to be interviewed. Then he sought out the opponents and the dissidents. Conservative MP Elmer MacKay was a constant critic, and he provided some leads. MacKay had championed the case of two Mounties who had been thrown out of the Security Service, and Sawatsky interviewed them as well. He began approaching current and former Security Service personnel with the seemingly impossible task of getting them to talk about the most secretive affairs of the RCMP. Sawatsky said he needed the same kind of skills and patience he had honed selling encyclopedias in high school. While many people instantly say no, a handful leave the door open. He found some RCMP officers were eager to talk, telling him things they had never revealed even to their wives. He believed the professionalism of the approach, and a neutral, non-judgmental demeanour, were critical in winning the confidence of so many officers.

Sawatsky spent weeks chasing the APLQ story, trying to confirm what many considered to be an outlandish accusation by Robert Samson. Though he had arrived in Ottawa not knowing a single word of French, he found himself in Montreal trying to coax French-speaking Mounties to unload their secrets in English. Slowly, he accumulated enough information to corroborate the story. But there was a nagging doubt, as a current member of the force continued to deny adamantly that the operation had happened. Sawatsky went to one of the former Mounties who was providing him with information, asked him to call the current officer and tape-record the conversation. Sure enough, the same officer who was denying it to Sawatsky not only confirmed the story privately but also bragged about the operation.

When the story finally appeared in the *Vancouver Sun* on 7 December 1976, Sawatsky had enough information to accuse police of an illegal break-in and a subsequent cover-up. What's more, he showed how higher authorities had directed the plan, called Operation Bricole, and how headquarters in Ottawa knew about the incident soon afterwards. 'It was the first public evidence of a Watergate in Canada since RCMP management had been for the first time implicated in methodical illegal activity.'[8] To Sawatsky's amazement, Canadian Press didn't carry the story. Even though the *Sun* had splashed it across the front page complete with a copyright, the major national media organizations were reluctant to run with the information. Faith in the RCMP was so strong that it seemed preposterous to think the organization could be deliberately involved in flagrant law breaking. Sawatsky remembered giving his story to a prominent press gallery journalist on the day it came out, only to have him hand it back as he rushed to cover the routine rhetoric of the day's question period. He had even leaked the story to Tommy Douglas of the NDP, hoping it would trigger a question in the House. Douglas called back later in the day to tell him his caucus had decided to go with a question on housing policy instead.

The incident illustrated a typical occurrence in the world of competitive journalism. Faced with a scoop by a competitor, especially on a story that is difficult to duplicate independently, many journalists will simply ignore the issue altogether. Sometimes an extraordinary exclusive by a regional newspaper or broadcast outlet will be shunned on the basis that it couldn't possibly reflect accurately on the national scene. This is especially true of the major national media players, who largely determine the agenda. Sawatsky would routinely break important stories, only to have them ignored. When the Toronto media occasionally picked up his stories, they would draw attention and be raised in Parliament. But stories that are not followed can soon become non-stories, much to the delight of the targets of the investigations.

Sawatsky was determined not to let that happen with his RCMP investigation. His initial series won the Michener Award for journalism that year, with judges praising his tenacity and skill at finding the information.[9] National media attention on RCMP wrongdoing didn't really escalate until May 1977, when three police officers pleaded guilty to failing to obtain a search warrant in the APLQ case. They were given discharges and allowed to return to their duties, and the federal government repeatedly claimed the APLQ case was an isolated and exceptional one. But Sawatsky had already shown that it signaled the presence of systemic illegality within the RCMP. Quebec and Ottawa set up separate inquiries into RCMP wrongdoing, and soon further tales of illegal activities were emerging.

Realizing that revelations would be coming, especially from the Parti Québécois-appointed Keable commission in Quebec, the federal government began making admissions of its own. Solicitor General Francis Fox announced in the fall of 1977 that the Security Service had secretly stolen the PQ membership list years earlier in a clandestine venture known as Operation Ham. Other journalists joined in the investigation. At *the fifth estate*, Joe MacAnthony applied his considerable research skills to uncover new details. Like Sawatsky, he began his work by visiting the Library of Parliament in Ottawa, where he read more than 20 years of newspaper clippings about the RCMP. He built an inventory of every disgruntled and disaffected Mountie, and soon established a network of contacts across the country.[10] His work helped the CBC reveal the existence of Operation Cathedral, a longstanding scheme on the part of the RCMP to open mail illegally. There were stories about the RCMP burning a barn as a disruptive tactic, planting *agents provocateurs* in dissident groups, and stealing dynamite. The disclosures continued coming as the commissions heard more evidence.

Most reporters became content with covering the inquiries and reporting on the stories as they emerged in the testimony. But for Sawatsky, it was another example of how the media gravitated toward official sources. 'I really felt we had been handed information for too long', he said. 'I really believed we had to do investigating and not just totally accept what comes down. We were more than just secretaries. It's also our job to alert the public about what is going on. If we just accept information from establishment sources, we're allowing them to tell us what to cover.' He avoided attending the hearings, and he urged all his fellow journalists to rely less on officially sanctioned sources and more on independent investigation. The commissions became especially useful in an unexpected way. With each piece of new testimony, Sawatsky found more insiders willing to come out of the woodwork to dispute official statements or reveal their version of what had really taken place.

Sawatsky wanted to paint a complete picture of the RCMP Security Service, and decided a book was the best way to do it. The idea came from a Toronto publisher who called Sawatsky for advice on who might be capable of writing a book about the Mounties. He offered himself as the prime candidate, and the publisher arranged a $3,000 grant to help with the research. He realized the amount of time and effort needed to do a proper job made it a poor financial decision, but he felt the task had to be done. He took a leave of absence from the *Vancouver Sun* and threw himself into the work full time. He criss-crossed the country on his shoestring budget, interviewing current and former Mounties and tape-recording their answers, then meticulously transcribing the interviews. The methodology paid dividends, as with each new layer of understanding he achieved, Sawatsky would reread transcripts and find additional meaning in them.

When his book, *Men in the Shadows*, was released in March 1980, it stood out as a groundbreaking analysis of an important government institution that no one had written about before. It was a damning indictment of the RCMP, showing a history of wrongdoing stretching back decades. Among the revelations was a 1970 memo from the RCMP commissioner sanctioning illegal activity as a matter of policy. Still, Sawatsky was careful to maintain the disinterested posture of a social scientist and not an advocate. 'I have probably—but who knows for sure?—overstated the Security Service's weaknesses and understated its strengths. There is no mention of the fact that most Security Service members have qualities comprising of honesty and dedication, among others.'[11] He blamed the RCMP itself for not cooperating more fully with his research, and the 'inadequacies of journalism' for not presenting a fuller picture. Still, the even-handedness of the commentary and his neutral stance showed how he was able to win the confidence of so many working and retired officers.

The book gave a detailed guide to the Security Service's organizational structure and inner workings. It explained how the service's operations were specifically grouped into units devoted to counter-espionage, counter-subversion, electronic surveillance, physical surveillance, informants, counter-terrorism, and others. It detailed many illegal, clandestine activities never before revealed. The book showed how the CIA played an ongoing role in Canadian intelligence decisions, and how journalists were recruited as informers. The book, excerpted on its release in the *Toronto Star*, preceded the final reports of both RCMP inquiries. It gave the public a picture they had never seen before of their national police service.

While waiting for the book to be released, Sawatsky went back to work briefly at the *Vancouver Sun*. The newspaper had a new publisher, and Sawatsky was being recalled to Vancouver. Though he preferred Vancouver as a place to live, he realized that Ottawa was a more important location for his work. He quit in November 1979, and began working on a sequel to his book. He also developed a plan. He would do full-time investigative work and book writing for as long as his finances would allow, taking a newspaper reporting job only when he needed to supplement his income. As it turned out, he never had to return to newspapers full time.

Sawatsky considered his second book, *For Services Rendered*, his best work. It told the story of the RCMP's hunt for a KGB mole inside its ranks, and how that exercise ruined the RCMP career of Leslie James Bennett, the guru of Canadian counter-espionage. In the process, he continued the narrative of RCMP dirty tricks and illegal activities. 'Nobody has ever written a book quite like this in Canada', said Ian Adams in a *Globe and Mail* review. Adams was qualified to offer the opinion. He had written an earlier novel called *S: Portrait of a Spy*, with veiled references to Bennett. 'In terms of its revelations about the internal workings of the RCMP Security Services it is on par with the best books on the CIA.' But, as Adams noted, the American books were all written by insiders. 'Sawatsky is simply a freelance reporter, working alone, without the organizational support of a newspaper or a magazine, a fact which says a great deal about the corporate media. . . . John has given us what a Royal Commission would never do, the RCMP's secret case against Leslie James Bennett. *For Services Rendered* is a brilliant journalistic coup.'[12]

Sawatsky was the first to provide so much detail about how the RCMP hounded Bennett from his position as head of Russian counter-intelligence without any real evidence of treachery. It set in motion a long process that eventually led to Bennett's public exoneration.

But it was the story of James Morrison, code-named Long Knife, that generated most of the headlines surrounding *For Services Rendered*. In his research, Sawatsky had learned of a former Security Service corporal who had sold secret information to Soviet agents between 1955 and 1958. Morrison had been part of the RCMP's surveillance unit, following Soviet diplomats and agents around Ottawa. For $4,000, it was alleged, Morrison turned over sensitive information, including secret details about a KGB officer the Mounties had turned into a double agent. As a result of the betrayal, the officer had been recalled to Moscow for an uncertain fate. Although Morrison had been forced out of the RCMP, he was never charged with betraying state secrets and potentially putting someone's life at risk.

Finding Morrison after 25 years wasn't a simple task. The first obstacle was to overcome the assumption that someone like Morrison would never talk, an idea that prevents many journalists from making efforts to track down information. Sawatsky knew Morrison had served in World War II, so he surmised that he might be receiving a pension from the department of Veterans Affairs. He contacted the department and asked them to forward a letter to Morrison, assuming he was on their mailing list. A week later, Morrison called from a small town in BC where he worked as a safety officer for a construction company. It took all of Sawatsky's skills at handling sources and eliciting information to get the full story. He conducted three lengthy interviews in different locations. Finally, in return for a promise of anonymity, Morrison revealed the entire episode, and it became an important part of Sawatsky's book. With Sawatsky's help, *the fifth estate* interviewed a disguised Morrison on-camera just as the book was being released, and the story was also excerpted in the *Toronto Star*. Though the case was a quarter-century old, it caught the government and the RCMP off-guard, and the justice department re-opened its investigation into the Long Knife case.

Knowing the sensitivity of all the information he had collected, and his promises of confidentiality to many sources, Sawatsky took precautions. He carried key documents and records with him in a briefcase everywhere he went. Other documents were secretly stored in a neighbour's house across the street. Being such a prominent and public investigator of the RCMP, Sawatsky realized he would be under scrutiny himself. But he knew about the sheer cost and effort of physical surveillance, and didn't think it would be feasible for the RCMP to employ that tactic against him. Still, he wasn't oblivious to the possibility that the force would recruit people to feed him disinformation. And once the Long Knife story stirred so much controversy, he became aware of the likelihood of police intervention.

It came on a snowy April day in 1983. Sawatsky was at his Ottawa home, preparing to write up a loan application to finance future projects, when two Mounties appeared at his door with a warrant. They conducted a four-hour search, going through every drawer and file. He was confident they wouldn't find anything sensitive, until he realized to his dismay he had inadvertently left one copy of the first Long Knife interview in a drawer. As soon as they left, even before calling a lawyer, he phoned the CBC to warn them the Mounties might be on the way to conduct a similar search. They casually informed him the police had been there the day before. Had the CBC warned him immediately after that search, Sawatsky believes, he could have cleansed his house more thoroughly and avoided the disclosure of the transcript.

Two months later, police arrested Morrison and charged him under the Official Secrets Act with passing secret information to Soviet agents.[13] Sawatsky was critical of the action, saying the RCMP were wrong not to have charged him at the time, and again wrong to have done so after so many years had elapsed. In the drawn-out proceedings, Sawatsky was called to testify and repeatedly refused to answer questions that would compromise his confidential sources. The Crown didn't push the issue, and he was never cited for contempt. Eventually Morrison, at age 70, was sentenced to 18 months in jail for the episode.[14] But the two men retained a good relationship, a testament to the even-handed approach Sawatsky used in handling the research.

Sawatsky's legal problems also included a struggle with Igor Gouzenko, the Soviet cipher clerk who defected in 1945 and touched off a wave of Cold War spy hysteria. Gouzenko, who was notoriously litigious, claimed Sawatsky had defamed him. His death in 1982 put an end to the legal action, but Sawatsky had amassed a wealth of information in preparation for the defence. He turned the material into his third book, an oral history called *Gouzenko: The Untold Story*. But his success as a journalist and writer was beginning to turn his career in other directions, and away from the dogged pursuit of the RCMP. An offer to teach journalism part-time at Carleton University was the beginning of a long relationship, and an important stepping-stone to solidifying the theories he held about interviewing methodology.

Sawatsky had been fascinated with the mechanics of questions ever since he bought his first tape recorder and began listening to his own question lines. A shy person by nature, he could barely stand listening to his own voice. An initial observation was that the questions were random and not complete, so an obvious first solution was to prepare question lists before going into an interview. But it was the wording of the questions themselves that really intrigued him. This came into sharper focus when he covered Parliament Hill and attended regular press conferences with Prime Minister Pierre Trudeau. He would observe Trudeau listening attentively, thinking about the specific question, and providing an answer. He would hear some reporters asking long, rambling questions, hoping to impress their editors who might glimpse the press conference on television. Then he would try to correlate the responsiveness of the answer to the actual question asked. He credits the Trudeau experience with providing that flash of insight. 'It made me realize how important the questions are. One of the axioms I use is: answers are a function of the question asked. If there are problems in the answer it usually starts in the question.'

And it was his experience with his Carleton students that confirmed many of his suspicions. His central aim in teaching investigative journalism was in stressing the importance of getting people to reveal information that wasn't normally available. He would send students into the community to interview people, then ask for all interviews to be transcribed. 'Here is where my eyes really got opened. I was the guy seeing all the transcripts. Certain questions consistently got great answers, certain questions consistently bombed. I had never thought of that before. Neither had most other people.'

After more than a decade of working with students and applying his theories to his ongoing work, Sawatsky developed a methodology of questioning that he continued to refine. The essence of the theory is that every question has moving parts, including a topic and a query. If a question doesn't work, the idea is not to change the topic, but to change the query. And you keep changing the query until the question works. He derived some practical operating principles from the theory. Questions need to be neutral and open-ended, as those generally produce better results than value-laden or close-ended ones. He cautioned against questions that were double-barrelled or embedded with assumptions, or the use of hyperbole or trigger words to distract the interviewee. Unlike the rambling questioners at the Trudeau press conferences, interviewers should not concentrate on their output, but should be worried about input from the interviewee. It wasn't an absolutist approach. Sometimes a trigger word would be useful to shake an interviewee from a robotic set of answers, and close-ended questions were occasionally needed. Sawatsky also developed theories about macro-interviewing strategy, arguing that a successful interview proceeds gradually, with interviewers trying to establish factual consensus on key points with their subjects, and leaving only targeted, close-ended queries to the later stages, followed by final mop-up questions for any outstanding details.

Sawatsky began teaching his methods to journalists across Canada and the US. He used taped clips from television interviewers to illustrate his points. Many veteran reporters reacted negatively, assuming that the methods they had used for years, derived generally from their gut instincts, were better. It seemed counter-intuitive to some reporters that tough, accusatory questioning was usually the worst possible tactic. But others who began to adopt his principles noticed changes in the quality of their interviews. All the while, he continued to refine his principles. He expanded his teaching to Europe, and his seminars were in high demand throughout Scandinavia. 'Interviewing is the one aspect of journalism that has not improved in the last 50 years. Every other aspect has made vast strides. There's better journalists around who can do better stories and even investigations than me. But when it came to interviewing, nobody was doing it.'[15]

The methodology was applied to his work on *The Insiders*, a book about government lobbyists in Ottawa. But the most thoroughgoing and practical application of his theories came in the research he compiled for his unauthorized biography of Brian Mulroney, titled *Mulroney: The Politics of Ambition*.

Working with his Carleton students and a full-time researcher, Harvey Cashore, Sawatsky started out with a concept he calls pure research. The idea was to set about investigating the life of the prime minister, but there was no immediate defined goal in mind. It was broad inquiry at first, getting to know the lay of the land and building a database of potential interviewees, along with questions that needed to be asked. According to Sawatsky, many journalists go astray in this phase. If you begin the research with too narrow a goal, or with a pre-defined aim to try to pin down something, there's a danger of gathering only the information that appears to fit the hypothesis. There's also the danger of investing weeks or months of research, coming up empty on the original hypothesis, and then abandoning the project altogether, even though broader inquiry could have uncovered equally interesting angles. Only after the pure research phase can the applied research stage begin, where more targeted questions can be asked.

By the end of the project, which took nearly four years, Sawatsky and his students had conducted more than 600 interviews. All were transcribed, and each paragraph was identified in terms of specific aspects of Mulroney's career. The prime minister's life was divided into 17 distinct time periods that were arranged as columns in a database. Along the rows were subject categories with the tagged paragraphs from the transcripts. It was a powerful tool for calling up information about the prime minister's life, and it became vital in the writing process, as it eliminated the possibility of forgetting a fact or detail from any of the interviews. The timeline allowed him to uncover secrets of Mulroney's life that he had suppressed, such as his unsuccessful attempts at passing the bar exam. And it provided conclusive evidence of a politician who was driven to questionable personal and professional actions by his powerful ambition.

When the 576-page Mulroney book was published in 1991, it became the most comprehensive account Canadians had seen of their prime minister. Details of his lying, drinking, and womanizing were the most titillating. But it also gave a balanced picture of the pressures that come with the ambitions of being a successful politician. Mulroney, who refused to be interviewed for the book, devised a strategy to discredit it. Allan Fotheringham, Sawatsky's old colleague from the *Vancouver Sun* days, thought the response was telling.

It's not often that the subject of a book illustrates immediately that the book's assessment is bang-on correct. The super-sensitive reaction of a super-sensitive

John Sawatsky in his student days at Simon Fraser University, heading to the van that was his home for several months. (Courtesy of John Sawatsky)

prime minister to John Sawatsky is the greatest compliment Sawatsky could be paid. Brian Mulroney couldn't do more than if he'd gone on the book tour himself, or stood on the corner of the Sparks Street Mall flogging the soon-to-be best-seller. . . . The PMO . . . sends its hit men and disinformation friends out on the television, radio and press conference trail, trying to discredit a very good reporter who has got closer to the truth about the Prime Minister than anyone yet. Trying to discredit Sawatsky, a painfully meticulous reporter, is like trying to accuse Mother Teresa of stealing the loose cash.[16]

But even the most meticulous reporter can miss an important part of any story. One of Sawatsky's first and most important sources for his RCMP material was Gilles Brunet, son of the first head of the Security and Intelligence Directorate when it was established in 1956. 'He possessed the perfect combination of brilliance, drive, wit, family background, and good luck', Sawatsky said of his source.[17] Brunet died of a heart attack in 1984, and soon stories began to emerge about his alleged links to the KGB. Years earlier his wife had found an envelope in his glove compartment containing $2,000 in cash, one day after Soviet embassy officials had discovered and removed a long-standing eavesdropping device from the Ottawa embassy. Brunet was suspected of selling information about the bug to the Soviets, and a subsequent Soviet defector fingered him as a double agent. Ironically, it appeared the same man who provided so much information for Sawatsky's first book turned out to be the spy who should really have been the subject of the mole-hunt in his second book.[18] 'At first I didn't believe it, and I still have reservations about it', Sawatsky said about the Brunet revelations. 'It's partly because I liked the guy.' Still, Sawatsky recognized the story wasn't out of the realm of possibility, given that Brunet liked to party and had a reckless lifestyle. Whatever the truth of the matter, he never relied exclusively on Brunet's information, and found corroboration from multiple sources on the key pieces of information in his research. In any case, the story highlights an important reality about journalism: No matter how exhaustive the research, new information will inevitably come to light, often necessitating a re-interpretation.

After his Mulroney investigation, Sawatsky spent his time lecturing around the world on his interviewing techniques. In 2004, he surprised many of his friends and colleagues by moving to Connecticut and joining ESPN, where he became director of talent development at the cable sports network, working with staff on their interviewing skills. 'I'm an employee of the Walt Disney Company, and Mickey Mouse is on my paycheque literally. I love it here actually. I probably shouldn't be saying that. They're very open, they say this is a better way, that it's the way of the future. So they've given me carte blanche basically. It's really giving me an opportunity to implement the methodology that I've developed over the years.'

An Ongoing Legacy of Dirty Tricks

Andrew Mitrovica had already broken a number of key stories in the *Globe and Mail* about Canada's spy agency when he got an intriguing phone call in the summer of 2000. John Farrell claimed to be a former member of CSIS, the Canadian Security Intelligence Service. Disaffected and angry with his former bosses, he was willing to reveal secrets. Mitrovica listened, wrote an initial newspaper story, and embarked on a two-year investigation that included more than 150 hours of interviews with Farrell. He assembled notes, logs, and records along with corroborating interviews. The result was a 2002 book called *Covert Entry: Spies, Lies and Crimes Inside Canada's Secret Service*. In many respects, it became the most detailed look inside Canada's intelligence community since John Sawatsky's books of the early 1980s.

Mitrovica didn't leave room for doubt about the conclusions he wanted readers to draw. 'What I discovered behind the carefully constructed artifice is an intelligence service, still in its infancy, riddled by waste, extravagance, laziness, nepotism, incompetence, corruption, and law-breaking', he wrote.[19] 'Far from being a shining example to sister intelligence agencies, CSIS and its imperious leadership remain wedded to its predecessor's destructive habits.' Farrell worked for Canada Post as an intelligence officer for two years, then for CSIS for another eight. At the post office, he was assigned to spy on union leaders, building dossiers on their private lives and probing their affairs through legal and illegal means. That included breaking into cars, stealing their garbage, and intercepting their private mail. At CSIS, Farrell snooped on Russian spies and alleged terrorists. All the while, he said, CSIS engaged in routine law-breaking, abuses, and conduct that trampled the human rights of ordinary Canadians.

Farrell warned Mitrovica that his stories would be treated by CSIS with the same mantra it applied to any potential exposé of its activities: 'Lie, deny, and then act surprised.' The agency admitted no wrongdoing, trying at various times to discredit both Farrell and Mitrovica. Most large media outlets were reluctant to follow Mitrovica's allegations, an echo of the difficulties Sawatsky faced in getting the national media to pay attention to his RCMP exposés. But for those who had thought the intelligence scandals of the 1970s were mere historical oddities, Mitrovica's book came as a sober reminder. 'Farrell's tenure with CSIS shatters the illusion that it abandoned the criminal conduct that triggered the demise of the RCMP Security Service', he wrote. 'His story is also an indictment of the leadership of CSIS and its political masters, who repeatedly assure Canadians that the civilian spy agency is built on a foundation of integrity, professionalism, and profound respect for the rights and liberties of every Canadian.'

Chapter 11

Investigative Journalism Matures

Either you repeat the same conventional doctrines everybody is saying, or else you say something true, and it will sound like it's from Neptune.

Noam Chomsky[1]

Early in 1978, Henry Aubin walked into a CBC studio in Toronto for an interview about his investigative book, *City for Sale*. The interviewer was Jock Ferguson, one of the corporation's most enterprising reporters who had been the founding producer at *Marketplace*. The two men realized immediately they were kindred spirits. Aubin talked about the difficulties he had with his editors in convincing them of his project's value. Ferguson thought back to his own problems at the CBC, and his history of getting into trouble by pushing the boundaries of conventional journalism. They realized something else. Important journalism was being done in different parts of the country, but much of it remained localized and unknown to the broader community. They wondered whether something could be done to address the problem.

The idea of forming an organization to foster investigative journalism was born. Aubin continued on his book tour, not sure whether anything would ever come of the conversation. But a few weeks later, Ferguson called Aubin to talk once more about the concept, and they both set about building an organization in earnest.

'Those of us doing this kind of work felt very isolated', said Aubin.[2] 'We didn't have anyone to talk to in our newsrooms. We were somewhat pariahs of management.' Although the excitement of the 1960s and the events following Watergate inspired many journalists, they often made management feel nervous. The growth of investigative work in the 1970s was accompanied by a hesitation on the part of many news managers, and Aubin and Ferguson felt an organization of ordinary journalists would help alleviate the situation. 'We offered the possibility of allowing serious journalists to network with each other, pooling information for the greater good', Aubin said.

Ferguson's aggressive reporting would soon cause consternation once again inside his own organization. Working as a reporter in the local Toronto newsroom, he was in the middle of investigating a payoff scheme at city hall, when nervous managers decided to pull him from the story. Ferguson was angry. The CBC was scheduled to appear before the CRTC later that year for a license renewal, and Ferguson wrote a letter to the commission outlining his concern about how the payoff story was handled. Then he went public more directly, complaining about the situation to Global Television and the *Toronto Star*. The CBC fired him. Within two months, Ferguson had a front-page story in the *Star* outlining how three Toronto builders paid $25,000 in bribes to city hall inspectors for approving illegal conversions of their properties. It was an embarrassing episode for local CBC management, made even worse by an arbitrator's report months later upholding Ferguson's grievance and ruling that he showed the kind of professional dedication the CBC's success depended on.[3]

The incident was another illustration of how individual journalists, and not institutional structures, were driving much of the investigative work at the time. One of the most basic goals of Aubin and Ferguson's discussions was to identify the key people across the country doing investigative work, and then link them together more closely. They realized, as well, that not all the work was being done at the biggest newspapers or network programs.

In the Maritimes, Linden MacIntyre had emerged as a dogged and uncompromising reporter who had a wealth of sources and used them to break important stories routinely. A native of St. Lawrence, Newfoundland, he was raised in Cape Breton and began work at the *Halifax Chronicle-Herald* in 1964. A decade of newspaper reporting in Halifax and Ottawa, including a stint at the *Financial Times*, cemented his reputation as the leading journalist in the region. But friction with management, and a reluctance to do a series of stories that would buttress an editorial stance the newspaper wanted to take on the coal mining industry, led to his dismissal from the *Chronicle-Herald* in 1976. At 33, he was already a veteran newsman, but he needed a new job. He accepted a position as story editor with the CBC in Halifax, and it didn't take long for senior CBC management to recognize his potential.[4]

Linden MacIntyre, as host of The MacIntyre File. *(CBC Still Photo Collection)*

On a trip to Halifax in 1977, network executive Peter Herrndorf approached MacIntyre with the offer of doing work in the mould of *the fifth estate*. Herrndorf had a pot of money to invest, and he wanted to see if a regional program of hard-hitting journalism would work. *The MacIntyre File* was the result, a half-hour, single-subject program every two weeks that was broadcast throughout the Maritimes.

The very first program was an exposé of the mayor of Moncton and his close connections to businesses that were getting contracts from the city. The conflict-of-interest tale won an ACTRA award and immediately made *The MacIntyre File* a popular show in the region. MacIntyre and his small team turned out 20 episodes a year, sometimes exposing outright corruption, other times looking critically at important social policy issues in the Maritimes. MacIntyre's credo at the time was simple: 'Don't be scared of anybody, work like hell, get your facts right, be prepared for opposition, and be prepared to stand up to your own bosses if necessary.'[5]

There was important work going on in Quebec as well, both in the English-language press and the French media. Marc Laurendeau was breaking stories on the Front de Libération du Québec, including the revelation that a sixth person had been involved in the kidnapping of James Cross in 1970. Up until that time, everyone believed the FLQ's Liberation cell had only five members. Following interviews with exiled FLQ kidnappers in Paris, Laurendeau revealed the presence of a sixth member who been involved in the plot to grab the British trade commissioner. Nigel Barry Hamer had never been interviewed, despite being known to police, and Laurendeau's revelation eventually led to charges and jail time for Hamer. There were other journalistic coups. Louis-Gilles Francoeur of *Le Devoir* was investigating the construction industry, and Jean-Claude Leclerc had broken stories on the RCMP. A series of articles written by Gilles Paquin in *La Presse* in 1979 outlined a secret system to bankroll Ottawa's effort to defeat the planned Quebec independence referendum. In stories that would foretell many of the same shenanigans of the modern-day sponsorship scandal, Paquin showed how funds were being channeled to the Pro-Canada Foundation through federal agencies such as Air Canada, Canadian National Railway, and the Canada Development Corporation.

Investigative work was also making its presence felt in books. Lloyd Tataryn's *Dying for a Living* was a scathing indictment of environmental pollution, and it served as the basis for a *fifth estate* program. Brian McKenna, working in his spare time, spent four years investigating Montreal Mayor Jean Drapeau. He and his wife, Susan Purcell, finally produced a detailed, unauthorized biography that contained information never before known about Drapeau. And Walter Stewart was writing books to expose problems with Canadian social policy, government mismanagement, and the banking system.

After their initial discussions about forming a group, Aubin and Ferguson decided to see if they could interest others in the project. Ferguson recruited Nick Fillmore, former editor of the *4th Estate* in Halifax, while Aubin spoke to Jean-Claude Leclerc, and the four men met to formulate further ideas. They wrote to about 30 more journalists across the country, getting a positive response and encouragement to go further. They expanded the core group to about a dozen, adding John Sawatsky, Graham Fraser from *Maclean's*, Jean-Pierre Bonhomme from *La Presse*, Ellen Roseman from the *Globe*, and others. A bigger group of about 20 met in June 1978 and published a brochure proposing that the Centre for Investigative Journalism (CIJ) be founded.[6]

'The purpose of the Centre for Investigative Journalism would be to advance understanding of the concealed, obscure, or complex aspects of matters which significantly affect the public', read the document. The language had been borrowed almost word-for-word from the US-based Fund for Investigative Journalism.

> The Centre would try to end the isolation between investigative reporters across the country. As it stands now, there is virtually no communication between members of our trade in different cities and little familiarity with the kind of work others are producing. . . . The Centre would provide expert legal advice to journalists or their employers. As it stands now, many employers have inadequate understanding of the application of libel law and the Official Secrets Act . . . the Centre would provide funding for specific investigative projects which might otherwise not be undertaken.[7]

The document acknowledged there had been some retrenchment in recent times when it came to hard-hitting probes, partly because of 'careless errors of fact which have brought otherwise avoidable court actions or other forms of "trouble"'.[8] It pledged to help overcome this reticence by promoting high standards of journalism and fairness. A follow-up meeting of organizers in Montreal gauged the reaction to the proposal, which had been circulated widely in newsrooms across the country. It was decided to plan a founding conference early in 1979.

It wasn't the first time journalists had banded together to form some type of professional association. A decade earlier, the Canadian Society of Professional Journalists had been founded. While it grew to about 80 members, it never had mass appeal among journalists, and didn't survive for long. A more serious and long-lasting organization was the Fédération professionnelle des journalistes du Québec, started in 1969, which defended press freedoms and upheld the public's right to access information. An association of English-speaking journalists in Quebec sprung up as well, and its president was active in trying to bring journalists from across Canada together.[9] A series of Canadian journalism conferences was organized between 1971 and 1975, but the meetings lacked a strong focus, and the 1976 gathering was cancelled for lack of interest. The initiative to unite journalists under the banner of investigative journalism provided a broader appeal.

The same idea had worked in the US. A small group gathered in Reston, Virginia in 1975 to form Investigative Reporters and Editors (IRE). They deliberately chose a name whose acronym would describe the sense of outrage that drives many muckraking journalists. The group's founding conference had been planned for 1976, but the murder of an Arizona reporter, Don Bolles, prompted a more immediate response from organizers. The group coordinated an effort to bring journalists together with a view to completing the research Bolles had begun into corruption and organized crime in Arizona. In an unprecedented process, 38 journalists from 28 newspapers and broadcast stations gathered to conduct the research under the direction of *Newsday*'s Bob Greene. The effort was dubbed the Arizona Project, and it published a series of stories in March 1977.[10]

To Canadian investigative journalists, the formation of a group dedicated to furthering their work was long overdue. To the country's security service, it sparked fear that important secrets might be exposed. An RCMP Security Service internal memorandum in 1975 described with concern the formation of IRE in the US. It accurately predicted: 'It may be reasonable to assume that a similar group could make its appearance on the Canadian scene.'[11]

The founding conference was set for Montreal on 19–21 January 1979, and organizers booked a hall for 150 people. Nearly 350 delegates registered, and the meeting had to move to a bigger venue. There was representation from every province and territory. It was a grassroots affair, with conference registration just $25 and many delegates being billeted with local journalists. Henry Aubin and his wife hired two babysitters for the weekend to help out delegates who brought their children.[12] 'The convention's purpose was to gather those who feel the need for more and better investigative journalism into a group promoting that end. . . . The scale of the turnout reflected a strong feeling across the country that the news industry is doing a poor job and needs a boot in the pants', said the new organization's bulletin.[13]

The conference had as its keynote speaker an American journalist, Morton Mintz of the *Washington Post*. It was a choice indicative of the US influences on organizers such as Aubin and Ferguson, but it was also meant to highlight a crusading journalist who had maintained his muckraking zeal over a long career. Mintz, who had worked at the *Post* for nearly three decades, had a reputation for uncovering corporate crime and misconduct. He was also a self-described pain in the ass to his own managers. At the conference, he spoke about price-fixing, dangerous products, and unsafe drugs as big stories that were often ignored. And he also called for a redefinition of the way news was viewed, urging more attention to public policy issues that really matter. The rest of the conference had workshops devoted to police, consumer, financial, and city hall reporting, along with a session on the how-to of investigative research techniques.[14]

The excitement surrounding the founding conference inspired other journalists to get involved. Seminars were organized across the country, attracting more than 1,000 people in total, and the CIJ *Bulletin* began getting wider circulation. Nick Fillmore organized a service called Sourcefile. He compiled a list of hundreds of people who could provide expertise in various fields, and encouraged journalists to call him for references and phone numbers.[15] Inspired by the Fund for Investigative Journalism, which had seeded Seymour Hersh's My Lai exposé and more than 250 other projects, the CIJ offered to supply grants to worthwhile ideas that would otherwise not be funded. Despite the pressure to grow quickly, the CIJ was mindful of potential conflicts and compromises when it came to soliciting funding. It decided not to accept donations of any kind from government or non-media corporations.

Organizers were surprised at the interest in the second convention, held in Montreal in March 1980. Nearly 650 registered. The CIJ announced the first three grants under its program to fund investigative projects. Without revealing who the journalists were or the exact nature of the projects, it was reported that they dealt with safety regulations on chemical pollution, security problems in the Canadian nuclear establishment, and the nature of the sports industry.[16] To fulfill its aim of popularizing investigative work from across the country, the CIJ began publishing a review of the year's best stories. It also began lobbying for better access and freedom of information legislation in Canada. By the spring of 1981, the CIJ had more than 500 members, and counted 5,000 people in all its conferences and seminars to date. The volunteer board of directors could no longer handle all the organization's administrative work, so a full-time executive director was hired, and a process began to professionalize the services. It didn't engage in any modesty when it declared: 'CIJ is now the most important, most progressive media organization in Canada.'[16]

The CIJ's annual review became a barometer of the growth of the genre, and it was clear that the organization's activities were spurring more reporters into mounting investigations. By 1981, in addition to contributions from the major national media, the annual review included reports from Regina, London, Kingston, Sherbrooke, Winnipeg, and Edmonton. In the spring of 1981, the *Edmonton Journal* ran a series showing how politically connected businesspeople had taken options on farmland outside Edmonton in the weeks before the property was annexed to the city. It sparked a judicial inquiry. The *Regina Leader-Post* exposed deficient practices in laboratories charged with testing the health effects of pesticides. An Ottawa-based reporter for the *Kingston Whig-Standard* put together an exposé of Canada's acquiescence in Indonesia's invasion of East Timor. Even *Reader's Digest* was getting into the act, commissioning Maggie Siggins to write a detailed account of a murderer who fell between the cracks of the mental and criminal health systems. Publishers of large newspapers were trying to outdo each other on the investigative front. An advertisement by the *Edmonton Journal* in the 1982 *CIJ Review* is typical: 'There's a lot of muck around . . . and the *Journal* keeps raking. It's bad news for someone when we run stories which scandalize the politicians and bureaucrats. But it's the only hope for some of society's oppressed.'[18]

Early successes may have convinced the CIJ's directors that investigative reporting was a growth industry that would produce more and better stories with each successive year. But the economic and political realities of the early 1980s soon put an end to that optimism. The Thomson and Southam newspaper chains, the dominant players in Canadian daily newspapers, came together to carve out monopoly markets in several Canadian cities. Thomson agreed to shut the *Ottawa Journal* in August 1980, and a day later Southam reciprocated by closing the *Winnipeg Tribune*, creating exclusive daily markets in both cities. The move came within a year of the closing of the *Montreal Star*. At the same time, Southam bought out Thomson's interests in Vancouver to acquire sole ownership of the *Sun* and *Province*, and it also took control of the *Gazette* in Montreal. Thomson also merged the two Victoria papers to create one, and it closed its FP News Services. With one stroke the competition in several major Canadian cities, which drove much of the enterprise and investigative spirit, was ended. Rationalizations in newsrooms created fewer opportunities for in-depth reporting.

The recession of 1981–2 put severe economic pressure on news organizations, and many responded with hiring freezes and budget cuts. Suddenly, investigative work in many quarters was seen as a luxury. 'Investigative reporting on the country's dailies, always in fragile health, is wheezing worse than ever as the strangle is put to editorial budgets', wrote media pundit Barrie Zwicker in the Fall 1982 issue of the *CIJ Bulletin*.[19] Layoffs and cutbacks, combined with pressures to reduce overtime and travel expenses, meant fewer opportunities to do anything but conventional daily stories. Recognizing the trend, the CIJ named its 1983 conference 'Hard News: Hard Times', and tried to devise strategies to cope with the problems.[20]

At CBC Radio, the economic pressures produced a quick turnaround in attitude to investigative work. Paul Kells, head of the English-language current affairs department, decided in early 1981 to build an investigative unit. Originally designed to supply in-depth stories for the entire department, the team was eventually attached to one program, *Sunday Morning*. Kells recruited Nick Fillmore as part of a four-person team to begin work in November 1981. They produced a number of stories in the first few months, including an exposé on aerial pesticide bombardment in New Brunswick, and a story about radiation exposure and elevated cancer rates suffered by Canadian veterans as a result of nuclear accidents.[21] But in June 1982, seven months after the team began work, CBC decided to kill it.[22]

The CIJ mounted a lobbying effort to have the unit reinstated, but CBC president Al Johnson rejected the idea. 'I can assure you that this decision was not taken lightly, but the hard reality is that we could not justify the cost of a four-man team working on in-depth reports—some of which took months to prepare—for one program. Had we continued with the unit, in light of the financial restraints under which the Corporation is operating, other radio programs in the current affairs area would have suffered.'[23] Kells admitted the concept of investigative reporting was 'obviously not entrenched here yet'. He said he doubted whether he would be able to find the funding to create another team in the immediate future.[24] The CBC Radio experience became a common one. Newspapers or broadcast outlets would occasionally create an investigative unit, only to dismantle it a year or two later. There were a variety of reasons. In some cases, the teams drew resentment from other staff members in the office who felt they weren't pulling their weight. Management often believed it took too long to work up investigative stories. A team could typically work for weeks or months on a project, only to decide not to proceed. Some managers saw that as a waste of time and money. And the inevitable fear of libel suits and of disaffecting the business community, which provided needed advertising dollars, always held some outlets in check.

If the faltering economy was one reason for the diminution of investigative work, it didn't necessarily follow that an economic recovery would return the genre to its former plateau. By the mid 1980s, Fillmore was showing how profits had recovered at both Thomson and Southam, but with no corresponding increase in staff and resources. Elected as CIJ president, he wrote that a new conservatism was sweeping Canadian journalism. Fillmore lamented the lack of in-depth reporting at the *Globe and Mail* and CBC's *The Journal*, and said most newspapers were more interested in embracing 'yuppie journalism' with its emphasis on lifestyle and soft features. 'At the CBC the new conservatism has hit like a ton of bricks—the budget cuts and the accusation that the CBC has a left-leaning bias have led to self-censorship of the worst kind. Reporters and producers think twice before suggesting a story that is probing and hard-hitting—if the story might be viewed by management as left-wing.'[25]

In 1985, CBC was creating a new program called *Venture*, widely seen as an attempt to appease the business community by doing features on entrepreneurs. At the same time, Fillmore saw *Sunday Morning* doing fewer in-depth documentaries, especially if they related to government, while it cut back on its Latin American coverage, which had been criticized as being anti-American. It was clear he was becoming disaffected with the corporation, and he left soon afterwards. He considered his time at the *4th Estate* to be the most important work of his life. And he lamented the reality that many of the people involved in investigative work around the time of the founding of the CIJ, and the first two or three years afterwards, subsequently left the field.[26]

A common debate at the CIJ's founding conference, and one that would repeat itself over the next decade, revolved around the use of the word 'investigative' itself. 'I hate the word "investigative", I think the public hates it, and it's bullshit really', pronounced Gerald McAuliffe at the initial conference.[27] Some others agreed, arguing that it was too elitist and excluded too many journalists. At the next annual meeting, Walter Stewart took an opposing view. 'I heard someone from this rostrum this afternoon say that all journalism is investigative. Like hell it is. A great deal of journalism is simply reflex action. . . . It's not investigative to rewrite press releases.'

All of which led to an exercise on both sides of the border to define exactly what 'investigative journalism' meant. IRE initially adopted a definition written by *Newsday's* Bob Greene. It said an investigative story needed to embody three aspects: first, it had to come from the initiative and personal work of a reporter, as opposed to the work of another person or institution; secondly, it had to be important to readers and viewers; and thirdly, it had to reveal information someone or some institution was trying to keep secret.[28] The definition changed over the years, but this first incarnation clearly bore the influence of Watergate with its emphasis on secrecy and exposé. In fact, dozens of American reports throughout the 1970s affixed the word 'gate' to the story of the day, particularly when the report revealed a piece of secret information.

The CIJ description of investigative work was broader, and included all matters dealing with concealed, obscure, or complex aspects of issues that significantly affect the public. A definition adopted by the CBC was even more far-ranging, and sought to eliminate the preconception that investigative work dealt solely with wrongdoing and injustice: 'While all journalism is, in a wide sense, investigative, the term can be particularly applied to the vigorous, intense examination of institutions or activities which concern public policy or touch upon the lives of a large part of the population. Investigative journalism should bear in mind the relative importance of an issue and

Journalists gather in Henry Aubin's house in November 1978 to plan the founding convention of the Centre for Investigative Journalism. (Courtesy of Penelope Aubin)

concern public policy or touch upon the lives of a large part of the population. Investigative journalism should bear in mind the relative importance of an issue and should not be exclusively concerned with the revelation of errors, injustice, or wrongdoing. Minor matters should not be treated when more significant topics warrant attention.'[29]

The debate within the CIJ over the nature of the organization and exactly who it should include raged for a decade, finally culminating in elimination of the investigative title altogether. In 1990, the CIJ became the Canadian Association of Journalists, to the consternation of some of its founders. But it has continued to organize workshops and conferences on the techniques and practices of investigative journalism. It also encourages enterprise projects by holding an annual awards competition, and remains the only organization in the country to advocate for the professional interests of all Canadian journalists.

Investigative journalism came a long way in the 1970s, taking on new and more sophisticated forms, and reflecting the use of increasingly refined methodologies. At the same time, ever-widening divisions appeared between individual journalists and their institutions. In the post-Watergate era, mainstream media organizations saw investigative work as a valuable commodity to be exploited. At the same time, they were cautious about attacking the status quo too vigorously, since privately owned media groups were an integral part of the establishment. In Alasdair MacIntyre's analysis, those engaging in a social practice must pay attention to 'standards of excellence and obedience to rules as well as achievement of goods'.[30] He calls them 'internal goods', and for investigative journalists they might include holding powerful interests to account, everyone that participates in the practice. At the same time, MacIntyre notes that the institutions employing practitioners have a corrupting power to promote what he calls 'external goods'. In a journalistic frame, those might include fame, power, awards, or money. The more someone has of them, the less there are for other people, so 'external goods are therefore characteristically objects of competition in which there must be losers as well as winners.'[31] In the case of many Canadian investigative journalists of the 1970s, the schism between their desire to adhere to standards of excellence and the needs of their institutions was growing wide.

In describing the evolution of American journalism, James Aucoin points to the corrosive nature of this contradiction. 'The body of journalism is replete with examples of practices usurped for the purposes of the news institutions. Automotive, real estate, and sometimes health care reporters, for example, largely because these specialties have not successfully separated themselves from the institutions that support them, have been co-opted in many newsrooms, relegated to producing fluff news for the benefit of advertisers.'[32] He suggests that investigative journalism in the United States followed a different path, in part because of the development of an independent community of practitioners where standards of excellence could be discussed, promoted, and refined. That community was represented by the Investigative Reporters and Editors organization. In some ways, the Centre for Investigative Journalism fulfilled a similar role in Canada. By linking investigative journalists from different organizations, it allowed for a community of interests to develop outside the circumscribed boundaries of the individual media institutions. There is evidence that internal competition to create vibrant investigative reports helped enlarge the genre's sphere of influence. While emerging social and economic forces altered the landscape for investigative journalism by the 1980s, the CIJ continued to uphold a professional standard that provided a sense of shared community within a common practice.

Chapter 12

Undercover, Hidden-Camera, and Gotcha Journalism

As the wagon was rapidly driven through the beautiful lawns up to the asylum my feelings of satisfaction at having attained the object of my work were greatly dampened by the look of distress on the faces of my companions. . . . The Insane Asylum on Blackwell's Island is a human rat-trap. It is easy to get in, but once there it is impossible to get out.[1]

Nelly Bly's first-person description of her stay at Blackwell's Island insane asylum in New York was a colourful account of a Dickensian institution. In fact, Dickens himself had compared the place to London's Bedlam, and there had been many earlier reports of its horrific conditions. But only after Bly's 1887 story in the *New York World* did officials begin to pay attention and try to change the situation. Bly, after all, wasn't mentally ill at any point. She was a reporter who tricked doctors into declaring her insane so she could be shipped to the asylum. After a 10-day stay, a lawyer arrived to secure her release.

Bly, born Elizabeth Cochrane, was a reporter with a strong drive to denounce injustice. As a teenager, she was outraged by an article in the *Pittsburgh Dispatch* entitled 'What Girls Are Good For'. It ridiculed the idea of women in the workplace, saying girls were only fit for housework. She wrote an angry letter to the newspaper, which so impressed the editor he immediately offered her a job. She soon became one of America's best-known journalists. Her articles detailed women's working conditions, slum life, and wider social problems. She went to Mexico to do a series on corruption and how the poor lived. Within two years she was writing for Joseph Pulitzer's *New York World*, and her exposé of Blackwell's Island was the first of her many undercover reporting stories.

The idea of going undercover to report on a story seems simple enough, but it had never been tried in earnest before Bly's attempt. Even after her enormous successes, the technique was considered by many to be a stunt and appropriate only for 'sob sister' reporting. Yet it was a variation on the technique of novelists, who wrote about their own real-life experiences or inserted themselves into other situations to find colour for their stories. Upton Sinclair combined undercover muckraking journalism with fiction when he wrote *The Jungle* in 1906. He came to Chicago to discover conditions in the meatpacking industry, carrying a lunch bucket and wandering around the plants and neighbourhoods in workers' clothes. Then he decided to use his research to weave an epic tale of immigrant suffering and horrendous working conditions. *The Jungle* was read around the world, though more attention was paid to the unsanitary conditions in the food production process than to the plight of the workers. 'I aimed at the public's heart and by accident I hit it in the stomach', he said afterwards.[2]

Examining the history of undercover reporting throws light on one of the more controversial methodologies used in investigative journalism. As Ettema and Glasser point out, investigative reporters operate in a context that makes greater demands on journalists when it comes to justification of evidence. 'Daily reporters ordinarily accept at face value—not necessarily as true but at least as news—the claims they glean from the beats they cover.'[3] Investigative journalists need to go further, using increasingly sophisticated measures to collect and assess evidence. What level of truth they ultimately need to attain is the subject of both philosophical debate and potential legal wrangling.[4] For Michael Schudson, there is no textbook answer to the question of how investigative and enterprise journalists exercise judgment in relation to verification and truth. 'It requires mature subjectivity; subjectivity tempered by encounters with, and regard for, the views of significant others in the profession; and subjectivity aged by encounters with, and regard for, the facts of the world.'[5] Historians who are trying to understand the past do not have the luxury of time-travel, where they might journey to the scene of a battle to discover how it really unfolded. Journalists trying to unravel aspects of contemporary life sometimes do have this advantage. Instead of relying on a document or a second-hand account, or the testimony of a number of witnesses, they can occasionally observe a situation first-hand and determine what really is taking place. Going undercover is a means of doing so, though the ethical implications are complex. The technique inherently involves deception and lying, leading some to question how a pursuit of truth can be aided by a blatant disregard for honesty.

Following the early muckraking experiments, undercover reporting became a sporadic feature of American journalism, often practised at the margins of the mainstream. Marvel Cooke, the first black woman to work as a reporter at a white-owned New York daily, went undercover in the so-called Bronx Slave Market. It was established after the 1929 stock market crash when black women who had performed domestic work became unemployed. They congregated on the streets of New York in defined areas, waiting for someone to buy their services. 'I was a slave', she wrote in her story for the *New York Compass* in 1950. 'I was part of the "paper-bag brigade", waiting patiently in front of Woolworth's on 170th St., between Jerome and Walton Aves., for someone to "buy" me for an hour or two, or, if I were lucky, for a day. That is the Bronx Slave Market, where Negro women wait, in rain or shine, in bitter cold or under broiling sun, to be hired by local housewives looking for bargains in human labor.'[6]

On rare occasions a mainstream reporter would use the technique as a supplement to an in-depth report. In 1961, Edgar May won a Pulitzer Prize for a series on welfare. May convinced his superiors at the *Buffalo Evening News* to allow him to pose as a caseworker in a social welfare office for three months as part of the story. Over the years, other writers undertook more dangerous assignments. Some infiltrated the Ku Klux Klan and wrote about their experiences. John Howard Griffin, a white writer, underwent skin treatments to pose as a black in the southern US. His book, *Black Like Me*, caused a sensation when it appeared in 1959. Hunter S. Thompson, in creating his brand of gonzo journalism in the 1960s, infiltrated the Hell's Angels and rode with them for a year. And in Germany, journalist Gunter Wallraff was beginning to build his career as a reporter who infiltrated various organizations and institutions to see how they really worked. His first book, *Wallraff the Undesirable Journalist*, was published in 1969.

The whole concept didn't affect mainstream American journalism until the big newspapers began rediscovering the investigative genre towards the end of the 1960s. Of the major dailies, the *Chicago Tribune* was among the first to engage aggressively in undercover reporting. In 1970, William Jones posed as an ambulance driver for two months, investigating local companies. His stories earned the newspaper a Pulitzer Prize for exposing collusion between police and some of Chicago's largest private ambulance companies to restrict service in low-income areas. The newspaper also went undercover to expose nursing home abuses. For a 1972 investigation of voter fraud during a presidential primary election, the *Tribune* organized a massive clandestine operation. It sent 17 staff members and eight outside investigators into the election as judges and poll watchers. They discovered significant voting fraud, including cash payments to voters.[7] The newspaper was again rewarded with a Pulitzer, and undercover work achieved unprecedented attention.

Undercover reporting made sporadic appearances in Canada as well. In 1935, a young reporter with the *Winnipeg Tribune* put on a pair of patched trousers and a thick woolen coat to join the 'On to Ottawa' trek incognito. 'How long my identity will remain unknown I don't know', wrote Charles J. Woodsworth, son of CCF founder J.S. Woodsworth. 'For five days I've ridden the rods, eaten relief meals, and tramped in the long parades with young fellows to whom I'm just another comrade.'[8] Woodsworth produced a sympathetic portrait of the unemployed workers who were marching to Ottawa to present their grievances to the federal government. He described a group of young, clean-cut men from all over Canada who were sick of a life they characterized as full of discouragement and absolute hopelessness. But his stories revealed the anxiety of working in clandestine conditions to get closer to the truth. 'Slipping away from the ranks to wire dispatches back to Winnipeg means constant danger of exposure. I've come close to being discovered but so far I've escaped.'[9]

The technique wasn't used only by reporters. In January 1969, celebrity Toronto politician Morton Shulman grew a two-day beard and donned dirty coveralls and a safety helmet so he could sneak into Inco's Sudbury plant. Security checked his worker's badge, but he had borrowed one from a retired employee, so was let through. After an eight-hour midnight shift he reported finding unsafe levels of sulphur dioxide, and described the Copper Cliff plant as something out of Dante's Inferno.[10] Shulman, an NDP member of the Ontario legislature at the time, admitted his venture was a publicity stunt, but he said it allowed him to demonstrate in stark terms the unsafe conditions at the mine. There were other occasional instances of surreptitious work, but no one practised it with regularity.

An organized foray into the world of undercover reporting came in 1974, when *Montreal Star* reporter Sheila Arnopoulos spent two weeks in five factories to find out what life was like for thousands of immigrant workers. Arnopoulos worked the social welfare beat, and was particularly interested in minorities, immigrants, and poverty. She was one of the *Star*'s most incisive writers, and had won a National Newspaper Award in 1969 for a series called *The Immigrant's Dilemma*. She knew that many immigrants worked in factories and were not earning the minimum wage. At first, she pursued the story conventionally, interviewing members of the Greek, Portuguese, and Italian communities about conditions in the factories. Stories emerged about workers locked up and forced to work overtime, employees earning less than minimum wage, and factories closing to avoid unionization drives, only to re-open under new names. Arnopoulos contacted the provincial agency charged with enforcing the wage laws, only to find it responded just to complaints and wasn't taking action to enforce the minimums. Finally, she discovered that garment unions weren't dealing with the problem either, and at the time were not hiring immigrant union officers.[11]

'I felt it was necessary to get closer to the situation', said Arnopoulos of the undercover work. 'I don't think it presented problems for me. Actually I loved doing this. You can get stuff you just can't get interviewing people.'[12] The inspiration for the idea came from reading Tom Wolfe and other members of the American 'new journalism' trend. Those writers probed deeply inside their subject matter and used the techniques of novelists to spin their tales. Arnopoulos pitched the proposal to her managing editor, and despite some misgivings from the city desk, got the go-ahead.

Arnopoulos searched the job listings, put on some old work clothes, and boarded the bus at 7:30 a.m. one day for Atlantic Hosiery, which had run a simple newspaper ad: 'Pantyhose packers and general work. Good salary.' After a job interview of half a dozen questions, she was hired, without even providing her name or social insurance number. No forms were filled out. She was led down a rickety staircase to a black, windowless basement where women on 60 noisy machines were making snow-white stockings. Her job would involve counting and bundling the stockings.

> Atlantic Hosiery, it appeared, was a sordid mess. Surrounding the women counting a number of stockings, were old steel oil drums. On top of the drums there were discarded tools, dirty rags drenched in grease, and puddles of scummy oil. Half-filled oil tins, broken jars, plastic tubing, crunched metal waste baskets, cigarette butts, wads of gum, cast-off stockings, and hunks of cardboard littered the black cement floor.[13]

Arnopoulos drew the kind of scene that would have been impossible to describe without first-hand observation.

> At noon I went over to the foreman. 'How much do we get an hour?'

'It's by the piece . . . three cents a dozen . . . but I wash my hands of it', he smiled apologetically. 'You have to check with the boss . . . after you learn to go fast . . . you can make some money.'

He shrugged his shoulders. 'It's hard to make a dollar these days.'

I estimated that I was making 60 cents an hour. [At the time, minimum wage was $1.85 per hour.][14]

By the end of her nine-hour shift, Arnopoulos had processed 200 dozen stockings. Her wages for the day were $5.80. Other jobs proved equally oppressive. At one company, the 100 employees were allowed seven-minute breaks, and access to one toilet. In other locations, the bathroom became a useful haven where Arnopoulos scribbled notes, capturing the dialogue of the workers and the details of what she was seeing. She told the stories of her own experiences side-by-side with conventional reports on the conditions facing immigrant workers generally. She pointed out that more than a quarter of a million people in Montreal, working 40-hour weeks at minimum wage, earned $3,848 each per year. But those were the lucky ones who were aware of the minimum wage. Others who weren't, or were too intimidated to demand it, earned closer to 60 cents an hour. 'Mainly they are immigrants from the Caribbean, Latin America, India, Pakistan, Greece, Portugal, and Italy. Most come from villages and have no skills or basic education. Some cannot read, write, or do simple arithmetic. A large number speak neither English nor French, even after a number of years in Canada, because they are not exposed to either language on the job or at home. . . . They may never escape low wages, long weary hours, and poor housing, but they hope for a richer, more rewarding life for their children.'[15]

The stories proved popular with a group that didn't often see its interests represented in the daily press: the working poor. The next year Arnopoulos followed up with a series on restaurants and bars. Once again she went undercover, this time getting jobs in six different establishments. She found half of them paid less than the minimum wage. Some collected portions of tips from waiters and waitresses, supposedly to pass along to busboys, but she found management pocketed the money. And in other restaurants, waiters were being illegally hired to work for tips only.[16] The style of reporting Arnopoulos developed was popular with readers, but less so with business owners, and the people who controlled her own newspaper were no exception. A story she wrote on tenants who were being displaced by developers angered a senior manager, whose brother was involved with the same developers in the US. 'What I knew deep down was to shut up and be careful about writing about big business. Newspapers and government have elites that don't want reporters and researchers poking around and revealing stuff that shows the vulnerable are exploited—especially if it will interfere with them making a lot of money.' Soon management began to view her as a radical and a supporter of Quebec separatism. She was put on the overnight copy desk, and after taking a leave to finish her MA in sociology, she decided to quit. Arnopoulos went on to write books, one of which won a Governor-General's award, and to teach journalism at Concordia University.

Arnopoulos wasn't the only reporter stoking controversy with undercover reporting. In Chicago, where the *Tribune* had earned Pulitzer honours for its clandestine work, a proposed undercover project sparked a vigorous ethical debate. Pam Zekman, one of the veterans of the *Tribune's* investigative team, pitched the idea of doing a story on corruption among Chicago building inspectors. But the treatment would be unprecedented. She proposed the newspaper buy a bar, start to renovate it, and monitor the activities of the various city inspectors as they visited the premises. The *Tribune* wasn't interested, so when Zekman jumped to the rival *Chicago Sun-Times*, she revived the story idea. Working in collaboration with a civic watchdog group and television's *60 Minutes*, the newspaper bought a run-down tavern and gave it the cheeky name 'The Mirage'. In August 1977, the renovated bar opened for business with the blessing of a variety of city inspectors, despite having building code, fire, and venting violations. The newspaper documented inspectors soliciting bribes and shaking down the owners for payoffs. Hidden cameras in an upstairs loft recorded the transgressions. After the series ran, inspectors were fired and civic reforms were enacted.[17]

But the entire affair had the aura of a sting, and that didn't sit well with many journalists. The Mirage series became a Pulitzer finalist, but Ben Bradlee of the *Washington Post* and others voted against it. In the end, the board decided not to give it the award because of its level of deception and what some believed to be entrapment. The episode had a profound impact on newspaper journalism in Chicago, where newspapers largely abandoned undercover reporting as a result. But the journalists who worked on the original project still defended the idea. 'All we did', said Bill Recktenwald, a member of the team that organized the Mirage, 'was what any citizen should be able to do—open a business. We didn't hang out a poster that said "Bribes are welcome here", and we didn't offer money to people. But if people asked us, we gave them the money. If we'd been offering money we probably would have had a lot more people taking it, but they had to ask. When we tried to run a business we found out we couldn't run it honestly, so we documented it.'[18] The sentiment was echoed by Jim Hoge, the *Sun-Times* editor at the time, who went on to edit *Foreign Affairs*. 'I thought at the time and have ever since that the Mirage project was an exemplary example of dramatic investigative journalism that made a difference. The *Sun-Times'* resort to undercover work came only after traditional reporting efforts failed to sufficiently surface the relevant corruptions and their tie-ins.'[19]

The inherent intrusiveness of undercover reporting became especially controversial whenever entrapment or a sting was involved. Questions arose as to whether the journalist was uncovering an incident or creating it. One of the first recorded journalistic stings involved W.T. Stead, editor of the *Pall Mall Gazette* in Britain. In 1885, he sought out and bought a 12-year-old girl in the East End of London for sexual purposes. He was arrested and convicted, but served just a short sentence when he revealed the tactic in his publication. It became an important case in the campaign to end child prostitution.[20] Virtually the same story was done a century later in India, when a newspaper reporter in Madhya Pradesh bid for and purchased a young woman. The story showed how trafficking in women worked, and how prominent people were involved in the process.[21] But in both cases, the ethics and integrity of the journalists involved were called into question.

Adding cameras to the process of going undercover inevitably made for even noisier ethical debate. That became clear in the first-known instance of a hidden-camera shoot, at Sing Sing prison in 1928. Ruth Snyder was on death row and scheduled to be electrocuted for killing her husband Alfred. Although journalists were invited to witness the high-profile execution, there were strict prohibitions against cameras. Guards were instructed to search everyone entering the prison. Editors at the *New York Daily News* came up with a plan. They imported a photographer from the *Chicago Tribune*, Thomas Howard, hoping the New York prison authorities wouldn't recognize him. They rigged up a special miniature camera, strapped it to his ankle, and ran a shutter-release cable up his pant leg to his pocket. Howard practised for a month. When the moment came, he crossed his legs and lifted his pant leg to snap a photo. It captured Snyder's final gruesome moment, and was splashed on the *Daily News* front page with the single screaming headline: Dead. Many denounced the photo as both illegal and unethical. Others felt it threw new light on America's use of capital punishment. The controversy raged, but the practice of hidden-camera journalism became enshrined in popular culture. The incident inspired the 1933 movie *Picture Snatcher* with James Cagney, and Howard's actual camera remains on exhibit in the Smithsonian Institution.

By the late 1950s, technological changes made hidden-camera shooting for television and film increasingly feasible. The CBS documentary *Biography of a Bookie Joint* used hidden cameras extensively in 1961, as did NBC's *Business of Gambling* in 1963. At the CBC program *Inqui'ry*, reporter Warner Troyer wandered the floor of a political convention with a microphone wrapped in a newspaper and a small transmitter in his breast pocket. Douglas Leiterman and Beryl Fox made use of a hidden camera concealed in a car and a secret microphone disguised as a brooch to capture racial inequality in *One More River*, and the idea migrated to *Seven Days*, which used it in its effort to prove that Fred Fawcett should not be in a mental institution. Early in its existence, *W5* experimented with hidden cameras as well, employing them to show how unsafe cars ended up on the road.

But the increased use of the technique wasn't universally embraced, and some who engaged in hidden-camera shooting found themselves in trouble with the law. That was the case in 1963, when *Life* magazine ran an exposé of health quackery by telling the story of a plumber who claimed amazing healing powers with the aid of clay, minerals, and herbs. Two journalists, in cooperation with authorities, conducted a sting by entering the plumber's home and asking for a medical consultation. The plumber concluded that a supposed lump in the reporter's breast developed after she ate rancid butter nearly 12 years earlier. The other journalist snapped a surreptitious photo of the event, while the entire conversation was captured on a hidden recorder. The article led to quackery charges against the plumber, but he sued *Life* for invading his privacy. After eight years of legal wrangling, he won. The court didn't buy *Life*'s constitutional arguments for freedom of the press, and levied a fine of $1,000. 'We agree that newsgathering is an integral part of news dissemination. We strongly disagree, however, that the hidden mechanical contrivances are "indispensable tools" of newsgathering. Investigative reporting is an ancient art; its successful practice long antecedes the invention of miniature cameras and electronic devices. The First Amendment has never been construed to accord newsmen immunity from torts or crimes committed during the course of newsgathering. The First Amendment is not a license to trespass, to steal, or to intrude by electronic means into the precincts of another's home or office.'[22]

Under Peter Herrndorf's tenure, CBC pushed the boundaries of hidden-camera usage. Wide-ranging surveillance and journalistic sting techniques were used during the *Connections* series. But other programs were experimenting with hidden cameras as well, and they delved into areas not as morally clear-cut as catching organized crime figures at work. In 1979, Robert Cooper of *Ombudsman* began looking into a two-year-old city jail fire in Saint John, New Brunswick. Locked in their cells, the inmates were powerless to escape, and 21 men died. Some of the dead were young men who had been arrested on petty crime charges. The *MacIntyre File* had done a segment about the incident, and there was evidence of flammable material in the jail and poor emergency training among the staff. Cooper wanted to know why the relatives of the victims had never been compensated or given any clear information as to what went wrong. But the fire chief and police chief both refused to do on-camera interviews. Cooper decided to use deception in gathering the stories.

He took his crew to the jail, convincing authorities to give them a tour while they filmed without permission. Although both chiefs sat down and spoke to Cooper about what went on, neither realized a camera was rolling. Cooper produced a dramatic report that pointed the finger at systemic problems in Saint John. The police chief was flabbergasted to see himself on television.[23] The fire chief also formally complained, and CBC management began feeling pressure. When it worked its way to the top of CBC's bureaucracy, president Al Johnson began drafting a letter of apology. Cooper heard about the letter and threatened to resign. As a result, he said, it was watered down considerably. But Cooper said it was indicative of the president's mindset. 'I got the information from very high, very good sources that he had tremendous problems understanding the program or its utility. He couldn't understand the purpose behind a TV show that actually takes on top government ministers on the air. I kept hearing over and over again that he was dissatisfied.'[24]

The following year, *Ombudsman* was cancelled, though it still had a loyal audience of more than a million viewers. Many pointed to the hidden-camera controversy as a central reason. Ron Base, television critic of the *Toronto Star*, said the program had run seven seasons but did not die of natural causes. 'Instead, the show was murdered by nervous CBC network officials who could not countenance a show that continually took big government to task, forcing it to react for a change to the usually ignored needs of the little man.'[25] The CBC disagreed, arguing that the cancellation had more to do with 'a changing environment, a loss of audience acceptance, and with our plan to develop strong daily information programming in prime time'.[26] Part of the changing environment, according to the CBC, was the growth of official provincial ombudsman positions, from four when the program started to nine. Therefore, the corporation argued, the need for the program lessened. As for the hidden-camera flap, the CBC denied it had anything to do with the show's demise, though it said the filming had not received approval from senior officials and was used for an interview that contributed nothing to the story. Other media organizations didn't accept the CBC's argument that ombudsman-type programming was no longer needed. Dale Goldhawk, for instance, enjoyed a lengthy career of fighting battles on behalf of consumers. And the CBC's own *Marketplace* continued to pursue aggressive consumer reporting. Under Sig Gerber, executive producer from 1985 to 1996, the program consistently broke original, investigative stories. Cooper eventually moved to the US where he became a successful Hollywood producer, heading the HBO worldwide pictures division before moving to TriStar and Dreamworks studios.

Hidden-camera shooting continued to be used on occasion throughout the 1980s in the US and Canada, though its frequency varied from program to program. *The fifth estate* was never a heavy proponent of the technique, though it did use concealed cameras and microphones in exceptional cases. Former executive producer Robin Taylor recalled that he would only contemplate using them for known crooks in the first place.[27] *Marketplace* made more frequent use of hidden cameras in the context of consumer frauds and deception.

The next wave of major hidden-camera reporting began in the late 1980s, fuelled by competitive pressures in the newsmagazine environment of the US, and by techno- logical advances that made cameras smaller and cheaper. Regional television stations could now afford small-format cameras, and soon any reporter could be outfitted with a camera that attached to a pair of eyeglasses or a lapel. Some news directors in the US, having invested in the new technology, were demanding hidden-camera stories for their ratings periods. It led to a wave of 'gotcha' stories that documented abuse wherever a reporter could find it. There were favourite and easy targets: car repair shops, boiler room operations, psychics, and a variety of low-level con artists. Capturing wrongdoing made for dramatic television, but viewers were often treated to elaborate, high-tech sledgehammers being used to swat minor annoyances.

ABC's *PrimeTime Live*, which began in 1989, made hidden-camera shooting one of its signature techniques. Producers staged effective investigations into abuse at health care facilities and day care centres. They used hidden cameras to document disparity in treatment between whites and blacks. They also used the technology for the easy targets, spending large sums to nail small-time car repair crooks. But the program's 1992 investigation into the Food Lion supermarket chain became a flashpoint for a wide-ranging debate about hidden cameras, undercover reporting, and the ethics surrounding journalistic deception.

ABC had been told some stores in the supermarket chain, which had 1,100 outlets in 14 states, engaged in unsanitary and dangerous practices. As part of its inquiry, it asked two producers to apply for jobs with Food Lion and take hidden cameras into the workplace. With cameras under their wigs and batteries strapped to their backs, the producers captured scenes of outdated meat being repackaged and re-dated, old ground beef being mixed together with new, and workers bleaching rancid chicken to improve its look and remove the odour.[28] The report was a major blow to the chain, which closed dozens of stores and suffered a steep decline in its share price after the broadcast. Food Lion responded by taking the matter to court, but it did so in an innovative way. Instead of suing for defamation or challenging the truth of the broadcast, it accused ABC's producers of falsifying their employment applications to get jobs at the supermarket, trespassing, and not discharging their legal duty of loyalty to their employer. A jury in North Carolina, where Food Lion was based, bought the argument and awarded the company $5.5 million in damages in 1997. The judgment sent a chill through newsrooms across North America, leading news managers to reassess their standards for undercover and hidden-camera reporting. A judge subsequently reduced the fine to $315,000, and when the case was finally reviewed by a federal appeals court, all but $2 of the assessed penalties were thrown out.[29] But the message to news organizations hadn't been lost.

While many media outlets continue to use undercover and surveillance reporting, the legal and ethical risks have created a dampening effect. The BBC remains one of the most consistent practitioners of the technique. Its *MacIntyre Undercover* series featured lengthy exposés of such issues as neglect at a care home, the exploitation of models in the British fashion industry, and football hooliganism. As in other eras, the work continues to be viewed as stunt reporting by some journalists. But other BBC productions have produced tangible evidence of systemic societal problems. A documentary called *The Secret Policeman* featured an elaborate infiltration of the Greater Manchester Police Department. Journalist Mark Daly went undercover and took the entire police training course, then reported for duty, all the while documenting racism within the ranks of his fellow officers. The corporation even created a program called *Whistleblower*, dedicated exclusively to investigating anti-social or criminal practices in organizations and companies throughout the UK. Programs have included investigations into airport security, rail safety, and unethical practices in the real estate field.

In Canada, hidden-camera and undercover investigations are not as frequent, but they continue to be used to good effect. The *Toronto Star* and *W5* have both employed undercover reporting techniques, and they continue to make their appearances on CBC current affairs offerings. In his documentary *Big Sugar*, Brian McKenna sent a reporter undercover to document the slave-like working conditions of Haitian cane cutters on sugar plantations in the Dominican Republic.[30] Among those organizations that have written codes of conduct, most allow for undercover and hidden-camera reporting on a utilitarian basis, approving the practice generally if the benefits outweigh the negative effects. Sometimes that is tempered by the principle that the story carry significant public value. The CBC has explicit guidelines, though they leave the door open to subjective judgments:

> As a general rule, hidden cameras and microphones should not be used to gather information. The CBC commonly operates openly where it can see and be seen. . . .

There may be occasions when the use of hidden cameras or microphones may be regarded as being in the public interest.

Examples of the latter include subjects such as illegal, anti-social, or fraudulent activity or clear and significant abuses of public trust. In these circumstances, it should be determined that the information gained serves an important journalistic purpose, is indispensable to that purpose, and cannot be obtained by more open means.[31]

Though undercover journalism has a long history, the ethical debate surrounding its usage has never subsided. At the centre of the discussion is a seemingly paradoxical question—can truth be discovered by telling lies? The reporter who goes undercover or carries a hidden camera is using deception and misrepresentation. Even if a greater truth is uncovered in the process, it puts the credibility of the reporter at risk. Most philosophers who have considered this situation conclude that lying in order to expose other lies is not necessarily hypocritical, and may be morally necessary in some cases.[32] At the same time, technological advances have made undercover and surreptitious reporting extremely easy. This has led to unwarranted use of the technique and a whole genre of 'gotcha' journalism that does not pass the utilitarian test of achieving greater good. While some journalistic organizations employ codes of conduct that set out strict guidelines for undercover work, others leave it to the moral judgment of individual practitioners.[33] In the end, investigative journalists have used undercover and other deceptive techniques when important truths needed to be discovered and when no other practical means were available to confirm them.[34]

Bugs in High Places

CTV reporter Tim Ralfe's most publicized moment came during the 1970 October crisis, when he asked Prime Minister Pierre Trudeau how far he would go in dealing with the FLQ. 'Just watch me', replied Trudeau. Three years later, Ralfe decided to see how far he himself could go in testing Canada's wiretap laws. At the time, the law actually permitted wiretaps in certain circumstances. Working for CTV *Inquiry* and producer Jack McGaw, Ralfe installed a matchbox-size radio transmitter where NDP caucus held its regular Ottawa meetings. The bug worked, and everything was recorded in a van parked outside the building. But then caucus chairman Ed Broadbent reached under the table and felt something unusual. Ralfe was busted.

NDP leader David Lewis stood up in the House of Commons on a point of privilege, denouncing the bugging and demanding the tapes be returned. The motion passed unanimously, and Ralfe immediately complied. CTV president Murray Chercover hadn't been told about the plan, and exploded when he found out. Ralfe argued the stunt was meant to demonstrate that Canada's anti-eavesdropping laws were not up to standard. Many of the MPs agreed, and Lewis granted Ralfe an interview on the subject. Other instances of invasion of privacy were investigated, and McGaw produced an hour-long program on the topic called *Hear No Evil, See No Evil, Speak No Evil.*

Was Ralfe's placement of the bug an example of solid investigative journalism, or a cheap form of 'gotcha' reporting? There were differing views. Columnist Geoffrey Stevens, writing in *The Globe and Mail,* called it a 'distressing, disgusting episode'. He said CTV knew the wiretap laws were scheduled to change soon anyway, and urged the network to offer an 'abject apology' for the bugging.[35] But judges in the annual Michener Awards for meritorious public service journalism thought differently. They chose the documentary for their 1973 award, inviting McGaw to Government House in Ottawa to accept the prize. 'I hope you haven't got an electronic bug on you', said Governor General Jules Léger. 'No sir, not today', replied McGaw. The judges for the award said the story was an outstanding example of in-depth reporting, and praised the producers for not being content with superficial skimming of the surface.[36]

Chapter 13

The Chilling Effect

Democracy has always recognized and cherished the fundamental importance of an individual. The importance must, in turn, be based upon the good repute of a person. It is that good repute which enhances an individual's sense of worth and value. False allegations can so very quickly and completely destroy a good reputation. A reputation tarnished by libel can seldom regain its former lustre. A democratic society, therefore, has an interest in ensuring that its members can enjoy and protect their good reputation so long as it is merited.

Former Supreme Court Justice Peter Cory[1]

Daniel Henry, an affable in-house lawyer for the CBC, routinely shows a documentary during training sessions for staff reporters and producers. It's presented as a segment from the program *The Skewerer*, a weekly show 'where the truth is never skewed, and wrongdoers are skewered'. *The Skewerer* is the flagship investigative program for a public broadcaster called TV8. And Hartley Cashman has come to the program to make a name for himself. He is trying to help the network boost its ratings to avoid a threatened government sell-off. His effort is a sensational story about payoffs in the provincial paving industry.[2]

The Skewerer, of course, is not a real program, but a mockumentary. Henry himself plays the role of Cashman, the intrepid reporter who makes sweeping allegations and chases after bad guys. The item has everything one might expect in the clichéd version of a television investigative report: crooked politicians, illegal payoffs, whistle-blowers, silhouette interviews, secret bank accounts in 'Spritzerland', and angry confrontations. Henry is gently poking fun at the entire genre, but he is also weaving a cautionary narrative about the pitfalls inherent in aggressive inquiry. 'It's a cornucopia of blatant political corruption', the anchor says in introducing the item, exact wording Henry took from an actual broadcast report.[3]

The mockumentary is filled with journalistic excesses, and Henry deconstructs the segment to illustrate all the legal problems. Along the way he explains and reinforces the various defences available to journalists who are sued for defamation: truth, fair comment, privilege, and consent. The program's main whistle-blower, a paving contractor who appears in silhouette, says that his rival paid off a former government minister to get contracts. Henry notes that the statement can't be proved on the basis of the evidence the reporter gathered. And even if it were an opinion, it wouldn't hold up to the defence of fair comment if the dominant motive of the whistle-blower were to injure his competitor. In the end, Henry cautions that the documentary could never have been broadcast in the way he produced it. But he says a version of the story would definitely be possible, if it paid close attention to all the necessary legal cautions and constraints.[4]

Since the radical colonial editors were fined and jailed for their writings, libel has been a concern for Canadian journalists.[5] Although criminal libels have become increasingly rare, civil judgments have made media organizations cautious when it comes to leveling serious accusations against individuals or organizations. As investigative journalism expanded in the 1970s, judgments for defamation actions began growing to major proportions in the US. But, in Canada, the monetary penalties were modest. Before 1978, the highest recorded defamation award was $35,000, and that related to a publication in 1962. By the late 1970s, the landscape began to change. In 1978, a judge awarded $135,000 to Gerald Snyder, a man prominent in business and public life in Montreal. He was defamed by the Montreal *Gazette* three years earlier in a story imputing connections with organized crime.[6] And in 1980, a CBC television broadcast in British Columbia became the focus of a defamation action that turned into a leading decision for years afterwards.

'This is the CBC Evening News', began the British Columbia regional supper-hour broadcast on 6 March 1980. 'British Columbia's deputy attorney general has interfered with the judicial system. Tonight, a detailed report.' Reporter Chris Bird proceeded to tell a sensational story of political interference. In a 14-minute report, he alleged that Dick Vogel, the province's deputy attorney general, influenced or tried to influence the course of justice in three specific cases. He also showed how Vogel had discretionary powers in deciding whether court cases should proceed or be halted. 'However, it seems Vogel took advantage of those powers in these specific cases', Bird said, particularly when matters involved friends.

The broadcast created a firestorm in BC political circles. The Opposition demanded the offices of the attorney general be padlocked, and called for the province's chief justice to take control of the ministry. Other media picked up on CBC's story, and there were calls for Vogel's head. The attorney general suspended Vogel with pay pending an investigation into the allegations. The story quickly became major news across the country, and CBC reporter Colin Hoath proclaimed on the CBC National: 'While no cabinet ministers have been implicated in the allegations so far, the whole business is obviously embarrassing to the Social Credit government.'[7]

Less than two weeks after the initial report, BC's attorney general announced the result of his inquiry. He said he had found no impropriety in Vogel's conduct, and he re-instated him immediately. There were comments in the media suggesting the investigation was a whitewash. Vogel called on the CBC to apologize and pay him compensation. The corporation responded by saying it stood behind the story.

Vogel sued, and the facts slowly began to emerge of how the media investigation was conducted.[8] It began with the hiring of Bird, who had about 10 years of experience with the *Victoria Colonist* and *Vancouver Province* before joining CBC in 1979. CBC was trailing BCTV in the ratings, and its new executive producer wanted to close the gap. One of the ways he thought that could happen was with more hard-hitting reports, so he hired Bird and designated him an investigative reporter. Bird cultivated senior prosecutor Bruce Donald as a source, and soon heard about a series of allegations of misconduct on the part of Vogel. Donald agreed to become a secret source, and the two began meeting in deserted areas of Stanley Park and in parts of the city where they were unlikely to be recognized.

No doubt inspired by images of Deep Throat and the *Washington Post*'s Watergate exploits, the two men devised clandestine means of exchanging information. Donald wanted to provide Bird with a memo he had written to the attorney general outlining allegations against Vogel, but he didn't want to be accused of giving it to him directly. According to the testimony, Donald left a copy of the letter in a plain brown envelope in a locker at the bus depot, hiding the locker key in the angle of a Y-shaped beam in an unfinished building. He told Bird he might find something interesting if he looked there. Bird looked in the wrong beam and puzzled over the old furniture store invoice he had found. He then called Donald who directed him to the right place, and Bird finally found the key, the locker, and the letter.

It turned out Donald was the reporter's only real source for the story, and Bird never revealed the source's identity to his superiors. If he had, they surely would have questioned Donald's presence in the story. He was shown, on-camera, firmly refusing to answer any questions about the case. In fact, Bird's final question was shouted through a door as Donald fled from the seemingly confrontational encounter. The entire interview had been stage-managed to help deflect attention away from Donald as the source.

It wasn't the only unusual technique Bird used in reporting the story. He interviewed several prosecutors while outfitted with a body pack to record their conversations, and showed one of them a bogus script to encourage him to think the CBC already had solid evidence for some of its allegations. Bird maintained the phony script procedure was standard practice for investigative reporters. In another case, he rehearsed an on-camera performance with a young man who was a participant in one of the incidents Vogel was alleged to have influenced. On tape, it's made to appear as if the young man has been taken by surprise and blurts out revealing information, only to clam up afterwards. Soon after the story went to air, Bird burned all his notes, dummy scripts, and other documents relating to the program.

BC Supreme Court Justice William Esson, in a judgment released in 1982, was merciless in his dissection of the program. He said Bird constructed a misleading and inaccurate narrative comprising good guys vs. bad guys, using the techniques of television to buttress his preconceived notions. The first example was how Bird portrayed himself early in the story, standing in the CBC newsroom with shirtsleeves rolled up and leaning on his typewriter, his expression grave and his voice serious. Esson said sympathetic characters in the story were portrayed visually with seriousness, while others were shot with hidden cameras looking guilty. In one case, a man was shown walking across the parking lot. 'His hat is pulled down over his eyes, his shoulders are hunched into his coat, his hands are in his pockets and a cigarette dangles from his lips. The impression given is one of shiftiness. The fact apparently is that he was on his way to his office on a cold morning, unaware that he was being watched. In those circumstances, few would come off better either in appearance or in reacting to the series of questions put sternly by the reporter while a camera is pointed from over his shoulder.'[9]

Under older legal definitions, libel was held to be defamation in print while slander was associated with verbal and generally more transitory insults.[10] While both were later rolled into a single definition of defamation in many jurisdictions, Esson stressed that the power of gestures, intonations, and images, which were important in slanders, had to be assessed in cases involving television. Programs on television, he said, 'tend to leave the audience with an impression rather than a firm understanding of what was said. Images, facial expressions, tones of voice, symbols, and the dramatic effect which can be achieved by juxtaposition of segments may be more important than the meaning derived from careful reading of the words of the script.'[11]

In finding that the broadcast was defamatory, Esson pointed out how Bird ignored evidence that tended to discredit his hypothesis. He also found there was malice, ruling that the motive of the defendants was to enhance their own reputations by producing a sensational program. He assessed damages against Bird and the CBC at $100,000, and tacked on an additional $25,000 in exemplary damages against the corporation. By the end of the case, Esson clearly had an opinion about how some CBC programs did their work. 'This is not the first, although it is the most serious, case disclosing what may be a tendency on the part of CBC in some of its programs to proclaim its view of the truth with righteous zeal but scant regard for the facts and for the reputations of those of whose conduct it disapproves.'[12]

The CBC felt blindsided by some of Bird's actions, and fired him after the judgment was released. Vogel's bosses were especially unhappy with his decision to burn his notes, withhold information favourable to Vogel, and stage the interview with Donald. 'We all wanted the story a little too badly', Bird reflected afterwards, though he questioned why he was the only one fired 'by faceless bureaucrats who came out of the hills in the east and killed the wounded.'[13] The Vogel case was an important precedent, and served as a wake-up call to news organizations that were beginning to practise investigative work but hadn't put necessary controls into place. It also emboldened people who felt aggrieved by media reports, and triggered more lawsuits. Esson himself later voiced judicial concern over 'the parade of libel plaintiffs for years afterwards, all claiming their case is "just like Vogel"'.[14] There was widespread misinterpretation of his ruling that the desire to create a blockbuster story could be considered malicious. Esson himself pointed out that there is nothing inherently wrong with a news organization seeking to advance its reputation with an interesting story. Malice is only present when the reporter's *primary* motivation is to produce a sensational story at the expense of fairness, he said.[15]

The lessons of the Vogel case didn't arrive in time for the *Toronto Sun*. 'Almost every week an editor or reporter somewhere seems to add yet another episode to a permanent serial entitled The Press Eats Its Own Words', said *Time* magazine in June 1981.[16] It was referring to a spectacular scandal unearthed by the *Toronto Sun* that month, a story made even more breathtaking when the newspaper retracted it in its entirety exactly one week later. The story alleged senior Liberals made secret profits when the federal government bought the Belgian oil company Petrofina. The most startling claim was that John Munro, Indian and northern affairs minister at the time, was a director of a company that had profited to the tune of $116,000.

The Munro story was a massive scoop, exactly the kind of piece editor Peter Worthington was looking for when he hired the two reporters who wrote it. Worthington always viewed the *Sun* as a mixture of the profound and the profane. In addition to scantily clad Sunshine girls, fires, and axe murders, he wanted a quotient of serious stories that could make an impact in Ottawa and beyond.[17] To achieve the aim, he hired Bob Reguly, the man who had tracked down Hal Banks and Gerda Munsinger. Reguly had left the *Star* in 1973 and worked with CTV for a number of years, appearing on *W5* and *CTV Reports*. The two men shared common interests in espionage and intelligence stories, and Reguly was keen to resume a career in newspapers. Worthington's other hire was less conventional. Donald Ramsay, at 28, had no political reporting experience, but was seen as a go-getter. Jean Sonmor, in her commissioned history of the *Toronto Sun*, said Ramsay's arrival was like a shot in the arm to the *Sun* newsroom. 'Ramsay—handsome, charming and hip—was everybody's image of the "Investigative Reporter". In the newsroom he was admired, sometimes extravagantly so. He knew everyone: mobsters, rock stars, hockey players.'[18]

Soon after joining the newspaper in 1981, Ramsay claimed to have received a tip that Liberal insiders profited when Crown-owned Petro-Canada bought Petrofina. In April, Ramsay came into Reguly's office brandishing a microfiche and announced: 'I've got that fucking Munro.' Ramsay said the microfiche was a corporate record showing Munro was a director of Molly Investments, a company that had allegedly traded in Petrofina shares at the time of the takeover.[19] The allegation was believable. Rumours had swirled for years about Munro's links with organized crime figures. And in 1978, he resigned his cabinet post after admitting he had called a judge to give a character reference for a constituent who was then being tried. 'Everybody viewed John Munro as a crook anyway', Worthington said.[20] 'I was willing to believe anything about Munro', Reguly added. Editors encouraged Ramsay to keep digging, and they assigned Reguly to help with the research.

As soon as the story was published, the denials came quickly. Munro, who wasn't quoted in the original piece, said he knew nothing about the affair. Prime Minister Pierre Trudeau called it 'garbage'. Worthington thought a follow-up story should show a picture of the microfiche evidence. But Ramsay couldn't find it, saying it was either lost or stolen. Nervous tension turned to panic among *Sun* editors when Ramsay suddenly disappeared and couldn't be located for a few days. Reguly said he had never looked at the microfiche, nor had anyone else at the newspaper. In a briefing memo requested by his editors, Reguly said the story rested largely on Ramsay's notes and documents, none of which could be found. Reguly acknowledged that Molly

Investments didn't exist. He said his request for more time on the story had been overruled because senior editors felt the details were already all over Ottawa. Reguly still thought the story was accurate, and might be salvaged if proof could be found of the sale of shares connected to Munro. He cautioned the newspaper not to overreact: 'If we can get our hands on the buy-and-sell order—and we're pulling all the strings—we could come up roses. The big worry is that an abject apology for a sleaze like Munro would destroy the credibility of the story—and any bulletproof revelations of the big fish who were involved would be dismissed. I think we should hang tough.'[21]

Worthington, meanwhile, called former defence minister James Richardson to ask whether his securities firm had any knowledge of the affair, as Ramsay had alleged. Richardson said no record could be found. At the same time, Worthington got a friendly call from one of Ramsay's former employers, telling him that the reporter couldn't be trusted.[22] But it was too late for the *Sun*. Ramsay was fired, and Reguly was asked to quit. 'It was put to me that it would be nice if I would resign, and I simply said fine. I saw no reason to whimper about it.'[23] The *Sun* ran a complete and abject apology one week after the article appeared, saying it had no evidence against Munro or any of the other prominent business people named in the story. On Trudeau's characterization of the story as 'garbage', the editorial said: 'It appears on this particular story that he was not far from the truth. We are very sorry.'[24] The apology didn't stop Munro from suing. He might have had a harder time with his lawsuit in the United States. Since 1964, American media organizations have benefited from a landmark precedent known as *New York Times* v. Sullivan, which makes it extremely difficult for libel charges to be filed by public officials. Journalists are allowed to publish reports about public figures, even if they turn out to be wrong, so long as they don't display a malicious and reckless disregard for the truth.[25] The idea is that citizens should have leeway to criticize their elected representatives. But even under those rules, it would have been challenging for the *Sun* to demonstrate an absence of malice. A year later, Munro was awarded $75,000 in damages in a judgment that said the reporters were driven by a desire to destroy reputations and gain notoriety.

The *Sun* refused to defend the reporters in court, one of the only times a media organization has ever taken such a stand in Canada. 'The result was that, with two children in university, I couldn't afford a lawyer and so didn't attend the trial, except for my brief testimony. Failure to do so was the biggest mistake in my life', Reguly said.[26] After a spectacular early career, the 50-year-old Reguly realized he would never get another newspaper job. He ended up freelancing, teaching journalism, writing speeches, and doing public relations for government. Twenty-five years after the incident, he still believed insiders made fortunes on the Petrofina deal, and that Munro was involved. Ramsay surfaced some time after the scandal as a public relations spokesman for the Winnipeg Jets hockey club. He died in Vancouver of liver failure at the age of 41.

With the Vogel and Munro cases coming in such quick succession, libel lawyers and their clients began wondering whether the media were becoming easy prey. In 1984, a court found *W5* libeled a quarry company and its president over a broadcast four years earlier. The program reported the company was taking toxic liquid wastes for disposal to a site designated for solid wastes. The company said its explanations were not adequately represented, and it called into question the honesty of *W5*'s techniques and procedures. The jury was told the program's audience was 883,000 people, so it multiplied the number by $1 per viewer, added additional penalties, and came up with a fine of $958,000.[27] At the time, it exceeded the largest previous Canadian libel award by more than seven times. When the case was appealed two years later, CTV lawyers argued the penalty would have a chilling effect on investigative journalism. 'There should be a deep chill on this sort of journalism', said lawyer Julian Porter, who represented the quarry company. 'It's my submission this is really the most wicked show possible.'[28] The appeal court thought Porter's characterization went too far. It set aside the jury award, gave $25,000 to the company president and ordered a new trial, which subsequently awarded an additional $90,000. A decade after the first court judgment, nearly $300,000 more was levied against CTV in costs.

Even those stakes were relatively paltry when compared to the amount of money at issue in a lawsuit launched by one of Canada's richest families against *Toronto Life* magazine. After his tenure at the CBC, Peter Herrndorf became publisher of *Toronto Life* and continued to encourage serious, challenging work. He found just the right journalist in freelancer Elaine Dewar, an experienced magazine researcher and writer. In 1987, Dewar wrote a story that Herrndorf called the ultimate example of investigative reporting, the longest, most complex, and documented article he had ever seen in Canadian magazine journalism.[29] Entitled 'The Mysterious Reichmanns: The Untold Story', the mini-book length article told the tale of the billionaire Reichmann family of Toronto, which controlled massive real estate and other corporate holdings. The Reichmanns didn't appreciate Dewar's interest in business dealings the family had in Europe and Africa before coming to Canada. They felt the article implied the family's wealth had illicit origins.[30] The Reichmanns responded with a $102-million lawsuit.

As a former researcher and fact-checker, Dewar knew the importance of getting every detail right. It came from real-life experience of verifying facts before a story was published. 'You listen to someone you call up to check a story and hear them explode. They're scared and angry. The story is dead wrong. You become aware of how it affects their lives, career, and standing in the community. You learn a respect for what you are doing because you realize you're messing with important business and must take care.'[31] Dewar was about to discover how a determined plaintiff could ruin her career and standing in the community. Over the next four years, millions were spent on the lawsuit by both sides. According to court records, the Reichmanns sent private investigators to the US, Europe, and Africa retracing Dewar's research steps.[32] They forced her to turn over thousands of pages of notes and documents, and engaged her in lengthy examinations for discovery. Meanwhile, the National Business Writing Awards rejected Dewar's article as an entry for its annual competition. The awards co-sponsor, the Royal Bank, provided a legal opinion that said circulating the article to judges could be held to be republication, which would put the awards organization at legal risk. *Toronto Life* and a number of other publications withdrew all their entries from the awards in protest, but Dewar's state of limbo over the story continued for years.

The legal fight exhausted the magazine's libel insurance, and began to threaten its financial stability. Finally, in early 1991, an out-of-court settlement was reached. The magazine agreed to publish an apology and make a donation to four Canadian charities. In March 1991, the magazine said, 'Any and all negative insinuations and allegations in the article . . . are totally false.' A gag order prevented much further detail from being revealed about the case. Herrndorf said the magazine discovered how difficult it was to sustain a lengthy fight against people with significant resources. 'Other publications looked at the battle between *Toronto Life* and the Reichmanns and began to wonder whether it made sense from an economic point of view to take on these causes.'[33] Proof of that assessment came rapidly. Macmillan of Canada was planning to publish a book by Kimberley Noble about the Bronfman family and its business interests. But a lawyer's letter warning the publisher that any mistakes might prompt a lawsuit convinced Macmillan it couldn't afford to defend itself in any action. It cancelled the project.[34] And if entries to the National Newspaper Awards were any indication, editors seemed to be commissioning fewer investigative stories. By 1993, there were only 52 entries in the Enterprise Reporting category, down from a high of 103 in 1988.[35]

Mistakes were one matter, but investigative journalists also started coming under fire for stories that were apparently error-free. A CBC *Marketplace* story in 1990 had looked at the issue of mercury in paint, and the potential for dangerous health effects. The Color Your World corporation sued, and a judge ruled in its favour. The court didn't find fault with any of the individual statements made in the story. At issue was the entire innuendo supposedly created by the item, which the judge agreed was defamatory. The plaintiff called an expert in communications to show how the program craftily arranged its pictures to heighten its defamatory message.[36] The testimony came as a surprise to the program's producers, who hadn't heard of, much less used, the cunning production techniques.[37] The judgment was overturned on appeal, but journalists were on notice that meticulously correct statements of fact might not be sufficient to defend against lawsuits.

Perhaps the most troublesome and costly defamation lawsuit in Canadian history came following broadcast of the *fifth estate* segment called 'The Heart of the Matter' in February 1996. It looked at questions being raised in the medical community about the safety of heart medications known as calcium channel blockers, specifically one called nifedipine. The focus of the broadcast was the response of Health Canada's Health Protection Branch to potential safety issues surrounding different formulations of the drug. Varying opinions about the drugs were highlighted, and issues of potential conflict of interest surrounding doctors who took part in Health Canada committee meetings were also explored. The lawsuits that followed didn't come from Health Canada, but from two doctors who said they had been maligned.

Dr Martin Myers and Dr Frans Leenen were both successful in their lawsuits, and the CBC was ordered to pay about $3 million in damages and legal costs. The Ontario Court of Appeal upheld the decisions, and the Supreme Court of Canada refused to hear any further appeal. The judge's comments in the Leenen case were especially critical of the CBC. Even though the program was an exploration of an issue that might be of significant public interest, and could be defended on the basis of fair comment, Justice J. Douglas Cunningham noted that an honest belief in the truth of the comment is essential in the defence of fair comment. 'Sadly, those involved in the production of this program could not have believed what they were doing', he asserted. He criticized various production techniques, including a portion of the program that showed Leenen fumbling for his glasses so he could read a document. 'This emphasis on trying to portray Dr Leenen's ineptitude with a most fundamental function in life goes to the depth to which the defendants tried to destroy the plaintiff not just professionally but as a human being.'[38] He called the production team 'parasitic sensationalists'.

The judge's vitriolic language shocked many journalists, but it caused others to reflect on exactly what kind of journalism the courts deemed acceptable. Tony Burman, executive director of CBC Television News at the time, defended the broadcast and said it was the result of careful research by a team that conducted dozens of interviews and looked at thousands of documents. He paid tribute to the quality of work *the fifth estate* was known for, and took issue with the judgment's finding of malice. An important issue for journalists, he said, is how they are to report on matters of conflict of interest. 'We believe that the legal and popular use of the term "conflict of interest" is clear, and that an allegation of conflict does not imply actual dishonesty or corruption. The judge's findings to the contrary may have grave implications for the media's ability to report on conflict of interest. The judgment can be read as favouring a circumscribed "he said, she said" formula, with no journalistic analysis applied.'[39] Burman said the ruling had the potential to have a dramatic effect on Canadian journalism.

Still, the judgment was far from the final word on how the courts viewed investigative television reports. In 2004, a judge from the Ontario Superior Court of Justice dismissed a defamation case against *the fifth estate* that complained of a 1998 broadcast called 'Prove It if You Can'. In that story, the program showed how insurance companies did not always treat accident victims fairly, alleging that they sometimes relied on assessment firms to dispute claims of disability. After a trial lasting 76 days, the courts found that the program treated the plaintiffs fairly. 'CBC was attempting to produce a program which was interesting and informative on an issue of public interest, but I do not accept that its predominant motive was to produce a sensational program rather than a show which served the public', wrote Justice Paul Rivard.[40] Even so, the harsh language of the Leenen judgment offered ongoing ammunition to defamation plaintiffs. It's hard to imagine how senior managers of Canadian media organizations could ignore such a precedent.

Far from a modern concept, libel chill is as old as journalism itself in Canada. Early colonial editors had to contend with heavy-handed administrators who were quick to arrest journalists for seditious libel. Between 1794 and 1829, there were more than 30 common-law sedition prosecutions in Upper Canada.[41] With the arrival of responsible government, the threat shifted to civil defamation actions. But until the 1980s, Canadian court judgments rarely served as a significant deterrent. The commodification of investigative journalism in the post-Watergate era encouraged all kinds of aggressive and often clumsy reporting. The rush to set up investigative teams often outpaced sober consideration of careful methodologies and standards. A number of high-profile cases at the beginning of the 1980s shook journalism and emboldened plaintiffs to take on reporters who became too aggressive. It didn't help that Canadian courts, unlike their American counterparts, weren't interested in affording journalists greater leeway when it came to public figures of any kind. As one Canadian judge said:

> If society wants, as it should, that its best citizens turn to public affairs, it must show the high esteem in which it holds them; and those who would imprudently risk, by a stroke of the pen, to destroy the reputation of such dedicated men ought to pay the high price that such a misdeed deserves.[42]

Suddenly, institutions had to weigh the possibility of extensive legal actions when they contemplated taking on projects. As we have seen, this occasionally meant stories were killed even before they were created. This process only exacerbated the tensions between practitioners, eager to attain their aim of penetrating investigative journalism, and institutions that were mindful of their bottom lines. The prospect of multi-million dollar lawsuits is always a sobering one when budgets are drawn up and projects planned. For independent journalists hoping to sell projects to institutions on a freelance basis, the high cost of libel insurance usually rules out risky investigative stories. Yet some media organizations, despite the inherent risks and liabilities, continue to commission aggressive investigations. And for CBC lawyer Daniel Henry, each new case produces more examples and lessons to incorporate into his training sessions for the next generation of journalists.

Chapter 14

Attacking the Messenger

> The politician seeks to lull the people with the pleasantries of government. The journalist seeks the cold, hard facts of government. Sometimes these don't jibe, whereupon the politician reaches for the nearest microphone and assures the people that the journalist is the worst sort of skunk.
>
> Ithiel de Sola Pool, political scientist[1]

Defamation lawsuits are by no means the only effective method of attacking investigative journalists. Those on the receiving end of pointed investigations have found novel ways to exact revenge on the people responsible for exposing their activities to the public. Organized-crime figures generally take the most blunt route. When a teenage Mafia bodyguard shot Montreal crime reporter Jean-Pierre Charbonneau in 1973, it was seen as a warning to other journalists at the time. But reporters continued to investigate the world of crime, even in the face of persistent attacks. In 1995, Robert Monastesse was shot in both legs after his freelance articles in *La Presse* exposed details of the turf battles between biker gangs in Montreal.[2] In 1998, Greg Rasmussen of CBC Radio in Vancouver worked on a Hell's Angels investigation, and then had his house broken into and vandalized.[3] And in 2000, veteran crime reporter Michel Auger, who had done pioneering investigative work into organized crime in the 1970s, pulled into the parking lot at *Le Journal de Montréal* and was shot in the back six times. His attacker used a .22 calibre assassin's pistol fitted with a silencer.[4] Although Charbonneau, Monastesse, and Auger survived, Tara Singh Hayer was not so fortunate. The founder of the *Indo-Canadian Times*, Hayer was a controversial figure and an outspoken critic of violence in the Sikh separatist movement. He also offered incriminating evidence involving suspects in the 1985 Air India bombing case, in which 329 people died. An assassination attempt in 1988 left him paralyzed, and 10 years later he was murdered at his Surrey, BC home.[5]

When guns aren't being brandished, other techniques emerge. Campaigns are mounted to discredit the credibility of journalists. Some are accused of bias or incompetence. In other cases, when the accuracy of the reports isn't at issue, it is the methods used by the journalists that come in for criticism. If an ethically questionable tactic can be found in the journalist's methodology, it can be used to discount an entire report. Complaints are lodged with an employer, an ombudsman, a commission of inquiry, or directly with the public, all in an effort to negate the initial sting of a story and deter further investigation. When the government is involved, the pressure can become oppressive. In 1971, John Zaritsky wrote a front-page story for the *Globe and Mail* detailing the Ontario Conservative government's role in shady land transactions. The story was a major embarrassment for Premier Bill Davis, and he immediately called a commission of inquiry. As the politicians emerged from the legislative chamber following the announcement of the inquiry, Zaritsky triumphantly approached the premier, only to have Davis poke him in the chest and say: 'You know something, you're going to be the first witness we subpoena.'[6] Davis made good on his promise. The inquiry decided it was important to know how Zaritsky got the story, and demanded to know his sources. Zaritsky refused to say, and even though his lawyer decried the 'witch hunt' atmosphere of the proceedings, he was held in contempt. In the end, the reporter who had broken the story and was responsible for creating the inquiry in the first place was fined $500 for his insolence.[7]

Two case studies, 30 years apart, demonstrate the kind of counter-offensives that can be triggered when investigative journalists aggressively pursue controversial stories. Both grew into far bigger affairs than the journalists could ever have originally imagined, and both touched on the complex interplay between journalists, their institutions, and government.

On 22 October 1967, viewers tuning in to CBC television expected to see the Ed Sullivan show. Instead, the coveted 8 p.m. timeslot on Sunday was reserved for a special documentary called *Air of Death*. Before viewers could get over the shock of missing their weekly fix of comedy, circus performers, and Topo Gigio, they were transfixed by a dramatic program on air pollution. It was a topic that journalists hadn't yet explored in great detail in Canada, and the CBC was determined to place it firmly on the national agenda. The host was Stanley Burke, anchor of the CBC national news, and in publicity before the telecast a CBC publication proclaimed: 'Air pollution is a social disease we must talk about.'[8]

The documentary opened with ominous music over images of belching smokestacks in a polluted city. Then, a nurse led an elderly man into a breathing chamber in a hospital. Burke provided the initial voice-over: 'Every day your lungs inhale 15,000 quarts of air, and poison. If you're an old man in a box, or a child at play, you can't choose not to breathe. You must breathe: 15,000 quarts a day, air and poison. . . . Air pollution stops your breath.' Early in the documentary, it became clear the broadcast wasn't a dispassionate account of just another scientific debate. Burke appeared on-camera to make the point in a personal way: 'For the past six months we've been researching this program, and frankly it's been a frightening experience. I don't smoke myself, but I now know I'm getting the equivalent of two packs a day right out of the air. I'm inhaling a cup full of dirt plus poison. I didn't know what emphysema was and perhaps you don't either, but you will. It's becoming one of the major killers.'[9]

The documentary was produced by Larry Gosnell of the CBC's farm and fisheries department. A talented and visionary producer, Gosnell had a degree in agricultural economics. Even before the publication of Rachel Carson's environmental warnings in

Silent Spring, he had produced *Poisons, Pests and People*, warning of the risks posed by pesticides.[10] For *Air of Death*, he conducted 70 interviews and shot footage in 19 locations including Windsor, Sarnia, Port Huron, Hamilton, Toronto, Montreal, Sydney, Port Alberni, and in the US. Burke, who also had a degree in agriculture, called *Air of Death* his proudest achievement in 20 years. And Murray Creed, network supervisor of the CBC department that produced it, explained why the project was initiated: 'In the view of the farm department, we have as much responsibility to do everything in our power to ensure that the natural resources are protected as we have to provide farmers with day-to-day information. At the present time, these resources are being wasted.'[11]

The documentary examined pollution around the world, with a particular emphasis on large Canadian cities. It investigated the specific contaminants released into the air and the health effects associated with them. But then the documentary changed direction, and set in motion a controversy that unleashed the biggest reaction against CBC producers since the firestorm that engulfed *This Hour Has Seven Days*. 'Air pollution isn't just a big-city problem', Burke said. 'A new phosphate plant back in 1960 brought a welcome boost to the economy of the quiet agricultural area around Dunnville in southern Ontario—new paycheques, new life. Ever since the pioneer days, generations had dwelt in the security and peace of rural living. Pandora's box was opened. . . . They don't like to talk about it, even now. You have to persuade them to tell you what it was that came out of the box. Something mysterious burned the peppers, burned the fruit, dwarfed and shriveled the grains, damaged everything that grew. Something in the air destroyed the crops. Anyone could see it. You can see it now.' The documentary examined the effect of fluoride emissions from the Electric Reduction Co. of Canada. It concluded that the pollution was harmful not only to the land and animals, but to humans as well. It suggested government and industry weren't doing enough to curb pollution, and highlighted a way the situation might change. Burke interviewed an environmental activist in New York who said: 'Nothing really will be done until the citizens begin to get involved and begin to let everybody know that they do care about having clean air to breathe, and for their children to breathe.'[12]

Air of Death drew an audience of one and a half million people, and reaction to it 'was sudden and prolonged and widespread'.[13] It sparked commentators across Canada to question what the government was doing about pollution. At the University of Toronto campus, it inspired activists to hold meetings and eventually create the organization known as Pollution Probe.[14] In Ottawa, federal NDP leader Tommy Douglas called for national pollution standards and legislation to criminalize pollution. The federal government responded with a promise to enact a national Clean Air act. The Ontario health department felt the greatest heat. Opposition parties denounced the government for lacking the guts to enforce anti-pollution laws, accusing it of a cover-up to protect a company. 'Shut the Electric Reduction Company today', pronounced Morton Shulman, a New Democrat MPP. 'They are killing their whole environment and should not be given another day's grace.'[15] The company, meanwhile, worked quietly behind the scenes to minimize the public relations damage and use its contacts with government to find a way out of the sea of negative publicity. Within a week of the broadcast, the government proposed a public inquiry. It soon became clear exactly what kind of inquiry it would be.

Executives of the Electric Reduction Co. knew who would chair the inquiry before it was made public.[16] 'We have heard privately that Dr Ed Hall is to be chairman. . . . I know him well and think he will probably give us a very fair hearing', wrote the company vice-chair at the time.[17] Hall was a known advocate for fluoridation who had been honourary head of the Pro-Fluoridation League. A second member of the inquiry, W.C. Winegard, had been given the Alcan award for 'the advancement of metallurgy in Canada' just before the broadcast. And the third commissioner was Alex McKinney, who was referred to in the press as a 'conservative stalwart', as were the other two members. In her doctoral thesis investigating the Hall commission, Ella Haley analyzed the various 'negation strategies' that were employed to attack the documentary. One of them involved appointing, as an advisory expert to the commission, a man who consistently dismissed critics of air pollution as 'cranks, layabouts, psychopaths'. The expert, Dr Patrick Lawther, argued that smog only killed the weak. 'We used to let people die with chronic bronchial pneumonia. Now we don't let them. We bring them back with antibiotics—and it is people like these who are the ones to go during severe smog attacks.'[18]

Predictably, when the commission reported at the end of 1968, it reserved its harshest criticism not for the polluters but for the CBC. The program 'treated a complex problem in a way designed to create alarm and fear', said the report. In denying there were human health problems in Dunnville, the commission said *Air of Death* was based on 'unwarranted, untruthful, and irresponsible statements'. It virtually invited those Dunnville residents whose businesses had been negatively affected by the publicity to sue the CBC. The headline writers turned their attention away from polluters and towards the public broadcaster. Some writers, though, detected the hint of a whitewash. 'Errors in fact, errors in scientific method, and plain political bias are to be found throughout the Royal Commission on Pollution, the so-called Hall Report', wrote Ron Haggart in the *Star*. '. . . [It] utters not one word of criticism of the inaction of the provincial government. Instead the Hall Report criticizes those who brought the scandal to light.'[19]

A few days after the report, the CRTC announced it would hold a special hearing into the circumstances surrounding the production of the broadcast. What followed was a first for the regulatory agency: a full-scale inquisition into a documentary. The commission was less interested in the extent of pollution in Dunnville and more concerned with how a broadcaster went about putting together a documentary. The CBC, which had refused to participate in the Hall inquiry, testified in force at the CRTC. Program producers vigorously defended the documentary. Stanley Burke said it was a carefully planned and responsible piece of work. 'This is the kind of television of the future. It begins a dialogue. Previously, television has been passive', he said.[20] When the commission reported in January 1970, it had significantly different conclusions than the Ontario committee. It described the documentary as 'one of the most thoroughly researched programs in the history of television broadcasting'. And it said it adequately reflected the information reasonably available at the time. While it was critical of the program's use of an expert known for his outspoken views against fluoridation, without providing viewers with sufficient context about his career, the commission said the program 'is well able to stand as an example of informational programming backed by a wealth of research and serving a useful purpose.'[21]

If Gosnell felt vindicated by the CRTC decision, he was exhausted by the intense scrutiny and criticism his documentary had undergone for more than two years. At one point, following the Hall report, he wondered if people would simply dismiss his future work as the product of 'that well-known CBC liar'. But the legacy of that single documentary remained significant, and when he died in 2004, many people said his work had paved the way for an increased awareness of pollution throughout Canadian society. 'He was a lot of trouble, but he was worth every second of it and more . . . trouble in the sense that what he wrote, what he did, was controversial, was argumentative', said Knowlton Nash, former CBC anchor and news executive. 'He was really one of the great pioneering, investigative producers, certainly one of the greatest.'[22]

Three decades later, a complex series of events in Vancouver led to an episode with interesting parallels to the *Air of Death* controversy. Once again, it was a CBC journalist who presented information that stirred discussion and emotions on a topic of great importance. And government again responded by focusing the debate back on the journalism itself. This time, however, the counter-attack was lodged from the highest political pulpit in the country, the Prime Minister's Office.

The story began in November 1997 with the annual gathering of the heads of the Asia-Pacific Economic Cooperation (APEC) countries in Vancouver. It was a routine meeting, held on the campus of the University of British Columbia, and most of the media coverage centred on the crisis in Asian economies at the time. There were protests by students and other activists, demonstrating against the lack of human rights and democracy in some of the participating nations. There was particular anger at the presence of Indonesian President Suharto, whose authoritarian regime and occupation of East Timor had drawn international condemnation. Police cracked down firmly on protesters, using pepper spray and pre-emptive arrests. The heavy-handed RCMP response drew considerable media coverage and complaints from protesters, eventually triggering an inquiry by the RCMP's Public Complaints Commission. Questioned by reporters about the police actions and the pepper spraying, Prime Minister Jean Chrétien famously replied: 'For me, pepper, I put it on my plate.'[23]

'It emerged that we'd all missed something', said Terry Milewski of CBC Television, one of the reporters who had covered the summit. He interviewed a protester who said police had told her that, on orders from the Prime Minister's Office, protest signs weren't allowed on the motorcade route. Another student, Craig Jones, spent 14 hours in jail for refusing to give up signs that advocated free speech, democracy, and human rights. Police had also seized another sign that said 'Dictators Not Welcome at UBC'.[24] Milewski began reporting these stories, along with denials from the Prime Minister's Office that it had been involved in any of the security arrangements. In a short story on 18 December, he reported on further indications that the Prime Minister's Office wanted stringent security. His report also asked some questions: 'If the security plan was good enough for the RCMP, why was it not good enough for the Prime Minister's Office? Did the prime minister offer any assurances to visiting leaders that demonstrators would be kept out of sight?'[25]

Milewski kept on the story, aggressively pursuing information and working his sources. Born in the UK and trained at Oxford, Milewski had a reputation for critical thinking and dogged pursuit. He had spent the last two decades reporting from around the world, and had a keen sense of when a story required further digging. Eventually he was able to answer the questions he himself had posed in his December report. In the fall of 1998, he broadcast a series of stories based on internal government documents from the Prime Minister's Office and the RCMP 'showing that they were determined to keep a lid on protests even if they had no legitimate security grounds for doing so'.[26] He showed an internal RCMP memo saying 'PM wants the tenters out . . . PM wanted everyone removed.' He also quoted another memo acknowledging the difficulty of removing banners for political reasons only: '. . . we do not want banners nor would the PMO's office. Having said that, banners are not a security issue. They are a political issue. If they are not going to be permitted what is the authority for removing them and who is going to do it?'[27] It emerged that Suharto had repeatedly expressed concerns about the potential for demonstrations and embarrassment. He had threatened to boycott the meeting if his worries couldn't be adequately addressed. An internal memo from the prime minister's top APEC official said: 'PMO has expressed concerns about the security perimeter at UBC, not so much from a security point of view but to avoid embarrassments to APEC leaders . . . we do not wish student demonstrations and efforts by the gov't to suppress the freedom of expression to become a major media story.'[28] Clearly the government's efforts to prevent a media backlash had failed. Milewski and producer Carmen Merrifield won a Gemini award for their initial APEC documentary. But as Milewski said: 'We should have remembered that pride goeth before a fall.'[29]

As part of the RCMP complaint inquiry, George MacIntosh, lawyer for RCMP officers, asked for an order compelling Craig Jones to turn over any documents he had on the APEC affair. They included e-mail exchanges between Jones and Milewski, which MacIntosh tabled at the inquiry. Even though Milewski's e-mails were considered irrelevant to the inquiry, they had entered the public record. In what Milewski characterized as an old-fashioned dirty trick, it was later revealed that MacIntosh had leaked the e-mails to the *Vancouver Sun*, and both the *Sun* and *Province* ran stories about the Milewski-Jones exchanges. The stories alleged that Milewski had been advising one of the protesters, and had provided him information from confidential documents. A *Sun* editorial condemned 'a worrying traffic in confidential documents' between the two men. Milewski wasn't pleased that his private e-mails had been made public, and he took issue with the interpretation the Vancouver newspapers were giving them. He said it was ironic the *Sun* was criticizing the traffic in confidential documents, since the newspaper itself had used Milewski's documents in a story it had done earlier on APEC.[30] But the story remained a minor, local sidebar to the bigger APEC affair.

That changed when the Prime Minister's Office issued a press release on 17 October. The media had identified APEC as the most difficult issue facing the Chrétien government in its second mandate. At the time, Solicitor General Andy Scott was under pressure to resign after he was overheard making questionable comments about the inquiry in public. And Ottawa was coming under fire for refusing to pay the legal fees of the student complainants at the inquiry. As this was unfolding, the prime minister's director of communications, Peter Donolo, launched a complaint with the CBC's ombudsman, charging bias on the part of Milewski. In what the *Globe and Mail* called one of the prime minister's sharpest attacks ever against the CBC, Donolo accused Milewski of having a one-sided agenda. 'It appears Mr Milewski has set out from the beginning to side with complainants, that he has secretly conspired with a complainant on legal strategies, and that he has sought to portray the government, in his own words, as "the Forces of Darkness"'.[31]

Suddenly, as in the *Air of Death* controversy, the CBC and its journalism became the story. Milewski was front page news the next day, as were excerpts from his e-mails. In one of his messages to Jones, Milewski had said: 'Thanks again for your help on this story. Not much new in tonight's, I'm afraid—we only just got on the air at all—so we must await Jones vs. the Forces of Darkness in the courts for our next attempt to milk it.' In another e-mail, Milewski reiterated a list of questions he had posed to the Prime Minister's Office that hadn't been answered. Donolo hadn't raised any complaints about errors of fact in Milewski's stories. The CBC responded by defending its journalism and rejecting the notion of bias. But it had a problem with the e-mails. 'We cannot condone a reporter offering or seem [*sic*] to be offering advice on legal strategy to anyone involved in a story. Also, we cannot condone a reporter sharing questions submitted to one party in a story to [*sic*] another party in the story.'[32] Milewski considered the allegation unfounded, as the information he supposedly shared with Jones had been shared three weeks earlier with the entire country in his documentary. But his bosses held a different view. The CBC suspended Milewski for three days without pay and removed him from further coverage of the APEC story.[33]

What followed was a noisy debate about journalism ethics and the methods reporters use to secure information. There was also sustained commentary about the power of the Prime Minister's Office to influence editorial policy at its Crown broadcaster, whose president and board are appointed by the government of the day. Milewski himself waded into the debate with an opinion piece in the *Globe and Mail* entitled 'Who's Next?' He suggested the government didn't appreciate aggressive reporting, and preferred handout journalism instead. 'Which journalist will be the target of a personal attack by the PMO, forcing his (or her) employer to pull him off the story, even when the substance of his reporting is unchallenged?' He lauded the CBC for standing behind him, but added, 'Let's hope the next reporter to get Donoloed has a powerful organization behind him.'[34] Because he hadn't cleared the piece with his superiors in advance, Milewski was suspended for another 15 days.

Milewski spent a nervous few months waiting for the CBC Ombudsman to render a judgment. The case had been passed to Marcel Pépin of Radio-Canada to decide. In

March of 1999, Pépin delivered a 14,000-word report that dealt not just with the specifics of Donolo's complaints, but the complexities and nuances in all investigative journalism. Although he said Donolo's arguments seemed convincing at first glance, an exhaustive review of all the documents and facts of the case led him to conclude that Milewski had not breached CBC's journalistic policies and was not guilty of inaccurate or unfair reporting. Calling the government the 'forces of darkness' was merely a joke, and Pépin rejected the idea that Milewski was offering advice on any legal strategies. He said he couldn't subscribe to CBC management's interpretation that by sending Jones the questions he had submitted to the prime minister he was breaching ethics. Pépin also objected to Donolo's characterization of Milewski's relationship with Jones as a secret conspiracy. 'The confidential nature of the relations between a journalist and his source gives them a secret nature; that is obvious. But there is nothing blameworthy in this since it involves not plot, but an exchange of courtesies.'[35] At most, said Pépin, Milewski was guilty of maladroit and imprudent language in his e-mails, and he said the tone in his stories might have sounded vindictive. But he was quick to point out that it was natural for the emphasis in the stories to be on the actions of the government and police.

One of the key questions Pépin tackled was whether Milewski was being unethical by seeming to espouse the point of view of the protesters. Here is how he addressed the complainant's arguments:

> Does the obvious sympathy he feels for those who maintain they were victimized constitute professional misconduct? What you are maintaining, basically, is that the reporter should have been strictly neutral, kept his distance from his sources and settled for reporting the opinions of the 'parties concerned'. There seems to be confusion here between objectivity and indifference. The parties concerned are not only persons and institutions, but also questions as basic as respect for civil rights guaranteed by the Constitution. This is not just another news item, like a car accident in which it must be determined which driver was at fault, but rather a matter of finding out whether rights as basic as freedom of expression or demonstration have been unjustly limited or denied.
>
> The history of journalism abounds in examples of journalists lending a particularly sympathetic ear to those who claim to be victims of abuses of power. To give just a few examples, let us recall the anti-apartheid movement in South Africa, the struggle of the Blacks in the US, the denunciation of working conditions in sweatshops, etc. If it is the media's duty to be faithful to the facts, the media also have a social responsibility, and that is what informs the approach of a journalist who is attentive to the cause of a group or a person dealing with any form of power.[36]

And elsewhere in the report, on the issue of Milewski's famous skepticism towards authorities and the official versions of events they disseminate, Pépin said:

That he could have a penchant towards respect for basic rights and be constantly skeptical regarding official explanations does not constitute, in my opinion, a breach of conduct. No one is asking journalists to pretend they are indifferent and blasé when covering events as controversial as those concerned here. Objectivity must not be confused with dull and pale neutrality.[37]

Milewski took the report as a complete exoneration. The CBC was less enthusiastic. In a note to staff, Bob Culbert, head of news and current affairs, said the report confirmed that CBC News had broadcast fair and accurate reports. But he said Pépin had no power to change or set new policy, and he disputed the statement of others that it represented a 'landmark ruling'. CBC was still defending its decision to suspend Milewski. 'If some believe that in this case management enforced the current policy too strictly, then so be it', Culbert told staff.[38] A year later, before the issue of Milewski's suspensions was scheduled to go to arbitration, CBC agreed to revoke his suspensions and provide financial compensation. The corporation said he would be free to cover the APEC story once again, though he never did.[39] The Law Society of British Columbia eventually determined it was an 'error in judgment' for George MacIntosh to have provided Milewski's e-mails to the press.[40]

Almost lost in the whole episode was the APEC incident itself and the result of the RCMP inquiry. Former judge Ted Hughes found widespread incompetence on the part of the RCMP, and in some cases violations of the constitutional rights of demonstrators. But his report came in the middle of summer in 2001, nearly four years after the Vancouver summit, and critics lambasted it for not holding the prime minister responsible. Milewski, meanwhile, had gone on to other assignments. Like Larry Gosnell, he wondered how his future career would play out following all the controversy. But he continued to pursue important stories aggressively, and said he hadn't changed any of his methods or techniques as a result.

Attacks on investigative journalists are common throughout the world. These can take many forms: physical assaults and murder, legal actions, campaigns of vilification, cancellation of advertising, and other more subtle forms of pressure. Journalists working for private media institutions, particularly in an era when print and broadcast conglomerates form part of the economic establishment, must tread warily when conducting their investigations. Local reporters who take on corporations that advertise heavily in their media outlets can find their investigations shut down. Often the pressure is less overt, with publishers and news directors gently urging their senior editors to concentrate on lifestyle and feature stories rather than aggressive inquiry. The situation is somewhat different when it comes to publicly owned media. This chapter focuses on two examples, 30 years apart, from the Canadian Broadcasting Corporation. In a sense, the main stakeholder in the CBC is the government of Canada, and it hasn't been shy about exercising its influence when its interests have been threatened. According to CBC historian and former executive Knowlton Nash, 'Inquisitions will always occur whenever the public broadcasting system offers challenges to conventional wisdom.'[41]Inquisitions of different kinds occurred in the *Air of Death* affair and the APEC controversy. In both cases, journalists had brought uncomfortable truths to light, and powerful interests were intent on blunting the message by attacking the messenger. The reaction of the media institution, in this case the CBC itself, is instructive. How fully it supported and endorsed its reporters sent a signal to other practitioners about the kind of aggressive inquiry it wanted to encourage. It showed, once more, the contradictions between the aims of practitioners and institutions in pursuing the objectives of the social practice of investigative journalism. How should any media institution react when one of its journalists comes under sustained attack? Should it avoid situations in the first place that might give rise to such pressure? In 1965, the Fowler Committee on broadcasting in Canada had some pointed advice for broadcasters, both public and private.

> A broadcasting system must not minister solely to the comfort of the people. It must not always play safe. Its guiding rule cannot be to give the people what they want, for at best this can be only what the broadcasters think the people want; they may not know, and the people themselves may not know. One of the essential tasks of a broadcasting system is to stir up the minds and emotions of the people and occasionally to make large numbers of them acutely uncomfortable. . . . In a vital broadcasting system, there must be room for the thinker, the disturber, and the creator of new forms and ideas.[42]

Men in Black

Ottawa Citizen reporter Juliet O'Neill was lying in bed on a cold January morning in 2004 when the doorbell rang. She wasn't expecting anyone, so she peeked out the window to see cars full of shadowy figures and men in black standing in her doorway. RCMP officers had arrived with a search warrant. Ten officers spent the next five hours rifling through everything in her home. They combed through her underwear drawer, checked under the bed sheets, copied the hard drive in her laptop, and examined love letters from her partner. It was all because of an article she had written on 8 November 2003 about the case involving Maher Arar, the Canadian engineer who was detained in New York and deported to Syria, where he was tortured.

Arar claimed he had been unjustly targeted as a terrorist suspect, and that Canadian and American authorities deliberately sent him to Syria where they knew he would be tortured. He was calling for a public inquiry. O'Neill's story quoted an unnamed security source who said the government feared an inquiry might reveal details of a suspected Ottawa-based al-Qaeda cell. She also quoted from an alleged leaked document, suggesting Arar confessed to terrorist activity while in Syrian captivity. The RCMP were at her door trying to find the source of her information.

For some, O'Neill's case was a classic example of attacking the messenger. Instead of trying to find the anonymous sources themselves, the government went after the reporter. It turned out the sources were spinning disinformation to cover their tracks on the Arar case. Arar was subsequently exonerated, and the government issued an apology together with a compensation settlement. But the search at O'Neill's home sent a message to journalists that reporting sensitive government information might result in police officers at the door. Police had secured their warrant using provisions of the Security of Information Act, legislation passed after the September 11 attack on the US. But O'Neill took the case to court, and in October 2006 an Ontario Superior Court judge quashed three sections of the so-called leakage provisions of the act. The judge said the warrants amounted to 'intimidation of the press and an infringement of the constitutional right of freedom of the press'. The judgment rendered the warrants used to search O'Neill's home null and void, and ordered police to return everything they had seized.

Chapter 15

Access to Information

This is a lonely existence. The only pats on the back I get are when somebody says, 'You're a bastard, you're a son-of-a-bitch.' That's when I feel what I'm doing is understood.

Ken Rubin[1]

Ken Rubin describes himself as a public interest researcher, citizens' advocate, author, civil libertarian, and organic farmer. He is also one of the country's foremost experts on how to pry information loose from different levels of government. From his Ottawa home, he devises strategies to extract documents from suspicious and reluctant government functionaries. When he succeeds at finding something important, which he routinely does, he turns it over to a public interest group, sells it to a media organization, or helps out someone who has been battling government bureaucracy. Since the federal government introduced its access to information legislation, Rubin has made more than 20,000 formal requests for documents. They have produced hundreds of vital stories that might otherwise never have come to light. It has all resulted in an important contribution to Canadian muckraking from a man who doesn't even consider himself a journalist.

Born in Winnipeg, Rubin studied history and political science at the University of Manitoba in the 1960s, but spent most of his spare time in community development and activism. In 1968, while studying for his second master's degree at Southern Illinois University, he worked in low-income neighbourhoods, ghettoes, and with would-be draft dodgers. By the early 1970s he moved to Ottawa and became involved in a variety of community and public interest groups. He was often the designated member to analyze data, do background research, and prepare materials for news releases. He began to realize that documents represent one of the most important tools of corroboration for researchers. While interviews and contacts with human sources are crucial, it is often more important to verify information by consulting internal government documents and official records. Journalists and researchers who are skilled at encouraging people to provide them information will often get important records in that way. But many other documents are buried away in filing cabinets and hard drives that are inaccessible to the public. At a time when John Sawatsky and other investigative journalists were refining their interviewing methodology and constructing effective question lines, Rubin was analyzing the role of public information and how best to access it.[2]

In 1972, Rubin joined a group promoting the creation of a freedom of information act for Canada. The federal government was the biggest repository of information in Canada, but its records were largely inaccessible to the public. A handful of other countries had already adopted legislation allowing for access to public records. The oldest such law was in Sweden, where wide-scale access was guaranteed under the Freedom of the Press Act of 1766. The US adopted its freedom of information law in 1966, Denmark and Norway followed soon afterwards, and other European countries began studying the issue in the early 1970s.[3] In Canada, an NDP member of Parliament, Barry Mather, introduced a private member's bill in 1965 that would have created an access to information act. He reintroduced it each year until 1970, but it never succeeded in moving beyond second reading. Progressive Conservative MP Gerald Baldwin tried the same technique each year between 1969 and 1974, and also failed to convince government to act.[4] Rubin joined Baldwin and others in lobbying for the legislation. As part of the work, he surveyed all MPs and senators, asking for examples of when they themselves had tried and failed to get government information.[5] Though many elected members were sympathetic, the federal government continued to find reasons not to act on the recommendations.

Some provincial governments, meanwhile, were faster off the mark. In 1977, Nova Scotia became the first province, and the first jurisdiction in the Commonwealth, to enact a freedom of information act.[6] New Brunswick followed by passing a law in 1978 that came into effect in 1980. In the following two years, Newfoundland and Quebec also introduced legislation. But if journalists thought the mere passage of a law would trigger a flood of new documents and stories, they were quickly dissuaded of the notion. A reporter in Nova Scotia asked to see a report into the investigation of an explosion at the provincially owned Sydney Steel Co. in 1977. The labour minister said the Freedom of Information Act actually barred him from providing it, citing a section that prohibited release of 'information obtained or prepared during the conduct of an investigation concerning alleged violations of any enactment'.[7] In another case, a reporter was denied results of provincial air testing to determine the source of noxious fumes at a Sydney hospital. 'The main weakness of the legislation is that it manages to circumscribe and remove from the public eye all but the most routine information', said Wendy Jackson, who chaired the Centre for Investigative Journalism's freedom of information committee. 'Many civil servants are more cautious about providing information now than they were before the legislation was passed.'[8] The success rate was no better in the United States. Eight years of experience with freedom of information wasn't enough to convince many critics that the law was having much effect. In urging Canada to adopt a bill, Baldwin was quick to advocate something radically different. 'We must go a lot further than the United States. The United States has an act which is virtually useless and is very rarely used. It does not cover many subject matters and it is easy to escape its provisions.'[9]

By the second half of the 1970s, Ottawa began paying lip service to the need for legislation, but the process of drafting a bill was laborious. It would not receive royal assent until 1982, with implementation for 1 July 1983. In the meantime, Rubin was acquiring the knowledge and tools that would make him an early and effective user. Throughout the 1970s, he worked at a variety of jobs with government and private groups. A short-term contract with the federal Metric Commission gave him an insider's look at how bureaucracy dealt with the flow of information. Another federal government job gave him the chance to write internal memos and speeches for ministers. It offered him an education into how government organized its information, and where to look for obscure data. In 1978, working with a national civil rights group, he applied for 59 different government files on himself. It was a test of newly enacted privacy legislation, and it also gave bureaucrats a taste of how careful they needed to be when complying with requests from Rubin. He called a press conference to tell the world what had been released, including what he described as inaccurate, outdated, and second-hand information. He also revealed that he had been given part of another man's medical record, complete with personal details of his health problems.[10]

Rubin didn't even wait for the act to be officially proclaimed before filing his first batch of requests. He asked departments to fulfill them in the spirit of the proposed legislation, and many did. Some early requests revealed information about the extent of the dangers of urea-formaldehyde foam insulation in government buildings. Rubin was also able to access meeting minutes of the Atomic Energy Control Board, opening a public window for the first time into how nuclear reactors were being regulated in Canada. He found reports on inadequate safety systems at some nuclear reactors and problems with radioactive waste disposal. Still, he considered the exemptions and overall operation of the machinery surrounding the act to be too restrictive. 'These are more secrecy acts than anything else . . . they're meant more to hide things than to release them', he said.[11] The act provided for a host of mandatory and discretionary exemptions, protecting against release of information surrounding national security, active law enforcement, advice to ministers, certain communications between Ottawa and the provinces, and many other categories.[12] There were also provisions allowing exemption of material when disclosure would have an adverse effect on a third party. By assessing costs for research time and copying, the act legitimized the practice of charging for government information, and also discouraged journalists from proceeding with requests that were too expensive. And by legislating a 30-day limit for providing an initial response, along with provisions for routine extensions, it also legitimized long delays in responding to requests for information. That prompted many journalists to abandon requests or avoid making them in the first place.

In a way, formal access to information acts provided a political legitimization for governments to deny requests for information altogether. In the absence of legislation, they would be subject to criticism inside Parliament or the legislature, and in the arena of public opinion, if they refused to release a requested report or document. But with a clear set of mandatory exemptions enshrined in law, they could deflect political criticism by pointing to the legislation as a reason for refusing access. Appeal processes in the federal and provincial acts usually were lengthy and complex. Outside the provisions of freedom of information acts, though, journalists were free to lobby for release of documents or head to court much more quickly to secure access.

That is exactly what happened when Linden MacIntyre was investigating political kickbacks and influence peddling among distillers and wineries in Nova Scotia in 1979. He became aware that the RCMP was conducting a series of raids across the province, but the details were cloaked in secrecy. A senior Mountie repeatedly told MacIntyre he couldn't give him details, but at the same time hinted strongly that the journalist had the right to the information if he looked carefully. It eventually led MacIntyre to the clerk of the courts, where he asked to see the information used by RCMP to obtain their search warrants. The clerk refused. An angry MacIntyre walked out of the courthouse and dialed his legal counsel, and a young lawyer patiently listened to the journalist's story. Soon the lawyer, Gordon Proudfoot, was arguing the case in court and MacIntyre won the legal right to inspect the documents. But the clerk who had originally denied MacIntyre access wasn't ready to admit defeat. He scrutinized MacIntyre's winning judgment and spotted a typographical error, refusing to comply with its terms until the mistake was corrected.

Before that happened, the provincial justice department appealed the decision to the Supreme Court of Nova Scotia. An interim order prevented disclosure before the case could be settled.

When the Nova Scotia higher court also ruled in favour of releasing the documents, the same clerk once again informed MacIntyre he would have to wait until the Supreme Court in Ottawa heard the case. None of this was helping him produce his item on *The MacIntyre File*, but the case had now assumed great importance in legal circles. Six provincial governments along with the federal justice department argued strenuously that information about search warrants should remain secret because investigations could otherwise be damaged. But Proudfoot and his legal team defended the principle of opening all documents to the widest scrutiny. They found a British statute from 1372, written in Norman French, saying all court documents were public. In January 1982 the Supreme Court of Canada ruled 5–4 that the information underlying search warrants should be open for inspection. Though warrants continue to be occasionally sealed, and court administrators still create problems regarding access, the ruling established an important principle and provided a tool for journalists to use. By the time of the final judgment, MacIntyre had moved to Toronto and was denied the final satisfaction of seeing how his nemesis in the Nova Scotia court office reacted to the Supreme Court's decision.[13]

Rubin, meanwhile, was busy making life miserable for access to information coordinators across Ottawa. In the first 10 years of the act's existence, there were about 70,000 requests—more than 3,000 from Rubin alone. Rubin rarely took no for an answer. He would negotiate firmly with the coordinators, bargaining for the greatest access and attempting at all times to minimize his costs. When he was met with a refusal he considered unreasonable, he filed a complaint to the Information Commissioner, and there were more than 400 in the first 10 years.[14] He didn't hesitate to go to court, taking part in 30 federal court actions to challenge refusals to disclose information. Rubin felt that in more than half of his requests, he had been met with 'denials, delays, and creative avoidance'.[15] Discretionary exemptions in the act, which related to records dealing with advice to government, or accounts of consultations and deliberations, were so vague and sweeping that they could be applied to virtually anything a department truly wished to hide. Still, while maintaining a healthy skepticism about the act's efficacy, he always cautioned against becoming so cynical as to stop using it. Rubin built a cottage industry of mining the act for information. If a startling story based on access documents appeared in the media, more often than not the request had originated with Rubin. Among his favourite discoveries in his first decade were the following:

- Proof that pressure from lobby groups and industry was involved in changing nutritional recommendations in Canada's Food Guide.
- Documentation showing how the Canadian government, in an effort to protect the domestic asbestos industry, tried to dissuade the US Environmental Protection Agency from a ban on asbestos products.
- A ministerial briefing note showing the Pentagon had approached Ottawa to test an advanced version of the nuclear cruise missile in Canada, at a time the proposal was unknown in the country.
- Disclosure of a Transport Canada audit of Air Canada in 1988 revealing serious concerns, including careless maintenance.
- Documentation showing the federal health department ignored warnings about potential dangers of Meme breast implants, which were finally withdrawn from the market in 1992.[16]

His early successes led to more requests and more disclosures. Rubin obtained data showing serious contamination in national parks. He revealed how government had aided the sale and development of tobacco products. And he has had a hand in providing journalists with documentation for many of Ottawa's political scandals.

The political headaches caused by Rubin's activities were clear when one of his requests turned up a letter from the Privy Council Office to senior bureaucrats, asking them to consult with the Prime Minister's Office before releasing potentially embarrassing information under the access legislation. In 1986, the defence and external affairs departments had released information about the costs of Prime Minister Brian Mulroney's foreign trips, causing critics to question why he needed to pay for the travel of a maid and butler on a two-week Asian jaunt. In response, Paul Tellier, clerk of the Privy Council Office, wrote to senior officials with a clear instruction: 'Where the records being requested relate to the Prime Minister or to the operations of his Office . . . you should arrange for consultations with Dr J.A. Doucet, Senior Adviser to the Prime Minister.'[17] To Rubin, it was evidence of political interference in a process that was designed to be independent of the government in power. An even clearer case of political meddling came in Manitoba, which proclaimed its own freedom of information act in 1988. A request from the opposition Liberal caucus to the culture department came back with a fax cover sheet inadvertently included. It was a message from the department's access coordinator to an aide for Progressive Conservative Premier Gary Filmon, setting out two options for disclosure and asking for advice on how to proceed. It was the most blatant indication yet that political considerations were paramount in deciding disclosure, not the spirit or letter of the legislation.[18]

Rubin's appeals to courts have established a number of important precedents for disclosure of information. During the 1980s, he worked with a *Kitchener-Waterloo Record* reporter to get meat inspection reports from Agriculture Canada. The battle went all the way to the Federal Court of Appeal in 1989, and they succeeded in winning fuller access to the information. Another victory came in Rubin's attempt to see board and executive committee minutes of the Canada Mortgage and Housing Corporation. After initial blanket refusals and a federal trial division's dismissal of his application to review the denial, Rubin took his case to the Federal Court of Appeal, which granted him the documents. An even more prolonged fight took place over Rubin's desire to see Transport Canada reports on a 1991 Nationair crash in Saudi Arabia that killed 262 people. After years of delays and refusals, Rubin finally argued his case in Federal Court and won, securing release of the reports that showed serious maintenance problems and deficiencies that were known to regulators before the crash.[19]

Even though Rubin found time to file thousands of requests, only a handful of journalists have ever taken up the task of asking for government data with any consistency. Statistics from 1999–2000 show media requests made up fewer than 15 per cent of all access filings.[20] Of those, many were filed by daily reporters looking for quick-hit stories on expense accounts and travel costs. 'Making freeloading politicians look foolish on the front page when they stay at expensive hotels and wear free athletic uniforms, like they did at the Salt Lake City Olympics, gets the point across', Rubin said.[21] But there needs to be more. 'Going after data, however, is not just about government waste and scandals. For me, it's about matters vital to Canadians' health, safety, and welfare.'[22]

When Michael McAuliffe of the CBC turned to the Access to Information Act in 1993, he was also pursuing an issue he considered vital to Canadian society. It stirred a deep sense of moral outrage in him, and a desire to unravel a cover-up that offended his sense of justice. It came at the beginning of April when he read a Canadian Press story quoting an article in the *Pembroke Observer* about what reporter Jim Day had seen while in Belet Huen, Somalia. Day was at the Canadian military base, reporting on Operation Deliverance, in which 900 Canadians and as many as 37,000 forces from around the world had been dispatched to Somalia to stem the effects of famine and civil war. The stated aim of the mission, which was originally under the auspices of the US and later taken over by the United Nations, was to restore order and bring assistance to the war-ravaged African country. Day was observing the Canadian contingent when he noticed an unconscious soldier being whisked from a holding cell on a stretcher. After days of stalling by National Defence, the department finally confirmed that a Somalian teenager had been detained and killed by Canadian soldiers in Belet Huen. One of the assailants was Master Corporal Clayton Matchee, who then attempted suicide by trying to hang himself. As McAuliffe read the story, he was amazed that the teenager's death had occurred 16 March, but that no public confirmation came until more than two weeks later.

McAuliffe and other reporters jumped on the story, and the sad fate of 16-year-old Shidane Arone became major news in Canada. Arone had entered the Canadian compound and was detained by soldiers. What followed was a cruel and horrific story of unprovoked torture. The soldiers kicked and punched him, smashed him with an iron bar, applied lit cigarettes to his body, and pointed a gun at his head. The full extent of the barbarity wasn't revealed until photos of the tortured boy later surfaced. Although a number of soldiers were quickly charged with murder, there was considerable confusion and deliberate obfuscation at first. Defence officials in Canada, including the minister, Kim Campbell, claimed there had been a communication mix-up and a delay in relaying the information about the death back to Ottawa. The opposition wasn't buying that explanation, but there was no proof to the contrary. McAuliffe set about trying to determine when the news was transmitted, and who would have known. His first step was to understand how the mission in Belet Huen communicated with Ottawa. He learned that any major event would trigger the production of a document called a Significant Incident Report. Soon after the news broke, he filed an access to information request for the report into Arone's death. When he received the document in July, he knew he had an explosive story.[23]

On 13 July, McAuliffe reported that the Canadian commander in Belet Huen had sent a Telex to Ottawa with full details of the incident within four hours of Arone's death. From the note's distribution list, he could authoritatively report that 10 different people at national defence headquarters in Ottawa were aware of the information, including ministerial staff. That raised questions about exactly when the full details became known to Kim Campbell, who by now had succeeded Brian Mulroney as Progressive Conservative leader and prime minister. The report mentioned that Arone had cuts and bruises to his body, and that his cause of death was believed to be head injuries. It was the first major indication of a cover-up, and sparked further stories throughout the summer and into the fall about Canadian activities in Somalia. Dr Barry Armstrong, an army surgeon, began blowing the whistle on cases of abuse he had witnessed. There were stories about the shooting of other Somali intruders found in the Canadian compound. Videotapes of hazing activities involving members of the Canadian Airborne Regiment surfaced. McAuliffe kept on the story, continuing to break additional elements, and all the while filing more requests under the act for documentation. As other reporters came up against official stonewalling and moved onto other stories, he felt compelled to keep the pressure going. Somebody, he thought to himself, had to be the voice of the 16-year-old kid who died in a bunker in Somalia at the hands of Canadian soldiers.[24]

Twenty years earlier, McAuliffe's father, Gerald, had felt the very same urge as he documented cases of police brutality in his series for the *Globe and Mail*. McAuliffe acknowledges that growing up in the home of a relentless investigative reporter inevitably had a profound effect on him. 'As a kid, watching my father work, I saw the moral imperative behind a lot of what he was doing. He was trying to shine some light on people who, for example, had been brutalized by Canadian police officers, and tried to expose their stories. It was difficult and occasionally dangerous work, but they were important stories for the public to know about. That resonated quite a bit. Having had that model growing up played a role when you had the death of Shidane Arone.'[25] He also observed his father's techniques in action. Sitting at the kitchen table and eating dinner, he would listen as his father conducted interviews or spoke with sources. It was an education in when to push, when to pull back, when to create some distance, and when to offer support. But in two decades, investigative techniques had changed. McAuliffe joked that his father once offered him the advice that 'whenever you're in an office, grab a fistful of paper from the garbage can next to the photocopier'.[26] It was a method he never tried. But he did engage in a more sophisticated attempt to secure documents that proved crucial to confirming details in his stories.

By the end of the summer of 1993, officials at the defence department were feeling besieged by McAuliffe's dogged reporting. They switched tactics, trying to win his sympathies by inviting him on a tour of the national defence headquarters building in Ottawa. 'Their attempt was to dazzle me a bit, take me into all the secret rooms, and make me feel I was getting a glimpse into something secret.'[27] Instead, they inadvertently revealed to McAuliffe how their systems worked and what kinds of documents they routinely generated. He asked them for a description of how a typical day unfolded, and their explanations gave him ideas for further requests. A daily morning operational briefing gave rise to a written record, and a daily executive meeting produced documents called 'DEM notes'. McAuliffe nonchalantly scribbled notes on a napkin, thanked his guests for the tour, and spent the next 36 hours writing several dozen new access requests. He delivered them all within two days, and then got a call from a public affairs spokesman who told him: 'Jesus Christ, you should see what's happening over here. It's like a bomb has gone off.'

The military was convinced McAuliffe had well-placed sources inside the department feeding him information and telling him which documents to request. Secret investigations were ordered, which McAuliffe assumed were accompanied by wiretaps, surveillance, and aggressive attempts to discover his contacts. Later it was revealed the military considered administering lie detector tests to find the leak, and they were worried the CBC was intercepting and taping cell phone conversations. In fact, he got the vast majority of his information through the front door, and largely because of his research into how the department worked. While he did have some inside sources, McAuliffe said the key to unraveling the full extent of the Somalia story was understanding the different mechanisms inside the department and the reports that were available. Later, when courts martial began, he spent a productive day in the Library of Parliament reading the army's Code of Service Discipline. It showed him how accountability was designed to work in the military, and where the chain of command ultimately led, allowing him to file even more requests.

McAuliffe learned of the existence of RTQs, or Responses to Queries, which the department routinely drew up in anticipation of questions from media or politicians. He asked for copies, a request that was to create turmoil inside the department. The turmoil turned to panic as departmental officials tampered with the documents, providing McAuliffe with altered records in an effort to mislead him about the full extent of the unfolding scandal. Later, they told him the RTQs no longer existed. What they failed to say was that the department had simply changed their name to MRLs, or Media Response Lines. It was an attempt to throw him off the trail. But the tempo of revelations continued. Officials resigned, the Canadian Airborne Regiment was disbanded, and the government convened a commission of inquiry to discover what had gone wrong with Canada's Somalia deployment.

When testimony at the inquiry revealed the alteration of records, McAuliffe suddenly became part of the story. He told commission staff he would refuse to disclose any of his sources if they called him to testify, a prospect that would undoubtedly have created a dilemma for commissioner Peter Desbarats, dean of the journalism department at the University of Western Ontario. The prospect of one journalist holding another in contempt never materialized, as the commission decided not to call him as a witness. But McAuliffe's name became a routine topic of conversation during testimony, forcing him to withdraw from covering the inquiry and into a position of observing it from the sidelines.

General Jean Boyle, chief of defence staff, offered a *mea culpa* at the inquiry for misleading McAuliffe. But he blamed his subordinates. 'You don't alter documents. . . . I've been at wit's end to understand why this happened in the first place.'[28] Boyle was on the stand for nine days, longer than any other witness, as proceedings were televised across the country. In its final report, the commission left no doubt about what it thought of his testimony. 'Boyle was described to us as a meticulous man, a micro manager, a man who was a stickler for details. It is unthinkable that a new Director General would have wished or been able to run altered documents by him without his knowledge, especially since these documents were to be the subject of release to the media.'[29] Boyle resigned. The commission said the altered documents amounted to deliberate deception, and it called the name change of RTQs to MRLs a vulgar scheme. 'The activities of DND at this time cannot be viewed as other than an attempt to frustrate the proper functioning of our access to information laws. For example, the estimate of the cost of searching for and analyzing documents subject to the first formal request established an inordinate number of hours and prohibitively high costs (413 hours and $4080). In point of fact, these documents were readily available.'[30]

In the middle of the inquiry, McAuliffe received a Michener award for his Somalia coverage. Desbarats would often look across the room and observe McAuliffe soaking in the testimony. In his diary, Desbarats reflected on the role of journalism in the entire affair. 'Commissioners and lawyers, I'm sure, have now lost sight of McAuliffe's role as we try to unravel the complexities of the story, but without McAuliffe there might well have been no inquiry at all. This great, awkward, expensive, and unwieldy mechanism that I'm now part of is very much a journalist's creation.'[31] McAuliffe was disappointed that Desbarats and the other commissioners felt the media should step aside and let the inquiry do the rest of the work. The disappointment turned to frustration when the inquiry began spending more time examining alteration of documents than the Canadian military's activities in Somalia. Before the substantive issues could be revisited, the federal government announced in January 1997 that it was effectively invoking closure, requiring the commission to conclude hearings by the end of March and deliver a final report on 30 June, six months before the inquiry's requested extension. Desbarats called it unprecedented and outrageous, and considered resigning, but the government succeeded in putting an end to the daily revelations and embarrassments.

McAuliffe believed his early successes with access requests were critical in the development of the story, and were only possible due to the orientation of defence officials who are trained to go by the book and assess matters in black and white terms.[32] Their thinking was simple: If the requested information was covered by the act, and no exemptions applied, it had to be released. Once the awkward stories began flowing, however, exemptions began to be enforced more stringently. By the end, the stream of information had completely stopped. Researchers have pointed to the Somalia affair as a reason for a spike in access requests in later years. But McAuliffe said his success came with a price—it provided bureaucrats with lessons in more creative ways to deny disclosure in the future. His attitude towards the Access to Information Act soured. 'I concluded that it became a waste of time. I'd never be inclined to rely on it as a major investigative tool again.'[33]

McAuliffe's grim assessment was endorsed by many journalists across the country. Even the Information Commissioner, whose task is to review the operation of the act and hear appeals, saw more problems than victories. In his 2005–06 annual report, John Reid said that 'after almost 23 years of living with the *Access to Information Act*, the name of the game, all too often, is how to resist transparency and engage in damage control by ignoring response deadlines, blacking out the embarrassing bits, conducting business orally, excluding records and institutions from the coverage of the *Access to Information Act*, and keeping the system's watchdog overworked and under-funded'.[34] In 1998, the Information Commissioner began grading departments on their compliance track records. In 2005–06, not a single major department earned an A. High profile areas such as justice, foreign affairs, and the Privy Council Office were given F.

Only a handful of Canadian journalists have made sustained use of the Access to Information Act. Jim Bronskill and Dean Beeby of Canadian Press incorporated it in their daily routine, filing requests whenever they felt an underlying document or record might illuminate a potential news story. Occasionally, an access request gives rise to a groundbreaking story, as it did when David McKie and a team of CBC journalists accessed Health Canada's database of adverse drug reactions.[35] But politicians and bureaucrats have devised mechanisms to minimize the flow. Each department flags sensitive requests from the media or opposition members, referring to them with such designations as 'amberlight' or 'red files' or simply 'interesting'.[36] Research has shown that this process delays the release of information, and gives government time to draft replies before any disclosures are made.[37] While some aspects of the sponsorship scandal came to light through access requests, the civil servants in charge of the program tried to ensure years earlier that it wouldn't be a major concern. Chuck Guité, who was eventually convicted for his role in the affair, told Parliament's public accounts committee in 2004: 'The reason we kept minimum information on the file was in case we have an access to information (request).'[38] In 2004–05, of the 25,207 requests filed under the act, a little more than 10 per cent came from the media. It seemed businesses were gleaning far better information from the legislation, as they accounted for 47 per cent of all inquiries.[39]

The doctrine of a people's right to know seems implicit in many of the theories underpinning journalism in general and investigative journalism in particular. If John Milton's self-righting principle is to work, for instance, how could truth ever enter the marketplace without a public right to information?[40] And how else would the media exercise its watchdog role without significant access to government documents? A government shrouded in secrecy might seem appropriate to monarchies and feudal regimes, but Enlightenment ideals dictated a freer exchange of ideas. Even so, the notion of enshrining these rights in legislation didn't begin surfacing until the second half of the twentieth century. Sweden was the notable exception to this process, producing an early and unique Freedom of the Press Act in 1766. But the next country to enact a similar law was the United States in 1966, and only then did many other countries begin taking action. In Canada, a persistent member of parliament introduced a private member's bill in 1965 'to better assure the public's rights to freedom of access to public documents and information about government adminis-tration'.[41] It took another 17 years until Canada's Access to Information Act finally received royal assent.

The best investigative journalists recognize the importance of written records and possess a 'documents state of mind' when it comes to their research.[42] Unlike human sources, official documents rarely lie or change their minds. They are often the smoking guns in a good investigative story. As arguably the largest repository of documents in any country, the government holds the key to many important investigations. But the complexity and bureaucratic nature of the Canadian Access to Information Act, together with a continued tendency on the part of government officials to deny access and frustrate the process, has led many journalists to underutilize the legislation as an everyday tool. There are some exceptions, and this chapter has attempted to document the kind of successes that resourceful reporters can achieve. Many of those reporters are also active in lobbying for continued improvements in access, but the process has been slow and frustrating. Still, the tool remains available for anyone to employ. Ken Rubin, for instance, has continued to file requests and use the information to advance what he calls his own form of Prairie populism.

The act was never really intended to primarily open up government. Yet it has allowed glimpses of goings-on even though Ottawa has much data it would rather forget or at least not make public. Nobody ever said gathering access would be easy. But by making queries you can make a difference.[43]

Accessing Government Secrets

In 2005, Canadian Press reporter Jim Bronskill began investigating the controversial question of CIA aircraft activity in Canada. US media reports suggested the CIA secretly owned and controlled a number of aircraft companies, and that some were used for renditions—ferrying terrorism suspects to foreign countries where they were subject to torture. Bronskill, who routinely filed about 200 access to information requests a year, began using the legislation to see what he could discover about aircraft operations in Canada. He soon had his hands on a number of documents that led to a series of exclusive stories about CIA plane landings in Canada.

One government document, stamped secret, showed that 20 planes with alleged CIA ties made 74 flights to Canada over the previous four years. In another story, Bronskill reported that a mysterious Twin Otter plane linked to the CIA had spent four months in a small Ontario town near Sault Ste. Marie. He showed how the airplane had left Bar River, Ontario for an airstrip in North Carolina that is known to be an aviation hub for US intelligence. Then it flew to a Virginia airport not far from CIA headquarters. No one would provide any details about the plane's activities in Canada. But Bronskill continued writing stories, and filing further access requests.

Then came a disturbing, but not altogether surprising development. It was revealed that Bronskill's identity in requesting further information was apparently leaked to the prime minister's political staff, a violation of the Privacy Act. Another newspaper had requested government documents on a related issue, and came across an e-mail informing government insiders: 'Noted there will shortly be another Bronskill/CIA Planes article, as new ATIP (access to information) info is going out . . .' The identity of requesters under the act is supposed to remain confidential, but the e-mail was widely distributed to bureaucrats, including officials in the Privy Council and Prime Minister's Office. Bronskill expressed displeasure at the leak, but few journalists who use the act were surprised. Keeping close tabs on investigative journalists, and others whose requests might pry loose embarrassing information, is seen as routine by governments of all political stripes.

Chapter 16

Bringing Down a Former Government

Genuinely objective journalism not only gets the facts right, it gets the meaning of events right. It is compelling not only today, but stands the test of time.

T.D. Allman, American journalist[1]

Harvey Cashore, one of Canada's leading investigative journalists, makes a habit of sharing his expertise with students and fellow journalists. When it comes to dealing with sources, his lessons are a mixture of solid advice and moral imperatives. Don't lie, don't steal, don't break the law, don't misrepresent yourself, don't argue, and don't grill your subject, he advises. Instead, he urges journalists to be neutral, honest, polite, curious, and patient. There are two further lessons he never fails to mention: tape all your interviews, and respect a source's confidentiality when given a piece of information that is off the record. If the students pay close attention, they will notice some irony in the last point. One of Cashore's biggest journalistic coups came after he decided to broadcast a tape-recorded, off the record comment without his subject's permission.

To understand Cashore's action, and to realize why it was the right call, it is necessary to examine one of the most complex and perplexing scandals in Canadian political history: the Airbus affair. From a journalistic point of view, Airbus initially seemed like a story that might topple a government. Later, it had the makings of an affair that could tarnish the reputation of a former government. In the end, it remained an unsolved mystery, but one in which a former prime minister was left trying to explain why he had secretly received hundreds of thousands of dollars in cash from a less than reputable source.

Cashore learned about Airbus even before his career in professional journalism began. As a student in John Sawatsky's class at Carleton University, he was recruited to conduct research for his teacher's book about the lobbying scene in Ottawa.[2] One of the people profiled in the 1987 book was Frank Moores, former Tory premier of Newfoundland and a close friend to Prime Minister Brian Mulroney. After Mulroney swept to power in 1984, Moores established a lobbying firm in Ottawa called Government Consultants International. He began signing clients and pushing their interests in the corridors of influence. Sawatsky's book recounted how Moores represented a German partner of the European consortium known as Airbus Industrie, which was trying to sell A320 passenger jets to Air Canada. This put Moores in a clear conflict, as he was simultaneously a board member at Air Canada, which was still a Crown corporation at the time. Moores resigned from Air Canada, but media coverage of the affair was the first indication that news involving Airbus needed to be scrutinized carefully. This became even more pronounced in 1988, when Air Canada finally made the decision to buy 34 Airbus planes for $1.8 billion.

Cashore's early immersion in the world of insider Ottawa politics would serve him well throughout his career. But it was Sawatsky's methods and mentorship that had a more lasting impact on his work. Sawatsky taught him the power of preparation and meticulous research, and the importance of carefully crafting questions before approaching sources. He also instilled the need for an open mind at all times. Transcribing interviews and building detailed chronologies were tedious tasks, but Cashore mastered the methodology and used it to potent effect for the rest of his career. Soon after joining CBC's *the fifth estate* in 1991, he earned a reputation as one of the corporation's most skilled investigators.

Airbus remained a subject of continuous speculation and innuendo for years after the Air Canada purchase. How had the consortium won the contract over its more established rival, Boeing? Did political connections play an important part in the sale? Were commissions or kickbacks involved? Airline executives in the US were suspicious, and there were brief but inconclusive investigations by the FBI and the RCMP into whether any commissions had been paid. Rumours abounded, but journalists could never accumulate enough information for an authoritative story. Mulroney, meanwhile, left office in 1993 and saw his party decimated at the polls. His administration had been hit with a variety of corruption scandals, and voters opted for a return to Liberal Party rule. The Airbus story seemed destined to occupy a minor footnote in his government's political history. All that changed, though, as a result of a dispute between two shady business figures in Europe.

The businessmen were Karlheinz Schreiber and Giorgio Pelossi. Schreiber was a lobbyist and promoter who unabashedly doled out commissions to grease the wheels of business deals for the benefit of his large corporate clients. He had a close relationship with Bavarian Premier Franz Josef Strauss, and eventually represented the interests of German companies such as Thyssen and Messerschmitt Bolkow Blohm. He also had deep roots in Canada, and had recruited a legion of political friends through the years. Pelossi was Schreiber's accountant. From his base in Switzerland, he was an expert at creating shadowy corporations and concealing money in confidential bank accounts. The two had a falling out over money, and by 1994 Pelossi was telling his story to the media.

Reporters for the German magazine *Der Spiegel* interviewed Pelossi and learned that Airbus had paid millions of dollars in secret commissions to win the Air Canada deal. The payments, averaging about $500,000 per plane, went to one of Schreiber's companies in Liechtenstein, and finally to his bank account in Switzerland. What's more, Pelossi said some of that money was destined for Canadian politicians in the form of kickbacks. Pelossi implicated Frank Moores in the scheme, telling reporters that

Moores and Schreiber had set up secret accounts in Switzerland for payoff purposes. One of the accounts, he alleged, was for Mulroney. He also said Schreiber received commissions for a German helicopter sale to the Canadian coast guard, and for lobbying to build a German tank-manufacturing plant in Nova Scotia. *Der Spiegel* knew Pelossi had an axe to grind, but he supplied them with convincing documentation. Realizing they needed some expertise on the ground in Canada, they searched for a journalistic partnership and contacted Jock Ferguson. By coincidence, Ferguson was working at the time with Cashore on a *fifth estate* story dealing with allegations of kickbacks in the airline industry, though Airbus wasn't the focus of their inquiries.[3] By late 1994 and early 1995, a team of investigative journalists at *Der Spiegel* and *the fifth estate* was digging into Pelossi's accusations and trying to find supporting evidence. The journalists felt confident about the facts surrounding secret commissions, but didn't have any way of corroborating the allegation against Mulroney. *Der Spiegel*'s story in late March of 1995, titled 'The Tycoon from Alberta', detailed the commissions.[4] Schreiber denied the story and said he wasn't connected to the Liechtenstein company.[5] The *fifth estate* story, called 'Sealed in Silence', ran shortly afterwards, making it the first Canadian report with substantive evidence of secret commissions in the Airbus affair.[6] Still, Cashore said both stories were understated and cautious, deliberately not mentioning Pelossi's allegations against Mulroney.[7] The complexity of the story, and its reliance on unnamed sources, may have dissuaded other journalists from trying to match it. In fact, there was virtually no media follow-up to the revelations. But Cashore knew police agencies would be interested in the story. He hid his documents at his aunt's house in Scarborough, just in case.[8]

Police already had a head start. In January 1995, they had visited journalist Stevie Cameron following an interview she had given on CBC about her recently published book, *On the Take*. The book, subtitled *Crime, Corruption and Greed in the Mulroney Years*, had devoted eight pages to the Airbus affair, but revealed little new information, noting that Airbus had generated 'the most gossip and the wildest innuendoes in Mulroney's Ottawa'.[9] RCMP wanted to see if Cameron could help them re-ignite an Airbus investigation. Cameron told police she had lent her Airbus files to former *Globe and Mail* colleague Jock Ferguson, who was part of a larger team investigating Pelossi's allegations. Ferguson promised to return the files along with information they had dug up after *Der Spiegel* and the CBC ran their stories. Once she got her files back, Cameron said, she would share them with RCMP. Similar police requests for information from Ferguson and Cashore were rebuffed, but Cameron says she cooperated with the officers and turned over material. She believed most of it was in the public domain, though some had originated with Pelossi.[10] 'I was surprised by how often the police called me at first and I pointed them to articles or books I had written, to work in Germany and, or, to the CBC documentaries. On one occasion I received a call asking me if I knew Brian Mulroney's birth date and I told the officer to look it up in the Parliamentary Guide.'[11] Cameron would eventually be designated a confidential RCMP informant, leading to a spirited debate in the journalistic community about how closely journalists should cooperate with police.[12]

Mulroney's alleged connection to the case went public in November that year, when Philip Mathias of the *Financial Post* revealed a letter the justice department had sent Swiss authorities asking for assistance in the investigation of Schreiber, Moores, and Mulroney.[13] Many believe Mulroney himself leaked the letter to Mathias, because it allowed him to claim he was being unfairly targeted.[14] On the very same day of the Mathias story, Mulroney announced a $50 million defamation suit against the federal government. Early in 1997, the government apologized to Mulroney for the wording in the letter, and agreed to pay him more than $2 million in compensation. But the Airbus investigation kept going on both sides of the Atlantic.[15]

While Canadian authorities were struggling to pry Schreiber's banking records out of Switzerland, the Germans were having more success. In May 1999, two Thyssen managers who were given money by Schreiber were charged with tax evasion. The next day, a German newspaper revealed that Schreiber had paid millions of German marks to high-ranking members of Helmut Kohl's Christian Democratic Party. The revelations sparked one of Germany's biggest post-war scandals. Cashore knew there had to be more information about Schreiber's Canadian capers. He flew to Germany and teamed up with reporter John Goetz, scouring the country in search of more information. They made a wide range of calls and checks, and in September of that year the work yielded what Cashore calls one of his most exciting moments in journalism. 'A source as unlikely as you can ever imagine' provided them with Schreiber's private bank account information, a treasure chest of data that allowed them to correlate commissions and payments that Pelossi could not even have known.[16] Back at *the fifth estate*, Cashore covered an office wall with chronologies, using pieces of string to connect transactions. Schreiber had set up coded bank accounts that German authorities speculated were directly related to key Canadian lobbyists and politicians. The most interesting revelation was the existence of an account code-named 'Britan', which German authorities didn't immediately connect to anyone, though it seemed suspiciously close to 'Brian'.[17] The net was closing on Schreiber, who was arrested in Toronto at the request of German authorities. Germany wanted him extradited to face fraud and tax evasion charges. But the elusive link to Mulroney was still missing. Cashore's next step was to call the former prime minister himself and put the evidence directly to him.

The closest he could get was Mulroney's public relations consultant, Luc Lavoie. Over three days in October 1999, the two engaged in a verbal dance around the allegations, with Cashore trying persistently to obtain an interview with Mulroney, and Lavoie attempting to find out as much as he could about what Cashore had gleaned from Schreiber's banking documents. At one point, Lavoie decided to offer some off the record comments in an effort to discredit any allegations Schreiber might make about Mulroney. 'Karlheinz Schreiber is the biggest fucking liar the world has ever seen. That's what we believe', Lavoie said. The Mulroney interview never materialized, and *the fifth estate* prepared to broadcast its story with the revelations about Schreiber's secret account. On the day the item was set to air, Cashore was surprised to read a story in the *National Post* discrediting the documentary in advance. Philip Mathias reported that the CBC was set to disclose the existence of an account code-named Britan, which some might suggest was connected to Mulroney. Mathias mockingly threw out some other suggestions. 'Others have pointed out that Britan is also similar to the name of a country, Britain, and a region of France, Brittany. It is also close to the name of the Brita water filter and other commercial products.' In the same piece, Mathias offered his assessment of efforts to implicate the former prime minister in the scandal. 'The so-called Airbus affair has generated a series of allegations against Mr Mulroney, each one followed by revelations that prove the allegation to be false.'[18] The CBC concluded that someone in the Mulroney camp had tipped off the *Post* to the story, even though Lavoie had promised they wouldn't discuss Cashore's information with any other reporter. That meant the corporation no longer had a duty to respect Lavoie's off the record comments about Schreiber. For Cashore, it was a difficult decision that appeared to run against his general practice of honouring agreements with sources. But the time had come for aggressive action, and Lavoie's epithet against Schreiber was inserted into the broadcast.

Schreiber considered Mulroney a friend. He had played a role in helping him win the leadership of the Progressive Conservative Party. Being called a liar on national television was not what he expected from a friend. Schreiber wanted to ensure the comments were genuine and not somehow manipulated by the CBC. Cashore played him the entire audiotape so he could hear the full context of the Lavoie interview. Efforts by Lavoie and Mulroney to apologize for the remarks and retract them had little effect. Cashore believed the incident changed their relationship fundamentally, eventually paving the way for Schreiber to talk about the cash payments he provided to Mulroney after the prime minister left office. Ironically, the reporter who nailed the story about Schreiber's secret payments to Mulroney was the man who had been one of the prime minister's staunchest defenders, Philip Mathias. How did he get the story? Mathias said it was the culmination of a year-long process involving 'painstakingly collecting tiny slivers of information from a number of sources'.[19] Others believed an enraged Schreiber, stung by Lavoie's crude attack, simply leaked it. Schreiber had coyly hinted to Cashore that he had given money to Mulroney, and he mentioned the same story to a former CTV reporter. Mathias, though, had all the facts, and they weren't being denied. But getting the story and having his newspaper publish it were two different matters. The *National Post* didn't think it was newsworthy to report that the former prime minister of Canada had received $300,000 in secret cash disbursements from a man who was ultimately accused of fraud, bribery, and tax evasion. The newspaper, after all, had campaigned relentlessly against any suggestion that Mulroney was involved in the Airbus scandal. Mathias retired without ever seeing his story in print. 'I would have liked to have had that feather in my cap', he said. Still, he remained neutral on the meaning of the payments. They might have been for legitimate lobbying or consulting work, and cash payments were the European way of doing things. Mathias continued to believe there was no evidence Mulroney ever received a bribe, or had any improper involvement in the Airbus affair.[20]

It was left to Toronto lawyer and author William Kaplan to get the scoop. Kaplan was another early Mulroney defender, having written a book that discredited all the attempts to link him to any alleged Airbus corruption. Mulroney had given Kaplan his full cooperation, and was pleased with the outcome. Before leaving the *Post*, Mathias had called Kaplan to tell him what he learned. 'I could not believe what I was hearing when Mathias read me his story', Kaplan later wrote. 'After spending the better part of a year working on a book that defended the former prime minister and severely criticized the then current one, Jean Chrétien, among others, I learned that Mulroney and Schreiber enjoyed something considerably more than a casual, nodding acquaintance. . . . I had been duped.'[21] In November 2003, Kaplan broke the story for the *Globe and Mail*, the same story Mathias couldn't convince the *National Post* to publish. For the first time, it was revealed that Schreiber had passed money to Mulroney, in circumstances no one could adequately explain. Mulroney's spokesman, Luc Lavoie, suggested it was for Mulroney's assistance in Schreiber's newly formed pasta business, and to facilitate international contacts. Whatever the reason, the acknowledgement of a financial relationship was in direct contradiction to statements Mulroney had made in the past. During his sworn testimony at his defamation proceeding against the government in 1996, Mulroney said of Schreiber: 'I had never had any dealings with him.' When specifically asked what contacts he had with Schreiber after leaving office, Mulroney said he thought he might have met him once or twice for coffee.[22]

All the while, Cashore kept investigating. In January 2005 he met Lavoie for dinner, trying once more to secure an interview with Mulroney. During the course of their conversation, Lavoie said that he knew Cashore's father was a former cabinet minister in BC, and that his brother was a professor at Yale. 'What are you implying?' Cashore asked. 'That we can investigate you too', replied Lavoie.[23] Cashore told him it would be a good idea to leave his family out of the situation. But the conversation, and a follow-up letter from Mulroney's lawyer to the CBC president and chair accusing him of boundless zeal in his anti-Mulroney bias, made Cashore think carefully about the consequences of further stories. He visited his executive producer, David Studer, and said he might not be able to handle the Airbus story any more. It was a Friday, and Studer told him to take the weekend to think about it. 'By Monday I had done a full reversal', Cashore said. 'I knew I couldn't live with myself if I didn't forge ahead with the story. Imagine telling my kids years later that I chickened out on one of the most important political stories of my generation. I think David knew full well that I would change my mind. He had that "I knew you would say that" smile when I came into his office on Monday.'[24]

Early in 2006, Cashore produced another documentary that took the story one step further. In a rare on-camera interview, Schreiber acknowledged that the cash payments he provided Mulroney came from the infamous Britan account. Monies from that account had originated with the secret commissions Schreiber earned for snagging Canadian government business. It still wasn't a smoking gun, and the program carefully acknowledged there was no evidence Mulroney knew where the money had come from.[25] But it was the closest link yet of a payment to Mulroney that had a connection to the commissions. As with many of the previous Airbus stories both in the print and broadcast media, *the fifth estate*'s report drew little public reaction. The government's Airbus investigation, by this time, had long since been abandoned, and Mulroney had been cleared of any wrongdoing. Instead, one author, William Kaplan, suffered the humiliation of admitting he was duped into writing a book that didn't tell a full and completely truthful story. And a second author, Stevie Cameron, endured public condemnation for collaborating with the police. New developments in the Airbus story and Schreiber's cash payments to the former prime minister continued to surface throughout 2007, even as Brian Mulroney tried to rehabilitate his public image with the publication of his memoirs. Reports by the CBC and the *Globe and Mail* late in the year prompted the government to call a public inquiry into Schreiber's payments to Mulroney, and the RCMP said it would review the matter, including allegations that Mulroney was still in office when the deal to provide him with $300,000 in cash was struck.

The Airbus affair provides a fascinating backdrop for the examination of a refined methodology of investigative journalism. The details of what happened are murky and mostly hidden, yet they involve powerful forces in society that journalists must hold to account. In such cases, the highest degree of skill and method are required. 'It does not matter that the news is not susceptible of mathematical statement', wrote American journalist Walter Lippmann. 'In fact, just because news is complex and slippery, good reporting requires the exercise of the highest scientific virtues.'[26] The scientific sensibility is what leads Bill Kovach and Tom Rosenstiel to describe a discipline of verification, a practice that ultimately separates journalism from entertainment, propaganda, fiction, or art.[27] Such a discipline ensures an objectivity of method that leads journalists to discover the truth, no matter what their original aim might be. In the case of William Kaplan, for instance, the desire to defend Brian Mulroney was ultimately dashed by the intrusion of facts negating Kaplan's original hypothesis. Of course, the journalist must always remain open to such disconfirmatory evidence. Otherwise, journalists can suffer from the same kind of tunnel vision that besets police officers, prosecutors, and other investigators who sometimes rush to judgment without a full perspective.

Cashore's methodology built upon the lessons and distilled wisdom of his predecessors. From John Sawatsky, he learned the importance of questions and human sources, and the necessity to tape and transcribe interviews. A militant neutrality in the interview process guarantees that people maintain trust and provide information, even if it doesn't always serve their best interests to do so. Interviews lead to the uncovering of new documents, some of which can be crucial in the verification process. For each of his stories, Cashore maintains and constantly builds a series of key documents: a question list composed of points he needs answered; a source list of people to be interviewed; a 'to do' list of tasks to be accomplished; and an annotated chronology of events that can grow to enormous size. Constantly examining the chronology provides clues to the timing and meaning of events. Accompanying the method is a morality of fair dealing with sources, an ethic that can be severely tested when sources begin to play by other rules.

If bringing down a government is a difficult task for investigative reporting, bringing down a former government, even one that was tarnished with documented charges of corruption, is no less daunting. All the while, Harvey Cashore keeps his Airbus file open for future developments.

Chapter 17

Modern Tools

Blacks arrested by Toronto police are treated more harshly than whites . . .
Black people, charged with simple drug possession, are taken to police stations
more often than whites facing the same charge.
Once at the station, accused blacks are held overnight, for a bail hearing, at twice
the rate of whites.

The statements in the *Toronto Star* article of 19 October 2002 were unequivocal. This was not a journalistic report of a survey, a collection of opinions, or yet another 'he said, she said' account of race relations in Canada's biggest city. Nor was it an investigative account in which readers were being invited to favour one set of interpretations over another. The conclusions were stated up-front. Justice is different for blacks and whites, said the headline for the opening piece in a series titled 'Race and Crime'. The story didn't rely on anyone else's opinion or study to make its point. 'The findings provide hard evidence of what blacks have long suspected—race matters in Canadian society especially when dealing with police.'[1]

The *Star* was comfortable making such strong statements because its investigation was based on an analysis of data that had come directly from Toronto police. It employed the techniques of computer-assisted reporting to analyze a police database containing more than 480,000 incidents in which someone had been arrested or ticketed for an offence. More than 800,000 charges were sifted, sorted, and analyzed to derive the final stories. The newspaper looked at offences, such as simple drug possession, where police had some discretion in how to deal with offenders. It found police often came down harder on blacks than whites. Whites, for instance, were released on a promise to appear in court 76.5 per cent of the time. For blacks, the number was 61.8 per cent. Of those taken to the station, blacks were held in jail awaiting bail 15.5 per cent of the time, compared to 7.3 per cent for whites. If the accused of either race had a police history, they were treated more harshly, but the difference in treatment between whites and blacks remained, the stories said.[2]

The newspaper had been fighting for more than two years to get the stories into print. In March 2000, the *Star* asked for the police database known as the Criminal Information Processing System. The request was initially denied, but following an appeal and a ruling by the province's privacy commissioner, a version of the database stripped of personal information was released in June 2002. Through the summer, reporter Jim Rankin and librarian Andrea Hall analyzed the database. An independent expert in statistical methodology and analysis was brought in to check the numbers. Mary Deanne Shears, the newspaper's managing editor at the time, explained why they had gone to so much trouble. 'At various times, concerns about relations between the police and minorities, questions about arrests and charges, have been raised by the city's minority communities. We believe it is the duty of a newspaper and its journalists to seek out the truth, to focus attention on practices and issues that need to be discussed and addressed.'[3] For the *Star*, seeking out the truth meant finding the empirical data that would show whether blacks were treated any differently than whites.

Inevitably, the analysis meant using subjective determinations to create categories for comparisons. The newspaper was guided by previous examinations into racial profiling in the US. For instance, the *Star* believed it was useful to look at what it called 'out-of-sight' violations, or offences that normally come to light only after a vehicle is stopped. These offences include driving without a licence or insurance. 'It's assumed random checks would generate a pattern of charges that mimics the racial distribution of drivers in society as a whole', the newspaper said. 'Almost 34 per cent of all drivers charged with out-of-sight violations were black, in the group where race was listed. Yet, according to the latest census figures, Toronto's black community represents just 8.1 per cent of the city's population.' It concluded the evidence showed police had been targeting black drivers in Toronto.[4] Not surprisingly, Toronto police categorically rejected the charge of racial profiling. Noting that they are prohibited from analyzing crime data from a racial point of view for fear of stoking racism, they accused the newspaper of doing just that. Police Chief Julian Fantino was emphatic: 'We do not do racial profiling. We do not deal with people on the basis of their ethnicity, their race, or any other factor. We're not perfect people but you're barking up the wrong tree. There's no racism.'[5]

Fantino went further, hiring a University of Toronto sociologist to review the analysis. After alleging the methodology was flawed, the police began labeling the *Star*'s series as junk science. The Toronto Police Association launched a $2.7 billion class-action lawsuit, suggesting the newspaper had defamed every member of the Toronto police service. For months, controversy raged. The *Star* assembled its own experts to verify the validity of its study. A judge eventually threw out the lawsuit, saying the stories did not implicate each and every police officer.[6] It was by no means the first time that an issue dealing with race had been so prominently debated in Canada's most ethnically diverse city. But when it came to relations with police, it was the first time some hard numbers were available to add context to opinion and rhetoric. It made sense for the newspaper to use the computer as a tool for this type of investigative work.

The idea of using computers to assist in the process of journalism was hardly new. Fifty years earlier, during coverage of the 1952 presidential election, CBS used the Remington Rand UNIVAC computer to analyze early returns and predict the outcome of the race. Before 9 p.m., UNIVAC predicted a landslide win for Dwight D. Eisenhower over Adlai Stevenson. Walter Cronkite and the CBS team were skeptical. The race was supposed to be far closer, and the computer was making its call with just seven per cent of the votes counted. They delayed reporting the computer's analysis, but finally told viewers later in the evening. In the end, UNIVAC turned out to be amazingly accurate. It had predicted 438 electoral votes for Eisenhower to 93 for Stevenson. The actual totals were 442 to 89.[7] By 1956, all three American networks were using computers on election night.

Whether it was the invention of the telegraph or the development of photography, technological advances have always had profound effects on the practice of reporting. In terms of investigative journalism, a number of advances in the second half of the twentieth century gave reporters the tools to do more complex inquiries. The widespread introduction of commercial photocopiers in the early 1960s changed the way people could access documents, and made it far simpler for whistleblowers to leak information to the press. Soon after, portable cassette tape recorders appeared. Now, a reporter could capture a complete and accurate record of conversations without relying on handwriting or bulky electronic newsgathering equipment.[8] As tape recorders and camera equipment became smaller, the possibilities for surreptitious journalism increased as well. Eventually, miniaturization made hidden-camera shooting and sting operations feasible for any media organization. At the annual meeting of Investigative Reporters and Editors in the US, a Manhattan-based company typically sets up a sales table offering a range of tiny cameras that can be concealed in shirts, handbags, eye-glasses, water bottles, pens, or specially modified iPods.

Computers seem like a natural aid to journalism, but the sheer size and complexity of early computing machines made it difficult for journalists to understand how they could harness the technology for their purposes in any practical way. Some pioneering efforts gave an indication of the possibilities. 'Some of my social scientist friends have made the flattering suggestion that people in their business could learn about fact-finding from newspapermen', wrote American journalist Philip Meyer in 1972. 'I wouldn't know. I do know that they have a few tricks which we can use to good advantage. . . . As our society becomes more intricate, we must find more intricate tools to describe and interpret it.'[9] Meyer felt journalists relied far too heavily on anecdotes, random opinions, and conventional wisdom in their reporting. By adopting the methods of social scientists, a process he referred to as 'precision journalism', he said 'we can follow their example by abandoning the philosopher's armchair, giving up the notion that a few facts and common sense will make any problem yield, and make the new, high-powered techniques our own.' Meyer had attended Harvard on a Nieman fellowship and was introduced to the IBM 7090 computer and programming language. During one of his lectures, Meyer realized the techniques were more than objects of news interest, but methods reporters could actually use.[10] He returned to his job as a national correspondent for the Knight-Ridder newspaper chain in 1967 and put his newfound learning into practice. Race riots had broken out in Detroit, and Meyer was dispatched to help the *Detroit Free Press* with its coverage. When the shooting had ended, he began designing a survey of Detroit neighbourhoods to discover some of the causes of the riot. Twenty-five researchers went into the field, conducting a total of

437 interviews. Keypunch operators coded the responses onto 1,311 cards, three for each of the interviews.[11] Survey results were entered into an IBM 360/40 computer for analysis. Some of the results ran counter to conventional wisdom at the time. He found college graduates were just as likely as school dropouts to have participated in the riots, and more of the rioters had been raised in the northern US than in the south. The story helped inaugurate a new era of computer-assisted reporting.

The following year, a reporter at the *Miami Herald* enlisted law students to computerize the paper records of 682 people who had been booked on vice charges in Florida's Dade County. His resulting analysis found bias in the justice system, and he published the story under the headline 'A Scientific Look at Dade Justice'.[12] It's believed to be the first time computers were used to analyze existing public records for a journalistic project.[13] The *Philadelphia Inquirer* took the idea one step further, identifying more than 1,000 defendants and following their progress through the court system. Reporters Donald Barlett and James Steele collected information from tens of thousands of court documents. They came up with 42 categories to define each case, including race and criminal history. Philip Meyer worked out the coding system and the analysis program, and an IBM computer was used to analyze the results. A series of stories in 1973 showed racial bias and politics were factors in dispensing unequal justice in the city.[14]

Computers, meanwhile, were beginning to affect journalism in other ways. By the mid-1970s, newsrooms started the process of converting from typewriters to video display terminals, with composing rooms moving from linotype machines to cold type. As stories began to be entered and stored electronically, the idea of online databases was born. By the early 1980s, companies such as Dow Jones and LexisNexis began offering electronic clipping services that would revolutionize journalistic research. The keyword became a powerful weapon as journalists used databases to retrieve information instantly. Suddenly it was possible to research individuals, companies, and topics with phenomenal speed and comprehensiveness. As government agencies and private institutions computerized their records, journalists realized there were increasing opportunities to request and analyze data. In the past, for instance, a land title search would yield one paper record at a time, and could only be done by requesting a specific legal description of a property. Now, a keyword search could determine all properties held by a single owner. New technologies opened avenues for investigative research that reporters of a previous era couldn't have imagined.

Soon journalists discovered that by comparing one database of information to another, useful overlapping information could be gleaned. Elliot Jaspin, a Rhode Island reporter and early user of computer-assisted journalism, collaborated with Maria Johnson to investigate a series of school bus accidents in 1985. They obtained a database of the state's traffic violations for the previous three years, and compared it to a database of school bus drivers. They found more than 25 per cent of the drivers had at least one violation, and some had serious records. A further comparison with the criminal record database showed some of the drivers had been convicted of drug dealing and other major crimes.[15] By the end of the project, more than a million records had been compared. Jaspin's interest in computer analysis carried into other projects, and in 1989 he founded the precursor to a group that would later become a leading centre for such work, the National Institute for Computer-Assisted Reporting.

Using computers to crunch data and produce new information was coming to be seen as an important tool for investigative work. In an effort to increase the in-depth coverage at the *Atlanta Journal-Constitution*, for instance, the newspaper conducted a massive study of lending patterns at banks, credit unions, and savings and loan associations. It used the Freedom of Information Act to obtain transactions at all the institutions over a six-year period. That included 82,610 home purchase loans and 26,721 home improvement loans for a total of more than $6 billion in lending by banks and savings and loans. The newspaper matched the lending data with census information to determine which neighbourhoods were getting the loans. If more than 80 per cent of the residents in an area were of the same colour, the neighbourhood was classified that way, otherwise it was considered integrated. This allowed researchers to determine how the loans broke down by race. The computer analysis showed that whites got five times as many home loans as blacks of the same income. The 1988 series, entitled *The Color of Money*, provided objective information to critics who had long fought against such institutionalized racism. The series won a Pulitzer and became widely known in American journalism circles for its methodology.[16]

Canadian journalists were monitoring these developments, but significant progress didn't take root until the middle of the 1990s. Bill Doskoch of the *Regina Leader-Post* took an interest in the genre and wrote an early handbook on the methodology, while conducting some small experiments.[17] He and a handful of reporters who were interested in computing began to discuss possibilities, and formed a caucus within the Canadian Association of Journalists in 1994. It was recognized that the success of such reporting depended on access to government information in a format that could be analyzed with the aid of computers. That led to discussions about the adequacy of Canada's access legislation, and the more restrictive climate surrounding government databases. Canadian reporters routinely marveled at the kinds of databases their American counterparts were accessing, but which were deemed private back home. During the early 1990s, there was far more discussion about this kind of reporting than actual practice. A survey of 30 Canadian reporters at two major dailies in 1994 found little interest in computers beyond traditional word processing and background research functions.[18]

The situation began to change in mid-decade, when *Toronto Star* publisher John Honderich returned from a conference in the US where he had learned about developments in the genre. He relayed the information to Kevin Donovan, who had been the newspaper's lead investigative reporter since 1989. Donovan had no computer background, and hadn't yet considered the idea of using databases and spreadsheets in his work. He attended a conference and an intensive boot-camp training session in the US, where he picked up the basics of data analysis.[19] By the spring of 1995, an opportunity arrived to put the training into practice. Donovan and a team of *Star* reporters were looking into Ontario's non-profit housing industry, and suspicions of profiteering and mismanagement. He acquired some relevant databases, including the Public Accounts of Ontario, which listed all government payments, as well as the province's system of tracking details about non-profit housing. He manually assembled other data and entered everything in a relational database, allowing him to derive story ideas from the numbers. He discovered, for instance, the projects that had the highest subsidies, the projects that cost the most to build, and which consultants had made the most money. Armed with the analysis, he then began looking for interviews and seeking government accountability.

The *Star* ran a series with the findings of the investigation entitled 'The Money Pit' in May 1995. Donovan reported that Ontario's social housing system was 'sinking under a morass of profiteering, political favouritism, shady business deals, conflicts of interest, suspected fraud, spiraling debt, and lack of accountability'.[20] Donovan's data analysis had helped identify stories, and provided statistical backup in the finished product. From that point forward, computer-assisted reporting became a regular tool at the *Star*. The newspaper used data analysis in stories on domestic abuse, problems in group homes, and abuse in the province's nursing homes. A handful of other reporters across the country began trying projects in the mid-1990s. Paul Schneidereit of the *Halifax Chronicle-Herald* used computer analysis to assist in a demographic profile of the city, and later to create a report card on Halifax schools. Fred Vallance-Jones of CBC Radio in Winnipeg used database analysis to show how government infrastructure grants were going disproportionately to constituencies held by the governing Conservatives.[21]

By 2000, computer-assisted stories were becoming more sophisticated and complex. The *Star* continued to be a leader among newspapers in using it as a tool in its investigative work. Despite the difficulties of public access, reporters working in the field were constantly looking for databases that could yield useful stories. Donovan accessed the federal database of charities, exposing problems with the way many organizations raised funds and disbursed donations. The *Star* also obtained a copy of Toronto's apartment inspection database, showing squalid conditions in many buildings.

But the story that got the biggest public reaction was the one that hit people directly in the stomach. It began in 1999, when *Star* reporter Rob Cribb became violently ill after eating a chicken dinner in a downtown Toronto restaurant. He tried to access the city's inspection reports for the restaurant, but was told they weren't publicly available. 'I made all the standard arguments about how such a policy undermines the public's right to know', said Cribb. 'I gently pointed out that the information is collected and filed by public servants paid by me to act in my best interests. I concluded by strongly suggesting that the information rightfully belongs to the public. Their answer remained a firm and unequivocal "Sorry, no."'[22]

Instead of giving up, Cribb widened his request and asked under freedom of information provisions for all inspection reports in Toronto over the previous two years. A familiar process unfolded. There were initial denials, high fee requests, negotiations, and an eventual resolution. The request was narrowed to establishments in the old city of Toronto, prior to municipal amalgamation. Five months later, the city released records of restaurants that had at least one critical food safety problem. Sorting and analyzing the data, Cribb then chose 27 restaurants from that list and requested more detailed inspection reports. His series, called 'Dirty Dining', finally began running in February 2000. In a city with an ingrained culture of eating out, the stories provoked immediate outrage. Cribb reported that the city completed fewer than half the inspections required by provincial law, that it rarely issued fines, and hadn't shut down a single establishment in two years. Readers eagerly checked the results for their favourite restaurants. There were stomach-churning stories of countertops stained with rodent droppings and vermin being found near raw meat. 'Restaurants have at least one week to clean up their act and if they don't do it by March 1, we'll close them down', Toronto Mayor Mel Lastman declared after he read the initial stories. 'If it means bringing all the inspectors to downtown Toronto for a week or two weeks, we're going to do a sweep. . . . If we find cockroaches, if we find mice, if we find droppings, they're closed . . . until they clean up their act.'[23] The sweep led to dozens of closings and even more charges. Eventually, the city began posting the results of inspections in the front window of every establishment across town. 'All that from a bad chicken dinner', said Cribb.

Despite examples of journalistic successes, computer-assisted reporting that makes use of database analysis has never become widespread in Canada. The CBC has done some, most successfully in its examination of adverse drug reactions in Canada. The *Hamilton Spectator* conducted what was perhaps the largest analysis of records by a media outlet when reporters Fred Vallance-Jones and Steve Buist examined more than 12 million documents from Ontario's Drive Clean program. They found significant problems, including fraud, in the program that tests automobile emissions.[24] But the vast majority of media outlets don't make use of the tool. According to Kevin Donovan, there is reluctance on the part of some journalists to adopt the technology, and a fear by others. 'When I started doing computer-assisted reporting in Canada, colleagues at my paper generally treated it with disdain. That changed as people saw the effects. I was fortunate to have people at the *Star* who backed it, and several other reporters who embraced it, but it has not spread like wildfire.'[25] The Canadian Association of Journalists has tried to encourage more examples in the genre by offering a prize for projects that make use of the technique. But the guru of computer-assisted reporting, Philip Meyer, believes journalists are being pretentious by thinking the use of computers is anything more than one tool among many in the kit of a competent precision journalist.

> I was critiquing a couple of prominent investigative projects that used computers, and one of them said—very high up—that this is a computer-assisted reporting story. It just shows how naïve journalists are to think that using computers is a big deal and we ought to tell everyone about it. My cousins in Michigan use a computer to manage their farming operation, but when they go to market they don't pull up to the unloading dock and say: 'Hey, I've got these computer-assisted soybeans.'[26]

It is tempting to view technological change as paramount in determining historical causation. North American journalism, for instance, went through a revolutionary transformation as the telegraph virtually eliminated the Atlantic Ocean as a barrier in the transmission of overseas news.[27] For investigative journalists, the tape recorder, photocopy machine, and hidden camera all provided significant new tools in helping reporters get closer to the truth of any given situation. As far as journalism goes, the computer is arguably the most important invention of the last century. In addition to modernizing methods of mass media production, it has provided journalists with a way to research and analyze information that could not have been comprehended a generation earlier. The ability to harness computers to collate, sort, and compare vast amounts of data has provided investigative journalists with another way of going beyond competing opinions to find patterns of social realities. As we have seen in this chapter, significant investigative work can be enhanced with the power of computer-assisted reporting. No modern investigative reporter can remain ignorant of the latest techniques of data gathering and analysis that computer-assisted journalism affords. Still, it would be dangerous to conclude that technology alone can spur a new wave of investigative journalism. In analyzing the rebirth of investigative work in the United States during the second half of the twentieth century, James Aucoin rejected technological change as a sufficient cause, though he acknowledged the importance of tape recorders, cameras, computers, and other devices. 'At most, one can say that these devices made new subjects or different analyses available to investigators and made the chores of investigation easier, more efficient, and perhaps more accurate (computers, in particular, provided all of these advantages).'[28] Nor should it ever be forgotten that databases and computer analyses are only as good as the people behind them. There have been a number of documented cases of egregious errors creeping into journalistic accounts because of so-called 'dirty data' and errors in database analysis.[29] Though it is a relatively new field, and one that still isn't widely used in Canada, there is little doubt that computer-assisted reporting will be an increasingly important part of the investigative journalist's toolbox.

Forcing Government to Clean Up its Act

Everyone applauded when the Ontario government introduced a program in 1999 called Drive Clean—a plan to test vehicles in the highly polluted smog zone stretching from Windsor to Ottawa. The *Hamilton Spectator* saw an opportunity to put the scheme itself to the test. In December 2000, the newspaper asked for the database of test results. More than three years of denials, bureaucratic stonewalling, and appeals ensued. Finally, the province's information and privacy commissioner ordered the data released, and reporters Fred Vallance-Jones and Steve Buist set to work analyzing 12 million records.

It was an ideal subject for database analysis. The reporters began to see suspicious patterns. Cars that ought to have failed had passed the pollution tests. Some drivers kept retesting their cars until they passed, in some cases immediately after a failure. Certain garages rarely failed a vehicle. The newspaper discovered more than $1 billion had been spent on testing fees and emission repairs, yet some polluting cars were still being allowed back onto the road. The data also called into question why the province was spending money testing so many newer vehicles, when almost all of them easily passed. Armed with the database results, the reporters took to the field. They rigged a car to fail the emission test, then took it to area garages and asked what could be done. Some garages suggested repairs, while others offered to provide false test reports so the car could be passed. One man, working for a Kitchener used car dealer, had made as much as $100,000 by issuing fake certificates for cars. Buist and Vallance-Jones performed a simple but effective test every reader could quickly grasp. They took a 1993 Plymouth Sundance to four different Drive Clean facilities and got significantly different results each time, from easy passes to near failures.

The result was a five-part series in the *Spectator* during September 2004 called 'Smokescreen', which won a National Newspaper Award for investigations. Soon Drive Clean was being reviewed independently, and a year later the province announced sweeping changes to the testing scheme, including stiffer measures to combat fraud.

Chapter 18

The Road Ahead

While the Golden Age of journalism was marked by a fortuitous congruence of dedicated authors, courageous editors and publishers, progressive politicians, and an outraged public, the circumstances are far different now. Today we have journalists dedicated to the pursuit of high salaries and prestigious awards, a paucity of courageous editors and publishers, a near reactionary political environment, and a public distracted by junk food news about O.J. Simpson, JonBenet Ramsey, and Monica Lewinsky.

Carl Jensen, founder of Project Censored[1]

It is not entirely clear whether Canada ever experienced a 'Golden Age' of journalism in the sense Carl Jensen had in mind. What the survey in this book has made evident, I believe, is the existence of a number of unique and dedicated journalists who have steadily perfected the investigative genre in Canada. I began by attempting to define the set of practices known as investigative journalism, trying to analyze the genre as a cohesive social practice. In simplest terms, it is a form of journalism that aims to find the truth about issues of major importance to society. It consistently prods those in authority to be responsive and transparent, and it holds powerful institutions of all kinds to account. In its methodology, it adopts a scientific approach and uses forensic tools to get at the truth.[2] By delving into the specific lives and biographies of investigative journalists, I have tried to illuminate their motivations and show how their persistence and courage was often needed to overcome institutional barriers.

The historic struggle against colonial and feudal vestiges, and for responsible government, gave rise to the earliest examples of investigative journalism in Canada. By combining his penchant for holding the Family Compact to account, together with his rigorous digging, William Lyon Mackenzie created a form of journalism that resembles modern investigative reporting. What separated him from some of the other radical editors of the early nineteenth century was his devotion to facts, and his desire to move beyond rhetoric in his analysis of social conditions in Upper Canada. While his fellow radical journalists may have been muckrakers engaging in aggressive reporting that challenged the status quo, Mackenzie was all that and more. He used a methodology of open inquiry to sift the facts, adding a forensic element that elevated his work to the level of investigative reporting. Those two essential characteristics, the desire to hold powerful forces to account and the discipline of open-minded, scientific inquiry, were the legacies Mackenzie left to future investigative journalists. Both were firmly grounded in the traditions and ideals of the Enlightenment.

I have paid particular attention to the development of methodology through the years, as each incremental advance allowed future investigative journalists to stand on the shoulders of their predecessors and conduct better inquiries. Mackenzie's analysis of documents gave him insights into the nature of power in his society. The development of the journalistic interview later in the nineteenth century gave journalists more tools to discover facts. Gustavus Myers showed how delving into government and historical archives could reveal unreported truths. By the 1950s, enterprising reporters were using court records, public documents, and other tools to chase stories. The public broadcasting pioneers of the 1950s and 1960s developed unique methods to broaden their inquiries and enhance their pursuit of the truth. By the 1970s, academic research techniques were being applied to some investigative work, while inquiries lasting more than a year were calling for unique ways of organizing and distilling information. The television newsmagazines designed a team-based work process that was more rigorous than haphazard practices of many daily reporters. At the same time, undercover reporting and hidden-camera techniques added a new dimension to reporting. John Sawatsky's ideas surrounding the organization of research material and the mechanics of interviewing have been of lasting influence, and have provided new insights into how a rigorous methodology can get journalists closer to their goal of reporting the truth. The systematic mining of government information through freedom of information laws has given journalists additional means to hold powerful interests to account. In the current environment, the use of computer databases and search techniques, along with other aspects of computer-assisted reporting, promise to open more avenues for journalistic investigation.

History never moves in a straight line, and investigative journalism has tended to swell and subside, as Kovach and Rosenstiel have noted, 'like a theme in a Bach fugue'.[3] On the one hand, technological changes and the development of more refined journalistic methods allowed for more accurate probing. But another critical ingredient is always needed for the flourishing of investigative work—ripe social and economic conditions. Only then can there be an opportunity for a confluence of skilled practitioners eager to deliver content and an audience receptive to the message. By examining the conditions of different historical periods, I have attempted to illustrate the factors that both inhibited and encouraged aggressive journalistic inquiry. Sporadic examples of investigative work appeared at different stages in Canadian history, especially involving alternative media and maverick journalists. By the late 1950s and throughout the 1960s, a foundation was being set for more thoroughgoing investigative reporting. In Canada, the role of public broadcasters was critical in this era, as were alternative publications. The greatest quantity of investigative journalism in Canadian history came, arguably, in the 1970s. Part of the reason was that the mainstream media saw a commercial advantage in embracing it. Spurred by the alternative press, and fed by a public that was losing faith in the credibility of its political masters, the media spotted an advantage in joining the investigative bandwagon. That enthusiasm was never uniform, and it tended to flag with every lawsuit, corporate threat, and overt lobbying effort from powerful interests. But if the promise of a big jump in circulation or audience ratings was present, the budget could usually be found to fund a project. Investigative journalism assumed the status of a hot commodity.

Like all commodities, it fluctuated between highs and lows on the journalistic market. But it always held an inherent danger for mainstream media organizations, a dialectic that threatened to turn a profit centre into its opposite. Ever since the wide-scale commercialization of the press, there has been a contradiction between the need to maximize profits and every media institution's perceived desire to fulfill some kind of social responsibility to its audience. While this has been a feature of journalism generally, the conundrum is even more apparent when it comes to investigative journalism. By aiming at the truth, and holding power to account, investigative journalists often eroded the prestige of the economic and political structures that their own institutions embraced.[4] This led to conflict between journalists and their institutions, a theme I have repeatedly revisited in this book. Helpful in understanding the complexity of this process is Alasdair MacIntyre's analysis of social practices, which I have briefly highlighted at different points in the narrative.[5] As he points out, the internal goods sought by practitioners frequently clash with the external goods coveted by the institutions, necessitating virtuous behaviour on the part of practitioners to resist the corrupting power of institutions.[6] I have noted that investigative journalists are constantly under a variety of external pressures—ranging from threats of physical violence to the ever-present danger of libel suits. But the internal pressures exercised by institutions can be the most vexing of all, and how a journalist reacts to those pressures can be crucial in determining the ultimate value of the work. James Dygert, who documented American investigative journalism when it was in vogue, warned against the pressure to choose safe and predictable subjects. 'Few investigative reporters admit that their own employers hold them back', he said. 'Treading on the toes of a community's power structure, of which the publisher or station owner is a part, to investigate a prominent hometown business or institution, for instance, takes real courage.'[7] Carl Jensen puts it more plainly. 'Muckraking is most effective when done by individuals driven by social conscience who won't be deterred from their goals by corporate groupthink or allegiance to some corporate entity.'[8] Many of those practitioners found it easier to operate outside the boundaries of the mainstream press, and any examination of investigative work must take into account the alternative media, as I have done in this book.

Carl Jensen, founder of Project Censored, spent years cataloguing important stories that should have been widely circulated in the media, but weren't. He compiled an annual list of exposés that were censored, underreported, or sometimes treated with disdain by the mainstream media. In Jensen's view, the Golden Age of American journalism was the turn-of-the-century muckraking period of Sinclair, Steffens, and Tarbell. While the 1960s and 1970s provided a partial revival, he saw a variety of factors contributing to a modern-day dearth of investigative reporting. Among the influences were the growing monopolization of the media, the punishing impact of both litigation and judicial restrictions, private media's single-minded concern for their bottom line, and a general loss of public faith in the media's ability to act as a watchdog.[9] Jensen's worries are as applicable to Canada as they are to the United States.

Any attempt to predict a future for investigative work in Canada needs to examine the nature of media institutions in the country and the individuals who work for those institutions. And it needs to consider the economic, legal, and political influences on both. Extraordinary economic pressures on media organizations are forcing newspaper publishers to find ways of stemming circulation loss. Maintaining audience share is just as pressing a concern for radio and television stations, both public and private. The history of investigative journalism has shown that media organizations often look at the genre as expensive, time-consuming, inherently dangerous, and ultimately optional. During periods of economic downturn, investigative journalism has usually been curtailed. The rise and fall of investigative teams at different newspapers and broadcast outlets can often be matched to budgetary imperatives at the time. But the trends have also shown that even when budgets improve, the teams do not necessarily return, as other genres are considered more cost-effective. Media consultants are constantly advising that journalists producing lifestyle news, or celebrity features, or dramatic crime narratives are far more likely to attract readers or viewers on a consistent basis than an investigative team, with its unpredictable outcomes and more costly methods. And the threat of a catastrophic lawsuit, not to mention the potential for incurring the wrath of an angry advertiser or government minister, is much lower.

During the 1970s, many investigative projects had their origins in news stories that cried out for further inquiry. Beat reporters would spot a lead and file it away for further research, when they had time. But over the last few decades, there has been a trend to devote fewer journalists to key beats, thereby reducing the potential to collect the raw material needed for investigative reports. Most major newspapers assign far fewer reporters to local city halls and legislatures than they did 25 years ago. Collective media scrutiny of national institutions has also declined markedly. Some large media organizations don't even consider it necessary to have specialists covering major areas of society and the economy. The vast majority of Canadian newsrooms scramble every day to put a newspaper on the street or a newscast to air. In this context, it is seen as a luxury for a reporter to have more than a day or two to work on any given story.

If changes to Canadian media institutions have had an impact on investigative journalism, so too have changes in the nature of the journalists themselves. 'Increasingly, the type of person who becomes a journalist has more difficulty identifying with the underdog', according to veteran reporter Linden MacIntyre. Reflecting on his early career, MacIntyre remembered a different kind of reporter.

> Almost everyone I worked with was a sort-of grown-up underdog. They came
> from working class or agrarian families. Or they had been in the war or had been
> in hard labour themselves at one point in their lives. If you got fired by Paper A
> for being a shit disturber, you just tied one on and three days later you worked

for Paper B. People were not as afraid of losing their job. Nowadays, you're more inclined to come out of a middle-class or upper-middle-class family. As salaries have gone up and as the jobs have become more complicated, and the business has become more professionalized, people look upon the possible loss of their position with a lot more fear. That will come to bear on what you do.[10]

Neil MacDonald of the CBC has an even blunter assessment:

Canadian journalism is far too inclined to genuflect to power. Institutions are given the benefit of the doubt. Marginal voices, or voices of those who think too far outside the conventional box, are ignored. That isn't to say that Canadian journalism doesn't challenge our politicians. These challenges are well within the confines of convention, so Canadian journalists generally have a field day speaking their version of the truth to those in power. . . . When it comes to challenging conventional wisdom, or better, challenging the motives and practices of business, Canadian journalists are anemic. Partly, I suppose, because journalists are relatively affluent, and therefore tend toward fiscal conservatism. They have far less in common with the poor and disadvantaged, and far more in common with executives and the politically powerful.[11]

Australian-born journalist John Pilger believes some journalists are part of a propaganda apparatus in thrall to the politically powerful without knowing it, while others act more consciously. 'Power rewards their collusion with faint recognition: a place at the table, perhaps even a Companion of the British Empire. At their most supine, they are spokesmen of the spokesmen, de-briefers of the briefers, what the French call *functionnaires*.'[12]

Still, the last two centuries of Canadian history have also shown that individual journalists seized with the investigative impulse will sprout spontaneously. They will always be among us, no matter how crammed the news pages are with celebrity profiles or how many talent shows compete for ratings on television. How loudly their voices are heard depends somewhat on factors beyond their control, but also on circumstances of their own making. Steven Truscott might never have called his entire murder conviction into doubt had Isabel LeBourdais not persisted in her efforts to research every aspect of the case. Henry Aubin's analysis of Montreal's real estate world might never have reached a wider audience had he not convinced a book publisher to embrace the story. John Sawatsky might have cut short his investigation into RCMP wrongdoing had he become discouraged at the virtual boycott of his stories by the national media. Daniel Leblanc might have abandoned his inquiry into the sponsorship scandal if he had been dissuaded by the federal bureaucrats and politicians who were intent on subverting his access to information requests. And there's no telling how many investigative stories might have vanished had reporters been cowed by threats of lawsuits or pressure to name sources for fear of being held in contempt of court. In each case, the perseverance of the individual journalist proved to be the deciding factor.

Modern technology appears to offer investigative journalists unprecedented opportunities to disseminate their stories. While alternative media outlets have always played an important muckraking role, Internet websites and blogs now afford them the possibility of worldwide distribution. This has empowered a variety of organizations and foundations dedicated to creating investigative journalism free from any reliance on corporate or government funding. One such group in the US, called the Center for Public Integrity, has as its mission the creation of 'high-quality, accessible investigative reports, databases, and contextual analysis on issues of public importance'.[13] Canadian journalists have participated actively in the group's work, which has included investigations into topics ranging from drugs, oil, and armaments to the politics of the world's water supplies. Other organizations and websites are springing up with similar aims. How effective they will be depends on the level of long-term funding they can secure, because investigative work requires an extensive commitment of time and resources.

Beyond the media organizations and journalists who work for them, there is another player that will ensure the existence of Canadian investigative journalism in the future. That is the whistle-blower, the committed individual who is motivated to speak out against injustice. Whistle-blowers are found in every occupation and profession, and at all levels of society. They tend to lurk silently when the media are meek and respectful of the status quo. A steady diet of infotainment might even convince them not to bother reaching for the telephone to call a reporter. But as every investigative journalist knows, one exposé tends to spawn others. A potential whistle-blower will read a story in the newspaper about injustice or systemic problems in one field and feel a glimmer of optimism about his or her own situation. Soon the fear of a lawsuit, or job loss, melts away and a brown envelope is slipped into the mail. Then it's up to the journalist to complete the process.

If history is any guide to the future, investigative reporting will continue to be an ongoing aspect of Canadian journalism. Its ultimate power and vibrancy depend on a complex web of factors, the most important being the courage and tenacity of its practitioners.

Global Assault on a Global Problem

Bill Marsden, an investigative reporter with the Montreal *Gazette*, was intrigued to receive an invitation to take part in a world-wide investigation of tobacco companies. Marsden had written numerous stories about Big Tobacco, showing how companies were complicit in smuggling operations designed to skirt rising government taxes. Now the International Consortium of Investigative Journalists, a group organized by the Center for Public Integrity in the US, wanted Marsden to look at the picture globally. Working with journalists in a number of countries, Marsden eventually published findings of the year-long investigation in a special report on 3 March 2001. The conclusions were dramatic: 'Tobacco company officials at BAT, Phillip Morris, and R.J. Reynolds have worked closely with companies and individuals directly connected to organized crime in Hong Kong, Canada, Colombia, Italy, and the United States.'[14]

Marsden and his team showed how tobacco companies undercut government tax regimes by offering brands on the black market. The result was massive tax evasion that depleted many government treasuries. The investigation was based on a review of thousands of pages of corporate and government documents and dozens of interviews with law enforcement officials, smugglers, and other sources. They estimated one in every three cigarettes exported worldwide was sold on the black market. 'In some cases, tobacco industry executives actively played various gangs off against each other and solicited and received millions of dollars in kickbacks or bribes in return for selling to preferred criminal syndicates, according to court records and sources.' The series had separate chapters on China, North America, Italy, Latin America, Africa, Cyprus, and the United States, showing remarkable similarities in how the international smuggling worked. The major tobacco companies all vigorously denied any involvement in the smuggling of their products.

Marsden said it was challenging to coordinate the work of so many journalists around the world, some of whom he had never met. But rigorous research and fact-checking ensured the series was completely sound. He employed the same methodology he used in all his investigations: a line-by-line check, with facts of the story on one side of the page and corroborating evidence on the other. Lawyers for the organization then pored over the text to make sure there was no cause for legal action. For Marsden, it was his first involvement in such a wide-ranging example of international investigative work. Most journalists spend their careers reporting issues within their own borders. This series clearly demonstrated the need for coordinated journalistic action to investigate issues that transcend many national boundaries.

Notes

Preface

1. Mitchell Stephens, *A History of News* (Penguin Books, 1988), p. 267.
2. Barbie Zelizer, *Taking Journalism Seriously* (Sage Publications, 2004), p.1.
3. Ibid., p.32.
4. James Aucoin, *The Evolution of American Investigative Journalism* (University of Missouri Press, 2005), p. 10.
5. Alasdair MacIntyre, *After Virtue* (Duckworth, 1981), pp. 178—181. MacIntyre defines a virtue as 'an acquired human quality the possession and exercise of which tends to enable us to achieve those goods which are internal to practices and the lack of which effectively prevents us from achieving any such goods' (p.178). He says practices involve standards of excellence and obedience to rules, as well as achievement of goods, both internal and external.
6. Ibid., p. 181.
7. The term 'investigative journalism' does not appear to have been in common usage before the 1950s. One of the earliest references I have found was in a speech by Louis B. Seltzer, editor of the *Cleveland Press*, in 1952. He said government was increasingly setting up protective shields, such as press conferences and handouts, between itself and the press. As a result, reporters were rarely getting to the actual source of news, and were being manipulated. He said it was a disgrace there was not more investigative reporting in Washington and the state capitals (*New York Times*, 3 December 1952).
8. Herbert Altschull, *From Milton to McLuhan: The Ideas Behind American Journalism* (Longman, 1990), p. 36.
9. John Milton, *Areopagitica* (found at http://www.gutenberg.org/etext/608).
10. Altschull, pp. 40—41.
11. Ibid., p. 52.
12. John Locke, *Two Treatises of Government and a Letter Concerning Toleration* (Yale University, 2003), p. 197.
13. Ibid.
14. Altschull, p. 57.
15. Minko Sotiron, *From Politics to Profit* (McGill-Queen's University Press, 1997), p. 161.
16. Fred Siebert, et. al., *Four Theories of the Press* (University of Illinois Press, 1956).
17. John Merrill, *Journalism Ethics: Philosophical Foundations for News Media* (St. Martin's Press, 1997), pp. 13—18.
18. Ibid., p. 74.
19. John C. Nerone, ed., *Last Rights: Revisiting Four Theories of the Press* (University of Illinois Press, 1995), p. 125.
20. Ibid., p. 122.
21. Hugo de Burgh, *Investigative Journalism: Context and Practice* (Routledge, 2000), p. 68.
22. Edward Herman and Noam Chomsky, *Manufacturing Consent: The Political Economy of the Mass Media* (Pantheon Books, 1988), p. xi.
23. Ibid., p. 298.
24. Robert Babe, *Canadian Communication Thought: Ten Foundational Writers* (University of Toronto Press, 2000), pp. 51–86.

25. John C. Nerone, p. 133.
26. Herman and Chomsky, pp. 299-300.
27. Ibid.
28. Edward Herman, *The Myth of the Liberal Media*, (Peter Lang Publishing, 1999), pp. 270–71.
29. See, for instance, Herman, p. 32.
30. Robert Babe, p. 84.
31. There are a number of recent anthologies that provide excerpts of these and many other examples of investigative work, though most are principally American. They include *Shaking the Foundations*, edited by Bruce Shapiro (Thunder's Mouth Press, 2003), *Muckraking: The Journalism that Changed America*, edited by Judith and William Serrin (The New Press, 2002), and *Tell Me No Lies: Investigative Journalism and its Triumphs*, edited by John Pilger (Jonathan Cape, 2004).
32. Henry Aubin, *City for Sale* (Editions l'Etincelle, 1977).
33. Most of the source material for this narrative comes from the organization's newsletter, the *CIJ Bulletin*, along with audio tapes of the founding convention, 19–21 January 1979, Montreal.

Chapter 1

1. *Newsweek*, 19 November 1973, p. 139B.
2. Andrew McIntosh, Interview, 5 May 2005.
3. Altschull, *From Milton to McLuhan*, p. 51.
4. David Protess, et al., *The Journalism of Outrage*, p. 5.
5. Ibid., p. 15.
6. James Ettema and Theodore Glasser, *Custodians of Conscience*, p. 3.
7. Ibid., p. 61.
8. John Zaritsky, Interview, 14 July 2006.
9. Kathy English and Nick Russell, eds, *Page 1*, p. 363.
10. John Zaritsky, Interview.
11. Doug Smith, *As Many Liars*, p. 13.
12. CBC Radio, *World Report*, 22 June 1998.
13. See the Report of the Commission of Inquiry into Allegations of Infractions of The Elections Act and The Elections Finances Act during the 1995 Manitoba general elections, Winnipeg, Manitoba: The Commission, 1999.
14. Ibid., p. 5.
15. Ibid., p. 180.
16. http://www.michenerawards.ca/english/winaward1999.htm
17. Andrew McIntosh, Interview.
18. *Globe and Mail*, 15 September 1986.
19. Excerpted in Kathy English and Nick Russell, pp.55–73.
20. McIntosh Interview. See also Andrew McIntosh, 'Into the Rough,' *Media*, Summer 2000, pp. 6–7.
21. See Affidavit of *Andrew McIntosh, R* v. *National Post*, 21 January 2004 (Ont. SCJ) ONSC M86/02.
22. Andrew McIntosh, Interview.
23. *Globe and Mail*, 16 November 2000.
24. Andrew McIntosh, Interview.

25. Chris Cobb, *Ego and Ink*, p. 255.

26. Andrew McIntosh, 'Ignoring the paper trail,' *Media*, Spring 2000, p. 27.

27. Cobb, op. cit., p. 263.

28. Quoted in Elysse Zarek, 'The Wrong Arm of the Law,' *Ryerson Review of Journalism*, Summer 2005, p. 52.

29. Dean Jobb, 'Name Names or Do Time,' *Media* Magazine, Winter, 1995.

30. *Globe and Mail*, 15 March 1969.

31. *R* v. *National Post*, 21 January 2004 (Ont. SCJ) ONSC M86/02.

32. Daniel Leblanc, Interview, 2 August 2006.

33. Commission of Inquiry into the Sponsorship Program and Advertising Activities, Vol. 38, 23 November 2004, p. 6585.

34. Daniel Leblanc, 'The secret caller who exposed Adscam,' *Globe and Mail*, 21 October 2006.

35. Leblanc has detailed this story in his book *Nom de Code*.

36. Commission of Inquiry into the Sponsorship Program and Advertising Activities, 'Who is Responsible?' p. 6, http://epe.lac-bac.gc.ca/100/206/301/pco-bcp/commissions/sponsorship-ef/06-03-06/www.gomery.ca/en/phase1report/summary/es_major%20findings_v01.pdf, accessed 1 August 2006.

37. Daniel Leblanc, Interview.

Chapter 2

1. William Lyon Mackenzie, address to the Legislative Assembly, 11 December 1831, quoted in William Kilbourn, *The Firebrand*, p. 68. Mackenzie's debt to Enlightenment views of basic human rights and freedom of expression is clear.

2. *Welland Canal*, 16 December 1835.

3. A good description of Mackenzie's post-1837 work and writings is contained in Lillian Gates, *After the Rebellion*.

4. William Kesterton, *History of Journalism in Canada*, pp. 3–4. See also *Dictionary of Canadian Biography* entries on Anthony Henry, John Bushell, and Bartholomew Green, as well as Thomas' own writings.

5. Isaiah Thomas, *History of Printing in America*, available in http://www.assumption.edu/ahc/1770s/pprintthomasbio.html, accessed 15 June 2006.

6. Douglas Lochhead, Entry on Anthony Henry, *Dictionary of Canadian Biography Online*, http://www.biographi.ca/EN/ShowBio.asp?BioId=36066

7. Claude Galarneau, Entry on Fleury Mesplet, *Dictionary of Canadian Biography Online*, http://www.biographi.ca/EN/ShowBio.asp?BioId=36188. See also Montreal *Gazette*, 30 August 2003, and George Galt, 'The Untold Tale of Fleury Mesplet', *Content*, July 1974.

8. Altschull, p. 78.

9. Ibid.

10. Galarneau, Ibid.

11. See, for example, Kesterton, p. 20, and Stanley Ryerson, *Unequal Union* (Progress, 1968), pp. 194–5.

12. H.P. Gundy, Entry on Francis Collins, *Dictionary of Canadian Biography Online*, http://www.biographi.ca/EN/ShowBio.asp?BioId=36935

13. Leslie Harris, *Dictionary of Canadian Biography Online*, Entry on Robert Parsons, http://

www.biographi.ca/EN/ShowBio.asp?BioId=39873

14. The offending letter, Howe's defence and other materials relating to the case can be found at www.gov.ns.ca/legislature/Facts/Howebio.html

15 Ibid.

16. Gourlay surveyed settlers for an exhaustive 'Statistical Account of Upper Canada', one of the first sociological examinations of rural life in Canada.

17. Ryerson, p. 91, and Kilbourn, p. 16.

18. *Colonial Advocate*, 18 May 1824.

19. Quoted in Ryerson, *Unequal Union*, p. 91.

20. William Lyon Mackenzie, *Sketches of Canada and the United States*, 1833, p. 81.

21. Ibid.

22. Quoted in Kilbourn, p. 33.

23. *Colonial Advocate*, 10 May 1832.

24. 'To the People of the County of York', *The Constitution*, 24 May 1837.

25. Hugo de Burgh, p. 30.

26. *Colonial Advocate*, 15 November 1832.

27. *Welland Canal*, 16 December 1835, p. 1.

28. In addition to Kilbourn, source material for information on Mackenzie's life can be found in Charles Lindsey, *The Life and Times of William Lyon Mackenzie*; William LeSueur, *William Lyon Mackenzie*; Rick Salutin, *1837: William Lyon Mackenzie and the Canadian Revolution*; and Margaret Fairley, ed., *The Selected Writings of William Lyon Mackenzie* (Oxford University Press, 1960), among others.

Chapter 3

1. *Globe* Editorial, 1852.

2. Stephens, *A History of News*, p. 226.

3. J.M.S. Careless, *Brown of The Globe*, Vol. 1, p. 103.

4. de Burgh, *Investigative Journalism*, p. 38.

5. Stephens, p. 229.

6. de Burgh, p. 35.

7. For a full discussion of the development of the daily press in this period, see Paul Rutherford, *A Victorian Authority*.

8. Quoted in Ron Poulton, *The Paper Tyrant*, p. 7.

9. Poulton, pp. 79–82.

10. Quoted in Sotiron, *From Politics to Profits*, p. 12.

11. Quoted in Ron Verzuh, *Radical Rag*, pp. 54–5.

12. For a survey of these alternative publications, see David Spencer, 'Providing an Alternative Vision', *Content*, March/April 1987, pp. 13–16. See also Spencer's chapter called 'Alternative Visions: The Intellectual Heritage of Nonconformist Journalists in Canada', in Hanno Hardt and Bonnie Brennen, eds, *Newsworkers*.

13. Gregory S. Kealey, *Toronto Workers Respond to Industrial Capitalism 1867–1892* (University of Toronto Press, 1980), p. 328.

14. *The Globe*, 10 June 1882.

15. *The Globe*, 5 June 1882.

16. Ibid.

17. *The Globe*, 10 June 1882.
18. The lives of the muckrakers have been well-documented in a number of books, including: Louis Filler, *The Muckrakers* (1993), originally published in 1939; Robert Miraldi, *The Muckrakers: Evangelical Crusaders* (Praeger, 2000), Robert Miraldi, *Muckraking and Objectivity: Journalism's Colliding Traditions* (Greenwood Press, 1990) and Arthur and Lila Weinberg, *The Muckrakers* (University of Illinois Press, 2001).
19. Some historians see the *McClure's Magazine* issue of January 1903 as a seminal moment in American muckraking. The issue contained articles by Lincoln Steffens, Ida Tarbell, and Ray Stannard Baker, along with an editorial that says the three pieces together 'may set us thinking'. See Ellen Fitzpatrick, *Muckraking: Three Landmark Articles*.
20. Ida Tarbell, *The History of the Standard Oil Company*, preface, online version at http://www.history.rochester.edu/fuels/tarbell/MAIN.HTM
21. Ibid.
22. Quoted in Arthur and Lila Weinberg, eds, p. 69.
23. Ibid., p. 178.
24. Miraldi, *Muckraking and Objectivity*, pp. 57–75.
25. Fraser Sutherland, *The Monthly Epic*, p. 139.
26. *Toronto Daily Star*, 14 November 1905, p. 1.
27. Ross Harkness, *J.E. Atkinson of the Star*, p. 68.
28. *Toronto Star*, 16 February 1914, p. 2.
29. Louis Filler, *The Muckrakers*, p. 118.
30. Ibid., p. 119.
31. From the preface to *The History of the Great American Fortunes*, quoted in Stanley Ryerson introduction to Gustavus Myers, *A History of Canadian Wealth* (James Lewis and Samuel, 1972), pp. xiii–xiv.
32. Ibid., p. xxxiv.
33. *New York Times*, 5 July 1914.
34. *Ryerson Review of Journalism*, Summer 1996.

Chapter 4

1. Walter Stewart, ed., *Canadian Newspapers*, p. 11.
2. P. Eric Louw, *The Media and Political Process*, p. 64. Sabato provides an analysis of the different stages of press activity in *Feeding Frenzy* (Free Press, 1993) in which he characterizes many contemporary scandal-mongering exposés as little more than 'junkyard journalism'.
3. Sotiron, *From Politics to Profits*, p. 157.
4. American historians generally concur that muckraking and investigative journalism stagnated in the mainstream US press between the First World War and the 1960s. David Protess calls the period a 'return to quiescence' (p. 42) when uncritical and pack journalism held sway. Any investigative reporting that was done was largely achieved by independent publications and freelance journalists, he says. Aucoin also sees only sporadic and inconsistent investigative work in the decades after the First World War. 'Throughout most of the 1950s, reporting of an investigative nature in newspapers was rare, pushed to journalism's sidelines by the enduring criticism of crusades and a growing complacency in the press.' (p. 39) Miraldi has a similar analysis of what took place after the turn-of-the-century American muckraking movement subsided during the First World War. 'Muckraking disappeared and,

except for isolated muckraking episodes over the next forty years, it did not reappear as a movement until the world had gone through a period of business idolatry, through a stock market crash and a depression, and through another world war.' (*Muckraking and Objectivity*, p. 75)

5. Sutherland, *The Monthly Epic*, pp. 148–9.
6. Judith and William Serrin, *Muckraking: The Journalism that Changed America*, p. 34.
7. George Seldes, *Never Tire of Protesting*.
8. Clarke Davey, Interview, 8 April 2005.
9. *New York Times*, 3 December 1952.
10. *Toronto Telegram*, 22 April 1953.
11. *Toronto Star*, 23 April 1953.
12. *Globe and Mail*, 16 April 1954.
13. Ron Haggart, Interview, 14 February 2005.
14. Richard J. Doyle, *Hurly Burly*, p. 140.
15. William Blackstone, *Commentaries on the Laws of England*.
16. *Toronto Star*, 8 May 1958, p. 66.
17. Jacques Hébert, *I Accuse the Assassins of Coffin*, pp. 28 and 93.
18. *Globe and Mail*, 7 December 1964, p. 11.
19. *Globe and Mail*, 5 December 1964, p. 1.
20. Ibid., p. 168.
21. *Globe and Mail*, 28 October 1963, p. 7.
22. *Toronto Star*, 25 January 1966, p. 20.
23. William French, 'Behind the Triumph, an Author's Trials', *Globe and Mail*, 29 March 1966, p. 7.
24. Isabel LeBourdais, *The Trial of Steven Truscott*, p. 240.
25. Letter of Mr Justice Ronald Ferguson to Pierre Trudeau, 5 June 1967.
26. *The fifth estate*, CBC, 20 March 2000. See also www.cbc.ca/fifth/truscott/
27. Robert Reguly, Interview, 14–15 February 2005.
28. *Toronto Star*, 2 October 1964, p. 1.
29. MacIntyre, p. 181.

Chapter 5

1. Edward R. Murrow, *See It Now*, 9 March 1954.
2. Douglas Leiterman, Interview, 7, 22, 29 April 2005.
3. Quoted in Eric Koch, *Inside Seven Days*, p. 40.
4. Douglas Leiterman, Interview.
5. Quoted in Babe, *Canadian Communication Thought*, p. 41.
6. Ibid., p. 40.
7. David Hogarth, 'Public-Service Broadcasting as a Modern Project: A Case Study of Early Public-Affairs Television in Canada', reprinted in Daniel Robinson, ed., *Communication History in Canada*, p. 197.
8. *CBC Times*, 6 October 1957.
9. CBC Press Service, September 1957.
10. Quoted in Paul Rutherford, *When Television was Young*, p. 163.
11. CBC Press Service, September 1957, Ross McLean Biography. See also CBC Press Service, 21

August 1953, *Ottawa Citizen*, 13 November 2002 ('Life magazine for TV' by Tony Atherton), and *Globe and Mail*, 3 June 1987 ('TV pioneer fondly remembered', by John Haslett Cuff).

12. *Toronto Telegram*, 13 June 1959, p tv-11.
13. Patrick Watson, *This Life Has Seven Decades* (McClelland and Stewart, 2004), p. 144.
14. *Toronto Star*, 13 and 15 February 1956.
15. *Close-Up* Production File, CBC Research Library, Toronto.
16. *Globe and Mail*, 11 January 1958.
17. CBC Press Service, 3 April 1958.
18. *Globe and Mail*, 11 January 1958.
19. Rutherford, *When Television was Young*, p. 177.
20. *Toronto Telegram*, 3 August 1963.
21. Watson, e-mail of 7 April 2005.
22. Watson, *This Life Has Seven Decades*, p. 566.
23. National Archives, RG 41 v.230, 'Controversial Programs—English Networks, March 1961—January 1964.' A CBC memo says of the Cuba documentary that it was produced by a highly competent team, and was an excellent presentation of one aspect of an extremely important situation. But 'the final product, under examination, was not in itself a fair presentation of the complete and many-sided situation.'
24. Quoted in *Globe and Mail*, 1 July 1964, p. 29.
25. *Globe and Mail*, 29 June 1964.
26. *Globe and Mail*, 25 June 1964.
27. 1993 Granada publicity, quoted in de Burgh, p. 49.
28. Watson, *This Life Has Seven Decades*, p. 228.
29. National Archives, RG 41 v.232, 11-25-7.
30. Aucoin, p. 85.
31. Helen Carscallen, 'Nine Years and Seven Days Later', *Content Magazine*, August 1975.
32. Watson, *This Life Has Seven Decades*, p. 202.
33. National Archives, RG 146, v.115, AH-2001/0048.
34. Koch, *Inside Seven Days*, p. 93.
35. Ron Haggart, *Toronto Star*, 26 October 1964, p. 7.
36. Quoted in Koch, p. 87.
37. National Archives, RG 41 v.234, 11-25-7 (pt. ii).
38. Quoted in Frank Peers, *The Public Eye*, p. 334.
39. National Archives, RG 41 v.234, 11-25-7, memo dated 3 April 1966.
40. Helen Carscallen, 'Control in a Broadcasting System', MA thesis, University of Toronto, September 1966, pp. 101 and 130.
41. Ibid., p. 101.
42. National Archives, RG 41 v. 232 11-25-7 (pt. I), memo of 4 February 1966 from Reeves Haggan to Bill Hogg.
43. National Archives, RG 41 v. 234, 11-25-7 (pt. 10), telegram to Alphonse Ouimet from members of the Prairie Region Office of Public Affairs and of the department's Winnipeg and Edmonton production staff.
44. Ron Haggart, *Toronto Star*, 30 May 1966, p. 7.
45. *New York Times*, 30 January 1966.
46. Leiterman Interview.
47. *Toronto Telegram*, 9 October 1968.
48. *Toronto Star*, 16 December 1968.

49. Leiterman Interview.
50. *Toronto Star*, 25 August 1966; *Toronto Telegram*, 27 August 1966.
51. *Toronto Telegram*, 13 November 1967.
52. CBC Press Release no. 698, 19 October 1966.
53. *Globe and Mail*, 7 September 1968.

Chapter 6

1. *Toronto Star*, 30 May 1966.
2. Keith Davey, *The Uncertain Mirror: Report of the Special Senate Committee on Mass Media* (Information Canada, 1970), p. 85.
3. Seymour Lipset and William Schneider, *The Confidence Gap*. They argue that trust in government changed little between 1958 and 1964 in the US, while in the subsequent six years, 'there was a virtual explosion of anti-government feeling' (p. 16).
4. Safer, quoted at http://www.pbs.org/weta/reportingamericaatwar/reporters/safer/camne.html
5. Pilger, p. 71.
6. Protess, p. 49.
7. 'A Muckrakers' Guide to 1968 and Other Horrors', *Ramparts* magazine, Vol. 7, No. 10, p. 32.
8. Ibid., p. 46.
9. Michael Schudson, *Discovering the News*, p. 181.
10. Ibid., p. 189.
11. James Dygert, *The Investigative Journalist: Folk Heroes of a New Era*, p. 6.
12. Quoted in Ron Verzuh, *Underground Times*, p. 17.
13. Ibid., p. 187.
14. Interview with Nick Fillmore, 18 February 2005.
15. Keith Davey, *The Uncertain Mirror: Report of the Special Senate Committee on Mass Media* (Information Canada, 1970), p. 89.
16. Ibid.
17. Quoted in Verzuh, *Underground Times*, p. 89.
18. National Archives, RG 146, v. 123, AH-2001, 00234, pt. 24.
19. Allan M. Gould, 'Mark Starowicz, Whiz-Kid Producer', *Chatelaine*, September 1981.
20. Mark Starowicz, Interview, 9 February 2006.
21. *Last Post*, Vol. 2, February 1970.
22. 'CBW in Canada', *Last Post*, Vol. 1, p. 9.
23. *Last Post*, Vol. 4, inside front cover.
24. The English version of the film was called *Cotton Mill Treadmill*. See www.nfb.ca
25. Brian McKenna, Interview, 15 June 2005.
26. Mark Starowicz, Interview.
27. Mark Feldstein, 'A Muckraking Model', *Press/Politics* 11(2) Spring 2006 pp. 105–120.

Chapter 7

1. Quoted in Pilger, *Tell Me No Lies*, p. xv.
2. Seymour Hersh, quoted in John C. Behrens, *The Typewriter Guerrillas*, pp. 134–5.
3. See, for example, Michael Schudson, 'Watergate: a study in mythology', *Columbia Journalism*

Review, May/June 1992.

4. 'The J-School Explosion', *Time*, 11 November 1974.

5. 'The Pulitzer Flap', *Time*, 20 May 1974.

6. James Steele, quoted in Aucoin, *The Evolution of American Investigative Journalism*, p. 88.

7. CBC Press Release 491, 14 September 1972.

8. Jack Miller, 'Changing Times at CBC in Search of Excitement', *Toronto Star*, 25 January 1974, p. E5.

9. CBC Press Release #547, 20 November 1973.

10. 'Did Official Jitters Kill TV Ombudsman?' *Toronto Star*, 22 April 1980, p. E2.

11. Quoted in Marq de Villiers, 'The Squeak that Roared,' *Weekend Magazine*, 1 November 1975.

12. *Globe and Mail*, 24 January 1974, p. 15.

13. Lloyd Tataryn, 'A Watershed court case could cramp investigations', *CIJ Bulletin* 13, Summer, 1981, p. 12.

14. Henry Aubin, Interview, 24 March 2005.

15. Kathy English and Nick Russell, *Page 1*, pp. 291–4.

16. Henry Aubin, *City for Sale*, p. 11.

17. Ibid., pp.15–16.

18. Henry Aubin, Interview.

19. Ibid.

20. Aubin, *City for Sale*, pp. 386–7, 389.

21. *Washington Post*, 20 August 1978, p. e6.

Chapter 8

1. Stephens, *A History of News*, p. 102.

2. *Toronto Star*, 2 May 1973, p.15.

3. Jean-Pierre Charbonneau, Interview, 6 April 2005.

4. Stephens, pp. 98–102.

5. Rutherford, *A Victorian Authority*, p. 73.

6. Jocko Thomas, *From Police Headquarters*, p. 149.

7. Ibid., p. 211.

8. Jean-Pierre Charbonneau, *The Canadian Connection* (Optimum Publishing, 1976), pp. XIII-XIV.

9. Ibid., p. 507.

10. Ibid., pp. XVI-XVII.

11. Jeremy Lipschultz and Michael Hilt, *Crime and Local Television News*, p. 13. A research study showed that crime news accounted for nearly 20 per cent of total coverage at two Chicago television stations in 1976 (quoted on p. 15).

12. Michel Auger, *The Biker Who Shot Me*, p. 96.

13. *Toronto Star*, 13 June 1977, p. 1.

14. Quoted in Wade Rowland, *Making Connections*, p. 109.

15. Ibid.

16. William Macadam, Interview, 7 April 2005.

17. James Dubro, Interview, 24 March 2005.

18. 'US Electronic Espionage, a Memoir: An Interview With a Former NSA Analyst', *Ramparts*,

Vol. 11, No. 2 (August 1972), pp. 35–50.

19. James Dubro, *The IRE Journal*, Spring, 1981, Vol. 4, No. 2.

20. Ibid. See also Rowland, *Making Connections*, p. 27.

21. *Globe and Mail*, 10 January 1974, p. 2.

22. *Toronto Sun*, 11 January 1974.

23. *Globe and Mail*, 11 January 1974, p. 2.

24. James Dubro, William Macadam, Interviews.

25. Rowland, p. 29.

26. Ibid., p. 33.

27. Ibid., pp. 45–6.

28. William Macadam, Interview.

29. Peter Herrndorf, Interview, 23 June 2005.

30. William Macadam, Interview.

31. Peter Herrndorf, Interview.

32. CBC News Release d-19, 21 March 1979.

33. James Dubro, Interview.

34. Dubro, *IRE Journal*, op. cit.

35. *Globe and Mail*, 21 September 1984.

36. *Globe and Mail*, 6 September 1984.

37. William Macadam, Interview.

38. Peter Herrndorf, Interview.

39. Ibid.

40. Clark Davey, Interview.

41. Ibid.

42. Gerald McAuliffe, Interview, 10 February 2005.

43. Ibid.

44. Bonnie McAuliffe, Interview, 10 February 2005.

45. Doyle, *Hurly Burly*, p. 365.

46. *Globe and Mail*, 15 October 1974, Page 1.

47. Gerald McAuliffe, Interview.

48. Stephens, *A History of News*, p. 99.

49. Lipschultz and Hilt explain the appeal and steady progression of crime reporting in local television newscasts. 'Crime stories are easy to tell because they usually feature good and bad; innocent victims subjected to lawless behaviour by criminals. Society, in a sense, is victimized by the inability of government to protect us from crime.' (*Crime and Local Television News*, p. 10).

50. Kim Bolan, *Loss of Faith* (McClelland and Stewart, 2005), p. 365.

Chapter 9

1. Marilyn Greenwald and Joseph Bernt, eds, *The Big Chill*, p. vii.

2. *Globe and Mail*, 18 June 1973.

3. See, for instance, 'Give Us This Day Our Daily Bread', CTV, 25 February 1973, reviewed in *Globe and Mail*, 24 February 1973.

4. Jack McGaw, Interview, 28 January 2007.

5. *Globe and Mail*, 18 October 1973.

6. See, for instance, *Globe and Mail*, 12 September 1974.
7. Peter Herrndorf, Interview.
8. Ibid.
9. *The Current Affairs Magazine*, internal CBC document, undated.
10. Ibid.
11. Ibid.
12. Peter Herrndorf, Interview.
13. See Philip Mathias, *Forced Growth*.
14. Philip Mathias, Interview, 31 July 2006.
15. Ross McLean, 'CBC's fifth estate a success despite itself,' *Broadcast Week*, 14–20 September 1983, p. 13.
16. 'The Olympic Connection', *the fifth estate*, CBC Television, 13 January 1976.
17. Philip Mathias, Interview.
18. 'Citizen McCain', *the fifth estate*, CBC Television, 7 December 1976.
19. *Toronto Star*, 10 December 1976.
20. Stephen Godfrey, *the fifth estate*, unpublished manuscript, p. 132, Eric Malling papers, 98–53: TV General, Memos and Articles, University of Regina Archives.
21. 'Television, No News is Bad News,' *Maclean's*, 3 April 1978.
22. CBC Internal Memo, 6 March 1978.
23. CBC Internal Memo, Production Meeting, Park Plaza, 5 June 1979.
24. Robin Taylor, Interview, 12 April 2005.
25. 'A Resume for the CBC', Prepared by the Ad Hoc Committee for Improved Business Reporting, undated.
26. CBC Internal Memo, 3 October 1978, Eric Malling papers, 98–53: TV General, Memos and Articles, University of Regina Archives.
27. Peter Herrndorf, Interview.
28. *Globe and Mail*, 26 October 1982.
29. Eric Malling papers, op. cit.
30. Godfrey, op. cit., pp. 90–102.
31. Eric Malling papers, op. cit.
32. John Zaritsky, Interview.
33. *the fifth estate*, 17 September 1985.
34. *Globe and Mail*, 19 September 1985, p. 1.
35. *Globe and Mail*, 20 September 1985, p. 1.
36. Eric Malling, Internal CBC Memorandum, 10 June 1988.
37. Ibid.
38. CBC Internal Memorandum, 'Notes on Comparative Production Costs for the CBC Board of Directors', undated.
39. http://www.ctv.ca/servlet/ArticleNews/show/CTVShows/20031017/wfive-history/20030924
40. Malcolm Fox, Interview, 13 March 2007.

Chapter 10

1. Quoted in Valerie Alia, C.B. Hoffmaster, et al., *Deadlines and Diversity*, p. 105.
2. RCMP Memorandum, 11 August 1975, National Archives, RG 146, v118, AH 2001/100051.
3. John Sawatsky, Interview. Most of the biographical and career details were provided by

Sawatsky in interviews with the author, 22 February 2005, 3 March 2005, and 8 January 2007.

4. Ibid.
5. Ibid.
6. Ibid.
7. John Sawatsky, *Men in the Shadows*, p. 279.
8. Ibid.
9. http://michenerawards.ca/english/winaward1976.htm
10. Joe MacAnthony, Interview, 2 September 2006.
11. Sawatsky, *Men in the Shadows*, p. xi.
12. *Globe and Mail*, 20 November 1982.
13. *Globe and Mail*, 9 June 1983.
14. *Toronto Star*, 27 May 1986.
15. John Sawatsky, Interview.
16. Allan Fotheringham, *Maclean's*, 14 October 1991.
17. Sawatsky, *Men in the Shadows*, p. 215.
18. The revelations about Brunet were widely publicized in a *fifth estate* program of 30 March 1993.
19. Andrew Mitrovica, *Covert Entry* (Random House Canada, 2002), p. 5.

Chapter 11

1. *The Progressive*, September 1999.
2. Henry Aubin, Interview.
3. *Toronto Star*, 15 April 1979.
4. Linden MacIntyre, Interview, 18 April 2005.
5. Ibid.
6. Henry Aubin, Jock Ferguson (23 April 2005), and Nick Fillmore, Interviews.
7. 'A Proposal', The Centre for Investigative Journalism, undated.
8. Ibid.
9. *Content*, May 1971, p. 17.
10. Aucoin, *The Evolution of American Investigative Journalism*, pp. 117–70.
11. RCMP Memorandum, 11 August 1975, ibid.
12. Henry Aubin, Interview.
13. 'Bulletin 4', Centre for Investigative Journalism, 26 February 1979.
14. 'Opening Statements', Conference Tapes, Audio Tape of Conference Proceedings, CIJ 1979, Tape 1.
15. Nick Fillmore, Interview.
16. *CIJ Bulletin* 9, 18 May 1980.
17. *CIJ Bulletin* 11, Spring 1981.
18. *CIJ Review/Revue CJE* 1982, p. 27.
19. *CIJ Bulletin* 18, Fall 1982.
20. *CIJ Bulletin* 19, Winter 1982–83.
21. Nick Fillmore, Interview.
22. *CIJ Bulletin* 17, Summer 1982.
23. *CIJ Bulletin* 18, Fall 1982.

24. *CIJ Bulletin* 17, Summer 1982.

25. *CIJ Bulletin* 27, Spring 1985.

26. Nick Fillmore, Interview.

27. Conference Tapes, CIJ 1979, ibid.

28. Protess, p. 5.

29. 'CBC Journalistic Standards and Practices', www.cbc.radio-canada.ca/accountability/journalistic/index.shtml

30. Alasdair MacIntyre, p. 177.

31. Ibid. p. 178.

32. Aucoin, p. 210.

Chapter 12

1. Nelly Bly, 'Ten Days in a Mad-House', *New York World*, 16 October 1887.

2. Anthony Arthur, *Radical Innocent*, p. 83.

3. Ettema and Glasser, p. 159.

4. John C. Merrill has a useful discussion about his concept of five levels of truth in *Journalism Ethics*, pp. 113–17.

5. Schudson, *Discovering the News*, p. 192.

6. Marvel Cooke, quoted in Bruce Shapiro, ed., *Shaking the Foundations*, p. 245.

7. Aucoin, *The Evolution of American Investigative Journalism*, p. 96.

8. *Winnipeg Tribune*, 17 June 1935.

9. Ibid.

10. *Toronto Star*, 24 January 1969.

11. Sheila Arnopoulos, Interview, 10 May 2006.

12. Ibid.

13. *Montreal Star*, 27 March 1974.

14. Ibid.

15. Ibid.

16. *Montreal Star*, 12 November 1975.

17. Aucoin, *The Evolution of American Investigative Journalism*, pp. 78–9.

18. *Chicago Reader*, 4 October 2002, http://www.chicagoreader.com/hottype/2002/021004_2.html, accessed 10 July 2006.

19. *Chicago Reader*, 11 October 2002, http://www.chicagoreader.com/hottype/2002/021011_2.html, accessed 10 July 2006.

20. de Burgh, *Investigative Journalism*, p. 38.

21. 'Undercover Journalism and Ethics', *The Hindu*, 6 April 2005.

22. Dietemann v. *Time*, United States Court of Appeals for the Ninth Circuit, 449 F.2d 245, 23 August 1971.

23. *Globe and Mail*, 16 January 1979.

24. *Toronto Star*, 22 April 1980.

25. Ibid.

26. *Toronto Star*, 26 April 1980.

27. Robin Taylor, Interview.

28. *PrimeTimeLive*, ABC, 5 November 1992.

29. *New York Times*, 21 October 1999.

30. See www.cbc.ca/documentaries/bigsugar
31. CBC Journalistic Standards and Policies, http://cbc.radio-canada.ca/accountability/journalistic/index.shtml
32. See Jennifer Jackson, 'Honesty in Investigative Journalism', in Andrew Belsey and Ruth Chadwick, eds, *Ethical Issues in Journalism and the Media*, pp. 93–111.
33. Kovach and Rosenstiel argue that when reporters masquerade to get a story, they should reveal the deceptions to their audience, and explain the necessity of the technique. See Bill Kovach and Tom Rosenstiel, 'Journalism of Verification', in G. Stuart Adam and Roy Peter Clark, *Journalism: The Democratic Craft*, p. 179.
34. A useful and coherent set of guiding ethical principles for journalists is provided by the Poynter Institute for Media Studies (www.poynter.org). These principles include: 1. Seek truth and report it as fully as possible; 2. Act independently; 3. Minimize harm. In their handbook on ethics, Jay Black, Bob Steele and Ralph Barney add a fourth guideline to the list: Be accountable. See Jay Black, Bob Steele, Ralph Barney, *Doing Ethics in Journalism*, p. 28.
35. *Globe and Mail*, 19 October 1973.
36. http://www.michenerawards.ca/english/winaward1973.htm

Chapter 13

1. *Hill* v. *Church of Scientology of Toronto*, 1995, 2 S.C.R. 1130 at 1175.
2. Canadian Broadcasting Corporation, (2003), CD-ROM Law for Journalists in the Electronic Media: a Navigational Guide.
3. Ibid.
4. Ibid.
5. For a good discussion of the laws of libel in the context of nineteenth-century British and Upper Canadian constitutionalism, see Paul Ramsey, 'Upper Canada in the 1820s: Criminal Prosecution and the Case of Francis Collins,' in *Canadian State Trials*, edited by F. Murray Greenwood and Barry Wright, pp. 515–18.
6. *Snyder* v. *Montreal Gazette* (1978), 87 D.L.R. (3d) 5 (Québec S.C.).
7. CBC, *The National*, 7 March 1980.
8. This narrative is derived from *Vogel* v. *Canadian Broadcasting Corporation*, 1982, B.C.J. No. 1565.
9. Ibid.
10. Michael Crawford, *The Journalist's Legal Guide*, Third Edition, p. 21.
11. Ibid.
12. Ibid.
13. *CIJ Bulletin* 17, Summer 1982.
14. David Crerar, 'Recent Developments in the Defamation Defence of Qualified Privilege', http://www.blgcanada.com/publications/disclaimeraccept.asp?PublicationKey=636&LanguageKey=1, accessed 14 July 2006.
15. Ibid.
16. *Time*, 29 June 1981.
17. Peter Worthington, Interview, 28 April 2005.
18. Jean Sonmor, *The Little Paper That Grew*, p. 209.
19. Robert Reguly, Interview.

20. Peter Worthington, Interview.
21. *Munro* v. *Toronto Sun Publishing Corp.*, (1982), O.J. No. 765 at 35.
22. Peter Worthington, Interview.
23. Canadian Press, 11 June 1981.
24. Ibid., p. 39.
25. Marilyn Greenwald and Joseph Bernt, eds, *The Big Chill*, p. 138.
26. Robert Reguly, Interview.
27. *Walker* v. CFTO *Ltd.* (1987), 59 O.R. (2d).
28. *Globe and Mail*, 4 December 1986.
29. Peter Herrndorf, Interview.
30. Stephen Bindman, *CanWest News*, 22 March 1990.
31. *CIJ Bulletin* 11, Winter 1980–81.
32. Bindman, ibid.
33. Peter Herrndorf, Interview.
34. *Globe and Mail*, 24 January 1992.
35. Bryan Cantley, National Newspaper Awards, Interview, 5 April 2005.
36. Crawford, *The Journalist's Legal Guide*, p. 23.
37. Sig Gerber, Interview, 31 July 2006.
38. *Leenen* v. CBC (2000), 48 O.R. (3d) 656 (S.C.J.).
39. Tony Burman, 'CBC: At the heart of the legal matter,' *Globe and Mail*, 25 May 2000.
40. *Assessmed Inc. v. Canadian Broadcasting Corp.* (2004), O.J. No. 802 (Sup. Ct).
41. J. M. Bumsted, 'Liberty of the Press in Early Prince Edward Island, 1823–9,' in *Canadian State Trials*, edited by F. Murray Greenwood and Barry Wright, p. 523.
42. *Snyder* v. *Montreal* Gazette (1978), 87 D.L.R. (3d) 5 (Québec S.C.), per Deschenes, C.J.

Chapter 14

1. Quoted in Protess et al., *The Journalism of Outrage*, p. 20.
2. *Globe and Mail*, 3 March 1995.
3. 'Journalist Threatened', 6 March 1998, Canadian Journalists for Free Expression press release, http://www.cjfe.org/releases/1998/rasm.html
4. See Auger, *The Biker Who Shot Me*.
5. *Globe and Mail*, 20 November 1998.
6. John Zaritsky, Interview.
7. *Globe and Mail*, 20 July 1971.
8. CBC *Times*, 21–27 October 1967.
9. *Air of Death*, CBC Television, 22 October 1967.
10. National Film Board of Canada, 1960, http://www.nfb.ca/trouverunfilm/fichefilm.php?id=11575&v=h&lg=en&exp=
11. *Closed Circuit*, 6 November 1967.
12. *Air of Death*, ibid.
13. *Closed Circuit*, Vol. 3, #14.
14. *Toronto Star*, 22 April 2000.
15. *Globe and Mail*, 26 October 1967.
16. Ella Haley, 'Methodology to Deconstruct Environmental Inquiries Using the Hall Commis-

sion as a Case Study', PhD thesis, Graduate Program in Sociology, York University, Toronto, June 2000, p. 204.

17. Ibid.
18. Ibid., quoted on p. 207.
19. Ibid., quoted on p. 314.
20. *Globe and Mail*, 20 March 1969.
21. *Toronto Star*, 7 January 1970.
22. *Globe and Mail*, 1 April 2004.
23. *Globe and Mail*, 26 November 1997.
24. Terry Milewski, 'Forces of Journalism,' in Wesley Pue, ed., *Pepper in Our Eyes*, p. 145.
25. Ibid., p. 147.
26. CBC, *The National*, 8 September 1998.
27. Ibid.
28. Milewski, op. cit., p. 144.
29. Ibid., p. 150.
30. Terry Milewski, Interview, 19 July 2006.
31. *Globe and Mail*, 17 October 1998.
32. Government of Canada Privy Council Office, http://www.pco-bcp.gc.ca/default.asp?Language=E&Page=archivechretien&Sub=NewsReleases&Doc=news_re19981109862_e.htm, accessed 18 July 2006.
33. Terry Milewski, Interview.
34. *Globe and Mail*, 10 November 1998.
35. Marcel Pépin, *Concerning the coverage of events surrounding the APEC Summit by the CBC and its reporter Terry Milewski*, Montreal, 19 March 1999.
36. Ibid.
37. Ibid.
38. Note to Staff—Ombudsman Report, 24 March 1999.
39. Terry Milewski, Interview.
40. *Toronto Star*, 19 May 2000.
41. Knowlton Nash, *The Microphone Wars* (McClelland and Stewart, 1994), p. 552.
42. Quoted in Nash, ibid., p. 318.

Chapter 15

1. *Globe and Mail*, 3 October 1997.
2. In his 'Notes Towards a Definition of Journalism,' G. Stuart Adam identifies the primary devices of the reporter as observation, the interview, and the study of documents. While acknowledging that the interview is at the heart of the practice of journalism, he also says it is probably the least reliable instrument. 'It would take some time to document this, but I would guess that most of what is published as news and most of what is factually wrong in newspapers is based on interviews.' Public records, on the other hand, are often gold mines for investigative reporters, and the study of documents, along with first-hand observation, are crucial to the reporting process. See G. Stuart Adam, 'Notes Towards a Definition of Journalism,' in G. Stuart Adam and Roy Peter Clark, *The Democratic Craft*, pp. 356–7.
3. Michel Drapeau and Marc-Aurèle Racicot, *The Complete Annotated Guide to Federal Access to*

Information 2002, p. x.

4. Ibid., p. 130.
5. Ken Rubin, Interview, 16 February 2005.
6. Drapeau and Racicot, p. 188.
7. *CIJ Bulletin* 9, 18 May 1980.
8. Ibid.
9. Quoted in Drapeau and Racicot, p. 131.
10. Ken Rubin, Interview. See also *Globe and Mail*, 5 December 1978.
11. Ken Rubin, Interview.
12. For a summary of the mandatory and discretionary exemptions provided by the act, see Crawford, pp. 277–9.
13. Linden MacIntyre, Interview. See also Crawford, pp. 201–2.
14. Ken Rubin, Interview.
15. *Globe and Mail*, 3 July 1993.
16. Ibid.
17. *Globe and Mail*, 3 December 1986.
18. Memo from Linda Perreault's office, Culture, Heritage and Citizenship, Manitoba, to Barb Biggar, 7 January 1992.
19. Ken Rubin, Interview.
20. Drapeau and Racicot, p. 210.
21. *Toronto Star*, 2 July 2003.
22. Ibid.
23. Michael McAuliffe, Interview, 18 July 2006.
24. Ibid.
25. Ibid.
26. Ibid.
27. Ibid.
28. CBC-TV News, 14 August 1996.
29. Report of the Somalia Commission of Inquiry, http://www.dnd.ca/somalia/vol5/v5c39e.htm, accessed 21 July 2006.
30. Ibid.
31. Peter Desbarats, *Somalia Cover-Up*, p. 106.
32. Michael McAuliffe, Interview.
33. Ibid.
34. Office of the Information Commissioner of Canada, Annual Report 2005–06, http://www.infocom.gc.ca/reports/section_display-e.asp?intSectionId=470, accessed 22 July 2006.
35. The series of stories can be seen at http://www.cbc.ca/news/adr/
36. For a description of the 'amberlight' process, see Alasdair Roberts, *Blacked Out: Government Secrecy in the Information Age*, pp. 89–93.
37. Ibid., p. 92.
38. *The Hill Times*, 3 May 2004.
39. *Info Source Bulletin* No. 28, December 2005, http://www.infosource.gc.ca/bulletin/2005/bulletin03_e.asp, accessed 22 July 2006.
40. Altschull, *From Milton to McLuhan*, pp. 249–50.
41. Drapeau and Racicot, p. 128.
42. For a discussion of this concept, which was popularized by *Philadelphia Inquirer* reporters

James Steele and Donald Barlett, see Houston et al., *The Investigative Reporter's Handbook*, p. 5.

43.   *Toronto Star*, 2 July 2003.

Chapter 16

1.   Quoted in Pilger, *Tell Me No Lies*, p. xiii.
2.   John Sawatsky, *The Insiders*.
3.   Jock Ferguson, Interview, 23 April 2005.
4.   *Der Spiegel*, 'Tycoon von Alberta,' 20 March 1995.
5.   Stevie Cameron and Harvey Cashore, *The Last Amigo*, p. 253.
6.   CBC Television, *the fifth estate*, 'Sealed in Silence,' 28 March 1995.
7.   Harvey Cashore, Interview, 8 January 2007.
8.   Ibid.
9.   Stevie Cameron, *On the Take*, p. 382.
10.   'Stevie Cameron and the Mounties,' 1994–2004, found at http://www.steviecameron.com
11.   Stevie Cameron, 'Airbus, the Mounties and Me,' found at http://steviecameronblog.blogspot.com
12.   The intricacies of this debate surrounding journalistic practice are beyond the scope of this book. Further information can be found in the listserv archives of the Canadian Association of Journalists, William Kaplan's book, *A Secret Trial*, and on Stevie Cameron's website, www.steviecameron.com
13.   *Financial Post*, 18 November 1995.
14.   Mathias denies this charge.
15.   An extensive chronology of events in the Airbus affair is available at http://www.cbc.ca/fifth/moneytruthandspin—further details revealed in 2007 are available at http://www.cbc.ca/fifth/unauthorizedchapter.
16.   Harvey Cashore, Interview.
17.   Cameron and Cashore, *The Last Amigo*, p. 311.
18.   *National Post*, 20 October 1999.
19.   Philip Mathias, Interview, 31 July 2006.
20.   Ibid.
21.   William Kaplan, *A Secret Trial*, p. 13.
22.   Audio Transcript from 17 April 1996, Superior Court Case No. 500-05-012098-958, also found at http://www.cbc.ca/fifth/moneytruthandspin/transcript_april17.pdf
23.   Harvey Cashore, Interview.
24.   Ibid.
25.   CBC Television, *the fifth estate*, 'Money, Truth and Spin,' 8 February 2006.
26.   Quoted in Adam and Clark, p. 173.
27.   Bill Kovach and Tom Rosenstiel, 'Journalism of Verification,' in Adam and Clark, p. 171.

Chapter 17

1.   *Toronto Star*, 19 October 2002.
2.   Ibid.

3. Ibid.

4. Ibid.

5. Ibid.

6. 'Police lawsuit against Toronto Star dismissed,' CBC News, 24 June 2003, http://www.cbc.ca/canada/story/2003/06/24/toronto_star_suit030624.html

7. Margaret DeFleur, *Computer-Assisted Investigative Reporting*, pp. 38–9.

8. Aucoin, *The Evolution of American Investigative Journalism*, p. 77.

9. Philip Meyer, *Precision Journalism*, p. ix.

10. Philip Meyer, 'There are Always Antecedents: Late 20th Century Efforts to Bring Social Science Methodology to the Practice of Journalism', in J.T. Johnson, ed., *Proceedings: Ver 1.0*, p. 25.

11. Behrens, *The Typewriter Guerrillas*, p. 141.

12. Clarence Jones, 'A Scientific Look at Dade Justice', *Miami Herald*, 15 December 1968.

13. DeFleur, *Computer-Assisted Investigative Reporting*, p. 74.

14. Aucoin, pp. 79–80. See also DeFleur, p. 77.

15. DeFleur, p. 78.

16. To view the entire series, see http://www.powerreporting.com/color. See also DeFleur, pp. 89–120.

17. Bill Doskoch, *Computer-Assisted Reporting* (Self Published, 1992).

18. Catherine McKercher, 'Computers and Reporters: Newsroom Practices at Two Canadian Daily Newspapers', *Canadian Journal of Communication*, Vol. 20, No. 2 (1995). McKercher interviewed journalists at the *Ottawa Citizen* and *The Gazette* in Montreal. While she found some knowledge and interest in computer-assisted reporting, especially at the *Gazette*'s investigative team, the overall picture was one of ambivalence. 'Some of this ambivalence toward computers may be linked to newsroom culture, which sees reporters as wordsmiths rather than number crunchers. Reporters think of their computers (at work and at home) as writing devices rather than communications links or file-keeping systems or aids to financial planning. Reporters specialize in getting other people to give them information. Hence, they place an emphasis on interviewing as a key journalistic skill. Reporters work to daily deadlines and require instant answers to their questions, or instant solutions to their problems.'

19. Kevin Donovan, Interview, 3 May 2006.

20. *Toronto Star*, 20 May 1995.

21. Colin Putney, 'Mighty Mouse', *Ryerson Review of Journalism*, Summer 1998, http://www.rrj.ca/issue/1998/summer/272. For a description of some computer-assisted stories since 1995, see also http://www.carincanada.ca/Stories.htm

22. *Media Magazine*, Summer 2001.

23. *Toronto Star*, 21 February 2000.

24. See http://www.carincanada.ca/smokescreen.htm

25. Kevin Donovan, Interview.

26. *Columbia Journalism Review*, May/June 2001.

27. Stephens, p. 227.

28. Aucoin, p. 81.

29. See, for example, Marcus Messner and Bruce Garrison, 'The Literature of Journalism Pertaining to Public Agency Databases', in J.T. Johnson, ed., p. 51.

Chapter 18

1. Carl Jensen, 'What Happened to Good Old-Fashioned Muckraking?', in Kristina Borjesson, ed., *Into the Buzzsaw*, p. 424.

2. I have deliberately avoided the temptation to provide a single sentence definition of investigative journalism, though others have coined some thought-provoking phrases. 'An investigative journalist is a man or woman whose profession it is to discover the truth and to identify lapses from it in whatever media may be available.' (de Burgh, *Investigative Journalism*, p. 9) John Pilger's conception of the paramount role of investigative journalism is reporting that 'not only keeps the record straight but holds those in power to account.' (Pilger, *Tell Me No Lies*, p. xiv) The CBC has offered the following definition: 'While all journalism is, in a wide sense, investigative, the term can be particularly applied to the vigorous, intense examination of institutions or activities which concern public policy or touch upon the lives of a large part of the population.' (*Journalistic Standards and Practices*, IV, 11).

3. Bill Kovach and Tom Rosenstiel, *The Elements of Journalism*, p. 144.

4. John O'Neill argues that the market inherently causes disruption between journalism and democracy. He says 'the market imperative is incompatible with both the internal goods of journalism and the democratic function it is meant to serve.' That is because the marketplace encourages institutions to present news in a way that is congruent with society's values and beliefs. 'It does not pay to present news which is outside the dominant cultural framework of the audiences addressed.' (John O'Neill, 'Journalism in the Market Place', in Andrew Belsey and Ruth Chadwick, *Ethical Issues in Journalism and the Media*, p. 22.

5. MacIntyre, *After Virtue*, p. 181. Describing this relationship, MacIntyre says: 'Indeed so intimate is the relationship of practices to institutions—and consequently of the goods external to the goods internal to the practices in question—that institutions and practices characteristically form a single causal order in which the ideals and the creativity of the practice are always vulnerable to the acquisitiveness of the institution, in which the cooperative care for common goods of the practice is always vulnerable to the competitiveness of the institution.'

6. Ibid.

7. Dygert, *The Investigative Journalist*, p. 273.

8. Jensen, p. 426.

9. Jensen, pp. 425–8.

10. Linden MacIntyre, Interview.

11. 'Canadian Journalism', *Public Policy Forum*, Ottawa, October 2005, p. 6.

12. Pilger, *Tell Me No Lies*, p. xv.

13. www.publicintegrity.org

14. http://www.publicintegrity.org/report.aspx?aid=351, accessed 15 January, 2007.

Bibliography

Adam, G.S. (2005). *Journalism: the democratic craft.* New York: Oxford University Press.

Alia, V., Brennan, B., et al. (1996). *Deadlines and diversity: journalism ethics in a changing world.* Halifax, NS: Fernwood.

Altschull, J.H. (1990). *From Milton to McLuhan: the ideas behind American journalism.* New York: Longman.

Anderson, D. and Benjaminson, P. (1976). *Investigative reporting.* Bloomington: Indiana University Press.

Arthur, A. (2006). *Radical innocent: Upton Sinclair.* New York: Random House.

Aubin, H. (1977). *City for sale.* Montreal: Editions l'Etincelle.

Aucoin, J. (2005). *The evolution of American investigative journalism.* Columbia, MO: University of Missouri Press.

Auger, M. (2002). *The biker who shot me: recollections of a crime reporter.* Toronto: McClelland & Stewart.

Babe, R.E. (2000). *Canadian communication thought: ten foundational writers.* Toronto: University of Toronto Press.

Behrens, J.C. (1977). *The typewriter guerrillas: close-ups of 20 top investigative reporters.* Chicago: Nelson-Hall.

Belliveau, J.E. (1979). *The Coffin murder case.* Markham, ON: Paperjacks.

Belsey, A. and Chadwick, R.F. (1992). *Ethical issues in journalism and the media.* London: New York, Routledge.

Bernstein, C. and Woodward, B. (1974). *All the President's men.* New York: Simon & Schuster.

Black, J., et al. (1999). *Doing ethics in journalism: a handbook with case studies.* Boston: Allyn and Bacon.

Blackstone, W. (1979). *Commentaries on the laws of England.* Chicago: University of Chicago Press.

Bluem, A.W. (1965). *Documentary in American television: form, function, method.* New York: Hastings House.

Bok, S. (1984). *Secrets: on the ethics of concealment and revelation.* New York: Oxford University Press.

Bolan, K. (2005). *Loss of faith: how the Air India bombers got away with murder.* Toronto: McClelland & Stewart.

Börjesson, K. (2004). *Into the buzzsaw: leading journalists expose the myth of a free press.* New York: Prometheus Books.

Cameron, S. (1989). *Ottawa inside out: power, prestige and scandal in the nation's capital.* Toronto: Key Porter Books.

——— (1995). *On the take: crime, corruption and greed in the Mulroney years.* Toronto: Seal Books.

——— and Cashore, H. (2001). *The last amigo: Karlheinz Schreiber and the anatomy of a scandal.* Toronto: Macfarlane, Walter & Ross.

Canada. Commission of Inquiry into the Sponsorship Program and Advertising Activities. (2004). http://www.tbs-sct.gc.ca/gr-rg/gomery/fsag-rpg18_e.asp

Canada. Parliament. Senate. Special Committee on Mass Media. (1970). *Report of the Special Senate Committee on Mass Media.* Ottawa: Queen's Printer.

Canada. Royal Commission on Newspapers. (1981). *Journalists.* Ottawa: Supply and Services

Canada.

Canadian Broadcasting Corporation. (2004). *Journalistic standards and practices.* Ottawa: Canadian Broadcasting Corporation.

Careless, J.M.S. (1959). *Brown of the Globe.* Toronto: Macmillan Canada.

Carscallen, H. (1966). 'Control in a Broadcasting System.' MA Thesis.

Carson, R., L. Darling, et al. (1962). *Silent spring.* Boston: Houghton Mifflin.

Chalmers, F.S. (1969). *A gentleman of the press.* Toronto: Doubleday.

Charbonneau, J.-P. (1976). *The Canadian connection.* Ottawa: Optimum.

Cobb, C. (2004). *Ego and ink: the inside story of Canada's national newspaper war.* Toronto: McClelland & Stewart.

Cohen, E.D. (1992). *Philosophical issues in journalism.* New York: Oxford University Press.

Commission of Inquiry into Allegations of Infractions of the Elections Act and the Elections Finances Act during the 1995 Manitoba General Election. (1999). *Report of the Commission of Inquiry into Allegations of Infractions of the Elections Act and the Elections Finances Act during the 1995 Manitoba General Election.* Winnipeg: The Commission.

Commission of Inquiry into the Deployment of Canadian Forces to Somalia. (1997). *Dishonoured legacy: the lessons of the Somalia Affair: report of the Commission of Inquiry into the Deployment of Canadian Forces to Somalia.* Ottawa: The Commission.

Conboy, M. (2004). *Journalism: a critical history.* London: Sage Publications.

Crawford, M.G. (1996). *The journalist's legal guide.* Scarborough, ON: Carswell.

Cribb, R.M. (2006). *Digging deeper: a Canadian reporter's research guide.* Don Mills, ON: Oxford University Press.

De Burgh, H. (2000). *Investigative journalism: context and practice.* London: New York, Routledge.

DeFleur, M.H. (1997). *Computer-assisted investigative reporting: development and methodology.* Mahwah, NJ: Erlbaum.

Desbarats, P. (1997). *Somalia cover-up: a commissioner's journal.* Toronto: McClelland & Stewart.

Downard, P.A. (2003). *Libel.* Markham, ON.: Butterworths.

Downing, J. (1984). *Radical media: the political experience of alternative communication.* Boston, MA: South End Press.

Doyle, R.J. (1990). *Hurly-burly: a time at the Globe.* Toronto: Macmillan Canada.

Drapeau, M.W. (2001). *The complete annotated guide to federal access to information 2002.* Toronto: Carswell.

Dubro, J. (1985). *Mob rule: inside the Canadian Mafia.* Toronto: Macmillan Canada.

——— (1987). *King of the mob: Rocco Perri and the women who ran his rackets.* Markham, ON: Viking.

Dygert, J.H. (1976). *The investigative journalist: folk heroes of a new era.* Englewood Cliffs, N.J.: Prentice-Hall.

Edge, M. (2001). *Pacific Press: the unauthorized story of Vancouver's newspaper monopoly.* Vancouver: New Star Books.

English, K. and Russell, N. (1999). *Page 1: National Newspaper Awards.* Toronto: Canadian Newspaper Association/Association canadienne des journaux.

Ettema, J.S. and Glasser, T.L. (1998). *Custodians of conscience: investigative journalism and public virtue.* New York: Columbia University Press.

Fetherling, G. (1990). *The rise of the Canadian newspaper.* Don Mills, ON: Oxford University Press.

Filler, L. (1993). *The muckrakers.* Stanford, CA: Stanford University Press.

Fitzpatrick, E.F., L. Steffens, et al. (1994). *Muckraking: three landmark articles*. Boston: St. Martin's Press.

Gagnon, S. (1985). *Quebec and its historians: the twentieth century*. Montreal: Harvest House.

Gaines, W. (1998). *Investigative reporting for print and broadcast*. Chicago: Nelson-Hall.

Gates, L.F. (1988). *After the rebellion: the later years of William Lyon Mackenzie*. Toronto: Dundurn Press.

Gingras, P.P. (1985). *Le Devoir*. Montréal: Libre expression.

Gittins, S. (1999). *CTV: the television wars*. Toronto: Stoddart.

Goldstein, T. (1985). *The news at any cost: how journalists compromise their ethics to shape the news*. New York: Simon & Schuster.

Greenwald, M.S. and Bernt, J. (2000). *The big chill: investigative reporting in the current media environment*. Ames: Iowa State University Press.

Greenwood, F.M., et al. (1996). *Canadian state trials*. Toronto: Published for the Osgoode Society for Canadian Legal History by University of Toronto Press.

Hackett, R.A. (2000). *The missing news: filters and blind spots in Canada's media*. Ottawa: Canadian Centre for Policy Alternatives.

Halberstam, D. (1979). *The powers that be*. New York: Knopf.

Haley, E. (2000). *Methodology to deconstruct environmental inquiries using the Hall Commission as a case study*. Toronto: York University.

Hardin, H. (1985). *Closed circuits: the sellout of Canadian television*. Vancouver: Douglas & McIntyre.

Hardt, H. and Brennen, B. (1995). *Newsworkers: toward a history of the rank and file*. Minneapolis: University of Minnesota Press.

Harkness, R. (1963). *J.E. Atkinson of the Star*. Toronto: University of Toronto Press.

Hayes, D. (1992). *Power and influence*. Toronto: Key Porter Books.

Hébert, J. (1964). *I accuse the assassins of Coffin*. Montréal: Editions du Jour.

Herman, E.S. (1999). *The myth of the liberal media: an Edward Herman reader*. New York: P. Lang.

——— and Chomsky, N. (1988). *Manufacturing consent: the political economy of the mass media*. New York: Pantheon Books.

Hersh, S.M. (1970). *My Lai 4: a report on the massacre and its aftermath*. New York: Random House.

Hildebrandt, K. and Soderlund, W.C. (2005). *Canadian newspaper ownership in the era of convergence: rediscovering social responsibility*. Edmonton: University of Alberta Press.

Hoffmaster, C.B., et al. (1996). *Deadlines and diversity: journalism ethics in a changing world*. Halifax, NS: Fernwood.

Houston, B., et al. (2002). *The investigative reporter's handbook: a guide to documents, databases, and techniques*. Boston: Bedford/St. Martin's.

Innis, H.A. (1964). *The bias of communication*. Toronto: University of Toronto Press.

Jensen, C. (2000). *Stories that changed America: muckrakers of the 20th century*. New York: Seven Stories Press.

Johnson, J.T. (2006). 'Proceedings': Ver 1.0 (Santa Fe: Institute for Analytic Journalism).

Kaplan, W. (1998). *Presumed guilty: Brian Mulroney, the Airbus affair, and the government of Canada*. Toronto: McClelland & Stewart.

——— (2004). *A secret trial: Brian Mulroney, Stevie Cameron and the public trust*. Montreal: McGill-Queen's University Press.

Karp, C. and Rosner, C. (1998). *When justice fails: the David Milgaard story*. Toronto: McClelland & Stewart.

Kealey, G.S. (1980). *Toronto workers respond to industrial capitalism, 1867–1892*. Toronto: University of Toronto Press.

——— (1995). *Workers and Canadian history*. Montreal: McGill-Queen's University Press.

Kennedy, G., et al. (1993). *Beyond the inverted pyramid: effective writing for newspapers, magazines, and specialized publications*. New York: St. Martin's Press.

Kesterton, W.H. (1967). *A history of journalism in Canada*. Toronto: McClelland & Stewart.

Kilbourn, W. (1956). *The firebrand: William Lyon Mackenzie and the rebellion in Upper Canada*. Toronto: Clarke Irwin.

Koch, E. (1986). *Inside Seven Days: the show that shook the nation*. Scarborough, ON: Prentice-Hall.

Kovach, B. and Rosenstiel, T. (2007). *The elements of journalism: what newspeople should know and the public should expect*. New York: Three Rivers Press.

Lang, M.L. (1999). *Women who made the news: female journalists in Canada, 1880–1945*. Montreal: McGill-Queen's University Press.

Leblanc, D. (2006). *Nom de code, MaChouette: l'enquête sur le scandale des commandites*. Outremont, QC: Libre expression.

LeBourdais, I.R. (1966). *The trial of Steven Truscott*. Toronto: McClelland & Stewart.

LeSueur, W.D. (1979). *William Lyon Mackenzie: a reinterpretation*. Toronto: Macmillan Canada; Ottawa: Institute of Canadian Studies, Carleton University.

Lindsey, C. (1862). *The life and times of Wm. Lyon Mackenzie: with an account of the Canadian rebellion of 1837, and the subsequent frontier disturbances, chiefly from unpublished documents*. Toronto: P.R. Randall.

Lipschultz, J.H. and Hilt, M.L. (2002). *Crime and local television news: dramatic, breaking, and live from the scene*. Mahwah, NJ: L. Earlbaum Associates.

Lipset, S.M. and Schneider, W. (1987). *The confidence gap: business, labor, and government in the public mind*. Baltimore: Johns Hopkins University Press.

Locke, J., et al. (2003). *Two treatises of government: and a letter concerning toleration*. London: Yale University Press.

Louw, P.E. (2005). *The media and political process*. Thousand Oaks, CA: SAGE.

MacIntyre, A.C. (1981). *After virtue: a study in moral theory*. Notre Dame, IN: University of Notre Dame Press.

McKenna, B. and Purcell, S. (1980). *Drapeau*. Toronto: Clarke Irwin.

Mackenzie, W.L. (1833). *Sketches of Canada and the United States*. London: E. Wilson.

——— (1960). *The selected writings of William Lyon Mackenzie, 1824–1837*. Toronto: Oxford University Press.

McQuaig, L. (1987). *Behind closed doors: how the rich won control of Canada's tax system—and ended up richer*. Toronto: Viking.

——— (1999). *The cult of impotence: selling the myth of powerlessness in the global economy*. Toronto: Penguin.

——— (2001). *All you can eat: greed, lust, and the new capitalism*. Toronto: Viking.

——— (2005). *It's the crude, dude: war, big oil and the fight for the planet*. Toronto: Anchor Canada.

Malarek, V. (1985). *Hey Malarek!: the true story of a street kid who made it*. Halifax, NS: Goodread Biographies.

——— (1995). *Ferreting out the facts: the nature and practice of investigative journalism*. Kingston, ON: Kashtan Press.

——— (1996). *Gut instinct: the making of an investigative journalist.* Toronto: Macmillan Canada.

Manoff, R.K. and Schudson, M. (1986). *Reading the news: a Pantheon guide to popular culture.* New York: Pantheon Books.

Mathias, P. (1971). *Forced growth: five studies of government involvement in the development of Canada.* Toronto: J. Lewis & Samuel.

Merrill, J.C. (1989). *The dialectic in journalism: toward a responsible use of press freedom.* Baton Rouge: Louisiana State University Press.

——— (1997). *Journalism ethics: philosophical foundations for news media.* New York: St. Martin's Press.

Metcalfe, W.H. (1986). *The view from thirty.* Winnipeg: Wm. H. Metcalfe.

Meyer, P. (1973). *Precision journalism: a reporter's introduction to social science methods.* Bloomington: Indiana University Press.

Miraldi, R. (1990). *Muckraking and objectivity: journalism's colliding traditions.* New York: Greenwood Press.

Mitford, J. (1978). *The American way of death.* New York: Simon & Schuster.

Mitrovica, A. (2002). *Covert entry: spies, lies and crimes inside Canada's secret service.* Toronto: Random House Canada.

Mollenhoff, C.R. (1981). *Investigative reporting: from courthouse to White House.* New York: Macmillan.

Myers, G. (1972). *A history of Canadian wealth.* Toronto: J. Lorimer.

Nash, K. (1984). *History on the run: the trenchcoat memoirs of a foreign correspondent.* Toronto: McClelland & Stewart.

——— (1987). *Prime time at ten: behind-the-camera battles of Canadian TV journalism.* Toronto: McClelland & Stewart.

——— (1994). *The microphone wars: a history of triumph and betrayal at the CBC.* Toronto: McClelland & Stewart.

——— (1996). *Cue the elephant!: backstage tales at the CBC.* Toronto: McClelland & Stewart.

National Press Club of Canada and Brault, L. (1967). *A century of reporting: the National Press Club anthology.* Toronto: Clarke, Irwin.

Nerone, J.C. (1995). *Last rights: revisiting four theories of the press.* Urbana: University of Illinois Press.

Osler, A.M. (1993). *News: the evolution of journalism in Canada.* Toronto: Copp Clark Pitman.

Ouston, R. (1990). *Getting the goods: information in B.C.—how to find it, how to use it.* Vancouver: New Star Books.

Overbury, S. (1985). *Finding Canadian facts fast.* Toronto: Methuen.

Palango, P. (1994). *Above the law.* Toronto: McClelland & Stewart.

Peers, F.W. (1979). *The public eye: television and the politics of Canadian broadcasting, 1952–1968.* Toronto: University of Toronto Press.

Pépin, M. (1999). *Concerning the coverage of events surrounding the APEC Summit by the CBC and its reporter Terry Milewski.* Montreal: Canadian Broadcasting Corporation.

Pilger, J. (2005). *Tell me no lies: investigative journalism that changed the world.* New York: Thunder's Mouth Press.

Poulton, R. (1971). *The paper tyrant: John Ross Robertson of the Toronto Telegram.* Toronto: Clarke Irwin.

Protess, D., et al. (1991). *The Journalism of outrage: investigative reporting and agenda building in America.* New York: Guilford Press.

Pue, W.W. (2000). *Pepper in our eyes: the APEC affair.* Vancouver: UBC Press.

Reid, T.E.H. (1969). *Student power and the Canadian campus.* Toronto: Peter Martin.

Roberts, A. (2006). *Blacked out: government secrecy in the information age.* NY: Cambridge University Press.

Robinson, D.J. (2004). *Communication history in Canada.* Don Mills, ON: Oxford University Press.

Rosenstiel, T. and Mitchell, A.S. (2003). *Thinking clearly: cases in journalistic decision-making.* New York: Columbia University Press.

Rosenthal, A. (1980). *The Documentary conscience: a casebook in film making.* Berkeley: University of California Press.

Rowland, W. (1979). *Making Connections.* Toronto: Gage.

Russell, N. (1994). *Morals and the media: ethics in Canadian journalism.* Vancouver: UBC Press.

Rutherford, P. (1978). *The making of the Canadian media.* Toronto: McGraw-Hill Ryerson.

———— (1982). *A Victorian authority: the daily press in late nineteenth-century Canada.* Toronto: University of Toronto Press.

———— (1990). *When television was young: primetime Canada 1952–1967.* Toronto: University of Toronto Press.

Ryerson, S.B. (1968). *Unequal Union: Confederation and the roots of conflict in the Canadas 1815–1873.* Toronto: Progress.

Salutin, R. (1976). *1837: William Lyon Mackenzie and the Canadian revolution.* Toronto: J. Lorimer.

Sawatsky, J. (1980). *Men in the shadows: the RCMP Security Service.* Toronto: Doubleday Canada.

———— (1982). *For services rendered: Leslie James Bennett and the RCMP Security Service.* Toronto: Doubleday Canada.

———— (1984). *Gouzenko: the untold story.* Toronto: Macmillan Canada.

———— (1987). *The insiders: government, business, and the lobbyists.* Toronto: McClelland & Stewart.

———— (1991). *Mulroney: the politics of ambition.* Toronto: Macfarlane Walter & Ross.

Schudson, M. (1978). *Discovering the news: a social history of American newspapers.* New York: Basic Books.

Seldes, G. (1968). *Never tire of protesting.* New York: L. Stuart.

Serrin, J. and Serrin, W. (2002). *Muckraking!: the journalism that changed America.* New York: New Press.

Shapiro, B. (2003). *Shaking the foundations: 200 years of investigative journalism in America.* New York: Thunder's Mouth Press/Nation Books.

Sher, J. (2001). *Until you are dead: Steven Truscott's long ride into history.* Toronto: Knopf Canada.

Siebert, F.S. (1956). *Four theories of the press: the authoritarian, libertarian, social responsibility, and Soviet communist concepts of what the press should be and do.* Urbana: University of Illinois Press.

Sinclair, U. (1926). *The jungle.* New York: Vanguard.

———— (1970). *The brass check: a study of American journalism.* New York: Arno.

Smith, D. (2003). *As many liars: The Story of the 1995 Manitoba Vote-Splitting Scandal.* Winnipeg: Arbeiter Ring.

Sonmor, J. (1993). *The little paper that grew: inside the Toronto Sun Publishing Corporation.* Toronto: The Corporation.

Sotiron, M. (1997). *From politics to profits: the commercialization of Canadian daily newspapers, 1890–1920.* Montreal: McGill-Queen's University Press.

———— and Rabchuk, G. (1987). *An annotated bibliography of works on daily newspapers in Canada, 1914–1983.* Montréal: M. Sotiron.

Spark, D. (1999). *Investigative reporting: a study in technique.* Burlington, MA: Focal Press.

Stephens, M. (1988). *A history of news: from the drum to the satellite.* New York: Viking.

Stewart, W. (1980). *Canadian newspapers: the inside story.* Edmonton: Hurtig Publishers.

Streitmatter, R. (2001). *Voices of revolution: the dissident press in America.* New York: Columbia University Press.

Sutherland, F. (1989). *The monthly epic: a history of Canadian magazines.* Toronto: Fitzhenry & Whiteside.

Tarbell, I.M. (1904). *The history of the Standard oil company.* New York: McClure, Phillips.

Thomas, J. (1990). *From police headquarters: true tales from the big city crime beat.* Toronto: Stoddart.

Troyer, W. (1980). *The sound and the fury: an anecdotal history of Canadian broadcasting.* Toronto: Wiley.

Verzuh, R. (1988). *Radical rag: the pioneer labour press in Canada.* Ottawa: Steel Rail.

———— (1989). *Underground times: Canada's flower-child revolutionaries.* Toronto: Deneau.

Watson, P. (2004). *This life has seven decades.* Toronto: McArthur.

Weinberg, A. and Weinberg, L.S. (2001). *The Muckrakers.* Urbana: University of Illinois Press.

Williams, P.N. (1978). *Investigative reporting and editing.* Englewood Cliffs, NJ: Prentice-Hall.

Zelizer, B. (2004). *Taking journalism seriously: news and the academy.* Thousand Oaks, CA: Sage.

Zwicker, B. and MacDonald, D. (1982). *The News: inside the Canadian media.* Ottawa: Deneau.

Index